SAGE was founded in 1965 by Sara Miller McCune to support the dissemination of usable knowledge by publishing innovative and high-quality research and teaching content. Today, we publish over 900 journals, including those of more than 400 learned societies, more than 800 new books per year, and a growing range of library products including archives, data, case studies, reports, and video. SAGE remains majority-owned by our founder, and after Sara's lifetime will become owned by a charitable trust that secures our continued independence.

Los Angeles | London | New Delhi | Singapore | Washington DC | Melbourne

ADVANCE PRAISE

As I read Akhil Ranjan Dutta's *Hindutva Regime in Assam: Saffron in the Rainbow*, I am reminded of the glorious tradition of writing *buranjis* or current histories in Assam. The book effectively infuses politics with history—long lost especially in political writings. Dutta views history not in a historicist way but as a practice that also contributes to the making of history. The beauty of the book lies in its quiet elegance, in informing the text with theory without loudly foregrounding it.

—Samir Kumar Das
Professor in Political Science, University of Calcutta, India;
Former Vice-Chancellor, University of North Bengal, Siliguri, India

By 2014, the BJP had already made headway in Assam. Its victory in 2016 marked a major shift in the state's politics, challenging the consensus that sustained plurality of the state. Akhil Ranjan Dutta's competent work provides detailed assessment of the BJP's politics as the ruling party of Assam. *Hindutva Regime in Assam: Saffron in the Rainbow* is an important contribution because it meticulously shows how the BJP ruptured the consensus on key issues. The book is also important for the assessment of governance that predominantly operates in the dual universe of Hindutva and neoliberalism.

—Suhas Palshikar
Chief Editor, Studies in Indian Politics
Former Professor in Political Science,
Savitribai Phule University, Pune, India

Akhil Ranjan Dutta's *Hindutva Regime in Assam: Saffron in the Rainbow* is a meticulously researched book on politics in contemporary Assam. With the help of logical and intelligently crafted arguments, Dutta takes the reader along the different routes through which the BJP amassed power in Assam, riding on a populist strategy of appealing to an Assamese pride which overwhelmed the promised 'rainbow' with saffron nationalism. By examining the BJP's strategies of negotiations and alliances in the electoral domain, the 'resolution' of contests over citizenship through the NRC and CAA, and the homogenization of plural imaginaries of the Assamese identity, the book explains both the rise of the BJP to power and the challenges it may face in the coming years. Lucid and accessible, this book is an important contribution to the study of politics in India in general and of Assam in particular.

—**Anupama Roy**
Professor, Centre for Political Studies, School of Social Sciences,
Jawaharlal Nehru University, New Delhi

HINDUTVA REGIME
IN ASSAM

HINDUTVA REGIME IN ASSAM

IN ASSAM

Saffron in the Rainbow

SAGE STUDIES ON INDIA'S NORTH EAST

Akhil Ranjan Dutta

Los Angeles | London | New Delhi
Singapore | Washington DC | Melbourne

First published in 2021 by

SAGE Publications India Pvt Ltd
B1/I-1 Mohan Cooperative Industrial Area
Mathura Road, New Delhi 110 044, India
www.sagepub.in

SAGE Publications Inc
2455 Teller Road
Thousand Oaks, California 91320, USA

SAGE Publications Ltd
1 Oliver's Yard, 55 City Road
London EC1Y 1SP, United Kingdom

SAGE Publications Asia-Pacific Pte Ltd
18 Cross Street #10-10/11/12
China Square Central
Singapore 048423

Published by Vivek Mehra for SAGE Publications India Pvt Ltd and typeset in 10.5/13 pt Berkeley by AG Infographics, Delhi.

Library of Congress Control Number: 2021941243

ISBN: 978-93-91370-20-6 (HB)

SAGE Team: Amrita Dutta, Shipra Pant and Rajinder Kaur
Cover Image: Aarti David

To
Professor Hiren Gohain,
an unwavering custodian of the people's conscience,
whose writings and social commitments have had an immense
bearing on my intellectual pursuits.

Thank you for choosing a SAGE product!
If you have any comment, observation or feedback,
I would like to personally hear from you.

Please write to me at **contactceo@sagepub.in**

Vivek Mehra, Managing Director and CEO, SAGE India.

CONTENTS

LIST OF TABLES

LIST OF ABBREVIATIONS

AADSU	All Assam Deori Students' Union
AAGSP	All Assam Gana Sangram Parishad
AAHSU	All Assam Hajong Students' Union
AAKSA	All Assam Karbi Students' Association
AAMSU	All Assam Moran Students' Union
AAN	Assam Arogya Nidhi
AASA	All Adivasi Students' Association
AASKSU	All Assam Sonowal Kachari Students' Union
AASU	All Assam Students' Union
AATS	All Assam Tribal Sangha
AATYL	All Assam Tribal Youth League
ABSU	All Bodo Students' Union
ACTA	Assam College Teachers' Association
ADSU	All Dimasa Students' Union
AGP	Asom Gana Parishad
AGSU	All Gorkha Students' Union
AHLC	All Party Hill Leaders Conference
AIMIM	All India Majlis-e-Ittehadul Muslimeen
AIUDF	All India United Democratic Front
AJP	Asom Jatiya Parishad
AJYCP	Asom Jatiyatabadi Yuva Chatra Parishad
ANS	Asom Nagarik Samaj
APW	Assam Public Works
ASDC	Autonomous State Demand Committee
ASHDR	Assam State Human Development Report
BBC	British Broadcasting Corporation

BIRD	Brahmaputra Institute of Research and Development
BJP	Bharatiya Janata Party
BJS	Bharatiya Jana Sangh
BLD	Bharatiya Lok Dal
BPF	Bodo Peoples' Front
BPL	Below poverty line
BTAD	Bodoland Territorial Area Districts
BTC	Bodoland Territorial Council
BTR	Bodoland Territorial Region
CAA	Citizenship (Amendment) Act
CAB	Citizenship (Amendment) Bill
CIL	Coal India Limited
CMSGUY	Chief Minister Samagra Gramya Unnayan Yojana
CPI (ML)	Communist Party of India (Marxist–Leninist)
CPI	Communist Party of India
CrPC	Criminal Procedure Code
CSDS	Centre for the Study of Developing Societies
CSI	Composite SDG India
DA	Dearness allowances
DBHs	Displaced Bengali Hindus
DBT	Direct benefit transfer
DHD-J	Dima Halam Daogah (Jewel)
DUTA	Dibrugarh University Teachers' Association
EIA	Environment Impact Assessment
EPFO	Employees' Provident Fund Organisation
EPW	*Economic & Political Weekly*
FRA	Forest Rights Act
FT	Foreigners Tribunal
GMCH	Gauhati Medical College and Hospital
GSDP	Gross state domestic product
GSP	Gana Shakti Party
GST	Goods and Services Tax
GUTA	Gauhati University Teachers' Association
HPCL	Hindustan Paper Corporation Limited
HSDC	Hill State Demand Committee
IAs	Intervening applications
ICC	Indian Citizenship Certificates

IIMC	Indian Institute of Mass Communication
ILP	Inner Line Permit
IMDT Act	Illegal Migrants (Determination by Tribunals) Act
IPC	Indian Penal Code
IPTA	Indian People's Theatre Association
IUML	Indian Union Muslim League
J&K	Jammu and Kashmir
JNNURM	Jawaharlal Nehru National Urban Renewal Mission
JNU	Jawaharlal Nehru University
JPC	Joint parliamentary committee
KMSS	Krishak Mukti Sangram Samiti
KNP	Kaziranga National Park
KSU	Karbi Students' Union
KYC	Know your customer
LoC	Letter of credit
LSHPP	Lower Subansiri Hydroelectric Power Project
LTV	Long Term Visa
MHA	Ministry of Home Affairs
MoU	Memorandum of understanding
NBWL	National Board of Wild Life
NDA	National Democratic Alliance
NDFB	National Democratic Front of Bodoland
NEDA	North-East Democratic Alliance
NESO	North East Students' Organization
NFHS	National Family Health Survey
NHM	National Health Mission
NIA	National Investigation Agency
NRC	National Register of Citizens
NREGA	National Rural Employment Guarantee Act
NRHM	National Rural Health Mission
NSA	National Security Act
NTCA	National Tiger Conservation Authority
OKDISCD	Omeo Kumar Das Institute of Social Change and Development
PCG	People's Consultative Group
PCI	Per capita income
PCs	Parliamentary constituencies

PGR	Professional grazing reserve
PILs	Public interest litigations
PIP	Prevention of Infiltration into India of Pakistani Nationals
PLFS	Periodic Labour Force Survey
PPE	Personal protective equipment
PSP	Praja Socialist Party
PTCA	Plain Tribals Council of Assam
RD	Raijor Dal
RJD	Rashtriya Janata Dal
RoP Act	Representation of the People Act
RSS	Rashtriya Swayamsevak Sangh
RTI	Right to Information
SAGMDJP	Sadou Asom Goria–Moria–Deshi Jatiya Parishad
SC	Scheduled Caste
SDGs	Sustainable Development Goals
SITA	State Innovation and Transformation Aayog
SJA	Sanmilita Jatiya Abhibarttan
SSRC	Social Science Research Community
ST	Scheduled Tribe
SUCI	Socialist Unity Centre of India
SVAYEM	Swami Vivekananda Assam Youth Empowerment
TMC	Trinamool Congress
ToRs	Terms of references
UAPA	Unlawful Activities (Prevention) Act
ULFA	United Liberation Front of Asom
UN	United Nations
UPA	United Progressive Alliance
UPDS	United People's Democratic Solidarity
UPF	United People's Front
UPPL	United People's Party Liberal
VGR	Village grazing reserve

FOREWORD

This is an important book which convincingly explains the nature and dynamics of politics in contemporary India. Through an in-depth analysis of the rise of the BJP to power in Assam, it tells the story of present-day India where Hindutva politics builds a brand of cultural nationalism while doggedly pursuing a neoliberal economic agenda. As a major part of its mobilization strategy, in course of consolidating its influence among the Hindu majority, it addresses the specific concerns of select ethnic groups, thus building a 'rainbow coalition'. At the same time, it focuses on regional identity in a demonstratively massive manner, thus forging a vote bank effectively. This is done even while promoting a clearly centralized polity and economy despite the federal framework stipulated in the Indian Constitution. Emotional campaigns are carried out by sharply articulating a perception of an 'enemy'—the Muslim population—which defines the broad electoral strategy of Hindutva politics.

The high-voltage electoral mobilization on these issues is propelled by attacking the prevailing regime—in this case the Congress regime which was in power in Assam for three successive terms till 2016—as corrupt and incompetent, which had betrayed the local people. Since there is some basis for such accusation, it does appeal to the common people. In these circumstances, the BJP calls for a 'paradigm shift' affecting all sectors. All this was possible because of the decades-long work by the RSS on the ground through schools, welfare work and cadre-building, with incentives and network solidarity at the all-India level. Equally significant was the fact that the electoral strategy critically involved splitting the ruling party and engineering defections. A mobilization strategy which combines modern high-tech communication skills with local idiom is smartly operated by trained professionals and an army of social media personnel.

When all this results in successful assumption of power, a sleuth of populist measures is unleashed to show an ostensibly 'pro-people' face of the regime, while the neoliberal strategy of economic growth is vigorously pursued with leading Indian business houses extracting local natural resources. The regime heavily relies on using the coercive apparatus of the state, applying extraordinary laws such as UAPA, enforcing widespread surveillance and suppressing dissent. Media is tamed or won over in the name of maintaining stability and promoting growth, and the RSS, now with state resources, doubles its mobilization to support the regime; taking on the critics on the ground in every sphere all over the region. All these trends of social mobilization, neoliberal reforms and authoritarian governance were further strengthened during the COVID-19 pandemic, which gave an opportunity to the BJP to pursue its agenda even more vigorously.

This unfolding story of contemporary India with Narendra Modi's avowed determination to 'transform India' with the slogan 'Ek Bharat, Shrestha Bharat' is analysed in great detail by Akhil Ranjan Dutta taking the Assam case as the example.

BJP's decisive victory in the 2016 assembly elections is explained by the author in great detail. The party conducted the campaign, invoking the Battle of Saraighat of 1671 in which the Ahoms had defeated the Mughals and restored their rule. The cultural ethos of Assam was fully utilized by highlighting the Vaishnavite Satras on the one hand and assurance of protecting the identities of the ethnic groups such as the Bodos on the other hand. Tea garden workers with roots in Jharkhand and neighbouring areas where the BJP had already built up its base were promised fair wages and better working conditions. Thus, Bengali Muslims were identified as the 'other' (described as 'enemy' by the Hindutva discourse) against whom the BJP vote bank of a 'Hindu majority' was forged. Assam movement youth leader Sarbananda Sonowal had already joined the BJP. The Congress leader with a substantial support base, Himanta Biswa Sarma joining the BJP was a major political gain for the latter. Above all, the corruption and governance failure of the Congress regime was exposed in great detail. Already, the campaign against the delay in preparing a National

Register of Citizens (NRC) was a source of discontent. All these factors together with the impact of the Modi-led NDA government coming to power in the Centre in 2014 brought the BJP to power in Assam. The many subtle moves by the BJP to counter the Congress and the All India United Democratic Front (AIUDF) led by Badruddin Ajmal are explained insightfully in this book.

A very important contribution of this work is the analysis of the movement for NRC, which had represented a consensus among the Assamese people across Hindus, Muslims and ethnic groups and the way this was broken by the Modi–Shah regime with the Citizenship Amendment Act (CAA) passed in December 2019. This law communalized the issue of identifying 'illegal aliens' and thus led to a widespread protest in Assam. The original purpose of the Assam movement was to identify and isolate the illegal entrants into Assam, irrespective of their religion, and create some safeguards for local people's rights. The CAA, on the other hand, was an exclusivist measure to offer 'persecuted non-Muslims' of the neighbouring countries for Indian citizenship. That a vast number of the people recorded as lacking documents entitling them to citizenship were Hindus as recorded in the final round of enumeration for NRC embarrassed the BJP. The author persuasively addresses the concerns expressed in many quarters in India, who wondered about many democratic forces of Assam supporting NRC and shows how the consensus on securing a framework to protect the multicultural, multi-religious identity of Assam was seriously fractured by the Hindutva politics. According to the author, while NRC was a legitimate demand, the CAA introduced a highly divisive process which was widely opposed in Assam until the pandemic came.

We get in this book illuminating details about the BJP regime's governance strategy in Assam, which also tells us a lot about the Modi regime's way of governing India. A host of populist measures are introduced which are targeted at specific groups of beneficiaries, thus creating an aura of a caring government looking after people's welfare. This is combined with a series of big ticket projects given to some top industrial houses of India. As the author points out, the structural causes of poverty and unemployment in Assam leading to distress migration are not addressed. The miserable record of Assam in the realization of the targets envisaged in the Sustainable Development

Goals is a good testimony to this. The large-scale privatization drive and handing over of major natural resources to large corporates further consolidated the long-standing character of the extractive economy of a resource-rich region of India such as Assam. One may add that with the Act East policy under the Modi regime acquiring momentum, Assam and north-east playing the role of a corridor for Southeast Asia rather than an active development partner, this feature of exploitation may be accentuated. The author calls the regime's development policies a 'Dream Seller's Economy', which destroys the natural resources and causes huge harm to the ecology and livelihood of common people. When these policies are challenged by people's movements, the regime comes down heavily upon them. We get to know about the extent of people's resistance including the saga of the struggle waged by the Krishak Mukti Sangram Samiti (KMSS) led by Akhil Gogoi, who was arrested under UAPA along with many activists. Movements against big dams, mining projects which cause displacement and agricultural policies which go against the interest of the peasants, among others, are still going on. This is also the all-India story with some local variations.

The book is written by a reputed teacher and a well-known social scientist, who is also a public intellectual of Assam regularly participating in the debates on critical issues of the time in the newspapers as well as the electronic media. It is not surprising, therefore, that we find a lucid, non-jargon style of writing in which a responsible and factual narrative of the rise of Hindutva politics in a region of India is discussed in depth in this work. The multidimensional analysis giving an integrated picture of the path through which the BJP came to power and tried to maintain its base while in government is a significant contribution to the study of the contemporary phase of the Indian politics. Both the general reader and the specialist, the activist as well as the policy analyst, will find it an extremely informative reading, which is challenging at the same time.

—**Manoranjan Mohanty**
Distinguished Professor & Editor, Social Change *(SAGE),*
Council for Social Development, New Delhi, India;
Former Professor & Head, Department of
Political Science, University of Delhi;
Former Chairperson & Director, Institute of
Chinese Studies, New Delhi

ACKNOWLEDGEMENTS

This book is an outcome of the last several years of my engagement with and research on issues on the consolidation and rule of the BJP-led regime in the state of Assam in India. In the process of writing the book, I have been supported, guided and inspired by many people and institutions. It would be impossible to acknowledge everyone personally. However, I take the privilege to express my deep sense of gratitude to them without whom this book would not have been perceived, completed and published.

The process of writing the book started long back in 2014. It was Professor Paul Wallace from the University of Missouri, Columbia, USA, who fuelled in me the quest for writing on the politics of the BJP in Assam by inviting me to contribute a chapter on Assam in his book *India's 2014 Elections: A Modi-led BJP Sweep* (SAGE, 2015). My chapter was on BJP's consolidation and performance in Assam in the 2014 parliamentary elections. Professor Wallace also invited me to contribute a chapter on Assam in his edited volume *India's 2019 Elections: The Hindutva Wave and Indian Nationalism* (SAGE, 2019). Working with Professor Wallace was indeed a learning experience. He passed away just after the release of the book in early 2020. He was 90, but young in spirit, and I feel his absence immensely. I take this opportunity to pay my sincere tribute to him.

The force behind this manuscript, however, is Professor Manoranjan Mohanty, my teacher at the University of Delhi, now a friend and colleague, who for quite a long time had been insisting that I author a book on this. He had earlier persuaded me to write on

Assam's 2016 elections, and this piece was published in *Social Change* (SAGE) in March 2017. Both Professor Manoranjan Mohanty and Professor Bidyut Mohanty, an amazing couple, have been an inspiration in my academic and personal journeys in life. I feel humbled by their unfailing faith in me, and I hope this book lives up to their expectations.

Economic & Political Weekly (EPW) invited me to write an article in the commentary section just after the publication of the first draft of the Assam's NRC on 31 December 2017. This helped me to deeply think about the BJP-led regime in Assam, and I subsequently published a few articles in EPW on themes related to the NRC, CAB and popular resistance in Assam. I thank the editor and the editorial board members of EPW for offering me the pages of the prestigious journal.

I am indebted to Professor Rakhee Bhattacharya from Jawaharlal Nehru University (JNU), who invited me to contribute a chapter in the volume *Developmentalism as Strategy: Interrogating Post-colonial Narratives on India's North East* (SAGE, 2019), where I wrote a chapter around the debates on conservation versus people's rights—taking the Gauhati High Court verdict on Kaziranga and the subsequent political developments as reference points. All these chapters and articles have been reproduced, revised and integrated in various chapters in the present volume with due permission. I have duly acknowledged the original sources of publications in respective chapters. I am grateful to Professor Anupama Roy, JNU, New Delhi, and Professor Ujjwal Kumar Singh, University of Delhi, who have always been great sources of inspiration in my research pursuits. My interactions with both of them have helped me shape the present book.

My continuous engagement with the political issues in Assam has been influenced and guided by the political and intellectual pursuits of Professor Hiren Gohain, an eminent intellectual and voice of conscience of Assam. More than two and a half decades of my association with Professor Gohain have helped me to speak my mind without fear and favour. I am deeply indebted to him.

Professor P. J. Handique, Vice-Chancellor of Gauhati University, Guwahati, India, deserves special mention and acknowledgement for providing an environment of academic freedom and autonomy to the teaching community, which is now becoming a rare attribute in many

Indian universities. A Biotechnologist by profession, Professor Handique reads and analyses issues with deep political insights. His comments on my research publications have helped me to investigate issues from new perspectives, and I am greatly obliged to him.

Professor Samir Kumar Das, Department of Political Science, University of Calcutta, has always been a guiding force. I was privileged to have him as a reader and reviewer of the substantive part of the manuscript. His critical insights have helped me to review and revise a few of my arguments. Professor Nani Gopal Mahanta, my colleague in the Department of Political Science, Gauhati University, and a brother to me, has been a critic of my writings; always providing a lot of new insights. My regular conversation with him on several issues has helped me to rearticulate my position.

Several colleagues and friends from various universities and institutions read different draft chapters and commented on them. Professor Babu P. Remesh, Ambedkar University, Delhi, Dr Joydeep Baruah, Omeo Kumar Das Institute of Social Change and Development (OKDISCD), Guwahati; and Dr Rajib Sutradhar, Christ University, Bengaluru, read and commented on my chapter on development titled 'Dream Seller's Economy' (Chapter 4). Dr Baruah provided several suggestions to sharpen the arguments. While Dr Bornali Sharma of Cotton University, Guwahati, read and commented on my 'CAB-turned-CAA' chapter (Chapter 3), Professor Shashwati Goswami of the Indian Institute of Mass Communication (IIMC), New Delhi, reviewed the chapter 'Conservation, Peoples' Entitlements and National Security' (Chapter 5). Both Professor Madhushree Das of Gauhati University and Dr Joydeep Baruah of OKDISCD read and commented on my chapter 'Pandemic and Politics' (Chapter 6). Professor Padmini Bhuyan Boruah of Gauhati University read and edited the earlier versions of a few chapters of this book and provided a few relevant perspectives for streamlining the arguments. I must say that all these colleagues and friends have contributed a lot towards shaping the ideas and arguments in this book, for which I am deeply grateful to them.

My articulation on relevant issues has evolved through my engagement with the local news dailies and television channels. Both the print and electronic media have provided me a space to speak my mind.

For this, I am deeply indebted to Homen Borgohain, former Chief Editor of *Amar Asom* and presently the Chief Editor of *Niyomiya Barta*; Ajit Kumar Bhuyan, former Editor-in-Chief in Prag News and presently a member of the Rajya Sabha; Prasanta Rajguru, former Editor of *Amar Asom* and presently the Editor-in-Chief in Prag News; Nitumoni Saikia, Editor-in-Chief in Pratidin Time; Zarir Hussain, Managing Editor of News Live; and Wasbir Hussain, Editor-in-Chief of North East Live. My long-term association with *Natun Padatik*, Anwesha and Axom Nagarik Samaj helped me in putting my arguments in perspective. Regular conversation with Paresh Malakar, President, Anwesha, on the political scenario in Assam has been quite enriching.

The Department of Political Science, Gauhati University, India, provides a unique opportunity for critical debate among the faculty members and research scholars. The UGC-SAP (DRS I & II) programme has also contributed to consolidating this culture. I take the privilege to acknowledge my gratitude to all my esteemed colleagues for their critical engagement in the process of writing this book. Professor Sandhya Goswami, Professor Alaka Sarmah and Professor Nani Gopal Mahanta have always been greatly supportive. My contemporary and junior colleagues Professor Jayanta Krishna Sarmah, Dr Dhruba Pratim Sharma, Dr Shubhrajeet Konwer, Dr Rubul Patgiri, Dr Joanna Mahjebeen, Dr Barasa Deka, Dr Vikas Tripathi and Dr Sukanya Bharadwaj have been great sources of inspiration.

Bidhan Dev of Bhabani Offset and Imaging Systems Pvt. Ltd, Guwahati, has been the patron of the Brahmaputra Institute of Research and Development (BIRD), India, of which I am the chairperson. Due to a series of economic catastrophes—from demonetization to the COVID-19 pandemic—BIRD is yet to consolidate its position as envisaged. But Mr Dev stands committed to BIRD's objectives. The larger framework of the book emanated from the research initiatives of the institute, and I am truly grateful to Bidhan Dev for his continuous support.

Social Science Research Community (SSRC), India—transcending boundaries for sustainable development, a community of social scientists and critiques from across the country and beyond, has emerged as a unique platform for intellectual pursuits among social scientists worldwide. Associated with the community as a founder member, I have been immensely benefited from the debates on contemporary critical issues among the members. I take this privilege to thank them all for the opportunity.

I am also grateful to the staff of the Assam Legislative Assembly Library; K. K. Handiqui Central Library, Gauhati University; and the Departmental Library of Political Science, Gauhati University, for their cooperation and assistance. My research scholars have helped in various ways in preparing the manuscript. I am grateful to all of them.

It has been a great experience to work with Amrita Dutta, Associate Commissioning Editor (Academics) and Shipra Pant, Associate Production Editor, SAGE, who guided me at every stage while working on the book. The comments and observations of the two anonymous reviewers helped me to sharpen my arguments. Kamal K. Baruah has been the language editor for most of my academic writing. He has also been helpful in editing the manuscript of the present book. I am grateful to all of them.

At the family front, my wife, Mouchumee Dutta Borah, took absolute care that I complete the work on time. Her critical comments and sharp observations compelled me to be extremely careful in taking a position on larger social and political issues. Mouchumee and our children, Aranyak (Loy) and Arohan (Raag), provided me with an ambient environment to work on the book. To thank them here will be too formal and would do no justice to my gratitude.

My late mother, Padmawati Kalita, and father, Thaneswar Kalita, always wanted me to hold my head high. I am sincerely indebted to them for this moral insight.

Finally, there are a lot of limitations in the book, and I take sole responsibility for all of them.

Thank you, all.

Introduction

THE RAINBOW ALLIANCE IN ASSAM: PROMISES MADE AND BROKEN

Assam, a major state in India's north-east, witnessed a massive wave of enthusiasm in the legislative assembly elections 2016, leading to the landslide victory of the Bharatiya Janata Party (BJP)-led alliance and a humiliating defeat for the ruling Congress. The BJP alone won 60 seats and, with its allies, a total of 86 seats in the 126-member state assembly. The election was fought against the widespread discontent arising out of the alleged misrule and corruption of the 15-year long Congress-led regime (2001–2016). People's movements were ripe on several issues, particularly around large river dams, land entitlements, unchecked corruption and the killing of one-horned rhinos in the Kaziranga National Park (KNP). The failure to prepare the much-demanded National Register of Citizens (NRC) and the unchecked illegal migration to Assam from across the border, that is, present-day Bangladesh, also made the incumbent government vulnerable in public eyes. The poor performance of the Congress party in the 2014 parliamentary elections had already been a blow to its repute. The defeat of the Congress-led United Progressive Alliance (UPA) regime at the Centre and installation of the BJP-led National Democratic Alliance (NDA) regime in 2014 added to the state government's vulnerable position on different fronts, particularly in availing Central aid. To add to its woes, the ruling Congress was struggling with the organizational crisis provoked by the growing dissidence against the incumbent Chief Minister Tarun Gogoi and led by his most trusted colleague and powerful minister Dr Himanta Biswa Sarma. The crisis culminated in the breaking away of Dr Sarma along with a fraction of Congress's elected representatives in the assembly. Dr Sarma joined the BJP in August 2015 and emerged as a core electoral strategist for the party in the 2016 assembly elections. Prior to its landslide victory in 2016, the BJP had won 7 out of 14 parliamentary seats in Assam in the 2014 general elections with a lead in 69 assembly segments. In both 2014 and 2016, BJP's consolidation in upper Assam, where it had only a marginal presence in terms of electoral performance earlier, was phenomenal.

The BJP's performance in the assembly elections was quite a political feat, considering that disillusionment with the new BJP-led NDA government at the Centre had surfaced almost immediately, once the government issued notifications in September 2015 on granting citizenship to refugees belonging to six non-Muslim minority communities from Afghanistan, Pakistan and Bangladesh by amending the relevant rules of the Passport (Entry into India) Act, 1920, and Foreigners Act, 1946. The failure of the government to fulfil the promise of granting Scheduled Tribe (ST) status to six indigenous communities in the state had also added to the party's woes. However, as the assembly elections approached, these points of discontent were pushed to the periphery by strategic electoral tactics by the BJP. The most important move on the part of the BJP had been its much-publicized Rainbow Alliance, which brought in most of the ethnic tribal political outfits, including the Bodos, to its fold. This was accompanied by the intelligently framed political narrative in the form of the Last Battle of Saraighat[1] to oust illegal migrants that had posed a threat to both the political rights and cultural identities of the indigenous people of Assam. The BJP also promised to overhaul the internal security, economy and well-being of citizens through its ambitious vision document released on the eve of the elections. It categorically promised to solve the foreigners' issue and complete the process of the preparation of the NRC for the state. Prime Minister Narendra Modi's election campaign highlighted the national heroes and cultural ethos of the state and added vibrancy to the popular BJP wave, while the core ideology of Hindutva was kept under the radar. All these culminated in the landslide victory of the BJP in the elections and the formation of the first-ever BJP-led government in the state.

However, after the BJP had captured power, its promises took almost a U-turn. The core Hindutva agenda came to the forefront through the Citizenship (Amendment) Bill (CAB), 2016. Its relentless pursuit dismantled the long-drawn consensus in Assam among the governments, the civil society forces that steered the anti-foreigner movements and also its critics both around the Assam Accord, 1985, and the NRC. On the development front, nothing substantive was implemented or achieved. Individual beneficiary-oriented populist policies received more attention than structural issues of poverty and inequality. The fringe elements of Hindutva including the hate mongers in the social media became active in day-to-day politics. Political and cultural intolerance reached a new height. The state government resorted to coercive apparatuses including the National Security Act (NSA), 1980, to deal with the growing political dissent.[2] Despite these challenges, the BJP again registered a landslide victory in the 2019 general elections, winning 9 out of 14 parliamentary constituencies (PCs), with a lead in 69 assembly segments. The absence of a credible electoral force to represent a voice of dissent against the BJP-led regime, consolidation of the Rashtriya Swayamsevak Sangh (RSS) at the grassroots and targeted populist schemes contributed towards BJP's victory even amid popular dissent. However, the enactment of the Citizenship (Amendment) Act (CAA) on 11 December 2019 brought about an unprecedented resistance and paralysed the state administration for almost three months—from December 2019 to February 2020. It was the COVID-19 pandemic that deflected attention from the CAA and helped the state government to gradually regain its legitimacy. The 2021 assembly elections have been fought against the backdrop of the political equations that unfolded during this pandemic.

The present book journeys through these turnarounds of the BJP-led regime in Assam and investigates and analyses how the regime added new vulnerabilities to Assam by infusing religious polarizations and communal distrusts.

THE REGIME IN CONTEXT: THE NEOLIBERAL STATE AND THE SAFFRON WAVE

Prime Minister Narendra Modi actively campaigned in the 2016 Assam legislative assembly elections and fuelled the expectations of the voters. In an election rally in Guwahati on 8 April 2016, he said,

> I am grateful to the people of Assam for the faith they have bestowed on us. This election is not about winning or who comes to power. This largest democratic exercise is for deciding the future of Assam and I am sure the electorate will take the right decision in which direction Assam needs to go.[3]

Assam's electorate firmly reposed its faith in the BJP in general and in the leadership of Prime Minister Modi in particular to drive a safe political destiny for the state and to be rescued from corruption and the misrule of the incumbent Congress regime. In his words and gestures, Prime Minister Modi epitomized a sense of pride and affection for the people of Assam that Assam had not experienced with the other prime ministers in recent decades. He was able to read and express the social and cultural rhythms that resonated with the people of the state. Well versed with Assam's cultural diversity, and having a grip over the regional aspirations of its people, he knew what would touch the hearts and sentiments of the Assamese people.

However, politics is not all about personal love and affection alone; it is not about flattering the culture or fuelling the aspirations and sentiments of a region and its people. These are tactics of electoral mobilization, and an impassioned rhetoric helps to camouflage the real agenda at the core of politics. At its deeper roots, politics is about both pursuits of long-drawn ideological goals and multi-layered hegemonic interests.

From where it is currently poised, the ideological orientation of the Indian state is fully embedded in neoliberalism. Neoliberalism has two distinct manifestations—one is economic and the other cultural and political. The first is, however, not disconnected from the other; rather, both complement the other. The economic process under neoliberalism accentuates accumulation through dispossession. It is all about giving the market a free ride. However, under neoliberalism, the market is neither competitive nor transparent. In contrast to the dominant view, neoliberalism is also not necessarily the withdrawal of the state as a regulatory institution. Rather, it is more about the shift in regulation, priorities and the complete overhauling of the personnel in the state institutions, which favours big capital and the elite.[4] David Harvey argues that the neoliberal state collapses 'the notion of freedom into freedom for economic elites'. For him, the freedoms that neoliberalism embodies 'reflect the interests of private property owners, businesses, multinational corporations, and financial capital'.[5] This process includes

> commodification and privatisation of land and the forceful expulsion of peasant populations; the conversion of various forms of property rights (common, collective, state, etc.) into exclusive private property rights; the suppression of rights to the commons; the commodification of labor power and the suppression of alternative (indigenous) forms of production and consumption....[6]

How does a state respond under the neoliberal framework? It assumes an authoritarian posture but, at the same time, strives for social legitimacy. Prabhat Patnaik illustrates this structural shift in acquiring social legitimacy by the neoliberal state and argues that social legitimacy

> is sought to be acquired by such regimes through other means: by invoking an enemy that is a common foe of the entire society, against which the State is projected as engaging in the struggle; or by uniting society for a common purpose behind some imperialist project of acquiring 'glory' or 'national pride'.[7]

Neoliberalism also brings in a unique relationship between cultural majoritarianism and greed for consumerism even as it curtails civic and political liberty. As Gudavarthy has pointed out, even though majoritarianism curbs civil liberties, it does not impose limitations on the freedom to consume. Rather, 'cultural nationalism and majoritarianism require neoliberal reforms precisely because they provide for political practices that move away from the language of rights and entitlements to foreground consumerism over citizenship.'[8]

India experienced all these currents after economic reforms were launched in 1991. Resource appropriation by the elite and the corporate sector has been glaring. The economy experienced an almost remarkable growth under neoliberalism until COVID-19 shook the entire world. Obsession with growth is an important feature of a neoliberal economy. The Indian economy nurtured this obsession ever since the neoliberal reforms were launched. There have been difficulties, but the dream of a miracle was sustained through campaigns. In 2019, India unveiled its goal of making itself a $5 trillion economy by 2024–2025. Finance Minister Nirmala Sitharaman asserts that India's 'vision to become a 5 trillion dollar economy by 2024–25 is challenging, but it is realizable'.[9]

This obsession with growth was accompanied by a concentration of wealth and appropriation of resources by the economic elites and corporate sector at the cost of growing vulnerability of the common citizen and unprecedented inequality. In recent years, India has performed very poorly in handling hunger among the countries of the world. In the Global Hunger Index, India was ranked 83 out of 113 countries in 2000. In 2018, the country was ranked 103 out of 119 countries. In 2019, it dropped to 102 among 117 countries.[10] Oxfam International has pointed out that India is one of the fastest-growing economies in the world. But along with that, India also has huge inequalities. 'Inequality has been rising sharply for the last three decades. The richest have cornered a huge part of the wealth created through crony capitalism and inheritance.'[11] According to the report,

The top 10% of the Indian population holds 77% of the total national wealth. 73% of the wealth generated in 2017 went to the richest 1%, while 67 million Indians who comprise the poorest half of the population saw only a 1% increase in their wealth. There are 119 billionaires in India. Their number has increased from only 9 in 2000 to 101 in 2017. Between 2018 and 2022, India is estimated to produce 70 new millionaires every day.[12]

How does neoliberalism sustain despite such levels of inequality and vulnerability? These experiences surely invite public anger and resistance. Therefore, neoliberalism also necessitates curtailing collective bargaining and mobilization. This invites labour reforms as well as other austerity measures. Such requirements facilitate the process of political consolidation of the conservative and rightist forces and their capturing of the state power. In India too, the consolidation of Hindutva forces and eventually their capturing power has been facilitated by the neoliberal oligarchies. Anand Teltumbde calls it 'saffron neoliberalism' and argues that the saffron neoliberalism, apart from entailing 'a revamp of labour laws, simplification of other laws, and amendments to the Constitution in order to make India more business-friendly', would also be 'progressively positioning Hindutva supporters at all important nodes in the bureaucracy and saffronising educational and other research institutions.'[13] Saffron nationalism also propagates 'strengthening of the internal security apparatus and "zero tolerance" of any resistance'.[14]

The consolidation of Hindu majoritarianism and the pursuit of neoliberalism have brought a major shift in Indian politics. Along with revamping labour laws and transfer of the state and community resources to the private and the corporate, India has witnessed the process of upending the long-drawn consensus on citizenship and growing surveillance over intellectual freedom. The journey of the BJP-led regime in Assam has been defined by these macro-political dynamics and their inherent challenges and contradictions.

ASSAM'S AGONY: STATE POLITICS AND THE ROAD FROM HOPE TO DIVISIVE DESPAIR

Assam had been passing through a critical journey, in terms of handling both the internal law and order situation and the health of the economy, when India had launched the neoliberal economic reforms. In the last decades of the 20th century, Assam had struggled to survive through several crises. Insurgent activities of the United Liberation Front of Asom (ULFA) were at their peak by the late 1980s, inviting military operations in the form of Operation Bajrang and Operation Rhino in 1990 and 1991, respectively. The state government of the late 1980s led by Prafulla Kumar Mahanta of the Asom Gana Parishad (AGP) was dismissed on 28 November 1990. Operation Bajrang was launched soon after and continued till April 1991. Operation Rhino was launched in September 1991 after the new Congress government assumed power in July 1991.[15] These operations succeeded in weakening the bases of ULFA, but they also traumatized the common masses. In the second half of the 1990s, the state witnessed one of its darkest phases in the form of secret killings under the patronage of the state. A group of surrendered ULFA cadres was used to identify and kill their former comrades and their family members.[16]

Along with these issues concerning internal security in the late 1980s and early 1990s, the state had also witnessed the plundering of public funds. The issue of the letter of credit (LoC)[17] was a massive political earthquake. The LoC was a unique innovation by the state government of Assam purposely to check corruption. But rather than helping check corruption, LoC itself became a huge corruption, unveiling the shocking practices of plundering public funds, allegedly involving ₹400 crore (4 billion). 'An investigation showed that the expenditure against the LoCs was lower than the sums were withdrawn. Where did the money go? If the CBI file … is to be believed, some of it went into funding the AGP, specifically Mahanta's election expenses.'[18] The chief minister was alleged to have had a direct hand in the corruption. It was speculated that CBI would also prosecute the chief minister if sanctioned by the governor. However, Governor S. K. Sinha came to the rescue of Chief Minister Mahanta and refused to accord sanction for his prosecution.[19]

There was a near meltdown of the foundation of the economy during this period. The counter-insurgency operations took a toll on the state finances, and the state government was under pressure to sign the memorandum of understanding (MoU) on fiscal reforms. The chief minister of Assam, Prafulla Kumar Mahanta, acknowledged that signing the memorandum 'would necessitate harsh steps like freezing employment, hiking electricity tariff, and transferring the state transport corporation to the private sector'.[20] The state government had already frozen appointments except in some key departments like education.

> The monthly receipts of the state amount to Rs. 391 crore at present, while the monthly expenditure is Rs. 451 crore. As a result of this monthly deficit, the overdraft figures for every month have been increasing. This has led to a situation where we are unable to liquidate the overdraft….[21]

These MoUs on fiscal reforms had been a part of the neoliberal policies.

The state's economy gradually improved by the middle of the first decade of the 21st century under the new Congress-led regime that came to power in 2001. That was also the period when the Congress-led UPA assumed power at the Centre in 2004. This government, which was formed with the support of many regional parties and the left political parties, introduced several schemes aimed at alleviating the growing distresses of the common masses. Notable among them were the National Rural Employment Guarantee Act (NREGA), 2005; National Rural Health Mission (NRHM), 2005; and the Forest Rights Act (FRA), 2006. In 2005, the Right to Information (RTI) Act was also enacted aiming to bring transparency in governance and thereby to check corruption. Subsequently, the National Food Security Act, 2013, was also passed. While these schemes and Acts contributed towards relieving the distress of the people, particularly in semi-urban and rural areas, they were not aimed at dismantling the neoliberal framework of the economy. The popular schemes of the government worked hand in hand with the neoliberal policies.

The state government benefited from the schemes as these took care of many concerns such as healthcare and rural employment and contributed towards the revival of the economy of the state of Assam, yielding the steady growth of the gross state domestic product (GSDP).[22] But along with the upsurge in growth came the corporate drive to appropriate resources, which took a rapid turn during this period. From the beginning of the 21st century, the whole of Northeast India witnessed a huge intensification of state and corporate drives to control the hydro resources of the region. Pointing out that, 'there is to be a massive intervention in the hydrology of the region: schemes to dam almost every river, and channelizing the waters of the Brahmaputra into the Ganga, a key element in the plan to interlink India's rivers…', *Down to Earth* reported in 2015,

26 potential sites for mega-dams have been identified. They will generate 99,256 megawatts (mw) of electricity. Some of the dams are already at advanced stages of planning. These include Tipaimukh (1500mw) and Loktak Downstream (90mw) in Manipur and Kameng (600mw), Lower Subansiri (2000mw), Upper, Middle and Lower Siang (11,000mw, 750mw

and 1700mw respectively) and Ranganadi I and II (450 and 150mw respectively) in Arunachal Pradesh.[23]

The report also pointed out that as per the estimates of the Central and state governments, the energy requirements of the north-east would be only 5,700 mw by 2020, while the construction of these dams would adversely impact the biodiversity and the ecology of the region. Referring to the impact of the already-built dams, the report pointed out that the dam spots were already identified as important biodiversity hotspots of the world, and these dams had caused irreversible damage to the fragile ecosystems of the region. In Loktak, for example, the dam had caused extinction of at least 7 varieties of fish species, and 23 varieties of aquatic vegetation had either degenerated or become extinct. The impact of these ecological imbalances had also adversely affected the livelihood of many communities in the dam's vicinity.[24]

Northeast India, particularly Assam, witnessed massive resistance against the dam-building spree. In Assam, the Lower Subansiri Hydroelectric Power Project (LSHPP) emerged as a site of contestation. For almost 10 years, from the middle of the first decade to the middle of the second decade of the 21st century, the state saw a series of resistance movements against large river dams in general and the LSHPP in particular, both steered by the All Assam Students' Union (AASU) and Krishak Mukti Sangram Samiti (KMSS). Under the banner of the KMSS, land entitlement and forest dwellers' movements took a radical turn. During this period, Guwahati, the capital city of Assam, also witnessed a series of peasants' rallies, demanding land entitlements.

The Congress-led regime during its three tenures (2001–2016), however, succeeded in bringing relative peace in the state. The civil society played an important role in facilitating negotiations with the insurgent groups, including the ULFA. However, corruption remained a burning issue. The *Assam State Human Development Report (ASHDR), 2014*, recorded that the regime was ranked low in overall governance despite a positive opinion by the people on its development initiatives.

The BJP-led regime came to power in 2016 with a lot of promises endorsed by popular support and enthusiasm. On the development front, the regime succeeded in consolidating internal revenue. It also introduced several populist schemes to reach out to almost all sections of the society. Along with these schemes, the regime consistently pursued the core neoliberal schemes of facilitating the corporate and private agendas. However, it invited public wrath when it began aggressively pursuing the Hindutva agenda through CAB, 2016, which was later passed by both the houses of the Parliament even after widespread protests in Assam and other parts of the country. It also invoked an enemy: the 'illegal Muslim migrants' and the Bengali-speaking Muslims of the state. The All India United Democratic Front (AIUDF) of Badruddin Ajmal that largely represents this community has been dubbed by the BJP as the main enemy to the greater Assamese society.[25] A theory of 65 per cent versus 35 per cent has also been floated, suggesting that the 65 per cent 'Assamese' are divided today as against the 35 per cent Bengali Muslims who have been creating a new *jati* (nationality) through their consolidation in Central and Lower Assam and the Barak Valley. The BJP's biggest political objective is not to allow 'Ajmal's civilization and culture', that is, 'the Bengali Muslim community to occupy the seat of power in Dispur'.[26] However, the regime continues to enjoy electoral support through populist schemes and social, educational and cultural activities carried out by the RSS and other Hindutva outfits at the grassroots.

ORGANIZATION OF THE BOOK

Divided into six chapters, the book attempts to address the important issues and dimensions that define the core agenda of the BJP-led Hindutva regime.

The first chapter titled 'From the "Rainbow" to "Saffron": BJP's Changing Electoral Strategies' investigates the shifting electoral tactics of the BJP in the last three elections: 2014 and 2019 Lok Sabha elections and 2016 Assam assembly elections. The chapter examines how the BJP used its Hindutva agenda with much panache by intruding into the diverse ethnic and cultural fabrics of the state. The party built the Rainbow Alliance in the 2016 assembly elections and reached out to the religious and cultural institutions like the Satras (institutions for Ekasarana tradition of Vaishnavism) to push its agenda. The BJP's

landslide victory in 2016 was the outcome of these creative strategies of capturing the religious imagination of the people of Assam.
Besides these efforts, the party has consistently invoked the Bengali-
speaking Muslims in the state as the core enemy of the indigenous
people of Assam. The alleged encroachment of Satra lands by the
immigrant Muslims has been another reference point for projecting
the community as a threat to the greater Assamese society. The BJP
also succeeded in creating a solid vote bank among the tea tribes in
Assam. This happened in two ways. First, the RSS has been working
with these communities for several decades. Second, the BJP-led government has initiated several schemes since 2016 exclusively meant
for these communities. These schemes offer instant benefits to these
communities rather than striving to bring them out from the structural
roots of poverty and exploitations. The BJP's victory in the 2019 Lok
Sabha elections amid popular resistance against CAB owes a lot to
these policies and schemes.

Chapter 2 titled 'Unmaking the Consensus: The NRC Debacle'
analyses at length the critical journey of the NRC. The NRC has
been a long-standing demand of the people of Assam, but reaching a
consensus on it has been a challenging task. It took decades of negotiations at various levels to take forward the process. There are a lot of
limitations of the NRC process, as it has proved to be discriminatory
at points to a large number of Bengali populations of both Hindus
and Muslims. There are consistent campaigns against the exercise
from different quarters. The UN agencies on minority rights have also
been critical about the NRC. Despite the challenges and limitations,
the NRC updating process moved towards its culmination under the
supervision of the Supreme Court of India, and people in Assam at
large cooperated with the process. In contrast, the incumbent government, which initially supported the process, eventually rejected it as a
flawed document. With this move, the long-drawn consensus around
the NRC has been dismantled. Chapter 2 captures almost all crucial
standpoints but finally defends it as an instrument that carries the
prospect of bringing a solution to the illegal migrant issue.

At the end of 2019, Assam witnessed unprecedented resistance
against CAB-turned-CAA. People both spontaneously and under the

banners of different organizations protested against it at all levels—on the street as well as before the joint parliamentary committee (JPC) which was examining the Bill. The JPC incorporated the grievances of the Assamese as well as the indigenous tribal communities against the Bill elaborately in its report. However, it finally endorsed the Bill, rejecting the plea of the indigenous people of Assam and the whole of Northeast India. The enactment of CAA violated the consensus on the detection, deletion and deportation of foreigners as agreed upon by the Assam Accord of 1985. The Act is also a huge blow to the updated NRC. While enacting the CAA, the Union government declared on the floor of the Rajya Sabha on 11 December 2019 that the government had been sincerely concerned about the apprehensions of the people of Assam emanated from CAA and was committed to safeguard the interests of the 'Assamese people' by implementing Clause 6 of the Assam Accord. However, the government exhibited an attitude of indifference to the recommendations of the *Expert Committee Report* on the said clause. Chapter 3 titled 'Hindutva at the Core: CAB-turned-CAA and Assam's Political Destiny' journeys through the very inception of the CAA in 2015 in the form of two notifications, to its final culmination in 2019, and Assam's encounter with it throughout the process of making the law.

The BJP-led government succeeded in bringing in a new vocabulary and rhetoric to its development pursuits. The paradigm shift has been its sloganeering while talking about development. Self-glorification has been another important dimension of its development strategies. Over the last five years, the government introduced several populist schemes through which it has managed to reach almost all the sections of the society. Creating immediate individual beneficiaries is the most important objective of its development strategies. The government has fared better than the previous regime in generating internal revenue and sustained its capacity to pay a regular salary to the state government employees even during the COVID-19 pandemic. But in terms of GSDP (Gross State Domestic Product) growth as well as budgetary expenses, the previous Congress regime and the incumbent BJP-led regime are on an equal footing. By 2018–2019, the growth of GSDP declined and unemployment increased sharply. Whereas the government has repeatedly asserted that growth in agriculture has been its most important priority in terms of both investments and achievements in the agriculture and allied sectors, the outcome has been just the opposite. The government has pursued the corporate agenda in many ways. The international auctioning of selected oil fields is a glaring example in this regard. The unfolding events around coal mining in the Dehing Patkai range are another testimony to it. Chapter 4 titled 'Dream Seller's Economy: Promises and Populism' endeavours to capture these dimensions.

While the government is concerned about national pride and national security, it is critical about the popular resistance that questions structural inequities. That attitude is not specific to Assam; it is seen across the country. In Assam, KMSS has been a formidable force of resistance since 2005. It has challenged the state's approach to development, environment and conservation. During the Congress-led regime too, KMSS confronted the government on these issues. During the BJP-led regime, it came into confrontation with the government on several issues, particularly on the model of conservation in Kaziranga and CAB-turned-CAA. The government has acted with heavy-handedness, invoking the NSA and the Unlawful Activities (Prevention) Act (UAPA) to deal with the organization.

The Kaziranga conservation model raised a storm after the BBC telecast a film in February 2017 on how the guards in the park resorted to indiscriminate killings of human beings alleged to be poachers. Although the film was withdrawn after the controversy, the report on the issue is still available on the BBC website. Concerning the issues of conservation and national security, the government has had mixed experiences with the judiciary. While it converged with the judiciary on the issue of conservation and protection of one-horned rhinos in Kaziranga, it received flak from the judiciary on the issue of imposing NSA on KMSS leader Akhil Gogoi and the procedural lapses while taking recourse to the Act. Chapter 5 entitled 'Conservation, Peoples' Entitlements and National Security' examines these issues exhaustively.

Chapter 6, titled 'Pandemic and Politics: BJP's Electoral Prospects', provides a critical commentary on political dynamics in the state, building up to the 2021 assembly elections. The anti-CAB and anti-CAA resistance, which had almost paralysed the state government at the end of 2019 and eroded its popular legitimacy, became more assertive and widespread after the enactment of the CAA. It turned so powerful that it compelled the government to cancel the prime ministerial summit between Narendra Modi and his Japanese counterpart, scheduled to be held in Guwahati in the latter part of December 2019. The government resorted to imposing curfew and suspending internet services to calm the situation and immediately arrested the KMSS leadership. The most vocal voice against CAB and CAA, Akhil Gogoi, was booked under the UAPA for allegedly indulging in a war against the nation. People from all levels of the society came out against CAA and continued to protest throughout the Brahmaputra Valley, until COVID-19 hit the world in mid-2020 and brought normal life to a standstill.

COVID-19 was a blessing in disguise for the government. Even though the pandemic dealt a severe blow to the economy and created huge challenges in addressing healthcare emergencies as well as providing a safe passage to migrant returnees, it helped the government to regain its popular legitimacy. Till almost mid-March 2020, the government had struggled to reinforce its legitimate presence in the public domain, but after the pandemic, it emerged as an omnipotent and omnipresent legitimate entity in all public domains. Through a series of lockdowns, containments and curbs in public and political activities, the mobility of the common citizens came under strict vigilance and restrictions. The public protests against CAA immediately collapsed, and health emergencies and access to essential commodities turned into core concerns. The media also became dependent on the government for all sorts of news. As a result, there was no scope for an independent enquiry into the success or failure of the government in handling the public healthcare emergencies stemmed from the epidemic.

Amid the challenges of the pandemic, the state has gradually geared up for the ensuing 2021 assembly elections. The anti-CAA forces have become fragmented, and a few regional political parties have been formed. The government energized itself amid the pandemic and by August–September started re-launching the popular schemes. However, it has been very calculating in implementing them. Many schemes target the tea tribes, who have gradually become a solid vote bank for the party. There have been tensions in the alliance with the Bodo Peoples' Front (BPF). But the BJP has been endeavouring to bring new equations into its alliance in the Bodoland Territorial Area Districts (BTAD), now renamed Bodoland Territorial Region (BTR). While the BJP has been far ahead in terms of its electoral strategies and prospects so far, the alliance between the Congress and AIUDF may well become a formidable challenge to the BJP in the 2021 elections. This chapter attempts to critically capture these unfolding political dynamics in the state.

The Epilogue, which was written only after the declaration of the results of the state Assembly elections 2021 on 2 May, 2021, investigates and analyzes the political and electoral dynamics and the outcomes of the elections.

WRITING THE BOOK: AUTHOR'S NOTE

First of all, let me clarify for whom I have written this book. It is for a wide range of readers—researchers, students, journalists, policy analysts and policymakers, political commentators, political and social activists and all those who want to understand the overall politics of the BJP in Assam. The primary objective of the book has been to investigate and analyse the ideological and political pursuits of the BJP-led regime in Assam. Therefore, chronologies of events that unfolded and defined the ideological and political orientation of the regime constitute the core of the book. The book also intends to reach out to those, particularly the defenders of human and minority rights, who defame the Assamese people as chauvinist and xenophobic for defending the NRC for the state. My objective is to place before them the political and cultural plights of the Assamese people for which they have been defending NRC while building up a strong resistance against the CAB-turned-CAA.

The book is a product of my active academic engagement and encounter with the activities of the BJP-led regime on an almost day-to-day basis. My responsibility as a political commentator for local dailies and reputed journals like *Economic & Political Weekly* (*EPW*) necessitates that I critically read and understand almost all important issues of the regime. Compared to other political parties, the BJP has been very innovative and creative in capturing the local sentiments and cultural ethos while devising the political and electoral strategies. But the regime has been uncompromisingly committed to its core Hindutva ideology. This has been evident in its campaign strategies which have two diametrically opposite components: flattering the mass expectations and manufacturing and focusing on the core enemies in line with Hindutva. The East-Bengal-origin Muslims and the left-progressive political forces have been BJP's two targeted enemies.[27]

I have observed the election campaigns and the interface between the government and the mass resistance against CAB and CAA, KNP, Dehing Patkai and other issues from close quarters. I have followed the debates and reporting on all vital issues in national and international media and journals during this period. For example, I have followed the debates on the NRC and CAB-turned-CAA published in *Al Jazeera, The New York Times, The Hindu, The Indian Express, Hindustan Times,* Scroll.in, The Wire, *EPW* and various web portals apart from following them on local media, including social media. The archives of *The Assam Tribune* have been very useful; I have also followed the debates in the state legislative assembly and the Parliament on these critical issues for this book. The judgments and orders of the Supreme Court of India and the Gauhati High Court are crucial towards understanding the NRC updating process and the encounter between the government and the resistance forces. I have read them minutely and used them as important sources. Various reports and debates around them—particularly the *JPC Report* on CAB and the *Expert Committee Report* on Clause 6 of the Assam Accord—constitute a substantive part of a few chapters. I have used government data, reports, speeches, budgets, economic surveys and reports on the economy in the backdrop of the pandemic among many other documents, to counter various claims of the government. Authoring a book about a period that continues to unfold is a challenging task. I have tried my best not to be prejudiced on any issue that the present book covers.

NOTES

1. In the Battle of Saraighat fought in 1671, the Ahoms defeated the mighty Mughals under the commandership of iconic warrior Lachit Borphukan. Both the war and Lachit Borphukan are symbols of heroism and patriotism in the popular mindset of Assam. In 2016 assembly elections, the BJP reinforced this patriotism by calling this election the Last Battle of Saraighat, with its political pledge to dislodge the Congress-led regime which allegedly had patronized the illegal migrants and thereby posed a threat to the political and cultural security of the indigenous people of the state. Rajat Sethi and Shubhrastha in their book titled *The Last Battle of Saraighat: The Story of the BJP's Rise in the North-east* (2017) recount the construct and success of this narrative in the 2016 elections.

2. NSA was imposed on Akhil Gogoi, adviser of KMSS, in September 2017. He was detained in custody under Section 3(3) of the NSA by an order of detention on 24 September 2017 in the pretext that he 'has been actively abetting/ instigating/provoking/motivating and conspiring to wage war against the state on certain grounds'. Gauhati High Court granted bail to Mr Gogoi in its verdict dated 21 December 2017. For details, refer to Akhil Ranjan Dutta, 'Preventive Detention under Judicial Scrutiny: Akhil Gogoi vs the State of Assam', *Economic & Political Weekly* 53, no. 12 (24 March 2018): 20–23, with minor changes. The article is available at https://www.epw.in/journal/2018/12/commentary/ preventive-detention-under-judicial-scrutiny.html?0=ip_login_no_cache%3 D9858eaa1e958b13ab7f05a8fe2844e72.

3. *The Assam Tribune*, 'Modi Seeks Decisive Mandate', 9 April 2016, http://www. assamtribune.com/scripts/detailsnew.asp?id=apr0916/at050.

4. Akhil Ranjan Dutta, 'Poverty and Inequality in South Asia: State Responses', in *Migration in South Asia: Poverty and Vulnerability* (SAAPE Poverty and Vulnerability Report 2020), eds. Babu P. Remesh, Akhil Ranjan Dutta and Mohan Mani. (Kathmandu: South Asia Alliance for Poverty Eradication, 2020), 47.

5. David Harvey, *A Brief History of Neoliberalism* (Oxford: Oxford University Press, 2005), 7.

6. David Harvey, *The New Imperialism* (Oxford: Oxford University Press, 2003), 45.

7. Prabhat Patnaik, 'The State under Neo-liberalism', *Social Scientist* 35, no. 1/2 (January–February 2007): 4–15.

8. Ajay Gudavarthy, 'Neoliberalism Is Killing the Very Idea of Citizenship in India', Quartz India, 3 September 2019, https://qz.com/india/1700542/ neoliberalism-is-killing-the-very-idea-of-citizenship-in-india/.

9. *The Economic Times*, 'India's Aim of Being a $5 Trillion Economy "Challenging" but "Realisable": Nirmala Sitharaman', 16 October 2019, https://economictimes.indiatimes.com/news/economy/indicators/indias-aim-of-being-a-5-trillion-economy-challenging-but-realisable-nirmala-sitharaman/ articleshow/71621262.cms?from=mdr.

10. *The Hindu* 'Global Hunger Index 2019: India Ranked Lower than Nepal, Pakistan, Bangladesh', 16 October 2019, https://www.thehindu.com/news/national/global-hunger-index-2019-india-ranked-lower-than-nepal-pakistan-bangladesh/article29714429.ece.

11. Oxfam India, 'India: Extreme Inequality in Numbers', n.d., https://www.oxfam.org/en/india-extreme-inequality-numbers.

12. Ibid.

13. Anand Teltumbde, 'Saffron Neo-liberalism', *Economic & Political Weekly* 49, no. 31 (2 August 2014): 11, https://www.epw.in/journal/2014/31/margin-speak/saffron-neo-liberalism.html?0=ip_login_no_cache%3D5ea38a5c9b3 17e2310d941d9079bce20.

14. Ibid.

15. Akhil Ranjan Dutta, 'The ULFA and Indian State: Role of Civil Society in Conflict Resolution', in *Unheeded Hinterland: Identity and Sovereignty in Northeast India*, ed. Dilip Gogoi (Abingdon: Routledge, 2016), 193–194.

16. Ibid., 195.

17. This was a document issued by a government department for the release of funds earmarked under specific heads. It had to be first endorsed by the finance department and then dispatched to treasury offices located in the concerned district headquarters. The treasury office was entrusted to check the amount and the purpose mentioned in the document based on instructions received by it from the department concerned. If the treasury office found that the amount required to be released was in the order, it passed the LoC and released the amount.

18. Avirook Sen, 'Letter of Credit Scam: Assam CM Prafulla Kumar Mahanta Comes under CBI Lens', *India Today*, 1 December 1997, https://www.india-today.in/magazine/states/story/19971201-letter-of-credit-scam-assam-cm-prafulla-mahanta-comes-under-cbi-lens-830997-1997-12-01.

19. Avirook Sen, 'Clean Chit to Prafulla Kumar Mahanta Comes as a Poll-eve Bonanza for AGP', *India Today*, 16 February 1998, https://www.indiatoday.in/magazine/states/story/19980216-clean-chit-to-prafulla-kumar-mahanta-comes-as-a-poll-eve-bonanza-for-agp-825731-1998-02-16.

20. *The Telegraph Online*, 'Mahanta Hedges on Reforms', 21 November 1999, Guwahati, https://www.telegraphindia.com/india/mahanta-hedges-on-reforms/cid/910537.

21. Ibid.

22. These issues have been discussed at length in Chapter 4.

23. Smitu Kothari and Ramananda Wangkheirakpam, 'Dams in the North-east Will Also Ruin Livelihoods', Down To Earth, 7 June 2015, https://www.downtoearth.org.in/coverage/dams-in-the-northeast-will-also-ruin-livelihoods-13890.

24. Ibid.

25. In a meeting held in Sivasagar, the North-East Democratic Alliance (NEDA) Coordinator and State Finance Minister Dr Himanta Biswa Sarma labelled Badruddin Ajmal-led AIUDF as one of the core enemies of the Assamese community. Source: Kangkan Kalita, 'Assam: BJP Leader Himanta Biswa Sarma Hits Out at Ajmal, Says BJP Will Win 100 Seats', *Times of India*,

5 October 2020, https://timesofindia.indiatimes.com/city/guwahati/
assam-bjp-leader-himanta-biswa-sarma-hits-out-at-ajmal-says-bjp-will-win-
100-seats/articleshow/78484415.cms.

26. Badruddin Ajmal is the AIUDF supremo. The AIUDF primarily represents the
Bengali Muslims, and the BJP has constantly been projecting this community
as the threat to the culture and the identity of the Assamese people. In the
run up to the 2021 elections, the political rhetoric is now building up with
the BJP sharpening its attack on the AIUDF. By Ajmal civilization, the BJP
refers to the culture and politics of the Bengali Muslims—the political base
of the AIUDF. Dr Himanta Biswa Sarma made this statement in a meeting in
Jorhat. Source: *Niyomiya Barta*, 'Madhya-Namani Asom- Barakat Sristi Hoiche
AanEkJ atir' [A new nationality is in ascendance in middle and lower Assam
and in the Barak valley], 17 October 2020.

27. These two strategies are evident in the speeches and writings of Himanta Biswa
Sarma. His 2019 book *Bhinna Samay Abhinna Mat* [Changing times, consistent
views] (Guwahati: Saraswati Printers & Publishers) is a testimony to it.

From the 'Rainbow' to 'Saffron'

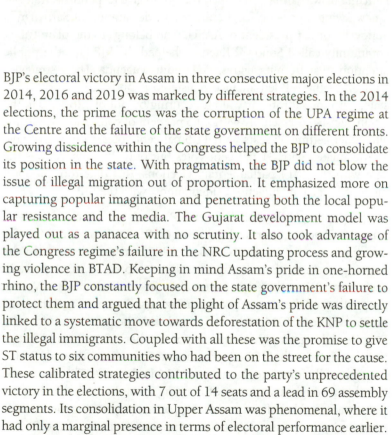

1

BJP's Changing Electoral Strategies

BJP's electoral victory in Assam in three consecutive major elections in 2014, 2016 and 2019 was marked by different strategies. In the 2014 elections, the prime focus was the corruption of the UPA regime at the Centre and the failure of the state government on different fronts. Growing dissidence within the Congress helped the BJP to consolidate its position in the state. With pragmatism, the BJP did not blow the issue of illegal migration out of proportion. It emphasized more on capturing popular imagination and penetrating both the local popular resistance and the media. The Gujarat development model was played out as a panacea with no scrutiny. It also took advantage of the Congress regime's failure in the NRC updating process and growing violence in BTAD. Keeping in mind Assam's pride in one-horned rhino, the BJP constantly focused on the state government's failure to protect them and argued that the plight of Assam's pride was directly linked to a systematic move towards deforestation of the KNP to settle the illegal immigrants. Coupled with all these was the promise to give ST status to six communities who had been on the street for the cause. These calibrated strategies contributed to the party's unprecedented victory in the elections, with 7 out of 14 seats and a lead in 69 assembly segments. Its consolidation in Upper Assam was phenomenal, where it had only a marginal presence in terms of electoral performance earlier.

But disillusionment with the new NDA government surfaced almost immediately once the government issued notifications on granting citizenship to six non-Muslim minority refugee communities by amending the relevant rules of the Passport (Entry into India) Act, 1920, and Foreigners Act, 1946. The failure of the government to fulfil the promise of granting ST status to six communities added woes to the party. It was amid these developments that the 2016 assembly elections were held. The BJP smartly changed its strategy and framed the Rainbow Alliance by bringing in almost all dominant political forces of major tribal-ethnic communities and the AGP, the major regional party in the state. The breakaway segment of the Congress along with Himanta Biswa Sarma also helped the BJP to give its political strategies a new swing. Focus on local culture and declaration of Sarbananda Sonowal, former president of AASU, who belongs to the plain tribes' community called Sonowal Kachari, helped the BJP take the public attention away from its aggressive Hindutva agenda. These strategies paid off as the BJP-led alliance registered a landslide victory in the state, with the saffron party alone securing 60 out of 126 seats in the Assam legislative assembly with 29.5 per cent of votes and the alliance altogether getting 86 seats with 41.5 per cent votes. Congress almost got decimated with 31 per cent votes but only 26 seats. As was the case with the 2014 parliamentary elections, this time too, the local media and local intelligentsia sided almost with the BJP.

The popular enthusiasm mover BJP's landslide victory, however, was short-lived. The introduction of CAB, 2016, that negated the consensus on the Assam Accord of 1985 and posed threat to the ongoing process of updating the NRC erupted in mass protests against the BJP in the state, particularly in the Brahmaputra Valley. People flocked the streets, protesting against the move, and the local media, unlike in 2014 and 2016, sided with the popular discontent. Despite the seemingly hostile response, the BJP registered better performance in the 2019 parliamentary elections than in 2014, taking its tally from 7 to 9 seats out of 14 in the state. This was made possible through its strategy of creating a solid vote bank through state-sponsored beneficiary schemes, particularly among the tea tribe community in Assam. Apart from the consolidation of the RSS at the grassroots and state's capacity to reach out different segments of the voters through the populist schemes, what helped the BJP most to win elections was the absence of a viable electoral alternative to represent the popular discontent.

This trajectory is marked by the party's shift in electoral strategies from the local-culture and community-centric Rainbow Alliance to that of hard Hindutva agenda accompanied by state's capacity to manoeuvre people's political decisions through state-sponsored schemes.

ELECTORAL BELTS: POLITICAL DOMINANCE AND CONTESTATIONS

Assam has a total of 14 PCs with 126 assembly segments. The electoral map of the state may be divided into total six belts. Each belt has unique demographic composition and thereby provides fertile grounds for electoral dominance and contestations. A brief reflection on the electoral belts will help us to understand the electoral strategies, consolidation and victory of the BJP in three consecutive elections.

1. Barak Valley has 2 PCs and 15 assembly segments with the dominance of Bengali-speaking population—both Hindus and Muslims sharing almost equal percentage, but a higher percentage of Muslims speaking Bengali than the Hindus. This belt witnessed the electoral penetration of the BJP in the 1990s. Subsequently, it became a battleground of three political parties—BJP, AIUDF and INC.

2. Autonomous District is the only hill constituency in the state, dominated by two hill tribes—Karbis and Dimasas—both having Sixth Schedule autonomous councils. This belt, having only one PC with five assembly segments, witnessed the consolidation of the Communist Party of India (Marxist–Leninist)—CPI (ML)—that steered the movement for the autonomous state under the banner of Autonomous State Demand Committee (ASDC), which challenged the dominance of the Congress from the mid-1980s. But by the beginning of the new century, the Congress re-established its dominance. From 2016, however, the BJP consolidated its base in this belt.

3. Kokrajhar is the epicentre of Bodo politics, which the Bodos dominate without a majority, and one of the conflict spots in Assam with rivalry among the Bodos and the non-Bodos. Koch-Rajbongshis

and Adivasis have a substantial presence in this belt, and they have been steering political movements for autonomy. Bodos are the first and only plain tribe community having granted an autonomous council under the Sixth Schedule in 2003. The community of Koch-Rajbongshis has also been granted an autonomous council through state legislation in 2020 in the name of Kamtapur Autonomous Council, the only council in Assam named after a geographical territory.[1] The Bodo community is also marked by intra-factionalism. But the ruling BPF emerged as an important political player in deciding the fortunes of the aspiring ruling party in the state since 2006. Created in 1967 as a PC and presently having 10 assembly segments, it was represented by a Bodo politician until 2014. In both 2014 and 2019, the constituency returned a non-Bodo candidate. However, elections to the councils and the assembly registered the dominance by BPF from 2005–2006. The parties allied with the Congress in both 2006 (post-poll) and 2011 (pre-poll) assembly elections. In the 2016 assembly elections and 2019 parliamentary elections, it allied with the BJP (pre-poll).

4. Lower Assam electoral belt has 2 PCs and 20 assembly seats. This belt is dominated by East-Bengal-origin Muslims and has been the main centre of the AIUDF politics since 2006. The belt used to have a substantive presence of left parties for quite a long time. At present, it is a battleground among the AIUDF, Congress and AGP, which is evident from the 2019 parliamentary election results.

5. Three PCs in Central Assam having a total of 29 assembly segments are mixed in demographic composition, with a substantive Bengali-speaking Muslim population along with ethnic tribes: the Rabhas and the Tiwas. These two communities have statutory non-territorial autonomous councils under the state Act. This belt has been a battleground between the Congress and non-Congress political parties since the first general elections. The Praja Socialist Party (PSP), Communist Party of India (CPI), Bharatiya Lok Dal (BLD), AGP and BJP had fought against the Congress in this belt during the latter's days of dominance. In parliamentary elections in the recent years, the BJP has become a dominating force. But in assembly elections, this belt has been a battleground of the Congress, BJP, AGP and AIUDF.

6. Upper Assam, with 5 PCs and 47 assembly segments, has played an important role in deciding the fortunes of the political parties in the state. This area has the highest number of tea gardens, 614 out of total 803 in the state,[2] and is the homeland of the tea tribes' politics. Besides, this belt has the dominance of the Ahoms along with other ethnic communities of Moran, Matak, Mising, Deori, Thengal-Kachari, Chutia and Koch-Rajbongshi. With the passage of autonomous council bills for Morans and Mataks in September 2020,[3] now this belt has six autonomous councils in total, created by the state legislature.[4] Earlier, Morans and Mataks along with Koch-Rajbongshis were granted the status of development councils along with other 30 development councils created by the state government since 2010.[5] The movements for the ST status for five out of six communities—Ahoms, Morans, Mataks, Chutias and Adivasi—have been quite strong in this belt. The BJP's growing dominance in this belt has been made possible through its penetration among the communities in tea gardens through both state-sponsored development activities in the post-2016 period and educational and cultural activities carried out by the RSS and other Hindutva affiliates for decades together.

The following sections endeavour to journey through the shift in strategic priorities of the BJP in the three elections through a comprehensive analysis of its campaign profiles, support base and performance.[6]

A SPECTACULAR VICTORY: BJP'S CONSOLIDATION IN 2014

Context and Dynamics

BJP's consolidation and victory in Assam in the 2014 parliamentary elections were spectacular. Apart from winning 7 out of 14 constituencies and registering the highest-ever percentage of votes (36.5%), it also led in 69 assembly segments. This election set the stage for its victory in the 2016 and 2019 elections. An analysis of the party's victory in 2014 invites a critical review of the context and dynamics of Assam's politics that shaped the electoral battle in 2014.

The 2011 state legislative assembly elections brought the Tarun Gogoi-led Congress government in the state to power for the third time in a row with a landslide majority of 78 seats. The election was billed as a 'mandate for peace and development'.[7] In 2001, when the Congress government assumed power, the state was facing severe economic contraction and deteriorating law and order. The Tarun Gogoi government was credited with bringing back normalcy to the state, and the economy also showed signs of resurgence. The government-initiated dialogue with various ethnic insurgent outfits brought them to the negotiation table. One of the important achievements was the signing of the Bodoland Territorial Council (BTC) Accord in 2003, which helped control Bodo militancy and violence to a great extent.

It was against this background that the Congress government under Tarun Gogoi's leadership was returned to power in 2006, although with a reduced majority, and the second consecutive government under his leadership was formed with a post-poll alliance with the BPF. This government, assisted by a series of Centre-sponsored popular initiatives such as MGNREGA, NRHM and Jawaharlal Nehru National Urban Renewal Mission (JNNURM), could reach out to the people with individual-oriented beneficiary schemes, which helped the government to sustain its popular bases. During the second tenure of the government, however, corruption became a huge issue and the government came into confrontation with the people's movements, particularly one led by KMSS on the issue of the LSHPP.

Assam witnessed a series of social resistance movements against the government. With the help of the newly enacted RTI Act, 2005, the corruption at different layers and levels of the government was exposed. The alleged ₹1,000 crore North Cachar Hills Autonomous Council scam elicited shocking waves of protest, and the government was put into the dock. On various other issues also, like granting land entitlement to the forest dwellers and implementation of FRA, 2006, various social groups continued to come into confrontation with the government. A series of conflicts in BTAD targeting primarily the Adivasis and Bengali-speaking Muslims also exposed the failure of the government in maintaining law and order.

Amid these challenges, with the initiative of Sanmilita Jatiya Abhibarttan (SJA) steered by a group of leading intellectuals, academics and social activists, the dialogue between ULFA and the Union government took off.[8] With P. C. Haldar (retired Intelligence Bureau chief) as the interlocutor, the initiative of dialogue and negotiation with a few other insurgent groups in the state including Dima Halam Daogah (Jewel)—(DHD-J)—United People's Democratic Solidarity (UPDS) and National Democratic Front of Bodoland (NDFB) was also undertaken.

It is against this background that the 2011 assembly elections were held. The ruling Congress not only won the election but with a spectacular majority of 78 seats in the 126-member legislative assembly. The state, however, witnessed the consolidation of both ethnic and religious polarization in Lower Assam during this election, which was already witnessed in the 2006 assembly elections. The AIUDF, representing the interests of the East-Bengal-origin Muslims, secured 18 seats and the BPF, the political organization of the Bodos, secured 12 seats in the assembly. The AGP was reduced to a total of 10 seats and the BJP was reduced to 5. One of the factors behind Congress's victory in 2011 amid challenges was the absence of a credible challenger apart from its much-publicized achievements towards development and peace in the state.

During 2011 and 2014, the country in general and Assam in particular witnessed many significant political developments. The Congress-led UPA government at the Centre was maligned with a number of scams and the infamous Nirbhaya case in Delhi in December 2012 that provoked mass reaction across the country. The state government's failure on the NRC update; the detection, deletion and deportation of foreigners; the land swap deal with Bangladesh (2011); and most importantly, the government's failure to stop killing of one-horned rhinos in KNP evoked large-scale protests.[9] Besides, price hikes and corruption further weakened the government. The 2012 violence in BTAD which displaced 392,000 persons[10] invited all-round condemnation and wrath from the people. The non-Bodos in BTAD, who now constitute more than 70 per cent of the total population,[11] were already challenging the BTC Accord that gives overriding powers to the Bodos in the council. Once the violence against the non-Bodos increased, they became more assertive and resistive against both the BTAD authority and the state government. The Congress–BPF alliance came under severe criticism as the violence exposed the unstable law and order situation in the state.

The state government also confronted with the much-energized people's resistance on a variety of issues, particularly related to the LSHPP, land entitlements, hike in the urban property tax and proposed water privatization in urban areas. Importing Sanjay Singh, a politician from Amethi, Uttar Pradesh, for the Rajya Sabha seat from the state legislative assembly, the election for which was held in February 2014, brought forth severe criticism in the civil society domain. It exposed the government's gross indifference towards Assamese feelings, feeding disillusionment with the party and the government.

While the government was almost dysfunctional in dealing with these challenges, the worst was yet to come. And it finally came in the form of dissidence from within the party when around 50 per cent of the Congress legislators including a few of his trusted colleagues publicly revolted against the incumbent Chief Minister Tarun Gogoi. The powerful Health and Education Minister Himanta Biswa Sarma led the dissident group. In the run-up to the Lok Sabha elections 2014, although the dissidence appeared to have disappeared, in reality, it was intact. It is the dissidents within the government and the party who caused more harm to the government, maligned it publicly and rendered it dysfunctional, resulting in the unprecedented defeat of the Congress in Assam. The Congress ended winning only three seats in the Lok Sabha elections, its lowest ever.

Verdict

With its victory in 7 out of 14 Lok Sabha seats[12] in Assam, BJP's upsurge in the state in the 2014 general elections had been spectacular. The BJP recorded the highest-ever percentage of votes (36.5%) so far in the 2014 general elections in the state, which was 20 per cent higher than the party polled in the 2009 Lok Sabha elections. It also led in 69 assembly segments out of 126. The party far surpassed poll predictions, possibly because of its previous election results, winning 4 seats in the 2009 Lok Sabha elections and only 5 seats in the 126-member legislative assembly elections in 2011. Voting percentages were 16.62 per cent and 11.47 per cent, respectively.

The BJP penetrated the Congress strongholds in Upper Assam for the first time, winning four constituencies: Tezpur, Jorhat, Dibrugarh and Lakhimpur. The other seat in the juncture between Upper Assam and Central Assam is Kaliabor, where the Congress had won since its formation in 1967 except in 1985 and 1996 when AGP candidates were returned to the Lok Sabha. It is now known as the dynastic constituency as Kaliabor was won by the former Chief Minister Tarun Gogoi in 1991, 1998 and 1999, his brother Dip Gogoi in 2004 and 2009 and has been won by his son Gourav Gogoi in both 2014 and 2019. However, in 2014, the BJP secured the second position and registered its lead in four assembly segments compared to three each by both the Congress and AIUDF.

In the three constituencies in Central Assam, Gauhati, Mangaldoi and Nowgong, the BJP won all as it did in the 2009 Lok Sabha elections. The Congress did not have a monopoly over these three constituencies, as non-Congress parties registered victories in them from time to time. The PSP won the Gauhati Lok Sabha seat twice in 1957 and 1962 with the CPI then winning it in 1967. In 1977, Guwahati returned the BLD candidate to the Lok Sabha, while the AGP won it in 1985 and 1996. In 1999 and 2009, BJP's Bijoya Chakraborty won it, as she did for the third time in 2014. The Mangaldoi constituency, formed in 1967, elected a PSP candidate in 1967; BLD won in 1977; and AGP won in 1985 and 1996. The BJP has been winning this seat consecutively for the third time since 2004. The Nowgong constituency elected AGP candidates in 1985, 1991 and 1996, but it has consecutively been won by the BJP since 1999. This is the only constituency in Assam where the BJP had won four consecutive times. The history of these three constituencies shows that BJP's consolidation has been both faster and wider in those seats where either the PSP or AGP could win in the past.

The BJP's only failure in the 2014 elections had been in the two Barak Valley constituencies, where the party registered its first victories in 1991 and won both seats—Silchar and Karimganj. Karimganj is the only Scheduled Caste (SC) reserved seat in the state. The BJP won Karimganj in the subsequent elections in 1996, whereas in Silchar it won in 1998 and 2009, while the Congress won the Silchar seat in 2014. The AIUDF, which primarily represents East-Bengal-origin Muslims, registered its first victory in the valley by winning the Karimganj seat in 2014. The BJP secured the second position in both constituencies. The AIUDF won in a dominate manner in two constituencies in Lower Assam, Dhubri and Barpeta, which witnessed the highest polling in the state, 88.49 per cent and 84.50 per cent, respectively. It registered its first victory in the Lok Sabha elections in Dhubri in 2009 and secured highest number of assembly seats in this Lok Sabha constituency in the 2011 assembly elections.

There are two ST constituencies in the state: the Autonomous District since the first election in 1951 and Kokrajhar established in 1967. Both are centres of hill tribes' and plain tribes' politics in the state respectively. The All Party Hill Leaders Conference (AHLC) dominated the Autonomous District constituency before the reorganization of Northeast India in 1972, while subsequently it became the battleground between the ASDC and Congress. The Congress won the seat in 1951, but in the subsequent four elections, AHLC candidates won them. In the next nine elections, Biren Singh Engti won it five times, and in the four elections from 1991 to 1999, it was won by Jayanta Rongpi, the leader of the ASDC and affiliated to CPI (ML). Rongpi fought the 1999 election under the CPI (ML) banner after the ASDC became divided. In the 2014 election, however, the BJP registered its presence by gaining the second position. In the Kokrajhar constituency, the Congress won only twice, in 1967 and 1971. In all subsequent elections from 1977 to 2009, candidates engaged in Bodo political mobilization won the seat. The year 2014 had been a watershed as for the first time this constituency had returned a non-Bodo candidate Naba Kumar Sarania, a former commander of the ULFA.[13]

The decline of the left parties has been phenomenal. The CPI won the Lok Sabha elections from the Gauhati constituency in 1967, and the CPI (M) won from the Barpeta constituency in 1991 and 1996. In the Autonomous District constituency, Rongpi, affiliated to CPI (ML), but under the ASDC label, won it in 1991, 1996 and 1998 and with the CPI (ML) ticket in 1999. Left parties together maintained 6–10 per cent votes from 1957 to 1991 in legislative assembly elections in Assam, winning 2–16 seats. In the 1978 assembly elections, it won the largest number of seats, 16 with a vote share of 9.71 per cent. From 1996, the left's vote share declined and in the 2011 assembly elections, the CPI and CPI (M) together polled 1.65 per cent votes. The decline continued. In 2014, the CPI (M) polled 0.4 per cent votes, and the CPI (ML) and Socialist Unity Centre of India (Communist)—SUCI— polled only 0.3 per cent votes each (see Table 1.1).

Consolidation of BJP

The Lok Sabha elections of 2014 were fought in the state of Assam at various levels with various strategies by the BJP, using all possible means and capturing both state and local dynamics. The ruling Congress was busy mostly in fighting the growing dissidents within the party, particularly the threat posed by almost half of the party legislators to the incumbent Chief Minister Tarun Gogoi and a few of his trusted colleagues. While the public grievances against the government were growing, both the media and the intelligentsia at large played a pro-BJP role and indulged in projecting the Gujarat development model as truly pro-people oriented and towards high growth and inclusive development.

The RSS, which was penetrating the social dynamics at various levels including through the educational network called Sankardev Sishu Niketan/Vidya Niketan,[14] which has over the years emerged almost as an alternative to the chaotic and discredited public school education system in the state, played an important role in social engineering for the political advantage of the BJP. Penetration of the Vanavasi Kalyan Ashram, an RSS affiliate, which has been working for economic and educational development of the tribal communities, particularly among the tea tribes in Assam, also helped the BJP to gain political mileage.[15] Violence in BTAD is not a conflict only between

Table 1.1 *Performance of Political Parties in Assam Lok Sabha Elections (1991–2019)*

Election	Voter %	Party	Seats Won	% of Votes
1991	75.3	INC	8	28.50
		AGP	1	17.60
		BJP	2	09.60
1996	78.5	INC	5	31.60
		AGP	5	27.20
		BJP	1	15.90
1998	61.1	INC	10	38.97
		AGP	0	12.70
		BJP	1	24.47
1999	71.30	INC	10	38.42
		AGP	0	11.92
		BJP	2	29.84
2004	69.08	INC	9	35.07
		AGP	2	19.95
		BJP	2	22.94
2009	69.52	INC	7	34.90
		AGP	1	14.60
		BJP	4	16.62
		AIUDF	1	16.10
2014	80.13	INC	3	29.60
		AGP	0	03.80
		BJP	7	36.50
		AIUDF	3	14.80
2019	81.00	INC	3	35.44
		AGP	0	8.23
		BJP	9	36.05
		AIUDF	1	7.80

Source: Compiled from Election Commission of India reports.

Hindus and Muslims, but it has also affected both Adivasis and other non-Bodo non-Muslim communities. The BJP, however, was successful in projecting violence in 2012 as a symbol and symptom of the attack on indigenous communities by illegal Muslim Bangladeshis.

BJP's consolidation in the state has a parallel to that of the decline of the AGP in the state. The Bharatiya Jana Sangh (BJS), the predecessor of the BJP, was present in Assam's electoral politics from 1951 although with an insignificant impact. The BJP for the first time contested in both Assam legislative assembly and Lok Sabha elections in 1985. In the legislative assembly elections, the party fielded 37 candidates and did not win a seat, registering 1.07 per cent votes. For the Lok Sabha, it contested two seats, forfeited deposits in both and registered 0.37 per cent votes. This election was fought after the six-year-long Assam agitation (1979–1985) on the illegal foreigners' issue. The BJP supported the movement, and its leaders including Atal Bihari Vajpayee visited the state and held discussions with the movement leaders. Among those who campaigned for the cause of the movement at the national level was Arun Shourie, a journalist by profession and an eminent BJP leader later on. It has been alleged that the RSS was instrumental in giving a communal face to the movement.

After the Assam agitation that ended in 1985 with the conclusion of the Assam Accord on 15 August 1985, the movement leaders formed a regional political party, the AGP. The party came to power in new elections held to the legislative assembly in December 1985. It won 63 seats in the 126-member assembly and registered 34.5 per cent votes. The AGP also won 7 out of 14 seats in Lok Sabha elections held in the same year. In the next assembly elections held in 1991, the BJP contested 48 seats, winning 10 with 6.55 per cent votes against the Congress and AGP, registering 29.35 per cent votes and 20 per cent votes and winning 66 and 19 seats, respectively. In the Lok Sabha elections held in the same year, the BJP won two seats with 9.6 per cent votes. The BJP maintained a steady growth, and the AGP experienced a decline after the 1996 elections. However, there is a difference in votes polled by the BJP in assembly and Lok Sabha elections. While the votes polled by the BJP in assembly elections were around 10 per cent from 1996 to 2011, the tally in the Lok Sabha elections was relatively higher.

The BJP's vote surge to 36.5 per cent in the 2014 elections, of course, was unprecedented. There are two possible explanations. One is the increase in total poll percentage (80.3%), and the other is an all-time low of votes for the AGP of only 3.8 per cent. The BJP has benefited from both. The BJP, with the help of the RSS network, penetrated in Northeast India in general and in Assam in particular, both through religious and educational institutions. The BJP re-organized itself in the run-up to the Lok Sabha elections. One of the important initiatives in this regard was the appointment of Sarbananda Sonowal as the president of the state BJP unit. Sonowal, former president of the AASU (1992–1999), joined the AGP after relinquishing his position in the AASU and was elected as an assembly member in 2001 and then to the Lok Sabha in 2004. One of the most important initiatives and achievements of Sarbananda Sonowal was to challenge the Illegal Migrants (Determination by Tribunals) Act (IMDT Act), 1983, in the Supreme Court of India. It was condemned as an infamous and discriminatory Act, which allegedly gave protection to foreigners in the state. The Supreme Court through its verdict in July 2005 struck down the Act. This achievement of Sonowal gave him a status of national hero (Jatiya Nayak) in the state. In 2011, Sonowal joined the BJP and became a national executive committee member of the BJP and the state's spokesperson. He was appointed as the president of the state BJP in 2012. He, then with the AGP, was the first leader to defeat the Congress in the Dibrugarh Lok Sabha constituency in 2004, which had been successively won by the Congress since 1951.

It was, however, the new political wave in the country generated by Narendra Modi's new avatar (incarnation), which added energy and vibrancy to the BJP's electoral consolidation in Assam. Modi, a pragmatist, did not blow the illegal migration issue in the state out of proportion. Rather, he used all rhetoric possible to mobilize the people against the Congress government both in the state and at the Centre. One-horned rhinos are Assam's pride. The state government failed to protect the rhinos over the years, and hundreds of them were killed. There were condemnations against the state government for its failure to protect Assam's pride. The government remained steadfast not to rise to the occasion. Modi, the pragmatist, took it as the Brahmastra against the state government and linked state government's indifference towards the protection of the one-horned rhino to that of the government's pro-Bangladeshi attitude.

In his electoral rally on 31 March 2014 at Gogamukh,[16] Modi 'accused the Congress led state government of trying to settle cheap Bangladeshi labourers in the forests of Assam by killing the endangered rhinos to clear the jungles'.[17] It was a mass appealing argument. Linking the issue of endangered Assam's pride with the incumbent government's plan to settle Bangladeshis re-energized people's distrust against the Congress regime. He was playing his communal card too by stating that the indigenous Muslims and East Bengali Hindu immigrants should take a unified stand against the Bangladeshi problem in Assam.[18]

On his first visit to Assam on 8 February 2014 after he was declared the NDA's prime ministerial candidate, Narendra Modi addressed the Maha Jagaran Rally in Guwahati, where he regretted that,

> Assam has great potential, as it is a land of tea and timber. He asked why is it that the same Assam, whose tea energizes the entire nation every morning is without energy and is facing power crisis. He further questioned why such a peace loving land was been full of violence and bloodshed?[19]

He questioned his commitment to the state from where he has been a Rajya Sabha member for the past 23 years. Calling Assam a peace-loving state, Modi attributed the state of conflict and violence in the Assam to the failure of the government.

With his political imagination and rhetoric, Modi touched the hearts of Assamese pride by citing the heroes of Assam's culture and politics. Praising the Assamese tradition in his hour-long speech, Modi said, 'Assam has a great tradition. It can boast personalities like Srimanta Sankardeva, Madhavdeva, Ajan Fakir, Joimoti, Bhaskar Barman, Sati Radhika, Naranarayan, Lachit Borphukan, Bishnu Rabha, Bhupen Hazarika etc. Under the Congress rule the tradition has been demolished.'[20]

Modi's maturity had grown in capturing the popular imagination and agony. This was evident from the advertisements published on the first day of polling on 7 April 2014, the day five PCs went to the polls: Tezpur, Kaliabor, Jorhat, Dibrugarh and Lakhimpur. These constituencies have a concentration of tea tribes[21] and the communities who have been struggling for the status of ST. The demand for the ST status by six communities was a burning issue at that point. The BJP unveiled its vision in the last page of its advertisement, which was in the form of a manifesto and commitment. It assured that 'For BJP, its manifesto shall be the basis of its governance agenda for a powerful, secure and insurgent India and Assam.'[22] The first commitment in the manifesto was to accord ST status to the Ahoms, Koch-Rajbongshis, Morans, Mataks, Chutias and tea tribes. All these communities except for the Koch-Rajbongshis had concentrations in these constituencies. Except for Kaliabor, in four other constituencies, the visibility of illegal Bangladeshis is not very strong. All the political outfits of the communities struggling for ST status are strong in those constituencies. Both small tea growers and tea tribes are concentrated in those areas. Several incidents were reported over the years where tea labourers resorted to violence on the issues of bonus and wages. Therefore, it was critical to focus on their problems. The BJP prioritized it very well and made it the second issue in its list of commitments. Both the issues of updating the NRC and the detection, deletion and deportation of illegal migrants were placed in the middle of the list of commitment. It, of course, promised that while updating NRC, it will take 1951 as the base year, as has been demanded by various nationality organizations in the state.

BJP's most important success was in the three Lok Sabha constituencies in Upper Assam: Jorhat, Dibrugarh and Lakhimpur, all of which have concentrations of tea tribe populations and tea estates. The Congress dominated all these constituencies from the time of their formation.

BJP candidates in these constituencies not only registered victories but had also won most votes in almost all assembly segments. In the Jorhat constituency, BJP candidate Kamakhya Prasad Tasa registered 49 per cent votes and defeated the Congress veteran Bijoy Krishna Handique, six-time MP from the constituency, by a margin of 1.02 lakh votes. He also secured most votes in 8 out of 10 assembly segments.

The Dibrugarh constituency was one of the strongholds of the Congress. Congress MP Paban Singh Ghatowar, former state Congress president and a minister of state in the UPA II, represented it five times. From 1951, only in 2004 did the seat go to another party, the AGP. In 2014, not only did Congress veteran Ghatowar lose the election, but the BJP candidate Rameswar Teli secured 55.5 per cent votes and defeated Ghatowar by a margin of 1.85 lakh votes and registered a lead in all 9 assembly segments. In Lakhimpur, Sarbananda Sonowal defeated his Congress rival Ranee Narah, three times Congress MP from the constituency and state minister in UPA II, by a margin of 2.92 lakh votes. While Sonowal secured 55 per cent votes, he led in 9 out of 10 assembly segments. In Lakhimpur, the political dynamics changed with an electoral understanding between the BJP and Gana Shakti, the political outfit of the Mising community in the constituency that registered a landslide victory in the Mising Autonomous Council election held in October 2013.

Growing Disappointment

Disillusionment with the BJP-led government grew in Assam almost immediately after it assumed power. In September 2014, Jammu and Kashmir (J&K), as well as Assam, suffered from heavy floods, which caused the loss of lives and property in both the states. While both Prime Minister Narendra Modi and Home Minister Rajnath Singh were prompt in responding to the woes of J&K, the Union government appeared to be indifferent to the woes of Assam. It caused adverse reactions in the state. The government failed to grant ST status to the six communities, which was the topmost promise given by the BJP in 2014. But the real disappointment came with the issuing of the two notifications by the Ministry of Home Affairs in September 2015, according citizenship to the refugees belonging to six non-Muslim minority communities from Afghanistan, Pakistan and Bangladesh till 31 December 2014. The notifications, which in 2016 incarnated in the form of CAB and finally got enacted into CAA in December 2019, triggered immediate reactions in Assam. The state witnessed resistance against the notifications on the ground that it violates the sanctity of the Assam Accord along with violating the secular foundation of citizenship as guaranteed by the Constitution of India.[23] However, in the run-up to the 2016 assembly elections, the BJP succeeded in subsiding these discontents by bringing in a discourse of *khilonjiya* (the indigenous) and building a much-publicized Rainbow Alliance which helped the party to register its landslide victory and to form the first-ever government in Assam. The assembly elections being close to the hearts of the people compared to a parliamentary election, the BJP had to be more strategic and comprehensive to win over the popular votes.

CO-OPTING THE KHILONJIYAS: LANDSLIDE VICTORY IN 2016

The landslide victory of the BJP in Assam in the April 2016 assembly elections provoked diametrically opposite interpretations. While for the rank and file of the Sangh Parivar the victory ascertained the consolidation of Hindutva in the state, on the other end of the spectrum, the intelligentsia who wanted to project the BJP as a changed and secular entity in the state asserted that the victory was not of Hindutva but of indigenous and identity politics. For the latter, the key to the victory was BJP's alliance with the regional-ethnic forces in the backdrop of growing insecurity of the indigenous people of Assam caused by unabated influx from Bangladesh. While Hindutva consolidation through different agencies and institutions gained momentum in the state, in the 2016 elections it was the charged campaign for the protection of the rights of the khilonjiyas, which added fortunes to the victory of BJP-led alliance. What is more important is to understand the way the 'indigenous' was constructed as an exclusionary category to bring in a communal divide in the electoral battle. The theory of 'indigenous' propagated during elections had, however, nothing to do with substantive rights like 'right to self-determination' or 'rights over resources' informed by international declarations on rights of the indigenous people. The international bidding for the auction of 12 oil fields in Assam by the BJP-led Union government immediately after the new government had assumed power in Assam and the resistance built by the nationalist and indigenous groups against the decision exposed the hollowness of the indigenous agenda of the BJP in Assam.

Rainbow Coalition

Ram Madhav, former National General Secretary of the BJP and also the north-east in-charge, counted three important factors that helped the BJP to register its victory in Assam in 2016: (a) success in forging 'a rainbow coalition' with the AGP and the BPF, (b) centring electoral strategies around local issues and concerns and not allowing the national issues to overshadow the campaign and also picking up a tribal leader Sarbananda Sonowal as the chief ministerial candidate and (c) inducting the Congress dissident Himanta Biswa Sarma to the party and making him a core strategist in the elections. They also asserted that the party planned its campaign so meticulously that ensured that the BJP 'did not make a single mistake that would have given the Congress any scope to gain political or electoral mileage'.[24]

The hallmark of the campaign for the 2016 Assam legislative assembly elections was the khilonjiya discourse. In the backdrop of the unabated influx from across the border and unproportionate growth of the Muslim population in the state, the demand for protection of the rights of the indigenous people in Assam was already ripe in the state. However, there were disagreements between the 'ethnic Assamese' and the 'ethnic-tribal communities' regarding who really constitute the true 'indigenous' communities in the state. During the run-up to the 2016 elections, Assam witnessed the consolidation of the tribal communities with the formation of the United People's Front (UPF) in September 2015. The UPF, floated on 9 September 2015 through a convention held in Guwahati, brought all the tribal communities of the hills and plains of Assam together on a single platform. The unification and resurgence of the tribal communities were perceived as the real threat by the BJP to its political fortune in the forthcoming assembly elections 2016. Therefore, the strategic campaign of the BJP started in January 2016 with a mission of bringing division within this grand tribal-ethnic alliance. A pre-election alliance between the BJP and BPF, the first alliance brokered by the BJP in Assam, was worked out on 17 January 2016, in New Delhi in the residence of BJP National President Amit Shah. Prime Minister Narendra Modi started the election campaign in Assam on 19 January 2016 in a rally organized by the BPF at Kokrajhar, the epicentre of Bodo politics. One of the significant announcements made by the prime minister in the rally was to grant ST status to the Bodos[25] living in two hill districts of Assam. The main objective behind this alliance was to capture the Bodo votes in around 12 assembly constituencies where BPF had its political control as well as in other 20 constituencies out of the total 126 constituencies where the Bodos were in a position to impact the poll outcomes in the state.[26] Besides, the substantive Bodo population in the hill districts was expected to add to the political fortunes of the BJP. The BPF was also struggling to overcome the electoral shock of 2014 Lok Sabha elections in which the party, in addition to losing the Kokrajhar constituency to a non-Bodo candidate[27] (that too in a constituency that returned BPF's candidate to the Lok Sabha in both 2004 and 2009 elections), even failed to register its lead in any assembly segment.

The resurgence of the ethnic-tribal communities through UPF collapsed immediately after the Hagrama Mohilary-led BPF joined hands with the BJP. Subsequently, the Rabha and Tiwa leadership also joined hands with the BJP. The Karbis and Misings, being led by Hill State Demand Committee (HSDC) and Gana Shakti respectively, both of which are known to be left-leaning political outfits, however, refrained from joining the BJP-led pre-poll alliance.[28] The decision to grant ST status to the Bodos in the hills immediately brought divisions between the tribes in the plains and the hills, with the tribes in the hills protesting the decision. Within a month and half of BJP–BPF alliance, the BJP also succeeded in striking an alliance with the AGP on 2 March 2016, again at the residence of the BJP National President Amit Shah. This grand alliance projected as Rainbow Coalition was necessary on the part of the BJP on two significant counts. First, the charged campaign by the BJP during 2014 Lok Sabha elections to grant ST status to six communities[29] was a key factor behind BJP's sweep in Upper Assam. This promise, however, created dissent among the existing ST communities in the state.[30] Second, the failure on the part of the BJP-led NDA government at the Centre to grant ST status to those communities so far also created enormous discontent. These twin reasons for discontent—from existing STs and aspiring STs—were perceived as a formidable challenge to BJP's political fortune in the 2016 assembly elections.

This strategic alliance completely transformed the electoral dynamics of the state and brought in the landslide victory to the BJP-led alliance with 86 seats in the 126-member Assam legislative assembly. The Hindutva forces played their active role at the grassroots,[31] but the party in the campaign kept these forces on a low profile by constantly harping on the '*Jati, Mati and Bheti*' (nationality, land and the hearth) slogan.[32] The demographic change as revealed by the successive censuses,[33] particularly by the census report of 2011 which shows a substantive increase of Muslim population in several districts, was a core issue in the campaign. A political fear psychosis was nurtured in a planned way by projecting how, in a near future, Assam's politics may go out of the control of the Assamese people and the 'Bangladeshis' may become the real political masters of the state. Such a campaign was already gaining momentum in the state, with leading nationalist organizations like the AASU projecting such apprehensions for quite a long time now. This was fully appropriated by the BJP in the campaign, and it was successful in transmitting this fear psychosis to almost all indigenous communities in the state. This particular issue came to the forefront to such an extent that all other issues such as the Land Swap Deal with Bangladesh, notification of granting refugee status to Hindu Bangladeshis, non-fulfilment of granting ST status to six communities and the Union government's determination to resume the construction of LSHPP, and the issues around which the discontents against the BJP-led Union government were gradually consolidating, were suddenly pushed to the periphery. The vocal and dominant forces in the civil society, including the media, openly exhibited their allegiance to the BJP. There was almost a complete alliance between the civil society forces and the political society being pushed by the BJP. This alliance became more tangible after a group of intellectuals and concerned citizens issued an appeal on 2 April 2016—two days ahead of the first phase of polling in the state—not to vote for the BJP owing to its communal agenda and its corporate pursuit.[34] Although the appeal was preceded by an analysis of the political situation in the country and the state on the issues that posed a serious threat to democracy and communal harmony in the country as a whole, the media at large focused on just the 'not to vote for BJP' portion of the appeal and unleashed a continuous attack on those who had signed the appeal.[35]

Appropriation of the Local Cultural Icons and Media

Malini Bhattacharjee pointed out that as against significant attention paid towards understanding BJP's electoral strategies and inroads in Assam's politics for the last one decade and so, 'There has surprisingly been little attention towards understanding the contribution of the social and cultural wings of its *parivar* in deepening the roots of Hindutva in Assam.'[36] Tracing the penetration of Hinduism in Assam since pre-historic period and consolidation of Hindutva since the late 1940s, Bhattacharjee also argued that the Hindutva brigade has extensively used 'local histories, myths and idioms' for its penetration in the state.[37] Hinduism is supposed to have entered the Brahmaputra Valley one or two centuries before Christ, but it was 'staggered with several cults gaining popularity in different periods'.[38] While immigrant Brahmins from North India played a missionary role in popularizing Hinduism in the state during the reign of Kumar Bhaskaravarman, it was during the Ahom dynasty rule from 13th to 18th century that different tribal communities were also brought into the fold of Hinduism. BJP's 'Assam Vision Document 2016–2025' traces the process of Aryanization in the state since pre-historic times, citing evidence from the popular myths and narratives that link Assam with the epics Ramayana and Mahabharata. The popular cult of Kamakhya, the *Saktipeeth* (seat of power) in the state, has also been extensively used by the Hindutva forces for its consolidation in Assam. Ambubachi Mela, held in this *peeth* every year in June, and which brings together thousands of sadhus and *sanyasis* (ascetics) from across the country, is used by Hindutva forces to show the commonality of the Hindu traditions between this part of the country and mainstream India.[39] The RSS, which was established in Assam in 1946, 20 years after the organization was founded in Nagpur in 1925, has indeed used the local notables for its penetration into the Assamese society. The most important among them was the appropriation of Sankardev, the religious and social reformer of medieval Assam. RSS's educational wing Vidya Bharati, which has established its school network in Assam, has also been named after Sankardev. These schools have now emerged as both popular and successful institutions and are used as a convenient means of consolidation of Hindutva in the state.

In the 2016 elections, the BJP both comprehensively and aggressively used these Hindutva strategies to bring about its electoral victory. But BJP's sloganeering was culturally contextualized by appropriating the popular cultural icons and lyrics, particularly of Srimanta Sankardev (1449–1568), the preacher of neo-Vaishnavaite movement in medieval Assam and Bhupen Hazarika (1926–2011), the 20th-century musical legend. While Sankardev's religion is anti-Brahminical in its substance and moved by the philosophy of mass emancipation in all domains of life, the RSS appropriated him to consolidate 'Hindutva' in the state. The Srimanta Sankaradeva Sangha (formed in 1930) is the largest religious conglomerate in the state and was brought into being to accommodate those who are not given due dignity by the more Brahminical *satras*, the religious monasteries in Assam which also claim to have represented the Sankari culture. The BJP left no stone unturned to appropriate both the satras and the Sangha for its political mileage. On 5 February 2016, Prime Minister Narendra Modi attended and addressed the 85th annual conference of the Sangha at Sivasagar, where he said, 'The strength of the government and society must combine so that we can create the India Srimanta Sankardeva envisioned.'[40] The satras have also been a core focus in the BJP's campaign. Apart from promising financial assistance to these monasteries, the issue of invasion of satra's land by illegal migrants was continuously played out by the party. The party chose Majuli, the capital of satras, as the constituency for the chief ministerial candidate Sarbananda Sonowal.

What the BJP did more tactfully was to appropriate the popular lyrics composed by Bhupen Hazarika. Hazarika, who was active in the Indian People's Theatre Association (IPTA) movement in Assam and represented the progressive cultural ethos with his inimitable compositions to fight both feudalism and state atrocities, had joined the BJP in 2004 to contest the general elections, which he however lost. In people's minds, the memory of Hazarika's BJP tag faded, and he continues to enjoy the respect and adulation accorded to him as a people's artiste. Assam cannot think of its identity without these two cultural icons—Sankardev and Hazarika—and the BJP used these icons to its clear advantage during the 2016 elections. In addressing four political rallies on 8 April 2016, while campaigning for the second phase of the elections, Prime Minister Narendra Modi started his speech by invoking a stanza from Hazarika's popular song: *Bohag matho eti ritu nohoi, nohoi bohag eti maah/Asomiya jatir ee ayush rekha, gana-jivanar ee saah* (Bohag, that ushers in the New Year, is not just a season or month, it is the lifeline of the Assamese people; it gives courage to community life).[41] In the run-up to the elections, the BJP bought either the full front page or the space at the top of the local dailies, both vernacular and English, for its campaign advertisements. Here too, the popular lyrics were extensively used.

The aggressive campaign in the media started on 31 March 2016, that is, four days ahead of the first phase of the elections scheduled for 4 March 2016. The caption for the advertisement in the front page of the local dailies was again appropriated from popular Assamese singer Jayanta Hazarika's *Akou natun prabhat hobo* (A new dawn will descend once more). It asserted that the corrupt Congress would be defeated, and a new Assam would be built—with an emphasis that if it did not happen this time, it will never happen. On 1 April 2016, the advertisement again appropriated the first lines of the Gauhati University anthem composed by Bhupen Hazarika, *Jilikaba Luitare paar* (The banks of the Luit will be illuminated). To these lyrics were added: *Samay ahil natun Asom garhar, Soudishe Sankhanaad, hobo eibar BJP-r sarkar* (This is the time to build a new Assam; the reverberation of the notes of the conch-shell heralds the formation of a BJP government in all directions). On the day of the elections, there were full-page advertisements for the party in all local dailies. Once the first phase of the elections was over, the campaign strategies changed. From 5 April 2016 onwards, the emphasis was on a sure victory in the already-concluded first phase. On 5 April 2016, the caption was 'The change has already come in Upper Assam, now it is time for Lower Assam to reciprocate.' On 8 and 10 April 2016, the BJP again bought full-page advertisements in local dailies. On 8 April 2016, the advertisements focused on the Parivattan Maharally of Prime Minister Narendra Modi. On 10 April 2016, it was on BJP's promises on 'Change will bring development', which focused on employment to 2.5 million youths, universal skill development training, free education and scooters to girls students' 24-hour electricity and safe drinking water to all households, MUDRA loans to the youth, doing away with interviews to the posts of third- and fourth-grade recruitment, 100 per cent irrigation to paddy fields, setting up of AIIMS and organic hub in Assam, one-time assistance of ₹1 lakh to each self-help group and ₹2 lakh health insurance to patients suffering from life-threatening diseases. The dominant local media houses, both print and electronic, particularly *Asomiya Pratidin*, the highest circulated daily in the state and its electronic channel Pratidin Time, and News Live, the highest watched electronic channel owned by the wife of BJP state election committee convener Himanta Biswa Sarma, and its daily paper *Niyomiya Barta*, took sides with the BJP. Ridiculing the BJP opponents, particularly the Left, was one of the dominant strategies used.

Khilonjiyas: The Context and the Construct

Udayon Misra[42] argues that the BJP's landslide victory in Assam 'was the result of the BJP's success in garnering the support of regional forces like the Asom Gana Parishad (AGP), the Bodoland People's Front (BPF) and the Rabha, Tiwa and other plains tribal organisations.'[43] He further asserts, 'There was no Hindutva agenda as such in these elections and the emphasis was clearly on preserving the identity and culture of the indigenous people of the state in the face of swift demographic change triggered by infiltration from neighbouring Bangladesh.'[44]

Prasanta Rajguru, the editor of a leading Assamese daily *Amar Asom,* also attributes the victory of the BJP-led alliance to the 'power of the indigenous'. Rajguru, in one of his columns titled 'Khilonjiyar Shakti', argues that the apprehensions of the khilonjiyas have been present in the state right from the moment of the formation of the AIUDF in 2006. Khilonjiyas were indeed looking for opportunities to strike against the growing political assertions of the Bengal-origin migrant Muslim community in the state. With no real alternative in hand, they voted for the Congress in 2006. The Congress won 53 seats and secured 31.08 per cent votes in 2006 elections, which, of course, was lower than its tally of 71 seats and 39.75 per cent votes in 2001. The Congress formed the government with the BPF, the newly formed

Bodo political party. The BPF was formed after the Bodos, the dominant plain tribes community in the state, were accommodated into the Sixth Schedule through an amendment to the Constitution and were granted the BTC in 2003. In the 2006 elections, the BPF secured 10 seats in the assembly. The AIUDF also, in the very first elections that it contested, got 10 seats and secured 9.03 per cent votes. The AGP won 24 seats and secured 20.39 votes. The BJP fought in 125 constituencies, won 10 seats, forfeited deposit in 87 constituencies and secured 11.98 per cent votes. The political assertions of the Bengali-speaking migrant Muslim community in this election frightened the indigenous people more. Having found no real alternative, Rajguru has pointed out, the khilonjiyas voted again for the Congress in 2011 in a big way in which the Congress won 78 seats in the assembly, securing 39.9 per cent votes. The AIUDF did assert itself convincingly by securing 18 seats (12.57% votes). The BPF, the Congress ally, won in 12 and secured 6.13 per cent votes. The AGP won only 10 seats and secured 16.29 per cent votes. The BJP's performance was indeed miserable. The party contested in 120 constituencies, won only in 5, forfeited deposit in 84 and secured 11.47 per cent votes. The AIUDF's growing dominance was perceived as a political threat across the society in Assam. It is against such a political backdrop that there emerged a growing affinity among the Assamese-speaking Hindu people, the ethnic tribal communities, tea tribes, Assamese Muslims and Bengali-speaking Hindus in recent times. During the run-up to the elections, when the concept of 'indigenous people of Assam' got a political fillip, the Bengal-origin Muslims began to be projected as the real political threat to Assam.

The term 'khilonjiyas' has been used extensively by both 'ethnic Assamese' and tribal ethnic groups in the state. In the recent past, AASU has been successful in building a broad alliance of indigenous communities in the state which accommodates 26 ethnic outfits. The important issues being raised by this alliance include indigenous people's ownership over land and other natural resources of the state, detection and deportation of foreigners, fighting against mega development projects including large river dams that pose both ecological threat and threat of displacement, implementation of all clauses of the Assam Accord, 1985, and granting more powers to the state. 'True Federal Republic' has been a demand of AASU, wherein it has strongly argued both for protection of the rights of the indigenous people and that of dual citizenship.[45] For AASU, this became more important in the context of large-scale illegal migration. In the same context, AASU also demanded that the sole authority of the Parliament on granting and terminating citizenship should be amended by introducing dual citizenship. On the issue of regularization of migrants from foreign countries, it stated that there must be a provision of ensuring concurrence of the affected states. The other two outfits that raised the issue of the rights of the indigenous people very strongly are Asom Jatiyatabadi Yuva Chatra Parishad (AJYCP) and KMSS. Three important demands being raised by AJYCP are as follows: inner line permit for Assam; dual citizenship and full autonomy for the state; and state government's control over oil and forest resources.[46] KMSS, primarily a peasant outfit, also raised a number of issues concerning control over natural resources. It has been very vocal on the large river dam issue, forest dwellers' rights and the land policy. It prepared a 52-page Draft Assam Land Bill, 2016, which was submitted to the Government of Assam on 17 December 2015. Seeking to replace the Assam Land and Revenue Regulation, 1886, enacted by the British government, the Draft Land Bill sought to 'mandate that only indigenous people of Assam, provided he/she is an Indian citizen as defined in the Indian citizenship Act or any relevant law of the State owing to its unique context may own, purchase and inherent land in the state of Assam'.[47]

While the issue of indigenous people's rights has been dominant in the nationalist discourse in the state, the core and burning political issue which brought in a broad consensus in the state in the recent history of Assam's politics was updating the NRC. The NRC had been prepared in accordance with the provisions of the 1986 Amendment incorporated into the Indian Citizenship Act, 1955. Anupama Roy[48] argues that a 'hyphenated-citizenship' has been worked out for Assam through the Amendment to the Indian Citizenship Act, 1986, to accommodate the provisions of the Assam Accord signed in 1985. Roy writes,

> The accord reached between the leaders of the movement and the Indian government in 1985, and the amendment in the Citizenship Act following the accord in 1986, put in place a template of graded citizenship in Assam, and shifted the chronological boundary of citizenship for the state to

25 March 1971, from 19 July 1948, which was the constitutional deadline for the rest of the country.[49]

Roy argues that a sixth category of citizenship was evolved through the Amendment to the Citizenship Act, 1955, by adding Section 6A in 1986. This category is in addition to the existing categories of getting citizenship by 'birth, descent, registration, naturalisation, and by incorporation of foreign territory into India'.[50]

In Assam, a broad political consensus evolved around this sixth category of citizenship. The core contention was around the IMDT Act, 1983, which was perceived as an obstacle of identification of foreigners as the Act imposed the onus of identification of the foreigner on the complainants. In 2005, the Supreme Court of India scrapped this Act in response to a petition seeking its repeal by Sarbananda Sonowal, a former president of AASU, a former member of the Assam legislative assembly and also a former MP from the AGP and currently the chief minister of Assam. In a much later period, the constitutional validity of this category of citizenship was challenged in the Supreme Court through a PIL filed by Assam Sanmilita Mahasangha, Assam Public Works and All Assam Ahom Association (in Assam Sanmilita Mahasangha and Others v Union of India and Another, 2014), which has now been referred to a constitutional bench.[51] Despite this legal/constitutional battle, Assam had undertaken the exercise towards preparation and updating of the NRC.

The consensus on updating NRC as per the Assam Accord, 1985, has been attempted to be undone by granting citizenship to the Hindu Bangladeshis and other minorities from 'undivided India' by the NDA regime at the Centre. In September 2015, the Union government sent a notification to the state government intimating its decision to grant citizenship to 'all Bangladeshi Hindus living in Assam who sought shelter before December 31, 2014.'[52] The notification invited wrath from different quarters, particularly from the nationalist organizations such as AASU, AJYCP and KMSS. These organizations came out on the streets demanding immediate implementation of the Assam Accord and detection and deportation of all illegal migrants who had entered Assam after 24 March 1971. It was reported that there are anywhere between 59 and 75 lakh displaced Bengali Hindus (DBHs) in Assam, out of a total of 3.5 crore said to be scattered across India, who are the victims of religious persecution in Bangladesh.[53]

The opposition to the notification also revealed the broad political consensus around updating the NRC as per the Assam Accord, 1985. It also exposed the BJP's political motives. However, surprisingly, during the run-up to the elections, contrary to the growing discontents of the nationalist and indigenous outfits in the state against BJP-led Union government, the party projected itself as the real champion of the indigenous people in the state. The political context in which such a political shift occurred cannot entirely be ignored. The issue of the indigenous people, although contentious, is indeed a legacy of the Assam Accord. Clause 6 of the Assam Accord, 1985, promised that 'constitutional, legislative and administrative safeguards, as may be appropriate, shall be provided to protect, preserve and promote the cultural, social and linguistic identity and heritage of the Assamese people.' While the Accord agreed to give citizenship to the pre-1971 'outsiders' through definite arrangements, Clause 6 of the Accord leaves behind a distinction between 'citizens' and 'Assamese people' pledging to give 'constitutional safeguards' to the latter, which will not be made available to all citizens in the state. However, the concepts of both 'Assamese people' and 'constitutional safeguards' are yet to be defined in categorical terms. The 'constitutional safeguards' have been attempted to be defined in terms of reservation of seats to the different layers of representational bodies, that is, from the panchayats to the Parliament only to the khilonjiyas. This is evident from public pronouncements made from time to time by AASU.

Although this has remained an issue of concern and contention since the Assam Accord was signed in 1985, it was in 2015 that Assam witnessed a charged debate on defining who constitutes the 'Assamese people'. It started with a debate in the Assam legislative assembly on 3 March 2015, when a member of the assembly belonging to AIUDF raised this issue in the House. Intervening in the debate, Speaker Pranab Gogoi said,

> We should remember that we emotionally made Assamese the state lan-
> guage, but today it is not there. All different communities have different
> languages. Some chauvinist forces tried to impose one language and all

people are going away. We cannot survive as a community with imposition by chauvinist elements.[54]

With the consent of the House, the speaker pledged to take an initiative to arrive at a broad consensus on the definition of Assam people.

The speaker, taking into considerations all shades of opinion, prepared and submitted his report on the last day of the budget session, that is, on 31 March 2015, where he recommended that

> the year 1951 be taken as the cut off period and the National Register of Citizens (NRC), 1951, be taken as the basis for the definition of the 'Assamese people' for the purpose of reservation of seats and constitutional safeguards as required by the Assam Accord.[55]

He also asserted that 'indigenous person of Assam means a person belonging to the state of Assam and speaking the Assamese language or any tribal dialect of Assam or, in case of Cachar, the language of the region'. Both the ruling Congress and the main opposition AIUDF strongly opposed the report of the speaker, arguing that it was done without consulting the political parties. However, the BJP, AGP and BPF backed the 'Speaker's definition of "Assamese people" and insisted that the Speaker's recommendation be accepted as the recommendation of the House'.[56] This was a turning point in Assam's politics. First, the new definition itself is a transformation of the 'Assamese people' as required under Clause 6 of the Assam Accord to that of 'indigenous people of Assam'. Second, as per this new definition, the Assamese language is no longer a criterion to be an 'Assamese'. A person speaking Assamese, tribal dialects or the language in Cachar, that is, Bangla, is also an 'indigenous person of Assam' provided his/her name figures in NRC, 1951.

As mentioned above, the political context of the debate is important here. Assam was struggling to update the NRC, taking 1971 as the reference year as per the provisions of the Assam Accord. Abdul Kalam Azad argued that the real motive of the definition was to undo the agreed framework of the Assam Accord to solve the foreigners' problem in the state. He was of the view that the safeguard under Assam Accord was meant only for the Assamese people and not for the foreigners which include 'all the communities irrespective of caste, creed, language or origin except those who entered the state illegally after 25th of March, 1971.'[57] However, as has been stated above, AASU, a signatory to the Assam Accord, is in disagreement with such an articulation. For it, there ought to be a distinction between 'Assamese people', who have been turned into 'indigenous people of Assam', and those guaranteed citizenship through the Assam Accord.

It was the BJP that engineered political fortunes out of this proclaimed distinction between 'citizens' and the 'indigenous people of Assam'. It also added new ambiguities to the whole issue by promising to give citizenship to the Hindu Bangladeshis as well as other minorities of 'undivided India'. In this whole articulation, the Bengal-origin Muslims became the 'other' and an excluded category in the political vocabulary of 'Jati, Mati, Bheti'.

The Landslide Victory

All these led to the landslide victory of BJP-led alliance in the elections in 2016, with the BJP alone winning 60 seats out of 89 seats that the party contested, and 86 seats altogether by the BJP-led alliance in the 126-member legislative assembly. Its ally AGP won 14 and the BPF won 12 seats, out of 24 (+6)[58] and 14 seats that the parties had contested respectively.

The BJP's first stint in the assembly in 1991 with 10 seats had never gone up till 2011. While in the 1996 and 2001 elections, the number had gone down to 4 and 8 respectively, in 2006 the party improved a little with 10 seats again. However, in 2011, the number again got reduced to 5. What was more remarkable was the forfeiting of deposits in and around 70 per cent seats that the party had contested in all those elections. The elections of 2016, therefore, have been unprecedented for the BJP in the true sense (see Table 1.2).

The BJP's poll percentage from 1991 to 2011 assembly elections moved from around 6 per cent to 12 per cent. In the Lok Sabha elections, the party had performed relatively better in almost all the elections. For example, in the 1998 and 1999 Lok Sabha elections, the party polled

Table 1.2 *Performance of Political Parties in Assam Legislative Assembly Elections (1985–2016)*

Election	Voter %	Party	Seats Contested	Seats Won	Forfeited Deposit	% of Votes
1985	79.21	INC	125	25	46	23.23
		AGP	NA	63	NA	34.54
		BJP	37	0	34	1.07
1991		INC	125	66	28	29.35
		AGP	121	19	57	17.93
		NAGP	85	5	76	5.45
		BJP	48	10	29	6.55
1996	78.92	INC	122	34	22	30.56
		AGP	96	59	10	29.70
		BJP	117	4	95	10.41
2001	75.05	INC	126	71	11	39.75
		AGP	77	20	13	20.02
		BJP	46	8	14	9.35
2006	75.77	INC	120	53	11	31.08
		AGP	100	24	28	20.39
		AGP(P)	93	1	88	2.58
		BJP	125	10	87	11.98
		AIUDF	69	10	36	9.03
		BPF	NA	11	NA	–
2011	75.92	INC	126	78	12	39.39
		AGP	104	10	46	16.29
		BJP	120	5	84	11.47
		AIUDF	78	18	41	12.57
		BPF	29	12	11	6.13
2016	82.20	INC	122	26	NA	31.00
		AGP	24 (+6)	14	NA	8.10
		BJP	89	60	NA	29.50
		AIUDF	73	13	NA	13.00
		BPF	13	12	NA	3.90

Source: Computed from the Election Commission of India database.

24.47 per cent and 29.84 per cent votes despite winning only 1 and 2 seats respectively. The total turnout of voters in both the elections were relatively lower—61.1 per cent and 71.30 per cent. In both the elections, the BJP came to power at the Centre. Therefore, 36.5 per cent votes in the 2014 Lok Sabha elections going in favour of the BJP—in the backdrop of enormous discontent against incumbent Congress-led UPA government at the Centre, and an all-India Modi wave—which registered total 81.3 per cent voter turnout in the state, was nothing spectacular. Of course, winning 7 out of 14 Lok Sabha seats was a milestone for the party. However, continuing that momentum in the assembly elections was unprecedented, particularly in the backdrop of BJP's humiliating defeat in assembly elections in both Delhi and Bihar in February and October–November 2015. In both these states, however, the BJP swept the 2014 Lok Sabha elections. What was remarkable in 2016 was the BJP's penetration into all electoral belts in the state of Assam.

Khilonjiyas' Tryst with the BJP

The BJP-led government took the oath of office in an unprecedented swearing-in ceremony on 24 May 2016 in an open venue at the Assam Veterinary College sports ground at Khanapara. This venue is used primarily for large political rallies and celebration of state functions such as Independence Day and Republic Day. The ceremony was attended by Prime Minister Narendra Modi, BJP National President Amit Shah, party veteran L. K. Advani, 12 chief ministers from the BJP and BJP-allies ruled states including Andhra Pradesh Chief Minister Chandrababu Naidu and Madhya Pradesh Chief Minister Shivraj Singh Chouhan, and Union Cabinet Ministers Arun Jaitley and Nitin Gadkari, among others. It was truly a grand oath-taking ceremony that Assam ever witnessed. In his speech just after taking the oath of office as the new chief minister, Sonowal said, 'I promise to strive to make Assam free of Bangladeshi infiltrators, corruption and pollution.'[59] In an interview to the NDTV hours before taking the oath, 'Mr Sonowal had listed addressing the issue of "illegal immigration" in Assam as his main priority as CM.'[60] Addressing the ceremony amid the crowd shouting 'Modi, Modi', the prime minister said, 'The people of Assam have voted for Assam and Sonowal is the perfect person to lead the state…. Sonowal will leave no stone unturned to change the destiny of Assam.'[61] But the destiny of Assam under the BJP-ruled government has not been as desired. The CAB 2016-turned Act in 2019 continued to trigger discontents and resistance almost throughout his tenure. Updating of the NRC, which was promised as one of the top priorities of the new government, was entirely rejected by the government after the final list had been published. The destiny of the report on Clause 6 of the Assam Accord, which the BJP-led Union government promised to implement with all sincerity while pushing the CAB, has almost been pushed to uncertainty. While the destiny of Assam defined by the BJP in its own terms during elections had been hanging, the party, however, sustained its electoral destiny by registering another landslide victory in 2019 general elections in Assam.

THE HINDUTVA WAVE: THE VICTORY IN 2019

The 2019 general elections in India were held at a time when Assam was in crisis. CAB 2016 was boiling Assam's politics, creating unprecedented dissent against the incumbent NDA governments both in the state and at the Centre led by the BJP. There was a loose coalition of civil and political forces against the BJP on the CAB issue, which proposed to grant citizenship to the illegal migrants of six non-Muslim minority religious communities of Afghanistan, Pakistan and Bangladesh. This proposition violated the Assam Accord, 1985, signed after the anti-foreigners agitation from 1979–1985. It established 24 March 1971 as the cut-off date for detecting, deleting and deporting foreigners from Assam, which legally became enacted in 1985 through the Amendment of Citizenship Act, 1955.

The Bill was also perceived to have derailed the ongoing process of updating the NRC, 1951, for the state of Assam carried out under the monitoring of the Supreme Court of India under the provisions of the Assam Accord. Despite the resistance, the government reiterated its commitment to grant citizenship to these non-Muslim communities through a Bill in the Lok Sabha in January 2019, shortly before the Lok Sabha elections. Three Ministers from the AGP in the Sarbananda Sonowal ministry in Assam resigned in protest. Due to political opposition, the Bill could not be introduced in the Rajya Sabha. The BJP during the 2019 election campaign reiterated its commitment to the Bill if returned to power.[62] It was also incorporated in its manifesto.

Despite the public outcry, the BJP improved politically winning nine seats, two more than in 2014. The BJP's victory, marked by polarization on religious lines, reduced its major opponent, the Congress party, primarily to an East-Bengal-origin Muslim base as viewed by the electorate. The Congress won three seats, maintaining its 2014 tally. The AIUDF, the party that benefited from the polarization of East-Bengal-origin Muslim votes since the 2006 assembly elections, witnessed the erosion of its vote banks which shifted towards the Congress. The party which had won 3 seats in 2014 was reduced to 1 in 2019.

The BJP registered this landslide victory in Assam despite the unprecedented dissent due to the interplay of social and political forces. These include certain developmental initiatives combined with hyper populism, the success of its long-term strategy of bringing the tea plantation workers and tribal communities into the Hindutva fold, Prime Minister Modi's leadership, its national security campaign capturing the popular imagination, the grassroots role of the RSS, and its rigid Hindutva agenda combined with a cultural and linguistic flavour.

The Verdict

The year 2019 marks another consecutive electoral success for the BJP in Assam following its ascendance in 2014. The BJP achieved a landslide victory in the 2016 assembly elections followed by a remarkable performance in the 2018 panchayat elections. Both the 2014 Lok Sabha elections and 2016 state assembly elections were fought around local issues, which earned a reputation for the BJP being committed towards the state's indigenous people, particularly in the Brahmaputra Valley. During both the elections, the Hindutva agenda was downplayed, as folk narratives, cultural ethos and historical legends were featured.[63] In 2019, the Hindutva agenda was emphasized by projecting CAB as a saviour of the linguistic and cultural identity of the indigenous people.[64] It also forced the AGP, the key regional ally of the BJP, to exit the BJP-led government in January 2019. The AGP had already fought the panchayat elections in December 2018 alone. The BJP then succeeded in persuading the AGP to return in March 2019, less than a month ahead of the elections. The BPF, the other regional ally, continued its ties with the BJP despite its reservations over the CAB.

Amid discontent around CAB on 6 January 2019, the Union government established a high-level committee chaired by a retired IAS officer to implement Clause 6 of the Assam Accord, which 'suggests that the government has to enact constitutional, legislative and administrative safeguards to protect, preserve and promote the cultural, social and linguistic identity and heritage of the Assamese people'.[65] The nine-member committee including eminent Assamese was expected to submit its report within six months. However, the initiative provoked such strong reactions as being a diversionary tactic that most of the committee members refused to be a part of it.

The mass discontent and protests, however, did not transform into votes in either the panchayat or the Lok Sabha elections. In panchayat elections, the BJP won around 50 per cent seats at all levels.[66] In 2019 Lok Sabha elections, the party won 9 out of 10 seats it contested out of 14 in the state. Four seats unsuccessfully went to its two allies—three for the AGP and one for the BPF (see Table 1.3).

Table 1.3 *Seats Won and Vote Share of Political Parties in 2019 Lok Sabha Elections*

Parties	Seats Contested	Won	Vote (%)	Vote % per Seat Contested
BJP	10	9	36.05	54.32
AGP	3	0	8.23	32.41
BPF	1	0	2.48	30.20
INC	14	3	35.44	35.44
AUDF	3	1	7.80	33.35
Independents	45	1	4.25	–

Source: Lokniti-CSDS Survey, accessed from https://www.thehindu.com/elections/lok-sabha-2019/post-poll-survey-bjps-polarisation-strategy-hits-the-mark-in-assam/article27267757.ece.

After 1991, the BJP regained both seats in Barak Valley (Karimganj and Silchar), registered its first victory in Lok Sabha elections in the hill districts (Autonomous District) and retained six seats (Tezpur, Dibrugarh, Lakhimpur, Jorhat, Guwahati and Mangaldoi) out of 7 seats that the party had won in 2014. It lost only in Nagaon constituency to the Congress, which it had won for four consecutive terms before 2019 elections. Victory in Karimganj constituency with a small margin was considered to be laudable by BJP's political strategists.[67] Shift of the AIUDF votes to the Congress also contributed towards the defeat of the AIUDF sitting MP in the constituency.

In both the constituencies in the valley having significant presence of Hindu Bengalis, the BJP used the CAB issue very prominently which pushed the Congress into an embarrassing situation. Officially, the Congress took a firm stand against CAB. However, to woo the Bengali Hindu voters, the Congress veteran and sitting MP of Silchar constituency Sushmita Dev took a position that contradicted her own party's official line.[68] BJP's victory in the Autonomous District was also remarkable. Apart from winning the constituency with 61.73 per cent votes by defeating the five times MP and Congress veteran Biren Singh Engti, the BJP registered its lead in all five assembly segments.

The Congress, which won only three seats in the present elections (Kaliabor, Nagaon and Barpeta), was reduced to a party dependent on immigrant Muslims as seen by the public. The AIUDF supposedly fought this election with a proclaimed strategy of unity against the BJP and therefore fielded its candidates in only three constituencies which the party had won in 2014 (Dhubri, Barpeta and Karimganj). The proposed unity, however, did not materialize allegedly due to betrayal by the Congress.[69] The party went from three to one seat.

The Kokrajhar constituency, which is largely under the administrative control of the BTAD, and controlled by BJP's ally BPF, returned the non-Bodo independent candidate Naba Kumar Sarania for the second consecutive term, although with a reduced majority from almost 52 per cent to 32.7 per cent in 2014 and 2019, respectively. The BPF won 9 out of 10 assembly segments of the constituency in 2016 assembly elections but won only 4 assembly segments in the 2019 general elections.

Anti-CAB Mobilizations: The Composition, Focus and Limitations

The question of how the BJP averted the unprecedented dissent against the CAB in Assam and registered a landslide victory in the 2019 Lok Sabha elections was debated comprehensively in the post-verdict period.[70] The analysts and commentators raised a set of critical questions about the electoral outcomes in the state and answered them using statistical evidence, primarily drawn from the CSDS survey data (2019). Although they provided important insights concerning the electoral processes and outcomes in the state, they, however, missed a few pressing political questions in their analyses.

While commenting on the failure of the anti-CAB protests to influence the electoral upshots, the analysts did not deeply probe into the nature of the anti-CAB mobilizations and the non-convergence of these movements from the larger electoral processes. The anti-CAB movements brought forth an unprecedented civil political alliance against the BJP-led incumbent governments. Although this alliance had an electoral ambition of teaching the BJP a lesson, it did not, however, have any electoral agency to carry out its objective. The mobilizations were primarily centred on the sanctity of the Assam Accord, 1985, which, among other things, called for the detection, deletion and deportation of illegal immigrants, setting 24 March 1971 as the cut-off date for all those purposes.

The anti-CAB alliance also did not have political coherence and consolidation. For example, two important nationalist organizations—the AASU and KMSS—pioneered the mobilizations against the Bill. While the AASU brought together almost all ethnic student outfits to its fold, the KMSS brought around 70 organizations, including the AJYCP, various ethnic outfits and organizations representing religious minorities to the table. Throughout the anti-CAB campaigns, these two alliances did not forge any unity. The third important face of the resistance against CAB was the Nagarikatwa Aain Songsudhan Birodhi Mancha (Forum against Citizenship Act Amendment Bill) led by eminent intellectual Hiren Gohain, which also brought several political and civic forces together. The Gohain-led forum was open to the forces led by both the ASSU and KMMS but failed to bring these two important forces on a common platform.

The resistance groups were hoping to transform the widespread anti-CAB sentiments into electoral results spontaneously. The AGP, which was also in the forefront of the anti-CAB mobilizations, left the BJP-led government in protest only to come back as the elections approached. Three important civil society groups—the North East Students' Organization (NESO) in which the AASU is a member, KMSS and Gohain-led anti-CAB forum—met Rahul Gandhi on 4 February 2019 to raise the issue of the CAB. This meeting was crucial, as it helped to stall the Bill in the Rajya Sabha. However, none of these outfits projected the Congress as an alternative to the BJP in the state. When there were public criticisms over the political motives of these outfits, they assumed a rather defensive posture. For example, AASU General Secretary Lurinjyoti Gogoi criticized Chief Minister Sonowal for his remarks that approaching Rahul Gandhi was 'a sad reflection on Assam'.[71] Gogoi asserted that the chief minister was trying 'to sieve out political meaning from the meeting'. He pointed that AASU 'had never toed the line of any political party, and we'll never do so in the future'.[72]

The KMSS, since its inception, has taken an anti-Congress position. In 2011, it published a list of 50 mega allegations against the Congress government and campaigned vigorously against the party. In 2014, too, its leader Gogoi took a very strong anti-Congress stand. Just before the elections, Gogoi declared, 'We will issue circular to our peoples spread across different areas of the state to campaign against Congress. We will distribute leaflets and reach out to the people in rive rine areas and tea gardens spread across the state.'[73] In March 2015, the KMSS declared that it would form its own political party which 'will fight for farmers, labourers, middle class—in short the exploited class of our society—and for the basic facilities they need. We will start a new politics, a new struggle'. The KMSS leader also declared that the objective of the new political outfit would be 'to snatch power from Congress, BJP, AGP, AIUDF and to throw them into the dustbin of politics'.[74]

The KMSS never had accepted the Congress as a credible pro-people party and perceived it to be pro-corporate and averse to the interests of the indigenous people. On its part, the Congress also never attempted to project itself as a reliable alternative to the BJP in the state. It did not have an agenda and organizational preparedness to confront the saffron party. The party was expecting a political miracle out of the anti-CAB mobilizations. While the BJP managed to keep its alliance with the BPF together, brought members from other ethnic outfits under its wings and succeeded in bringing the AGP back to its fold, the Congress did not even attempt to build any credible alliance with any political party in the state, and its indecisiveness about allying with the AIUDF (which finally did not happen) offered the perfect political fodder to the BJP to spread rumours that both the parties had *actually* formed a secret alliance. The Congress's failure to avert the propaganda helped the BJP to penetrate the anti-CAB social bases, particularly in Upper Assam.

All these factors partially explain why the majority of those who supported the anti-CAB mobilizations finally voted for the BJP. However, the real reasons behind the BJP's victory are its populist policies, its success in persuading the tea tribe communities to embrace the party, the gradual expansion of the Hindutva network and the role of the RSS in softening the blow of the anti-CAB protests in the elections.

Deep Roots among the Tea Tribe Communities

Based on decades of work carried out by the RSS in Northeast India in general and Assam in particular, the BJP succeeded in gaining support by the tribal and tea tribe communities in the state. An almost complete swing of votes occurred in 2019 by the tea tribe communities, traditional Congress supporters, towards the BJP. The BJP had two tea tribe candidates who polled very well; Rameswar Teli (Dibrugarh) and Pallab Lochan Das (Tezpur). In Dibrugarh, the BJP polled almost 65 per cent of the votes, leading in all 9 assembly segments as against 29 per cent secured by the Congress candidate. Teli's margin of victory was more than 3.6 lakh. He defeated the strong Congressman Paban Singh Ghatowar, also a member from the same community who had won the constituency five times and was a state minister in both Narasimha Rao and Manmohan Singh's council of ministers.

BJP's strategy to nominate Pallab Lochan Das, the state minister in the Sarbananda Sonowal's ministry in Assam, was both dramatic and strategic. It was reported that the BJP's state unit forwarded only the name of Himanta Biswa Sarma, the NEDA convener and the state finance minister, to the central election committee of the party. The central committee put aside the state unit's single nomination and selected Das as the candidate. The sitting BJP MP, R. P. Sarmah, an old RSS activist who belongs to the dominant Nepali community in the constituency, was also denied the ticket.[75] BJP's performance in this constituency was also extraordinary. The party registered more than 57 per cent votes as against 37 per cent by his Congress rival and led in all 9 assembly segments. The margin of victory was over 2.4 lakh votes.

Kamakhya Prasad Tasa, who was the BJP sitting MP from Jorhat constituency, and a member of the tea tribe's community, was denied the ticket for the 2019 elections. In this constituency, too, where the tea tribes have a substantive presence, the BJP registered a remarkable victory, securing more than 51 per cent of the votes polled as against 43.5 per cent by the Congress rival and led in 8 out of 10 assembly segments. The BJP might have played a strategic game plan by putting an Ahom candidate Topon Kumar Gogoi, former General Secretary of AASU, also an incumbent state minister in Sonowal government, against an Ahom candidate fielded by the Congress. Immediately after the Lok Sabha elections, Tasa was rewarded by electing him to the Rajya Sabha.

In the new Union ministry following the 2019 elections, Rameswar Teli became the lone representative from Assam. 'The BJP strategically chose Teli keeping the assembly polls in mind which are just two years away,' wrote The Wire in its report on the inclusion of Teli, the two times MP from Dibrugarh. In its report titled 'Rameshwar Teli's Inclusion in Govt Telling of BJP's Desire to Woo Assam's Tea Tribe',[76] Pisharoty writes:

> Both in the 2014 Lok Sabha and the 2016 assembly polls, the BJP could become victorious in the Brahmaputra Valley mainly due to the success of the RSS in channeling the tea tribe votes into BJP. With the Assamese community getting vocal against the BJP close to the 2019 Lok Sabha polls due to the Citizenship (Amendment) Bill, it became all the more vital for the BJP to hold on to its tea tribe votes.

In addition to the long-term RSS efforts within the community, the BJP also tried to shift the loyalty of the community from the Congress to the BJP.

A striking feature of the BJP-led state budgets is the numerous schemes announced for the tea tribe community, which has around 35–40 per cent vote share in the Brahmaputra Valley. The schemes favoured the tea tribe community that allegedly could become a solid electoral block for the party. In every budget, the government came up with schemes that also included the direct transfer of funds to the people belonging to the community. In 2017, the government launched the Chah Bagicha Dhan Puraskar Mela. In January 2018, the government transferred the first tranche of ₹2,500 through direct benefit transfer to over 7 lakh bank accounts of tea garden workers across 752 tea gardens. In 2018–2019, additional funds were scheduled to be released including to an expanded list of beneficiaries that included those who had been left out. Additional benefits were allocated for subsidized rice schemes.[77]

The government also introduced several populist schemes under Astadash Mukutar Unnoyonee Mala, 18 flagship schemes targeting different sections of the society. The government offered free textbooks up to degree level and fee waiver up to postgraduate levels for poor students, one tola gold for brides for all communities with a condition of marriage registration as well as further subsidy in rice under the National Food Security Act. These paid electoral dividends to the ruling party.

RSS at the Grassroots

Explaining the phenomenal success of the BJP in 2019, Bhattacharyya pointed out, 'The traditional bastions of the Congress in Assam's rural areas are being painted with a saffron hue, which helps to explain BJP's phenomenal success in the general elections.'[78] Bhattacharyya was investigating the role of the Ekal Vidyalayas, or single-teacher schools, which have mushroomed across almost all districts in Assam. Field reports suggest that the RSS played a significant role in the BJP's success as it built up a grassroots network to mitigate the discontent arising out of the CAB 2016. The Sangha reportedly organized around 600 small-scale meetings at the grassroots and distributed 90 lakh leaflets to allay the fear against the CAB 2016.[79] Eminent local persons participated in the meetings.

The RSS has been penetrating Assam's tribal communities as well as mainstream ethnic Assamese communities, particularly through educational and cultural means. Many educational institutions, including Sankardev Sishu Niketan, Ekal Vidyalayas and Vanavasi Kalyan Ashram are working in different locations in the state and have been instrumental in bringing legitimacy to the RSS agenda. In Assam, the RSS appears to have appropriated the name of the great 15th-century Assamese poet-saint Sri Sankardeva by naming its schools after him.[80] Sankardev Sishu Niketan, which has an affiliation to Vidya Bharati, has a large network in the state with 550 schools that enrol more than 1.60 lakh students.[81] These schools with Assamese medium of instruction are affiliated to the state board (SEBA), providing reasonably good quality education at affordable fees.

In relatively big towns, the children of middle and upper-middle classes gradually switched over to English medium. In small towns and villages, middle- and lower-income classes resorted to the Sishu Niketans in an environment of major problems with the state-aided schools throughout the state. Apart from the behavioural and cultural training, these schools performed well in final examinations at the secondary level. For example, in 2019, the pass percentage of the Sishu Niketans was almost 95 per cent, with more than 130 schools registering 100 per cent success. They have also retained a number of ranks with top 10–20, which are considered to be exceptional in Assam. In 2016, the state education minister publicly declared that these schools would spread to all 2,202 panchayats in the state.[82]

The RSS, under the banner of Purvottar Janajati Shiksha Samiti, established a large network of single-teacher schools named Ekal Vidyalayas. Quoting Karna Gaur, *prabhat pramukh* of the schools in the north-east, Bhattacharyya has pointed out that about 70 per cent of these schools are located in the tea belt and remaining are in the areas inhabited by different tribal communities such as Karbi, Dimasa, Mising, Rabha and Bodo. 'By the end of 2018, as many as 4,650 such schools were established in 22 districts out of a total of thirty-three in the state.'[83] The RSS is now planning to establish these schools in the districts of Dhubri, Nalbari and South Salmara in western Assam having sizeable Muslim populations.

Tea tribes have a decisive role in the electoral politics of the four Lok Sabha constituencies of Jorhat, Dibrugarh, Lakhimpur and Tezpur. BJP victory margins in these constituencies reveal the penetration of Hindutva forces into these communities. Ekal Vidyalayas played an important role in this penetration. Apart from the Sishu Niketans and Ekal Vidyalayas, the RSS also expanded its network through

shakhas, Vivekananda schools, balwadis, Kasturba Gandhi Balika Vidyalayas, tuition centres, study circles, vocational training centres and a hospital. The Vanvasi Kalyan Ashram (VKA), which works among tribal people, runs eight hostels, 42 nursery schools and coaching centres, holds medical camps and sends tribal teams to out-of-State sports events.[84]

Polarization along Religious and Linguistic Lines

CSDS-Lokniti post-poll survey suggests that BJP's campaign strategy remained focused on three major issues: (a) the leadership of Prime Minister Narendra Modi, (b) development activities by the Union government and (c) performance by the BJP-led government in the state since 2016. However, 'the reason for the party's success seems to have been the polarization it achieved.'[85]

With RSS networks on the ground and a firmly rooted electoral organization, the BJP succeeded in polarizing the electorate on religious lines. The Lokniti-CSDS post-poll survey[86] reveals that except for Muslims, all other social categories including the Dalits (66%) and Adivasis (86%) voted for the NDA. Altogether, 74 per cent Hindus voted for the NDA, and only 16 per cent of them voted for the Congress. A total of 70 per cent Muslims voted for the Congress, a significant trend, as only 20 per cent of them voted for the AIUDF. Seven per cent of Muslims voted for the NDA. This voting pattern illustrates the failure of the anti-CAB movement to translate into electoral outcomes. The Lokniti-CSDS survey also finds that 75 per cent of Assamese Hindus opposed the Bill. From that total, 56 per cent voted for the BJP and its allies, while only 28 per cent voted for the Congress. Twenty-five per cent Assamese Hindus supported CAB, but from that total, 88 per cent voted for the BJP and its allies.

The survey data provide evidence that in a socially diverse state that had undergone decades of ethnic conflict and insurgency, religion cutting across ethnic cleavages can be critically important. BJP's success lay in its ability to neutralize opposition to the CAB and divert the attention of Hindus towards the increase in the Muslim population, presumably due to influx from Bangladesh with Congress patronage. This reduced Congress into a Muslim-dependent party, which is particularly true in the Nagaon constituency. It is the single constituency in Assam which the BJP won for four consecutive terms, from 1999 to 2014. But the BJP lost this Muslim-dominant constituency to the Congress in the 2019 elections due to the religious bipolarization.

The BJP lost it despite leading in 6 assembly segments out of 9. The Congress won with a lead in only 3 assembly segments. In two of them, Laharighat and Jamunamukh, which are East-Bengal-origin Muslim-dominated constituencies, the Congress secured 71 per cent and 83 per cent votes respectively as against around 27 per cent and 15 per cent polled by the BJP. The margin of victory was low, less than 17,000. In the case of Kaliabor constituency, too, which the Congress won for the seventh consecutive term since 1998, victory was determined by the East-Bengal-origin Muslim-dominated constituencies, particularly in Dhing and Rupohihat assembly segments, where the party had registered around 90 per cent and 85 per cent votes, respectively. Out of the total 10 assembly segments, both the Congress and AGP, BJP's ally, had a lead in 5 segments each. The margin of victory was remarkable, more than 2 lakh, with the Congress securing 55.80 per cent votes as against 40.89 per cent secured by the AGP.[87]

Modi Magic and Hype over National Security

In both the 2014 Lok Sabha and 2016 assembly elections, Prime Minister Narendra Modi served as the core BJP campaign rallying point. The glorification of his leadership and creating hype around national security were two key BJPs strategies in Assam. Both Modi and BJP President Amit Shah took a keen and active interest in the electoral strategies. Modi campaigned in the state on 4 January, 30 March and 12 April 2019.

He also came on Christmas day, 25 December 2018, to inaugurate the Dhola–Sadiya Bridge, the longest bridge over the Brahmaputra. Naming the bridge after Bhupen Hazarika, the legendary Assamese musician, and awarding him with the Bharat Ratna evoked state-wide emotional sentiment. On 4 January, Modi addressed a rally in Silchar, primarily aimed at Bengali voters. He assured them that none of the Indian citizens will be left out of the NRC. He also stated that the Citizenship Bill would protect the rights of the Bengali Hindu refugees. On 30 March, he addressed two rallies in Upper Assam—one each in the northern and southern banks of the Brahmaputra.

Three issues figured prominently in his campaign: implementation of Clause 6 of the Assam Accord, ST status to six OBC communities and welfare of the tea tribe communities.[88] On 12 April 2019, Modi again came to Assam and addressed two rallies—one in Silchar and the other in Kendukana in Lower Assam. While in Silchar, his focus was on CAB, in Kendukana, it was on the identity and rights of the indigenous people. Modi got live coverage in electronic media and captured headlines in local dailies. The election campaign glorified Modi's leadership with its poll song *Akou Ebar Modi Sarkar* (Once again the Modi government). It immediately became viral in social media with the state finance minister singing and dancing and leading street marches across the state.

BJP President Amit Shah campaigned in Assam on 17 February 2019 in Lakhimpur, just after the Pulwama bombing on 14 February, killing 44 Indian paramilitaries, including Assam's Maneswar Basumatary. Shah asserted that both NRC and CAB are important to save Assam from becoming a state like J&K.[89] He again came to Assam on 28 March and 6 April and addressed three rallies in Central and Upper Assam. Basumatary's death evoked patriotic sentiments with the local media providing maximum coverage. He was cremated with full state honours on 17 February 2019.[90] India's Balakot airstrike in Pakistan also evoked strong sentiments. All these helped the BJP to counter anti-CAB sentiments.

Perpetual Poverty and the Populist Agenda

The hyper populism indulged in by the BJP-led state and Union governments surpassed the previous Congress-led government. One of the much-publicized epitomes of development of the new government has been the Astadash Mukutar Unnoyonee Mala, under which 18 flagship schemes have been launched. Under the National Food Security Act, the Government of India provides rice at ₹3 per kg to 5.7 million households in Assam. In the 2019–2020 budget speech, it was declared that the Government of Assam would provide rice at a further subsidized rate of ₹1 per kg instead of the earlier rate of ₹3 per kg, which would benefit 5.3 million households. The government has also announced that it would provide 'one tola of gold' (1 tola = 11.664 g) to brides belonging to all communities of the state (it is customary to provide gold at the time of wedding), provided the marriage is formally registered. Offering gold to the brides under the government scheme has come under criticisms; however, the government has remained steadfast on it. Admission fee waiver and free textbooks up to the degree levels to the students of economically backward families are some of the other initiatives that have attracted criticism. The government has launched schemes that may make both the students and teachers obliged to the incumbent government. It has also proposed giving a subsidy of ₹700 per student per month for 10 months a year on mess bills for the students staying in the hostels of government or provincialized colleges and universities.[91]

Post-2019 Elections

The post-2019 elections did not bring peace. The NRC final list published on 31 August 2019 was entirely rejected by the government. The state president of BJP said that his party would not accept the updated NRC and 'appealed to the central and the state governments to prepare a nationwide NRC'.[92] BJP strategist and NEDA convener, Sarma, said, 'The Centre and the State governments have been discussing new ways to eject foreigners after the "disappointment" with the NRC.' He also asserted, 'I don't think this is the final list. There are many more to come.'[93] But the BJP also attempted to leave no stone unturned to invoke its self-proclaimed love for the indigenous people by projecting the NRC as an instrument of protecting the illegal migrants rather than safeguarding the genuine Indians. In the meantime, the Union government formed an expert committee to suggest measures to ensure constitutional, legal and administrative safeguards for the Assamese people as per Clause 6 of the Assam Accord.[94]

However, the state plunged into a new wave of anti-CAB protests once the Union government introduced the Bill in the Parliament and finally got through both the houses on 11 December 2019. The new wave of protests has been spontaneous, and the initial lead was taken by the students' communities. Writers and artists also came out on the street, forcing many artists affiliated to the BJP to resign and join in the people's protests. On 11 December 2019, the day Bill was debated and passed in the Rajya Sabha, Assam saw unprecedented protests throughout the state, particularly in the Guwahati city. Paramilitary forces were deployed in the city, but the protestors stopped the regular lives in the city. Sporadic violence also erupted. In the evening, curfew was imposed in the city and other places of the state, subsequently being extended for an indefinite period. Internet services were withdrawn from the evening on 11 December in 10 districts in the pretext 'to prevent "misuse" of social media to disturb peace and tranquillity and to maintain law and order'.[95] The atmosphere hit such a level that the Government of India was forced to postpone the India–Japan summit which was scheduled to take place in Guwahati on 15–17 December and to be attended by Indian Prime Minister Narendra Modi and Japanese Prime Minister Shinzo Abe. The protests continued until February 2020 but suddenly disappeared with the spread of COVID-19. The pandemic proved to be a god-sent rescue for the government, as it helped the ruling party to regain legitimacy through its efforts to deal with the challenges emanated from the outbreak of coronavirus. The anti-CAA forces also got gradually fragmented, and in the run-up to the 2021 assembly elections, Assam witnesses the formation of a number of regional political parties with a proclaimed goal of unseating the BJP from power but refusing to bring in unity among themselves to fight against the common political enemy. These fragmentations may help the BJP to bounce back and reclaim the electoral supremacy. Chapter 6 deals with these issues in details.

NOTES

1. The Wire, 'Assam Assembly Passes Bills to Create Three Separate Autonomous Councils', 4 September 2020, https://thewire.in/government/assam-assembly-passes-bills-to-create-three-separate-autonomous-councils.
2. As per government data, there are 804 tea gardens in the state, of which 614 are located in the districts of Sivasagar (85), Tinsukia (122), Golaghat (74), Jorhat (88), Dibrugarh (177), Sonitpur (59) and undivided Lakhimpur (10). Information obtained from https://ttwd.assam.gov.in/frontimpotentdata/list-of-tea-garden-at-assam.
3. The Wire, 'Assam Assembly Passes Bills'.
4. Six autonomous councils are Mising Autonomous Council, Deori Autonomous Council, Thengal Kachari Autonomous Council, Sonowal Kachari Autonomous Council, Moran Autonomous Council and Matak Autonomous Council.
5. Government of Assam, 'Autonomous Councils', n.d., https://assam.gov.in/en/main/Autonomous%20Councils#:~:
6. This chapter has substantially drawn from two chapters and two articles already published. They are: 'BJP's Consolidation, AIUDF's Polarization and Congress Defeat in Assam', in *India's 2014 Elections: A Modi-led BJP Sweep*, ed. Paul Wallace (New Delhi: SAGE Publications, 2015), 381–403; 'Co-opting the Khilonjiyas BJP's Electoral Victory in Assam, 2016', *Social Change* 47, no. 1 (2017): 1–17; 'Assam Polls: The Hindutva Wave', in *India's 2019 Elections: The Hindutva Wave and Indian Nationalism*, ed. Paul Wallace (New Delhi: SAGE Publications, 2020); 'Assam's Verdict 2019: Why the Anti-CAB Mobilisations Failed?' *Economic & Political Weekly* 54, no. 51 (28 December 2019): 27–32, https://www.epw.in/system/files/pdf/2019_54/51/PE_LIV_51_281219_Akhil_Ranjan_Dutta.pdf.
7. Sandhya Goswami, 'Assam: Mandate for Peace and Development', *Economic & Political Weekly* 46, no. 23 (4 June 2011): 20–22.
8. Before the initiative of SJA, People's Consultative Group (PCG)—a nine member group constituted by ULFA in September 2005—had held three rounds of talks with the Government of India on 26 October 2005, 7 February 2006 and 22 June 2006. The first meeting was at the prime ministerial level. However, the talks failed to facilitate the dialogues between the Government of India and ULFA. Alleging that the Government of India failed to honour its own commitment through these talks towards creating a conducive environment for direct dialogue with the ULFA, PCG declared its decision to disassociate itself from any further dialogue with the government through a public statement issued on 28 September 2020. For details, please refer to Arup Borbora, *All about PCG & Talks* (Guwahati: Aank-Baak, 2010).
9. Quoting government sources, it was reported by *The Assam Tribune*, Guwahati, on 9 January 2014 that since 2001 around 170 rhinos were killed in the state, mostly in the KNP, and 43 rhinos were killed in 2013 alone.

10. For details, see Dola Mitra, Debarshi Dasgupta, and Uttam Sengupta, 'A Bridge Too Far', *Outlook India* (13 August 2012), https://magazine.outlookindia.com/story/a-bridge-too-far/281840.

11. According to the 2011 census, the ST population constitutes 31 per cent in four districts under BTAD. Zamser Ali, President of BTAD Citizens Rights Forum and Chief Spokesperson of Sanmilita Janagoshthiya Aikya Mancha, asserts that the non-Bodo ST population in BTAD is not less than 5 per cent. Therefore, the Bodos constitute only 26 per cent of the total population in the territory. (Information is based on personal discussion with Ali on 5 October 2014.)

12. The PCs in Assam were redrawn in 1962 and 1967. Assam started with 10 PCs in 1951 and 1957. Out of this, eight were single-member constituencies and rest were two-member constituencies. In 1951, all were general member constituencies, but in 1957 one single-member constituency was reserved for ST. In 1962, all were converted into single-member constituencies and the number increased to 12, out of which 1 was reserved for SC and 2 for ST. In 1967, the number of constituencies were increased to 14, out of which 11 were general, 1 was SC and 2 were ST constituencies. This arrangement continues till date.

13. Naba Kumar Sarania belongs to the community called Sarania Kachari, which was a part of the Bodo Kachari community. The community enjoys ST status. However, prior to the elections, an organization called Janajati Suraksha Samity challenged the credibility of the ST certificate of Sarania. The organization pointed out that 'All Assam Tribal Sangha, which had issued the ST certificate to the Sarania Kachari community, was not a competent authority to do so.' The members who issued the statement were Bodos. (Source: *The Telegraph*, Sarania ST status challenged. 22 April 2014, https://www.telegraphindia.com/northeast/sarania-st-status-challenged/cid/194951, accessed on 29 March 2021).

14. Sankardev, a Vaishnavite, is a social and religious reformer of the 15th-and 16th-century Assam, who is perceived as the most important cultural architect of the greater Assamese identity across communities. Hindutva ideologues appropriate Sankardev for its own mileage, and there are 477 Sankardev Sishu/Vidya Niketans affiliated to Vidya Bharati in the Brahmaputra Valley alone. These schools introduce students to the Hindutva ideology through discipline and prayer. (Information is based on interaction with Sada Dutta, Guwahati, a functionary of the school network, accessed on 1 October 2014.)

15. Based on discussion with Indibar Deori, Guwahati, on 1 October 2014, who is an authority on ethnic and tribal politics in Northeast India.

16. Gogamukh is around 400 km from Assam's capital city Guwahati, located in the Lakhimpur PC from where the then BJP State President Sarbananda Sonowal was contesting.

17. Farhana Ahmed, 'Rhinos Killed to Settle Bangladeshis', *The Assam Tribune*, 1 April 2014, Guwahati.

18. Ibid.

19. Narendra Modi (2014) 'Narendra Modi addresses rally in Assam, seeks support for BJP and attacks Congress for lack of development in Northeast India' 8 February. Available at https://www.narendramodi.in/

narendra-modi-addresses-rally-in-assam-seeks-support-for-bjp-attacks-congress-for-lack-of-development-in-northeast-5949, accessed on 29 March 2021.

20. *The Sentinel*, 'Modi Gives a Clarion Call, Blames Congress for its "Narrow Mindset"', 9 February 2014, Guwahati.

21. Tea tribes or tea tribe community is a composite group in Assam whose ancestors were brought to Assam from Central and Eastern India by the colonial authority as tea plantation migrant labourers. One of the most exploited communities in the state, the tea tribes lost their connection with their natives and became permanent settlers in the state. In their ancestors' place, these communities enjoy ST status. In Assam, they have been struggling for it.

22. *The Assam Tribune*, 'Our Manifesto, Our Commitment', 7 April 2014, Guwahati.

23. Chapter 3 on 'Hindutva at the Core: CAB-turned-CAA and Assam's Political Destiny' comprehensively discusses the resistance against these notifications.

24. Ram Madhab, 'Foreword', in *The Last Battle of Saraighat: The Story of the BJP's Rise in the North-east*, eds. Rajat Sethi and Shubhrastha (New Delhi: Penguin, 2017), xiii.

25. Bodos are the dominant plain tribe community in the state. They were granted Sixth Schedule status with a council called BTC in 2003. It was done by an amendment to the Constitution. Through Clause 8 of the Accord, the government 'agrees to consider sympathetically the inclusion of the Bodo Kacharis living in Karbi Anglong and NC Hills Autonomous Council area in the ST (Hill) List of State of Assam.' This was opposed by Jayanta Rongpi, the member in Lok Sabha elected from the Autonomous Hill constituency of the state while debating on the amendment.

26. Samudra Gupta Kashyap, 'Why Modi Launched His Campaign from Kokrajhar', *The Indian Express*, 19 January 2016, https://indianexpress.com/article/explained/why-modi-launched-his-assam-campaign-from-kokrajhar/.

27. In BTAD, the ruling BPF has been facing the wrath of different sections. Factionalism within Bodos has also been a challenge for the party. Today, the Bodos constitute around 25 per cent of the total population in BTAD but have overriding representation in the council. The non-Bodos, including the migrant Bengali-speaking Muslims who have been targeted by the Bodos frequently, showed solidarity on the eve of 2014 Lok Sabha elections and sponsored a non-Bodo tribal leader Naba Sarania, who registered a landslide victory.

28. Gana Shakti later became an ally of the BJP-led alliance and its leader Ranoj Pegu subsequently joined the BJP and was elected to the assembly in the by-poll held in April 2017. (Source: Ratnadip Choudhury, 'Assam By-Election Result 2017: Ranoj Pegu Retains Dhemaji Seat For BJP', NDTV, 13 April 2017, https://www.ndtv.com/india-news/assam-assembly-poll-result-2017-ranoj-pegu-retains-dhemaji-seat-for-bjp-1680872).

29. BJP promised to grant ST status to the Mataks, Morans, Ahoms, Chutias, tea tribes and the Koch-Rajbongshis during the campaign for the 2014 Lok Sabha elections. It was the first promise that the BJP made in its poll pledge published on 7 April 2014, that is, on the day of the first phase of the elections.

30. The Coordination Committee of the Tribal Organizations of Assam (CCTOA) in a convention held in Guwahati on 23 August 2016 strongly opposed the centre's move to grant Scheduled Tribe (ST) status to six communities in Assam and announced `to launch a series of agitation programmes including bandh and blocking of national highways'. CCTOA also remarked that this move will push the existing 14 scheduled tribes further backward. (Source: NDTV, 2016, `Tribal Bodies Oppose Granting Scheduled Tribe Status To 6 Communities In Assam', 23 August. Available at https://www.ndtv.com/india-news/tribal-bodies-oppose-granting-scheduled-tribe-status-to-6 communities-in-assam-1448737, accessed on 29 March 2021.

31. State Minister of Home, Government of India, Kiren Rijuju, claimed after the elections that 25,000 RSS workers worked day and night to ensure the victory in Assam.

32. Udayon Misra, 'Victory for Identity Politics, Not Hindutva in Assam', *Economic & Political Weekly* 51, no. 22 (28 May 2016), https://www.epw.in/journal/2016/22/2016-state-assembly-elections/victory-identity-politics-not-hindutva-assam.html.

33. According to the 2011 census data, the Hindu population constitutes 61.47 per cent of the total population in the state; the Muslims account for 34.22 per cent. In rural areas, Hindus constitute 58.57 per cent against 36.85 per cent of Muslims. The Muslims constituted 24.6 per cent of the total population in 1971. Available data suggests that in 1971, they were in majority in two districts, namely Dhubri and Hailakandi. In 1991, they became a majority in four districts: Dhubri, Goalpara, Barpeta and Hailakandi. In 2001, a total of six districts became Muslim dominated and in 2011 the number increased to nine districts. According to the 2011 census, the Muslim majority districts are Barpeta (70.74%), Bongaigaon (50.22%), Darrang (64.34%), Dhubri (79.67%), Goalpara (57.52%), Hailakandi (60.31%), Karimganj (58.36%), Morigaon (52.65%) and Nagaon (55.36%); Dutta 2016: *Sambhabana*, pp 53–55. (Source: Akhil Ranjan Dutta, 'Sambhawana: Asom Bidhan Sabha Nirbachan', 2016 (The Possibilities: Assam Legislative Assembly Elections 2016), Rainbow Publishers, Guwahati, India, pp 53–55).

34. Samudra Gupta Kashyap, 'Assam: Intellectuals Appeal to Vote against BJP Kicks Up Row', *The Indian Express*, 3 April 2016, https://indianexpress.com/article/elections-2016/india/india-news-india/assam-intellectuals-appeal-against-bjp-kicks-up-row/.

35. This appeal was signed by 43 citizens in the state and was led by Hiren Gohain, a leading leftist intellectual in the state. Prominent other signatories were Nalinidhar Bhattacharyya, Nilmoni Phukan and Nirupama Borgohain—all Sahitya Akademi awardees. The media played it out in such a way that both Bhattacharyya and Borgohain later distanced themselves from the appeal.

36. Malini Bhattacharjee, 'Tracing the Emergence and Consolidation of Hindutva in Assam', *Economic & Political Weekly* 51, no. 16 (16 April 2016): 80.

37. Ibid., 80.

38. Ibid., 81.

39. Ibid., 81.
40. PMINDIA, 'Text of PM's Address at 85th Annual Conference of Srimanta Sankaradeva Sangha at Sibsagar', 5 February 2016, https://www.pmindia. gov.in/en/news_updates/text-of-pms-address-at-85th-annual-conference-of-srimanta-sankaradeva-sangha-at-sibsagar-assam/.
41. Samudra Gupta Kashyap, 'Give Me Love in This Election, I Will Give You 5 Years of Development: PM Modi in Assam Election Rally', *The Indian Express*, 9 April 2016, http://indianexpress.com/article/elections-2016/india/india-news-india/pm-narendra-modi-assam-election-rally-country-suffered-due-to-remote-control-state-should-not/.
42. Misra, 'Victory for Identity Politics'.
43. Ibid., 20.
44. Ibid., 20.
45. All Assam Students' Union, 'Restructuring of Indian Constitution to Provide for a True Federal Republic', proposals presented by All Assam Students' Union in the National Seminar, held at Himachal Bhawan, New Delhi, 14–15 November 1992.
46. Dhruba Jyoti Borah, *Jatiya Prasna Aru Atmaniyantran* [The Nationality Question and Self-determination] (Guwahati: Radiant Impression, 1993), 127.
47. KMSS, 'Draft Assam Land Bill, 2016', 7.
48. Anupama Roy, 'Ambivalence of Citizenship in Assam', *Economic & Political Weekly* 51, no. 26–27 (25 June 2016): 45–51, 46.
49. Ibid.
50. Ibid.
51. Ibid., 47.
52. Sangeeta Barooah Pisharoty, 'Assam on the Boil Again, This Time over Hindu Migrants from Bangladesh', The Wire, 13 September 2015, http://thewire.in/10622/assam-on-the-boil-again-this-time-over-hindu-migrants-from-angladesh/.
53. Ibid.
54. *Business Standard*, 'Assam Speaker Initiates Steps for "Assamese" Definition', 4 March 2015, https://www.business-standard.com/article/pti-stories/assam-speaker-initiates-steps-for-assamese-definition-115030400784_1.html.
55. *The Hindu*, '"Assamese People" Definition Rocks Assembly', 1 April 2015, http://www.thehindu.com/news/national/other-states/assamese-people-definition-rocks-assembly/article7055297.ece.
56. Ibid.
57. Abdul Kalam Azad, 'Definition of Assamese People: NRC Updation and Recent Political Developments in Assam', 2015, https://abdulkazad.wordpress.com/tag/definition-of-assamese/.
58. The AGP contested in 24 seats as a part of the alliance and additional 6 seats independently.
59. Samudra Gupta Kashyap, 'Assam: Sonowal Takes Oath, Promises Bangladeshi-free Assam', *The Indian Express*, 25 May 2016, https://indianexpress.com/article/india/india-news-india/sarbananda-sonowal-my-govt-will-make-assam-free-of-bangladeshis-corruption-pollution-2817128/.

60. NDTV, 'In Sonowal's First Speech as Assam Chief Minister, a Plea and a Promise', 24 May 2016, https://www.ndtv.com/india-news/in-sonowals-first-speech-as-assam-chief-minister-a-plea-and-a-promise-1409718.

61. *Firstpost*, 'Sarbananda Sonowal Sworn-in as Assam Chief Minister in Grand Ceremony', 24 May 2016, https://www.firstpost.com/politics/sarbananda-sonowal-sworn-in-as-chief-minister-in-grand-ceremony-in-guwahati-2796748.html.

62. In an election rally in Lakhimpur, Upper Assam, Amit Shah declared that the BJP 'would bring the Citizenship (Amendment) Bill back if it returned to power'. The party also felt 'the Bill was necessary to prevent Assam from becoming a Muslim-majority state like Kashmir'. (Source: *The Hindu*, 'Amit Shah Swears by Citizenship Bill', 17 February 2019, https://www.thehindu.com/news/national/sacrifices-of-crpf-personnel-wont-go-in-vain-amit-shah/article26296689.ece).

63. Akhil Ranjan Dutta in his analysis of the 2014 Lok Sabha and 2016 assembly elections in Assam extensively deals with how the BJP used local issues and cultural ethos as electoral strategies. Akhil Ranjan Dutta, 'BJP's Consolidation, AIUDF's Polarization and Congress' Defeat in Assam', in *India's 2014 Elections: A Modi-led BJP Sweep*, ed. Paul Wallace (New Delhi: SAGE Publications, 2015), 381–403; Akhil Ranjan Dutta, 'BJP's Electoral Victory in Assam, 2016: Co-opting the Khilonjiyas', *Social Change* 47, no. 1 (2017): 108–124 https://journals.sagepub.com/doi/abs/10.1177/0049085716683114?journalCode=scha.

64. *The Sentinel*, 'Citizenship (Amendment) Bill Will Prevent Assam from Becoming: Kashmir": Himanta Biswa Sarma', 2019, https://www.sentinelassam.com/top-headlines/citizenship-amendment-bill-will-prevent-assam-from-becoming-kashmir-himanta-biswa-sarma/.

65. *The Economic Times*, 'Government Sets Up Panel to Implement Clause 6 of Assam Accord', 7 January 2019, https://economictimes.indiatimes.com/news/politics-and-nation/government-sets-up-panel-to-implement-clause-6-of-assam-accord/articleshow/67414320.cms.

66. Assam Election Commission, 'Press Release on Party-wise Results of Counting of Votes for Panchayat Election 2018', 15 December 2018, https://www.secassam.in/pdfnoti/Final-Result-21.pdf.

67. In a tweet, Himanta Biswa Sarma, BJP's political strategist in Assam, especially mentioned victory in Karimganj constituency. He also mentioned it in a series of interviews and comments. The tweet is available at https://twitter.com/himantabiswa/status/1131522057693360128.

68. *Northeast Today*, 'Dual Standard of INC Exposed on the Citizenship (Amendment) Bill', 10 January 2019, https://www.northeasttoday.in/dual-standard-of-inc-exposed-on-the-citizenship-amendment-bill/.

69. *The Economic Times*, 'Aiudf Wants Understanding with Congress to Stop BJP', 23 March 2019, http//economictimes.indiatimes.com/articleshow/68541724.cms?from=mdr&utm_source=contentofinterest&utm_medium=text&utm_campaign=cppst&; *The Economic Times*, 'Was Betrayed by Congress People:

AIUDF's Ajmal', 22 April 2019, https://economictimes.indiatimes.com/news/
elections/lok-sabha/india/was-betrayed-by-congress-people-aiudfs-ajmal/
articleshow/68983510.cms.

70. One can refer to two articles published in the *Economic & Political Weekly*, first
by Deepankar Basu and Debarshi Das entitled 'Assam: BJP's Consolidation,
Congress's Lost Opportunities' published on 22 June 2019 and the second by
Dhruba Pratim Sharma and Vikas Tripathi with the title 'Assam 2019: NDA
Deepens Its Dominance', which appeared on the 24 August 2019 issue.

71. *The Sentinel*, 'Chief Minister Says AASU Approaching Rahul Gandhi
Is Sad,' 7 February 2019, https://www.sentinelassam.com/news/
chief-minister-says-aasu-approaching-rahul-gandhi-is-sad/.

72. *The Sentinel*, 'Don't Give Political Tone to AICC Meeting over CAB: AASU to
Sarbananda Sonowal', 8 February 2019, https://www.sentinelassam.com/news/
dont-give-political-tone-to-aicc-meeting-over-cab-aasu-to-sarbananda-sonowal/.

73. *The Economic Times*, 'Akhil Gogoi to Campaign against Congress in
Assam', 2 April 2014, https://www.economictimes.indiatimes.com/article-
show/33125802.cms?from=mdr&utm_source=contentofinterest&utm_
medium=text&utm_campaign=cppst.

74. *The Economic Times*, 'Akhil Gogoi's KMSS to Float New Political Party to
Fight Polls', 18 March 2015, https://www.economictimes.indiatimes.com/
articleshow/46607907.cms?from=mdr&utm_source=contentofinterest&utm_
medium=text&utm_campaign=cppst.

75. News 18, 'Denied Ticket, BJP's Mission 20 Stands in the Way of Himanta
Biswa Sarma and a Delhi Berth', 22 March 2019, https://www.news18.com/
news/politics/denied-ticket-bjps-mission-20-stands-in-the-way-of-himanta-
biswa-sarma-and-a-delhi-berth-2074301.html.

76. Sangeeta Barooah Pisharoty, 'Rameshwar Teli's Inclusion in Govt Telling of BJP's
Desire to Woo Assam's Tea Tribe', The Wire, 31 May 2019, https://thewire.
in/politics/rameshwar-teli-inclusion-modi-govt-bjp-assam-tea-community.

77. Himanta Biswa Sarma, 'Assam Budget: Budget Speech 2019–20', 2019,
Department of Finance, Government of Assam, https://finassam.in/
budget_documents/.

78. Rajeev Bhattacharyya, 'Saffron Wave in Assam: Ekal Vidyalayas Helped BJP,
RSS Establish Strong Roots in Assam's Tribal Areas, Tea Estates', *Firstpost*, 24
May 2019, https://www.firstpost.com/politics/saffron-wave-in-assam-ekal-
vidyalayas-helped-bjp-rss-establish-strong-roots-in-assams-tribal-areas-tea-
estates-6696851.html.

79. *The Economic Times*, 'RSS Cleared the Air in Northeast, Assam on Citizenship
Bill', 27 May 2019, https://economictimes.indiatimes.com/news/elections/
lok-sabha/india/rss-cleared-the-air-in-northeast-assam-on-citizenship-bill/
articleshow/69511256.cms.

80. Hiren Gohain, 'The BJP's Plans for Assam: An RSS-run School in Every
Panchayat', The Wire, 15 June 2016, https://thewire.in/communalism/
the-bjps-plans-for-assam-an-rss-run-school-in-every-panchayat.

81. Information received from Sada Dutta (30 June 2019), who acted as the general secretary of these schools for nine years. Until the BJP came to power, these schools engaged eminent educationists. Although affiliated to Vidya Bharati, the presence of the RSS was not prominent. After the BJP came to power in 2016, the RSS increasingly became involved in running the schools.

82. Gohain, 'The BJP's Plans for Assam'.

83. Bhattacharyya, 'Saffron Wave in Assam'.

84. Smita Gupta, 'How the RSS Grew Roots in the North-East', 2019, https://www.thehindubusinessline.com/blink/know/how-the-rss-grew-roots-in-the-north-east/article22991950.ece.

85. Hilal Ahmed, Dhruba Patim Sharma, and Vikas Tripathi, 'Post-poll Survey: BJP's Polarization Strategy Hits the Mark in Assam', *The Hindu*, 28 May 2019, https://www.thehindu.com/elections/lok-sabha-2019/post-poll-survey-bjps-polarisation-strategy-hits-the-mark-in-assam/article27267757.ece.

86. Ibid.

87. Compiled from the statistics of Election Commission of India, http://results.eci.gov.in/pc/en/constituencywise/ConstituencywiseS033.htm?ac=3. Disaggregated lead in assembly segments compiled by Assam Pradesh Congress Committee, Guwahati.

88. *The Economic Times*, 'Narendra Modi Blames Congress for Assam Accord Delay in Northeast Rally', 30 March 2019, https://economictimes.indiatimes.com/news/elections/lok-sabha/india/narendra-modi-blames-congress-for-assam-accord-delay-in-northeast-rally/articleshow/68644339.cms?from=mdr.

89. *The Hindu*, 'Amit Shah Swears by Citizenship Bill'.

90. *The Sentinel*, 'Maneswar Basumatary Cremated with Full State Honour', 17 February, https://www.sentinelassam.com/news/maneswar-basumatary-cremated-with-full-state-honour/.

91. Sarma, 'Assam Budget'.

92. *The Hindu*, 'Assam NRC Final List Publication: Live Updates', 31 August 2019, https://www.thehindu.com/news/national/assam-nrc-fi nal-list2019-live-updates/article29307171.ece.

93. Ibid.

94. *The Economic Times*, 'Government Panel on Clause 6 of Assam Accord Reconstituted', 16 July 2019, https://economictimes.indiatimes.com/article-show/702 51 3- 25.cms?from=mdr&utm_source=con tent ofi - nterest&utm_medium=text&utm_campaign= - cppst.

95. *The Times of India*, 'Suspension of Internet in 10 Assam Districts Extended for 48 Hours', 12 December 2019, https://timesofi ndia.indiatimes.com/india/suspension-of-internet-in-10-assam-districtsextended-for-48-hrs/articleshow/72489742. cms.

Unmaking the Consensus

The NRC Debacle

2

The mounting attack on Assam's NRC—from UN human/minority rights agencies to various organizations and individuals engaged in defending the rights of the linguistic and religious minorities, particularly the Bengali Muslims—defamed the defenders of the NRC as xenophobic, exclusionist and intolerant. Such attacks also provoked certain sections of the Bengali Muslim community in Assam to express outrage against the NRC updating process. The lack of any agreement with the Government of Bangladesh for possible extradition of those who are made 'stateless' by the NRC process intensified the attacks. The initial defence of Assam's NRC by the incumbent governments that pursue the agenda of Hindu majoritarianism and its parallel efforts to grant citizenship to non-Muslim minority communities from Afghanistan, Pakistan and Bangladesh by amending the Citizenship Act made Assam's NRC updating process more vulnerable. Amid these challenges, the larger society in Assam rallied behind the NRC as a substantive move to settle the citizenship issue which has plagued the state for decades.

The NRC, an outcome of the Assam Accord of 1985 that attained the sanctity of a 'public law contract' in the recent past, was also considered to be an instrument to do away with the prejudices against the East-Bengal-origin Muslims in the state who had been accorded citizenship by the accord. It also became urgently necessary to counter any move towards abrogation of Section 6A of the Citizenship Act, 1955, which guarantees right to citizenship to the immigrants from East Pakistan (present-day Bangladesh) until 24 March 1971.

The overriding concerns of the critics of Assam's NRC also failed to distinguish the aspirations of the Assamese people from that of the communal and sectarian agenda of the incumbent NDA regime on citizenship. The critics have also perceived Assam's NRC as a blueprint of the national NRC as well as the other side of the CAA. Assam's demand for NRC was alleged to be narrow nationalism driven by xenophobic tendencies for which it has also been attempted to be equated with the inhumane tenets of Nazism. The critics also refused to credit the same Assamese people who built an unprecedented resistance against both CAB and CAA in parallel to its pursuit for the NRC. The escalating attacks made it quite easy for the incumbent government to entirely reject the Supreme Court-monitored NRC once the final document failed its vested agenda of making it a pro-Hindu Bengali citizenship register. These events contributed towards dismantling the consensus around the NRC which had been built through political understanding and negotiations in the post-Assam Accord period. The erosion of the consensus on NRC has a lot of implications. It may help in bringing back more chauvinist elements to the forefront and the resurgence of the demands for 1951 as the cut-off date for the detection, deletion and deportation of the foreigners. Such a possible reverse move towards an aggressive campaign against the immigrants is also the outcome of refusal of the humanitarians to recognize the historical context of the Assam's NRC.

The present chapter is an attempt to journey through this critical and contested trajectory of Assam's NRC.

WARRANTING THE NRC: THE BACKGROUND

Assam's politics has long been dominated by contestation over citizenship, resulting primarily from the unchecked illegal migration from across the border, particularly from erstwhile East Pakistan (present-day Bangladesh). Migration/immigration has been a burden of history since it became part of British India in 1826.[1] The British brought in migrant labourers, mostly tribals from the Chota Nagpur Plateau and its adjoining areas covering present-day Jharkhand and Chhattisgarh and parts of Bihar, West Bengal, Odisha, Telangana and Andhra

Pradesh, to work in the newly opened tea plantations from the mid-19th century. The colonial authority also encouraged the migration of Muslim farmers from East Bengal from the late 19th century and early 20th century to grow food and cultivate jute. The issue had been constantly debated in the Assam Legislative Council since 1912 and subsequently in the legislative assembly since 1937. After independence, it assumed even a wider dimension, which was evident from the debates in the Legislative Assembly. The colonial rulers also promoted the migrants to Assam, apprehending a massive peasant revolt. 'The British colonial rulers, after fleecing poor East Bengal peasants for more than a century apprehended a massive peasant revolt and promoted the latter's migration to Assam'.[2] It was again the colonial authority that had 'also set off an alarm among native Assamese people about their lands being "seized" and their culture "being" buried'. Provocative remarks by British official like Census superintendent C.S. Mullan in 1931 'made the situation worse, turning anxiety into panic'. Muslim leaders like Maulana Bhashani 'breathed fire into this by demanding both land for new immigrants and inclusion of Assam in Pakistan'.[3]

Harsh Mander, a staunch critic of Assam's NRC, also acknowledges the anxiety of the indigenous communities of Assam due to the unchecked migration since the colonial period. The roots of the NRC, Mander writes, may be traced back to the strategies of the colonial administration that indulged in clearing forest lands for the expansion of both food production and tea plantations. These projects facilitated 'a steady flow of land-hungry and industrious migrants from neighbouring East Bengal'. These hardworking migrants who helped convert forest land into paddy fields eventually settled in the state. The flow of migration continued even after the partition of the country. The continued brutality of the Pakistani regime on East Pakistan, which reached its height during the Liberation War in 1971, forced a huge number of them to migrate to Assam. While pointing out the contributions of the Bengali migrants to the Assam's economy and the culture 'with their toil and sweat as well as their lyrical music and poetry', Mander also points out, 'Their mounting numbers stirred anxieties among the indigenous Assamese people about the preservation of their distinct culture and ownership of land.'[4] These anxieties culminated in the anti-foreigner movement of 1979–1985, which primarily targeted the Bengali migrants. The Assam Accord, 1985, was an important milestone towards addressing these anxieties which agreed to accord citizenship to all immigrants till 24 March 1971 through amended provisions of the Indian Citizenship Act, 1955. Extending immigrants' right to citizenship till 24 March 1971 had been an exception only for the state of Assam, and this exception warranted the much-debated NRC for the state. There have always been contentions and debates regarding the actual number of the immigrants and refugees to Assam from across the border particularly since independence. The 'White Paper on Foreigners' Issue' published by the Government of Assam in 2012 provides the numbers along with different schemes undertaken by both the Union and state governments to deal with the anxieties caused by the influx of the migrants since India had achieved independence. In the decades-long process of dealing with the issues of immigrants and refugees, a citizens' register for Assam figured as one of the core concerns. The NRC 2019 is the culmination of this long process.

Following the partition and communal riots in the subcontinent, Assam initially saw an influx of refugees and other migrants from East Pakistan. The number of such people was initially reported by the state government to be between 150,000 and 200,000 but later estimated to be around 500,000.[5] It is around this time that on the issue of refugees, conflict erupted between the state government and the Union government. In 1949, Gopinath Bardoloi-led state government was beset with three major problems, of which the influx of refugees—both Hindus and Muslims—from the then East Pakistan was very crucial. The other two challenges were the paucity of funds for the state's development programme and the troubles created by the communist insurgents.[6] The Central government was making it almost a condition for Assam to accept the refugees from East Pakistan to receive central fund for development. The Bardoloi government insisted on the scarcity of land in Assam, as the state was also facing the challenges of the settlement of 186,121 landless peasant families and about 50,000 flood-displaced families.[7]

On 6 January 1950, in the month that the Constitution took effect, and five years ahead of the enactment of the Indian Citizenship Act,

1955, the intensity and accompanied apprehensions around immigration into Assam from across the border forced the Union government of India to promulgate an ordinance. Later, the ordinance was enacted into the Immigrants (Expulsion from Assam) Act that came into effect on 1 March 1950.

The 1950 Act was primarily enacted to 'provide for the expulsion of certain immigrants from Assam'. The Act mandated to expel those residents who had entered Assam, either before or after the commencement of the Act, from territories outside India, and whose stay in Assam was considered detrimental to the interests of the general public of India or any section thereof or any STs in Assam. However, the Act did not apply to 'any person who on account of civil disturbances or the fear of such disturbances in any area now forming part of Pakistan has been displaced from or has left his place of residence in such area and who has been subsequently residing in Assam'.[8] This was the provision which ensured that not all immigrants from across the border can be expelled. The persecution and atrocities in erstwhile East Pakistan by the Pakistani government forced huge influx to Assam, which the Indian government could not expel despite the 1950 Act.

Fresh communal disturbances occurred in the early 1950s in Assam along with East Pakistan, West Bengal and Tripura. The violence forced some immigrants living in the districts of Goalpara, Kamrup and Darrang to flee to East Pakistan, leaving their properties behind. It is in this context that the Nehru–Liaquat Agreement was signed on 8 April 1950. One of the basic objectives of the agreement was to protect the immovable property of those migrants and to restore to them when they return to the original homes. The government report suggests that 'there was net influx of 1,61,360 people into Assam who had entered Assam through recognized routes of travel'.[9] It is, of course, debatable whether these returnees may be termed as 'influx'.

It is under these circumstances and the directive of the Ministry of Home Affairs (MHA) that an NRC was prepared for Assam during the census of 1951. It was done by copying relevant information on every person enumerated in the census document. Apart from other relevant information like the name of the father or the husband, nationality, sex, age and means of livelihood of every person, the NRC particularly showed the houses or holdings in a serial order, mentioning the name and number of the person living therein. These registers, which were initially kept in the offices of Deputy Commissioners (DCs) and Sub Divisional Officers (SDOs), were transferred to the police for custody in the early 1960s to facilitate the verification of infiltration/illegal migrants.[10] It may be mentioned that there had been a number of hindrances towards driving out illegal migrants due to the continuance of the colonial regulations like the passport and visa regulations formulated under the Indian Passport Act, 1920, and the Foreigners Act, 1946. The regulations on passport and visa for India and Pakistan came into effect only in October 1952, and the definition of a foreigner to cover a Pakistani national under the Foreigners Act, 1946, was clearly spelt out only in 1957. Under the amended provision of the Act, a foreigner came to be defined 'as a person who is not a citizen of India'. Before this amendment, a foreigner was defined 'as a person who is not a natural-born British subject', a definition that was borrowed from relevant provisions of the British Nationality and Status of Aliens Act of 1914.[11] The amendment came into effect on 19 January 1957, and it relieved Pakistani nationals registering themselves with the registration officer of the respective districts which they had visited. In March 1957, detailed instructions were issued to the state governments to deport the Pakistani nationals living in India without proper authority or sanction. It may also be mentioned that the Indian Citizenship Act was enacted in 1955 and came into effect from 30 December 1955.

As the legal instruments of defining and deporting the foreign nationals, particularly from Pakistan, got streamlined, the process of identification and deportation started. The census report of the Registrar General of Census assessed that 220,691 infiltrators had entered India. Based on the reports, the police undertook initiatives during 1962–1964 to detect and deport such infiltrators. By 1964, the state government constituted four tribunals under special officers with judicial knowledge to cover the cases of suspected infiltrators who claimed to be Indians. Based on the decisions by these tribunals 'Quit India' notices were issued.[12] It had been reported that during 1961–1966, approximately 178,952 infiltrators were either deported or voluntarily left the country. These drives attracted a lot of criticisms, and the Government of Pakistan threatened to take the issue to the United Nations (UN). Under these circumstances, the government decided to introduce foolproof judicial scrutiny in the procedure of the eviction of Pakistani infiltrators to strengthen its legal–juridical position on infiltrators before international forums like the UN. It culminated in the issuing of a statutory order called Foreigners (Tribunal) Order in September 1964 and the creation of Foreigners Tribunal (FT) under it. It was also warranted by an international campaign against the harassment of bona fide Indian persons while issuing the Quit India notices. Under this order, four tribunals were constituted in Assam in 1964 which were extended to nine in 1968.[13] In 1969, the government also streamlined the process of deportation and decided that only three categories of foreigners could be summarily deported: (a) Pakistani nationals holding Pakistani passports, (b) re-infiltrators who were once deported and (c) fresh infiltrators who were caught in the border. More restrictions were imposed on checking and detaining people only on the ground of suspicion.[14]

In June 1962, the Ministry of Home Affairs of the Government of India approved a scheme called Prevention of Infiltration into India of Pakistani Nationals (PIP) through which the government intended to 'establish a security screen in depth to exercise a physical check and control over the number, identity and movement of existing inhabitants in the migrant settlements near the border making it impossible for any new entrants to go untraced and unnoticed'.[15] Initially, it was implemented in three border districts—Goalpara, Garo Hills and Cachar—and three interior districts of Kamrup, Nagaon and Darrang. Later, the Lakhimpur district was also brought under the scheme. Police infrastructure was expanded to keep vigilance over the movement of infiltrators across the border districts and to detect the arrival of new immigrants in existing immigrant settlements near the border. The scheme also facilitated the process of preparing a register of all residents in the areas covered by the scheme. Under this scheme, initially, 52 police posts were established which were extended to 180 by 1964. The scheme was initially made functional under the control of an assistant inspector general of police. The post was later upgraded to the level of deputy inspector general of police and finally to the additional director general of police.

In 1965, the Government of India also asked the Government of Assam to expedite the compilation of a register of citizens and to issue identity cards based on it to Indian nationals in select areas. The citizens having identity cards were supposed to carry it with them voluntarily to avoid any harassment being meted out to them on account of suspicion. The issue of barbed wire fencing along the border of Pakistan also came up during this period for which the Government of India proposed to the state government for clearance of a mile-deep belt along the border. The proposal could not be implemented as it involved shifting of 25,000 families (128,000 persons) along the 560 square mile belt on the Assam–East Pakistan border.[16] Eventually, both the ideas of issuing identity cards and installing barbed wire were dropped. It may be mentioned that although Bangladesh came into being in 1971, it was only in 1976 that the Central government authorized the appropriate authorities of the state government of Assam to issue orders against Bangladeshi nationals under Foreigners Act, 1946. It was also instructed that 'persons who (had) come to India from Erstwhile East Pakistan/Bangladesh prior to March 1971 are not to be sent back to Bangladesh'.[17]

These developments ultimately culminated in the six-year-long Assam Movement, which started in 1979. The immediate context was the by-elections in the Mangaldoi Lok Sabha constituency, which was necessitated by the death of the incumbent member Hiralal Patowari. It was reported by the Election Commission of India that names of suspected nationality entered the voters list, triggering the agitation instantly. The movement, although claimed to be non-violent, turned out to be violent in many instances. The 1983 Nellie massacre was indeed a black spot on the movement. The AASU and All Assam Gana Sangram Parishad (AAGSP) steered the movement and raised the issue of NRC in their letter to Prime Minister Indira Gandhi on 18 January 1980. 'They submitted some broad proposals for the purpose of detecting and deleting the names of foreigners from the electoral rolls based on the NRC of 1951 and thereafter deporting them.' Among the range of proposals submitted to the prime minister, two were related to NRC: (a) updating the NRC of 1951 and (c) cross-checking electoral rolls with the updated NRC.[18]

The six-year-long Assam agitation initially demanded 1951 as the cut-off year for the detection and deportation of foreigners. In its memorandum submitted to the prime minister of India dated 2 February 1980, AASU made its point clear. On the part of the government, 25 March 1971 was offered as the cut-off date for the detection and deportation of foreigners, which the AASU instantly rejected.

The Union government insisted on 25 March 1971 as it was on this day that Bangladesh declared its independence after the military junta in Pakistan refused to allow the Awami League led by Sheikh Mujibur Rahman to form the government despite securing the majority of seats in the Pakistan National Assembly. It was followed by Operation Searchlight by the Pakistani army that resulted in genocide in East Pakistan. There is no exact number of people being killed and the estimate varies from 3 lakh (0.3 million) to 30 lakh (3 million).

In a discussion held with AASU in April 1980, the Governor of Assam suggested that 1967 should be the cut-off year for the detection and deletion of foreigners and 1971 for the deportation of foreigners. This proposal was also rejected by the student body. Prime Minister Indira Gandhi held another round of discussion with them in Assam on 12 April 1980. It did not yield any positive outcome. In September 1980, the AASU proposed that the organization would agree to a negotiated settlement towards accepting the immigrants who came between 1951 and 1961, provided the government agreed to shift the 1961–1971 streams of immigrants to other states. The government disagreed to the proposal. From 1980 to 1982, as many as 23 rounds of negotiations took place at different levels but failed to come into a consensus.[19]

The Assam Movement was marked by the systematic targeting of East-Bengal-origin Muslims and sporadic violence. Apart from Nellie, where around 2,000 Muslims were massacred on 18 February 1983,[20] two days before this ghostly incident, that is, on 16 February 1983, 109 people were burnt alive in Nagabandha High School in the present-day Morigaon district.[21] The movement had a mass base and popular support. But the chauvinist character and the intolerance towards the opponents and critics of the movement brought divisions within the larger society. The 1983 elections for the legislative assembly were marked by social boycotts and violence, and the elected government headed by Hiteswar Saikia earned the title of 'people's enemy' throughout his tenure. The left and progressive forces were also boycotted and targeted for their insistence on 1971 as the cut-off year for the detection and deportation of foreigners. These forces were also critical of the chauvinist and intolerant attitudes of the movement leaders. Whereas in the popular discourse the 855 martyrs of Assam Movement remain a reference point, however, altogether 67 people belonging to different left political parties lost their lives in the hands of the violent elements of the movement. They were also targeted due to their participation in the 1983 assembly elections, which the movement supporters boycotted. For the left parties, participation in the election was important to defend the democratic system.[22] The government machinery was suppressive, and the common masses came under severe pressure. Finally, on 15 August 1985, the government and the agitating groups accepted 1966 as the cut-off year for granting citizenship to the immigrants and 24 March 1971 as the cut-off date for the detection, deletion and deportation of illegal migrants. The immigrants of the 1966–1971 period were also offered citizenship after disenfranchisement of 10 years and subject to registration. With these provisions, the accord extended the constitutionally mandated cut-off dates of granting Indian citizenship to the immigrants, resulting in the enactment of the first amendment of the Indian Citizenship Act, 1955, adopted in December 1985. This amendment made Assam a case of 'exception' as far as granting citizenship to the immigrants was concerned, by incorporating Section 6A into the Act. The new provisions extended the date of granting citizenship to the immigrants from the constitutionally mandated cut-off date of the 'day of enforcement of the Constitution', that is, 26 January 1950, to 24 March 1971. It is this exception that warranted the updating of the NRC, 1951, for Assam.

It should be mentioned that the Assam Accord did not have a provision on updating the NRC. There are two clauses on the 'issue of citizenship certificate' but none about the NRC. These two clauses are as follows: '8.1 The Government will arrange for the issue of citizenship certificate in future only by the authorities of the Central Government; 8.2 Specific complaints that may be made by AASU/

AAGSP about irregular issuance of Indian Citizenship Certificates (ICC) will be looked into.'

Regarding the implementation of these two clauses, the 2012 White Paper writes: 'The Citizenship Act has been amended and issuance of citizenship is done only by the authorities of the Central Government. The Government of India have informed that they have not received any specific complaints relating to irregular issuance of citizenship certificate.'[23]

It was in 1990s that the issue of NRC came up in a meeting between the AASU and the Union government that discussed the progress of the implementation of the Assam Accord. During an official-level tripartite talk held on 17 November 1999, a decision was taken to update the NRC. Finally, in a tripartite meeting involving the Central and state governments and the AASU on 5 May 2005, which was chaired by the then Prime Minister Manmohan Singh, a decision was taken to update the NRC within a couple of years and to issue identity cards to genuine Indian citizens living in the state on the basis of it.[24] Accordingly, based on the recommendation of the Group of Ministers in 2008, the Citizenship (Registration of Citizens and Issue of National Identity Cards) Rules, 2003, was amended in 2009, following which the legal framework for updating the NRC was put in place by inserting relevant rules and procedures.

Under the amended provisions of the citizenship rules, it has been stated that:

> The Central Government shall, for the purpose, of the National Register of Indian Citizens in the State of Assam, cause to carry out throughout the State of Assam for preparation of the National Register of Indian Citizens in the State of Assam by inviting applications from all the residents, for collection of specified particulars relating to each family and individual, residing in a local area in the State including the citizenship status based on the National Register of Citizens 1951, and the electoral rolls up to the midnight of the 24th day of March, 1971.[25]

On 22 April 2010, in another official-level tripartite meeting, a decision was taken to launch a pilot project in Chaygaon and Barpeta revenue circles. But the process was stalled after a violent protest in Barpeta.

The project was criticized and resisted, largely by the Bengali-speaking Muslim population.[26] It was resisted on many grounds. First, as a part of the process, the citizens were required to submit documents for verification where their names appeared. Three important documents meant for verification were the list of NRC 1951 and electoral rolls of 1966 and 1971. It was pointed out by the critics that there are a lot of anomalies in these documents for which genuine Indian citizens were served notices allegedly to be a foreigner. It was also questioned about why only Assam should have an updated NRC. They expressed the apprehensions that the basic objective was to identify a large number of Bengali-speaking Muslim population as non-citizens and drive them out. It was also alleged that the basic objective behind this exercise had been to underestimate the number of Bengali population in the state.[27] All these controversies and contestations resulted in dropping the pilot project.

However, a series of initiatives afterwards created a consensus on updating the NRC. But, it was only after the intervention of the Supreme Court of India that the preparing of the NRC process took off, and three lists were published, including the final list being published on 31 August 2019. After the publication of each list—the partial draft on 31 December 2017, the final draft on 30 July 2018 and the final list on 31 August 2019—a lot of debates and controversies surfaced. The incumbent government and the ruling BJP, which supported and endorsed both the partial and the final drafts, rejected the final list, calling it a flawed document and pleaded for Assam to be a part of all-India NRC. This idea of a national NRC, however, had to be abandoned due to the protests across the country.[28]

UPDATING THE NRC

The Partial Draft

Updating the NRC for Assam was one of the initial demands of the Assam Movement, and a series of initiatives were undertaken in the post-Assam Accord period towards its implementation. However, the process moved only after the intervention by the Supreme Court. The turning point in the process was the judgment delivered on

17 December 2014, which laid down a definite timeframe to publish the updated and final version of the NRC. This was a combined judgment on three writ petitions filed by Assam Sanmilita Mahasangha and Others (2012), Assam Public Works (APW; 2009) and All Assam Ahom Associations and Others (2014).[29] The hearing on the second petition started in 2009, and subsequently the hearing on the first petition was also combined with it. Regarding the third petition, notices were yet to be served to the respondents at the time of judgment. Union of India and others are the respondents in the three petitions. The 70-page judgment, apart from documenting various reports on immigration in Assam, also reflected on both legal and administrative initiatives towards resolving the issue. The seriousness of immigration as perceived by the judgment is evident from the opening remarks which state: 'A Prophet is without honour in his own country. Substitute "citizens" for "prophet" and you will get the gist of various writ petitions filed under Article 32 of the Constitution of India assailing Section 6A of the Citizenship Act.'[30] The judgment also remarked that while 'the Parliament has not enacted any law pertaining to refugees from other counties', through the Assam Accord 'a huge number of illegal migrants were made deemed citizens of India.'[31] This judgment also took cognizance of the Supreme Court's judgment in 2005 on the Writ Petition No. 131 of 2000 through which the controversial IMDT Act, 1983 was declared null and void on the ground that the

> Act and the rules made there under operated in the reverse direction i.e. instead of seeing that illegal migrants are deported, it did the opposite by placing the burden of proof on the State to prove that a person happens to be an illegal migrant.[32]

In the 2005 verdict, the Court, apart from asserting that the IMDT) Act, 1983, violated Article 355 of the Constitution of India, opined that 'the Union had failed to protect the State of Assam against external aggression and internal disturbance caused by huge influx of illegal migrants from Bangladesh to Assam....'[33] The Court, through the verdict, restored the Immigrants (Expulsion from Assam) Act, 1950, together with the Foreigners Act, 1946, and the Foreigners Tribunal Order, 1964, as the tools for both detecting and deporting illegal migrants.

The 2014 judgment dealt with two fundamental issues: constitutional validity of Clause 6A (first petition, 2012) and updating the NRC for Assam (second petition, 2009). The judgment, however, refrained from giving any order on the first question on the ground that the issues associated with it 'are substantial questions need to be answered by an appropriate bench as most of them are substantial questions as to the interpretations of the Constitution'[34] and, therefore, referred it to be decided by a constitution bench. The bench framed a total of 13 questions to be examined by the constitution bench. The Court, however, took Section 6A of the Act 'deemed to be valid'[35] and made a detailed note of the progress in implementing various clauses of Assam Accord and issued directions to the appropriate authorities to undertake necessary measures to expedite the process.[36] The Court noted,

> The implementation of the aforesaid directions will be monitored by this Court on the expiry of three months from today. In the event it becomes so necessary, the Court will entrust such monitoring to be undertaken by an empowered committee which will be constituted by this Court, if and when required.[37]

While considering the writ petition filed by APW (2009), the judgment laid down a schedule to govern the process of updating the NRC. It gave 11 months to finalize the updated NRC, which was to be completed by 1 January 2016.[38] From this point, the NRC updating process came under the scrutiny and monitoring of the two-judge bench of the Supreme Court, comprising Justice Ranjan Gogoi and Justice R. F. Nariman.

The NRC updating process has been both complex and contentious. With directions from the Supreme Court of India, the Government of Assam appointed Prateek Hajela, a 1995 batch IAS officer of the Assam–Meghalaya cadre, as the coordinator in September 2013. One of the first tasks before the government was to develop and finalize the modalities for updating the register. The Government of Assam developed the modalities through a Cabinet sub-committee in mid-2013, which were sent to the Union government for approval, which gave its go-ahead in November 2014.[39] Under those modalities, a total of 16 documents were identified and approved to be used by the applicants to include their names in the updated NRC. Out of the 16 documents, 12 are main documents and the remaining four are supporting documents. The main 12 documents are extract of NRC, 1951; extract/certified copy of electoral rolls; land/tenancy records; citizenship certificates; Permanent Residential Certificate (PRC); refugee registration certificate; Indian passport; LIC insurance policy; licence; service/employment records under government/public sector; bank/post office accounts; and birth certificates. The supporting documents are: certificate issued by village panchayat secretary; educational certificate issued by boards/universities; ration cards; and records/processes pertaining to the court.[40] Except for the NRC 1951 and village panchayat secretary certificate, the other documents would be valid only if issued up to 24 March 1971. The village panchayat certificate is issued for females who have migrated to other villages after marriage. In the case of urban areas, such certificates issued by jurisdictional circle officers would be accepted. Later, in the case of four districts in BTC, where there is no panchayat, the Lat Mandals have been allowed to issue such certificates. These certificates must be countersigned by the circle officer/revenue officer/executive magistrate.

The actual process of updating the NRC started with the invitation of applications in May–June 2015. The last date of submission of applications was 31 August 2015. Provisions of online applications were also made available, and the entire exercise culminated in receiving 3.29 crore (32.9 million) applications and over 6 crore (60 million) documents. The entire exercise was carried out by 52,000 officials of the state government. The decision to publish only the partial draft and not the full draft on the date decided by the Court, that is, 31 December 2017, was accepted due to an order of the Gauhati High Court in February 2017, in which it declared the village panchayat certificate an inadmissible public document, and also due to the non-receipt of verified documents sent to various authorities, including state governments and foreign governments.

The judgment of the Gauhati High Court on 28 February 2017 in the writ petition of *Manowara Bewa vs The Union of India* caused controversies and confusions. The Court order cited a few grounds while declaring the said certificate invalid as an admissible public document. It argued that the Assam Panchayat Act, 1994, does not authorize the village panchayat secretary to issue such a certificate and, under the Indian Evidence Act, 1872, such a certificate is not a public document. Besides, the Court asked why an exception had been made in the case of the panchayat certificate, while the cut-off date was 24 March 1971 for all other documents. The order quashing the village panchayat certificate made around 48 lakh (4.8 million) applications invalid, which used certificates issued by village panchayat secretary/ revenue official and the Lat Mandals as supporting documents. The order of the Gauhati High Court created a huge challenge to the process of updating the NRC which was nearing completion at that time.

The judgment of the High Court was challenged in the Supreme Court through several special leave petitions. Through its order dated 5 December 2017,[41] the Supreme Court finally set aside the judgment of the Gauhati High Court and reinstated the validity of village panchayat certificate as a supporting document. The Supreme Court pointed out that the certificate in contention was accepted as a supporting document in consultation with all the stakeholders involved in the process, including civil society organizations, which subsequently was approved by the state government, Union government and the Registrar General of India. Besides, the document itself is no proof of citizenship; it only establishes a link between the certificate holder and the person with whom legacy data is claimed. The Court also pointed out that the certificate would thoroughly be examined, including its authenticity, before it was accepted even as a supporting document.

However, in between these events, the issue of original inhabitants cropped up. Based on the information received from the NRC project coordinator, the Court recorded in its order on 24 August 2017 that out of the disputed 48 lakh applicants 'about 20 lakh claims to be in respect of "original inhabitants" which fact, if proved, will not require any further proof or inquiry and all such persons will be included in the draft NRC'. The Court ordered the coordinator to explore and segregate the original inhabitants of the state from among the 48 lakh applicants. The introduction of the 'original inhabitants' category in the NRC was, however, challenged in the Court by Kamalakhya Dey Purkayastha through a special leave petition. The Court, after a thorough examination, removed the tag of original inhabitants from the NRC updating process by its order dated 5 December 2017. The Court argued:

> The exercise of upgradation of NRC is not intended to be one of identification and determination of who are originally inhabitants of the State of Assam. The sole test for inclusion in the NRC is citizenship under the Constitution of India and under the Citizenship Act including Section 6A thereof. Citizens who are originally inhabitants/residents of the State of Assam and those who are not are at par for inclusion in the NRC.[42]

Thwarting the hindrances in the whole process, the Supreme Court finally facilitated the release of the first part draft of the NRC on 31 December 2017. The partial draft incorporated the names of only 1.90 crore (19 million) persons out of 3.29 core (32.9 million) applications. The New Year 2018 was unique for the state of Assam as it started with the news on the NRC partial draft. Run up to the release of the draft there were apprehensions regarding the possible outrage and communal tension. The tension was already building up. Therefore, the law and order-maintaining authorities kept strict vigilance over the social networking sites apart from monitoring the situation in sensitive areas. The chief minister

> assured that no genuine Indian citizens would be excluded from the NRC and if any name is left out from the part draft of the NRC, there is provision to submit claims and objections against the same. The government would also extend all support in this regard.[43]

While appreciating the people of Assam for their cooperation towards the entire process of NRC update, the chief minister, however, warned that the police was constantly monitoring the social media, including Facebook and Twitter, and anybody indulging in spreading of misinformation would invite strict action.

The AASU that spearheaded the Assam agitation and consistently demanded the NRC termed the publication of the partial draft as 'historic event' and also said, 'It is a tribute to the martyrs of the Assam agitation.'[44] The man behind the NRC update process, Prateek Hajela, the NRC coordinator, said that the 'legacy data' was the game-changer. In his interview to *The Assam Tribune*, Hajela said that while taking over the charge as the state coordinator of NRC in September 2013, 'It was thought that the project would be an impossible one as nowhere in the country such a mega project was launched.' He also pointed out, 'Mega projects are normally based on the success of pilot projects, but in case of Assam, the project started with the experience of an unsuccessful pilot project, which had to be suspended.' He asserted that two factors contributed to the success of the NRC update process. One was the 'digitization of the legacy data' and the other was the 'preparation of family tree' which played a 'key role in preparation of a correct NRC as a number of false or forged documents were detected'.[45] While almost all political parties welcomed the draft NRC, however, the non-inclusion of political personalities and apparently members from the Bengali-speaking community incited a lot of reactions. Among those whose names did not figure also included legislators and parliamentarians, including the chief of AIUDF Badruddin Ajmal. For the next few weeks, the newspapers and social media were filled with reports regarding the prominent figures whose names did not figure in the draft NRC. However, the publication of the draft did not evoke any communal tension in the state.

The most adverse reactions on the NRC came from the Chief Minister of West Bengal, Mamata Banerjee. She said that the NRC was the repeat of the '1960s "Bongal Kheda" ["Expelling of Bengalis"] ethnic cleansing movement in Assam' that forced nearly 50,000 Bengalis of Assam to flee the state and take shelter in West Bengal. She also alleged that another 14,000 Bengalis had to leave Assam and go to West Bengal during the 1972–1973 language riots in Assam. Her party, Trinamool Congress (TMC), also alleged that the names of more than 70 per cent of Bengali speakers did not figure in the first draft of NRC. Bengali-dominated Barak Valley in South Assam was the most affected for being a Bengali-speaking region.[46]

Sanjib Kumar Baruah, who was one of the intellectual ideologues supporting the cause of the Assam Movement, invoked Hannah Arendt in his article 'Stateless in Assam', published in *The Indian Express* on 19 January 2018. He started the article by referring to Hanif Khan, who had committed suicide before the first draft of the NRC which was published on 31 December 2017. Hanif Khan was reported to be 'extremely anxious about the whole NRC business. He and his family, he feared, would be promptly arrested and deported to Bangladesh if their names do not appear on it'.[47]

Pointing out that deportation of the detected foreigners will not be an easy task, and in the Indian context, it is next to impossible, as the Government of India is yet to take up the issue with the Bangladesh government, the destiny of the detected foreigners may be the detention camp and they will be stateless people. It is in this context that Baruah invoked Hannah Arendt and wrote:

> The political condition of a stateless person, as political theorist Hannah Arendt had memorably pointed out, is much worse than that of a prisoner. The person loses more than his or her freedom. A stateless person is no longer part of a legal and political order; he or she loses the 'right to have rights'. A stateless person wrote Arendt, represents 'a new kind of human being'—the kind that are put in concentration camps by their foes and in internment camps by their friends.[48]

Whereas the reactions on the NRC created political battles, Assam remained almost peaceful and nothing untoward happened. As I argue in the last part of the chapter, this was made possible through the interventions of the larger civil society who continued to defend the NRC as a rallying point of moving ahead for a peaceful and harmonious society.

Final Draft: Anxieties, Embracement and Rejections

In the whole process of updating Assam's NRC, the publication of the final draft on 30 July 2018 was the most critical and challenging one. There was unprecedented global dissent against the draft and battles among political parties in the run-up to the publication of the final draft and its aftermath. The journey towards the final draft itself started with a state of uncertainty. The Supreme Court in its order dated 5 February 2018 referred the matter relating to the issue of the validity of Section 6A of the Citizenship Act to a constitution bench. The three-judge bench headed by the Chief Justice of India in its short order said: 'As the matter has been referred to the Constitution Bench vide order dated 17.12.2014, let the matter be placed before Hon'ble the Chief Justice of India for constituting an appropriate Bench, on the administrative side.'[49] On 6 February 2018, 10 organizations of indigenous people of Assam pleaded before the Supreme Court 'to issue an order staying the ongoing process of updating the National Register of Certificates (NRC) in Assam ... until the cut-off date for the purpose is finalised by a Constitution Bench of the apex court'.[50] The apex court on 20 February 2018, however, directed the NRC state coordinator to complete the verification of all pending applications and fixed 30 June 2018 for publishing the final list of the NRC. The date was subsequently extended to 30 July 2018. The NRC special bench called for hearing on NRC for four times—20 February, 27 March, 8 May and 2 July—before the final draft was published. In each hearing, the NRC coordinator presented detailed reports on the progress of the process based on which the Court provided the necessary directions. On 20 February 2018, apart from the scrutiny over the progress of verification and necessary directions on how to move ahead, the Court noticed two developments and issued necessary orders accordingly. The Court noticed that the local body/municipal/panchayat elections were due in Assam in March/April 2018. The Court, while acknowledging the fact that the said elections would have to be held as per plans as scheduled by the State Election Commission, directed that holding of elections in no way would disrupt the process of updating the NRC. The Court ordered, 'Preparation/upgradation of the final draft NRC will continue as before with full deployment of manpower as on date.' The Court also halted the proposal mooted by the state government to appoint an additional state coordinator and directed that the NRC updating process till the final draft would be carried by Hajela, the incumbent NRC state coordinator. In its hearing on 27 March 2018, the Court particularly looked into non-receipt of responses from various issuing authorities such as banks, UIDAI (Aadhaar), Central Board of Secondary Education, Ministry of External Affairs, various Central and state government departments including railways, and various state governments. The NRC authority sent 572,809 queries to the state governments of India but received only 175,479 responses (30.63%) and 3,97,330 queries were still pending. Bengal had the highest number of queries to be replied. Out of the 114,971 queries sent, the NRC authority received only 7,430 responses, that is, 6.46 per cent, and 107,541 queries were yet to be replied by the West Bengal government. The Court asked all state chief secretaries and respective authorities and departments to ensure the verification of the pending data to do the needful. On the issue of panchayat/local body elections, the Court maintained its order of 20 February 2018 and said that it would not give any relaxation on using the NRC officials and employees for the elections except for the Additional Deputy Commissioners (ADCs).

The Court also fixed 30 July 2018 as the final date for the publication of the final draft. Earlier, it was proposed to be published on 30 June 2018. The Court strictly ordered that these dates would be maintained 'under any circumstances'. The coordinator also assured that the date fixed by the Court for publication of the final draft NRC would be adhered to without fail. Accordingly, the final draft was published on the day with the exclusion of 40.07 lakh (4.07 million) applicants.

As Assam approached the publication of the final draft of the NRC, the agony around the imminent exclusion of four million applicants from the draft erupted at both national and global levels. After the final draft was released on 30 July 2018, the anxiety, discontent and rejection further escalated, and the concerned individuals and organizations expressed serious apprehensions about the imminent violation of fundamental rights of the excluded applicants.

On 11 June 2018, UN special rapporteurs on minority issues—the special rapporteur on contemporary forms of racism, racial discrimination, xenophobia and related intolerance; the special rapporteur on the promotion and protection of the right to freedom of opinion and expression; and the special rapporteur on freedom of religion or belief—wrote an eight-page letter to the External Affairs Minister of Government of India, expressing serious apprehensions around the ongoing updating of NRC for Assam. The list of subjects represented by the rapporteurs gives the impression that the ongoing updating of the NRC has adverse implications on minority rights and may facilitate racism, racial discrimination, xenophobia and intolerance, which in turn will adversely impact the right of freedom and expression as well as the right to religion and belief of the particular minority communities. The letter asserted,

> The NRC update has generated increased anxiety and concerns among the Bengali Muslim minority in Assam, who have long been discriminated against due to their perceived status as foreigners, despite possessing the necessary documents to prove their citizenship. While it is acknowledged that the updating process is generally committed to retaining Indian citizens on the NRC, concerns have been raised that local authorities in Assam, which are deemed to be particularly hostile towards Muslims and people of Bengali descent, may manipulate the verification system in an attempt to exclude many genuine Indian citizens from the updated NRC, the special rapporteurs pointed out.[51]

It also asserted,

> It is alleged that the potential discriminatory effects of the updated NRC should be seen in light of the history of discrimination and violence faced by Muslims of Bengali origin due to their status as ethnic, religious and linguistic minority and their perceived foreignness.[52]

Digging history of discrimination against the Bengali Muslim community and also referring to the CAB, 2016, which aims to give Indian citizenship to six non-Muslim immigrant communities from Afghanistan, Pakistan and Bangladesh, the letter said,

> While we do not wish to prejudge the accuracy of these allegations, we would like to express serious concern that members of the Bengali Muslim minority in Assam have experienced discrimination in access to and enjoyment of citizenship status on the basis of their ethnic and religious minority status. We are particularly concerned that this discrimination is predicted to escalate as a result of the NRC.[53]

UN agencies apart, various other organizations came up sharply against the process. The most vocal was the petition mooted by Avaaz (the voice), which was signed by around 3.3 lakh (0.33 million) people. The petition was titled 'India: Stop Deleting Muslims!' Avaaz was termed as 'a campaigning community bringing people-powered politics to decision-making worldwide, against publication of National Register of Citizens (NRC) being prepared in Assam'. The campaign started on 12 July 2018.

The petition alleged,

In a few days, India will delete as many as 7 million Muslims in Assam State from its master list of 'citizens' because they speak the wrong language and worship the wrong God. Husbands, wives, and children could be torn apart and left to rot in prison camps.

It further asserted, 'This is how genocides begin—how the nightmare of the Rohingya began. But it's all unfolding quietly—if we raise a massive alarm calling for the UN Secretary-General and key governments to intervene—we can stop this horror before it starts.' The petition was addressed to the UN Secretary-General and the international community and urged: 'We urge you to issue an early warning about the publication of the National Register of Citizens (NRC) in Assam State in India—which will lead to mass violence, ethnic cleansing, and the transfer of minority Muslims to prison camps for life.'[54]

The final draft was published on 30 July 2018 amid the cacophony of allegations and discontent. The draft enumerated 28,983,677 people as valid citizens of India out of the total 32,991,384 people who had applied for it, leaving out 4,007,707 applicants. As expected, the final draft generated strong and adverse reactions from different quarters. Both the AASU and the Union government endorsed the NRC final draft in unequivocal terms. The student organization called it a historic event. The Union government defended it in the Parliament, suggesting that it was impartial, as it was an exercise monitored by the Supreme Court of India. Home Minister Rajnath Singh asserted,

The NRC exercise is being carried out under the aegis of the Supreme Court of India (SC); it is a sensitive issue and I would request all of you not to politicise it. Everyone will have full opportunity to file claims/objections as per provision in the law. Only after the disposal of claims and objections, will the final NRC be published.[55]

The criticisms against the final draft of NRC were centred on multiple issues. Apart from the alleged xenophobic character of the Assamese people, the NRC was perceived as an instrument driven by the majoritarian and anti-Muslim politics steered by the BJP and systematic targeting of the Bengali Muslims. The whole process was also equated with Myanmar's drive against the Rohingya Muslims. The NRC brought together diverse forces as its critics, who otherwise radically differed in their political and ideological orientations.

West Bengal Chief Minister and TMC Chief Mamata Banerjee alleged the NRC to be an instrument of pursuing political mileage and called it an 'an attempt to create a huge mass of refugees ... to create disturbance'. She said, 'This is most unfortunate as Bengali, Bihari, Hindu, Muslims—everyone—will be affected and we cannot do this kind of politics to identify people from other States and push them back'.[56]

Hartosh Singh Bal equated the NRC outcomes with the plight of the Rohingyas, as both target the Muslims of the Bengali ethnicity. In an article published in *The New York Times,* titled 'Is India Creating Its Own Rohingya?' Bal asserted,

> The Rohingya, like a huge number of those affected by the N.R.C. in Assam, are Muslims of Bengali ethnicity. The denial of citizenship, loss of rights and continued hostility against the Rohingya in Myanmar eventually led to the brutal violence and ethnic cleansing of the past few years. The excuses that majoritarian nationalists made in the context of the Rohingya in Myanmar—that outsiders don't understand the complexity of the problem and don't appreciate the anxieties and fears of the ethnic majority—are being repeated in Assam.[57]

Harsh Mander, who has always been a strong critic of the NRC, authored an article titled 'It's Time We Listened to the Plight of Assam's "Foreigners"' in *Al Jazeera* on 4 August 2018. He argued that the consolidation of majoritarian and anti-Muslim politics of the BJP escalated the anti-foreigner sentiments in Assam and paved the way for the devastation of millions of people through the NRC. He asserted,

> The protracted process to deem who are 'foreigners' in Assam, although conducted under the watchful eye of India's Supreme Court, could lead to more suffering and polarisation. If compassion is not placed at the centre of all efforts, the final NRC may set the stage for another round of blood-letting, akin to the one we witnessed in the 1980s and yet another harvest of electoral victories built ultimately on the further suffering of these impoverished communities.[58]

Three UN special rapporteurs on minority issues and freedom of religion or belief wrote a letter on 13 December 2018 to the Indian government as a follow-up to its previous letter of June 2018, expressing its serious concerns over the uncertainty around the status of those excluded from the final NRC. The letter pointed out that 'in a region with very poor record-keeping, the current status of the verification process has the potential to create a massive category of people who are on Indian Territory but cannot prove citizenship of either India or Bangladesh, thereby risking becoming stateless'. It also felt that the NRC update exercise 'is stoking ethnic tensions in a region that has already experienced a tumultuous history of identity-based tensions and suffered from strained inter-communal relationship, including multiple outbreaks of serious violence'.[59]

Sanjib Baruah, an ardent supporter of the Assam agitation and now a critic of the NRC, in his article published on 2 August 2018 in *Indian Express* titled 'The Missing 4,007,707' posed the following question: 'Can a democracy permit so many to be in a state of liminal legality? NRC poses a political and moral question.' He further wrote,

> The possibility—whether immediate or somewhat remote—that at the end of the process as many as 4 million people may lose their legal status as citizens should not be a cause of celebration in a democracy. Nor should it generate a mad rush among politicians competing for political credit.[60]

One of the consistent intellectual voices in the public domain who defended NRC at all stages of its preparation has been Hiren Gohain. He pointed out that NRC is an outcome of a long-drawn consensus around the Assam Accord. He says,

> Assam has been repeatedly plunged into blood-spattered chaos since the end of the Assam Movement. But Bengalis have lived for decades now without friction and in friendly relationships with the Assamese. Muslims of migrant origin, who suffered much more, such as in the *massacre at Nellie*, have also been living in peace and amity with the Assamese for decades now. All the hue and cry is outside the state.[61]

He reminds us that a society or nationality should not be held back by the ghosts of the past. Rather, we need to learn from the historical experiences of transcending the violence of the past and striving to live in peace.

> While the ghosts of the past need to be kept in mind, they need not be stirred back into action. The common man has repeatedly been whipped into hatred and blind spite by evil powers who escape indictment. Did ordinary Hindus and Muslims not indulge in an orgy of unimaginable violence in the 1946 Calcutta riots? And in the Partition 'holocaust', did ordinary Muslims, Sikhs and Hindus not rush into one of the most horrifying communal vendettas lasting weeks?[62]

For him,

> In that blood-besmeared fog of mistrust, suspicion and ill-will, the NRC appeared the only sane and tangible instrument for restoring peace and goodwill among communities. It is another thing that the state under its present leadership is trying every possible means to hijack or derail it. By painting it black outside Assam, the detractors of the NRC are only helping those who want to push Assam back into that boiling cauldron from which it had emerged scalded barely a decade or so ago.[63]

Udayon Misra, a historian and political commentator, points out that very often people from other parts of the country find it extremely difficult to understand 'the emotional response of the Assamese people to the question of identity and demographic change'. They often consider it to be 'an expression of an insular mindset, or even as a sign of xenophobia'. Asserting that for many people in Assam, the NRC is a lifeline, Misra reminds that to understand the reason behind such a conviction, 'there is a need to revisit some of the major events from 1920 to 1950 that centred around immigration, land and identity—moments which helped shape Assam's post-Independence history.'[64] Journeying through the historical trajectory he explains why Assam remained calm and peaceful despite speculation of violence after the publication of the NRC final draft. He writes,

> However, it is a positive sign that the state has been totally free of any violent incidents since the publication of the NRC. One major reason for this state of calm is that an overwhelmingly large section of pre-1971 people who have long been considered as illegal migrants or 'Bangladeshis' have made it to the NRC. This has given them a sense of security which they

had lacked all these years. The involvement of the Supreme Court seems to have lent a sort of sanctity to the entire process and initial apprehensions among linguistic and religious minorities after the first draft was published in January 2017 which had left out almost half of the state's population, seem to have been largely dispelled after the figures of the final draft were made public.[65]

Such assertions, of course, came under severe attack and a group of young scholars from Assam called such assertions 'intellectual racism'. We will take up these issues in the later part of the chapter.

The Final List: A U-turn by the Government

Amid the political and intellectual campaigns against the final NRC, the Supreme Court continued to monitor the process of updating the NRC and called for hearing 16 times between the publication of the final draft on 30 July 2018 and that of the final list on 30 August 2019.[66] The final list received a huge blow with the complete U-turn of the government that rejected the NRC altogether as a flawed document. The state coordinator of NRC also came under severe attack, which forced him to leave the state on deputation.[67]

As the final draft excluded more than 4.0 million applicants, therefore, there were apprehensions that those people will automatically become 'stateless'. Just to give examples, the headline of the Countercurrents.org on the NRC final draft was 'The Final Draft of State Sponsored Statelessness: NRC and the 4 Million "Stateless People" of India'.[68] Al Jazeera captioned it 'What's Next for the 4 Million Stripped of Citizenship in India?' as its lead news on 30 July 2018.[69] Therefore, in the hearing on 31 July 2018, the NRC bench of the Supreme Court categorically said, 'Court would like to observe that what has been published is only the Complete Draft NRC which naturally being a draft cannot be the basis of any action by any authority.'

The Court approved the modalities/standard operating procedure for filing and disposal of claims and objections leading to the publication of the final NRC after giving due time to various stakeholders to give their opinion. But the most crucial issue during this phase was the proposal submitted by the state NRC coordinator to approve only 10 out of 15 documents which had been used until the final draft of the NRC. The state coordinator, based on his assessments and apprehensions, proposed that five documents (a) names in NRC, 1951; (b) names in electoral roll up to 24 March 1971; (c) citizenship certificate and refugee registration certificate; (d) certified copies of pre-1971 electoral roll, particularly those issued from the state of Tripura; and (e) ration card may not be allowed to be used for entry into the final NRC. The Court initially allowed the process to move ahead only with the 10 documents. However, in its hearing on 1 November, it rejected the plea of the coordinator to exclude the five documents to be used for the inclusion of one's name in the NRC.

The coordinator objected to the use of these five documents primarily on two grounds: (a) his apprehensions regarding the abuse of two documents, that is, (i) names in NRC, 1951, and (ii) names in electoral roll up to 24 March 1971 and (b) the use of forged documents in the process of verification for the inclusion of names in the draft NRC belonging to the three categories, that is, (i) citizenship certificate and refugee registration certificate; (ii) certified copies of pre-1971 electoral roll, particularly those issued from the state of Tripura; and (iii) ration card. The Court rejected the coordinator's plea and argued that only because of apprehension and misuse of documents in the past the sanctity or authenticity of these documents could not be questioned. In case of the first two documents, the Court observed that the apprehension was 'based entirely on a possibility of abuse which, however, strong, cannot be an acceptable reason in law to exclude the documents from consideration'. In the case of the last three documents, the Court observed, 'It is our considered view that the mere possibility of filing of forged documents or that such documents were filed in the earlier exercise cannot be a ground to exclude the same from the impending process of filing of claims and objections.' The Court also extended the date for filing claims and objections until 31 December 2018. The coordinator also pleaded for stretching the date for the publication of the final list of NRC until the later part of September 2019 on the ground of the ensuing parliamentary elections. However, the Court fixed 30 July 2019 as the last date for the publication of the final list, which, however, was finally extended to 30 August 2020 in its hearing on 23 July 2019.

Out of the total 3.29 crore applicants, 3.11 crore (31.1 million) made it to the NRC in the final list published on 31 August 2019, leaving out a total of 1,906,657 people, including those who did not submit their claims. The excluded persons had the option to appeal before the FTs if they intended to do so.[70] There were two diametrically opposite reactions to the final list. Many stakeholders remained quite unhappy regarding the meagre number of those who were excluded. The critics of the NRC, on the other hand, weighed heavily on the document for making 1.9 lakh (0.19 million) applicants 'stateless' without any scheme of their rehabilitation. They pointed out that these people would finally be the captives in the detention camps, where they would be forced to live under inhuman conditions. The deaths of several doubtful voters in detention camps also contributed towards the sharp attack on the NRC.

The original petitioner of the NRC, president of APW, Abhijeet Sharma, expressed his complete disillusionment over the number of people excluded from the final list. For him, it was too small, and he termed the final list a 'flawed document'. He also raised questions regarding the software used in the process of the NRC updating. APW submitted five petitions in the Supreme Court pleading for re-verification of the draft NRC. The apex court rejected the plea on the ground that 27 per cent of samples of the final data had been re-verified. Casting his doubts on the final document, Sharma contended that the problem of illegal immigration would never be resolved in Assam.[71] The AASU also expressed its unhappiness over the excluded figures and reportedly said that it would appeal the apex court to remove the faults and deficiencies.[72] Reacting to the final list, its adviser Samujjal Bhattacharya said,

We are not happy with the outcome of the mammoth exercise and believe that there are a lot of deficiencies in the NRC. The final exclusion figure of 19.06 lakh is nowhere near the estimate given by the Union government from time to time. At one point of time, the Union Home Minister had said that the figure was approximately 50 lakh. Different estimates were given by the Union and the State governments, but none was as low as the one, which came out in the NRC.[73]

However, the AASU also stated that despite all its flaws and shortcomings,

> The NRC is the first and only systematic exercise undertaken on the foreigners' issue in the past 40 years. The process was monitored by the Supreme Court and supervised by the Registrar General of India, and we believe that our concerns could be addressed through the same channel.[74]

But the severe blow to the NRC came with the rejection of the final list by the government itself which called it a flawed document and pleaded for making Assam again a part of the national NRC, a proposal mooted by the Union government.

The government's U-turn on the NRC invites brief scrutiny about its shifting positions. In the vision document of the party, prepared on the eve of Assam state assembly elections of 2016, BJP declared,

> Citizens' participation is the bedrock of a democracy. It is important that as times evolve, the reflection of a democratic nation state moves beyond elections to people's participation and engagement in policy and governance. The first step towards fulfilling this adage is citizens' participation in the policy cycle. Making citizens active stakeholders in the decision making process by allowing them to set priorities and agendas for their elected representatives is the first towards citizens' engagement. Subsequently, people can be involved in later stages of the policy cycle like policy development, policy implementation and policy evaluation.[75]

The citizen-centric approach to governance was the highlight of the document, which was the outcome of a series of dialogues carried out under the banner of 'Assam Nirman Development Dialogues' to understand the expectations of the people of Assam from the party. 'State security' was the topmost priority in the document. Within this broader section, 'Assam Accord and dealing with infiltration' figured as the second item which categorically declared 'implementing the Assam Accord in its letter and spirit' and 'constitutional, legislative, social and cultural safeguard as per the clause 6 of Assam Accord' as its commitment. Along with it, the vision document committed to strictly adhere to 'scrutinizing the citizenship of all suspected residents of the state in conformity with the upgraded National Register of Citizens (NRC)'.[76]

In the first budget speech of the BJP-led government presented on 27 July 2016, the finance minister declared in the assembly,

> The Government wishes to convey that the ongoing exercise to update the National Register of Citizens (NRC) is the number one priority for the Government of Assam. The Hon'ble Chief Minister of Assam is personally monitoring the NRC updation process wherein the NRC data is expected to be published within the current financial year. I propose to allocate Rs. 24932 Lakhs from the State budget.[77]

Just after assuming the office, Chief Minister Sarbananda Sonowal took a keen interest on the completion of the NRC updating process. He visited NRC Seva Kendras to review the updating process. The BJP was enthusiastic over the final draft of the NRC, and the National President Amit Shah took pride in its execution. He said, 'Rajiv Gandhi signed the Assam Accord in 1985, which was similar to NRC. They did not have the courage to implement it, we did.'[78]

However, as the process of publication of the final list approached, the position of both government and the party towards NRC made a one-eighty degree turn. Four days ahead of the publication of the final draft, BJP's State President Ranjeet Kumar Daas declared, 'We don't believe that the NRC is going to be an error-free document. He contended that "names of genuine Indian citizens" would be left out of when it will be published on August 31.'[79] The government also took an antagonistic position in the Supreme Court towards the authority of the Court in deciding the date of publication of NRC.

After the publication of the final list, the BJP downplayed the sanctity of the NRC. The state finance minister declared,

> Assam state BJP [Bharatiya Janata Party] and Assam government opined that the NRC, which was prepared under the supervision of the Supreme Court and by the state coordinator Prateek Hajela in Assam, has failed to fulfill the aspiration of the people of Assam. There were many gaps and spaces and we have already pointed out in public and various forums. Various social organisations of Assam have already filed petitions before the Supreme Court seeking review of the present process. The present NRC process should be scrapped. We should be a part of the national NRC process. When the national NRC will be prepared, Assam should be made part it.[80]

More importantly, at the highest level of the government, the position on the NRC was not coherent and consistent. While the top brass of the party and top ministers spoke almost against the NRC, the External Affairs Ministry had to confront the international outrage against the exercise. The ministry publicly defended the NRC, calling it a Supreme Court-monitored document that does not bear political scoring. On 2 September 2019, the spokesperson of the Ministry of the External Affairs asserted,

> The NRC is not an executive-driven process. The process is being monitored by the Supreme Court directly and the government is acting in accordance with the directives issued by the court. The apex court of the land has itself set the deadlines for all steps that have been taken so far.[81]

The spokesperson further noted that no NRC-excluded person would automatically become stateless or foreigner until 'they have exhausted all the remedies available under the law'. He also categorically said that the method used for updating NRC is 'fair' and based on 'scientific methods' and the process of the NRC is 'non-discriminatory' that 'leaves no room for bias and injustice'.[82]

However, the process has not moved in the right direction. The fate of the excluded applicants has been hanging, as even after more than a year of the publication of the NRC final list, the NRC authorities are yet to issue the rejection slip that mentions the reason behind non-inclusion in the NRC. More ironic is the fact that the Registrar General of India also did not notify the final list of the NRC. Without this formal notification, the rejection slips cannot be issued.[83] Proposed 200 FTs to hear the cases of the excluded applicants have also not started functioning so far. Defenders of NRC suspect that these are tactics used by the incumbent government to de-legitimize the entire process of Assam's NRC. These developments have helped in consolidating the campaign against the NRC.

ALLEGED FUNDAMENTAL FLAWS AND THE XENOPHOBIC DESIGN

Deepankar Basu and Debarshi Das[84] raised a few critical issues regarding the fundamental flaws in the NRC updating process in Assam and emphasized building an alternative narrative. The authors came out with four critical observations on the process: (a) The first observation was on the alleged flaws in the premise of the NRC exercise itself through which the residents who sought their names to be included in the updated NRC had to take the burden of providing legitimate documents that showed that they or their parental ancestors were rightful citizens of India before 25 March 1971. (b) To substantiate their concerns, the authors have referred to the wave of massive protests across India against both NRC and CAA after the Union home minister's announcement about a nationwide NRC. They argued, 'There is palpable anxiety among the common people as to how they would show documentary evidence of antecedence.' (c) The authors have also asserted that the updated NRC has failed even to satisfy those who fought for it both politically and through judicial means, and therefore, 'It was naïve to expect that an issue as complex as anxiety over one's identity can be clinched through the judicio-bureaucratic exercise of an NRC.'[85] (d) Finally, they argued that the census data do not reveal large-scale migration to Assam after 1971. Considering this, the authors asked, 'What fuels the clamour for NRC and similar exercises, if immigration has ebbed?'[86] The authors came up with a hypothetical answer which lies in the 'economy and society'. They argued that the economy in Assam has witnessed radical transformations in the past years and the 'centre of gravity has moved away from agriculture and the rural economy'[87]. In the new economic milieu, the descendants of the Muslim peasants who migrated to Assam many decades ago 'have diversified to other occupations such as trade, transportation, and other skilled professions'. However, the descendants, who have acquired education and have been competing for the middle-class jobs, continue with the distinct descent of the community. For the authors, 'Greater presence and, visibility of the migrants' descendants in middle-class, urban spaces is being identified as illegal immigration from Bangladesh.'[88] They conclusively argued that 'the "indigenous"—who are often the victims of destructive economic policies—have directed their ire against migrants. But it is naïve to believe that cultural anxieties can be resolved through the NRC.'

Many other critics, apart from pointing out the alleged flawed process of the NRC, have also heavily criticized the xenophobic character of the indigenous communities of Assam and the exclusionary tendencies and an unwarranted insensitive attitude towards those who have been/will be stateless citizens as a result of the NRC. They have also pointed out that the FTs, which will now decide the destiny of the NRC-excluded applicants, have been both bias and incompetent. These critics also include a group of young scholars from Assam.

Suraj Gogoi, while arguing that the 'psychology behind NRC mirrors narrow, dominating side of Assamese language, and its fragile nationalism, cultural identity', also asserts that the 'psychology shares disturbing similarity with the history of Nazism whose sympathisers not only share similar profile with the well-wishers of NRC, but they shared the hatred against racial and political minorities, as well.'[89] For Angshuman Choudhury and Suraj Gogoi, the CAA and NRC 'are two sides of same coin; both seek to alienate India's Muslims'. They have also argued, 'If the National Register of Citizens (NRC) is the graveyard of Indian citizenship, the Citizenship Amendment Act (CAA), 2019 is the graveyard of Indian democracy.'[90] Choudhury and Gogoi, while refuting Hiren Gohain's contention of putting the NRC in its appropriate context, assert that 'Gohain's defence of the NRC comes from a chauvinist understanding of Assamese society that privileges the Assamese-speaking middle class elite over the "others" within the state's territorial space.'[91] Defining Assam's obsession with NRC as 'narrow nationalism', the authors also argue that 'the NRC is not just an isolated administrative exercise, but a process that is embedded in a history and the larger politics of Assamese nationalism, which is principally characterised by hatred towards the outsider, "the Bangladeshi"'.[92] Pointing out that the institutions—FTs, the Border Police, detention camps, doubtful voter—that continue to haunt the targeted people loom larger in the aftermath of the release of the final NRC list. Suraj Gogoi in a co-authored piece with Abhinav P. Borbora alleges that the NRC represents only a majoritarian consensus. They point out, 'Often, the lack of public disorder is used to draw a theory of consensus in society. Certain public intellectuals and stakeholders in Assam have chosen to interpret the relative calm as proof of support for the citizen mapping exercise across all sections of society.'[93]

The attack on NRC also traces its roots into the 'decades of anti-immigrant, xenophobic and chauvinist propaganda pushed into the public imagination of Assam by the mainstream civil society organisations, intelligentsia and political elites'.[94]

One of the major concerns of the humanists and advocates of the minority rights centred on the political destiny of those excluded from the NRC final list. Harsh Mander, for example, has pointed out that the destiny of the 'illegal migrants' will be hanging as there is no possibility of Bangladesh accepting them as their citizens. He has also pointed out that the Government of India is yet to initiate a dialogue with the Government of Bangladesh in this regard. While pointing out the statement of Home Minister Amit Shah in the Parliament where he categorically said that 'he would deport illegal immigrants from every square inch of Indian land', Mander has the following questions to ask: 'How would this be accomplished? Would these millions be pushed forcefully into Bangladesh? Or would they be locked in massive detention centres? If yes, for how long?' He is of the view that all the NRC-excluded applicants will finally be allowed to live in India 'but stripped of all citizenship rights. They would be a 'marked people', powerless and susceptible to social violence and intense state scrutiny'.[95]

The gender dimension of the issue did not figure adequately in the NRC debate despite the fact that the women are one of the most vulnerable categories in the process of the NRC. Ditilekha Sharma argues that the controversies around the panchayat certificate in the absence of birth or education certificates to establish linkage with the legacy holder is a glaring example in this regard. She has also argued that within women, Bengali Hindu and Muslim women were the most vulnerable. 'While communities that have been given the status of original inhabitants have not had to undergo stringent verification of their panchayat certificate, Muslim women and Bengali Hindu women who provided the same were put through a stringent verification process'.[96] The rights of the transgender did not figure at all in the whole NRC discourse. Sharma has pointed out that Assam has around 20,000 transgender persons and out of that, at least 2,000 transgender women had applied to be enlisted in the NRC. But their status remained unknown. Most of hijras 'leave their biological families when they are young and are left with no contacts and it is hence practically impossible for them to get access to legacy data establishing their link'.[97] Summing up all these challenges, *EPW*, in one of its editorials, writes,

> An exercise like the NRC, with its fundamental premises rooted in the binary of outsiders/insiders, cut-off dates, and primordial claims over land, threatens to aggravate the already existing social tensions. This is the case even if the intentions behind such an exercise were to bring to a closure the festering conflicts and dispel the atmosphere of mutual suspicion. Realising these intentions would demand a reconciliatory process within communities/social groups and coming to terms with the burden of history by arriving at a consensus in the present to fashion a common future. However, this would require painstaking efforts with an overarching normative vision for a decent society. With the ruling party's political agenda being shorn of such a vision and its evident attempts to use this exercise to consolidate its electoral prospects, the pious hopes of reconciliation harboured by a section of progressives in Assam are bound to be belied.[98]

DEFENDING THE NRC: THE CONTEXT AND THE POLITICAL TRAJECTORY

While the trepidations about the NRC are both logical and appreciable, the concerned parties either failed or refused to understand and recognize the critical political journey that Assam had passed through during the last four decades or so. The critics of NRC have also ignored the polyrhythm of the NRC process that facilitated a working consensus across different sections, including the East-Bengal-origin Muslims.

The critics also chose to ignore the fact that it was not NRC but the resistance against the CAB, 2016, that generated the momentum around the citizenship debate in Assam. Assam, particularly the Brahmaputra Valley, never had such a consensus on the Assam Accord and NRC as it has today. The accord has now been christened as 'public law contract',[99] a term that Assam did not hear until recently. It is this momentum that helped the state to avoid any possible communal holocaust after the final draft and the final list of the NRC had been published. Both the consensus on NRC as well as the relative peace today may be momentary, and it may break down at any moment due to the aggressive politics of polarization pursued by the current regime. However, understanding the critical journey to the working consensus on NRC is necessary to appreciate why relative peace prevails in the state despite serious apprehensions both inside the country and beyond.[100]

The humanists who were campaigning against updating the NRC and finally rejected the updated list have indulged in an abstract humanist approach. The humanists in Assam, who have been defending the NRC, are adopting a mature and pragmatic approach which is based on their long-term understanding of the ground reality. The Assam Movement, in its initial phase, was marked by violence and had a strong chauvinist agenda. It demanded 1951 as the cut-off date for the detection and deportation of the foreigners. The left political parties and the intellectuals were very critical of the movement at that time and protested the communal forces that had allegedly penetrated it. The left was completely cornered by the movement, as the mainstream narratives projected them as the real enemy to the greater cause of the Assamese nationality and labelled them as pro-Bengali and pro-Muslim. The debate in *EPW* in 1980 that started with an article by Hiren Gohain titled 'Cudgel of Chauvinism'[101] and culminated in a comprehensive debate entitled 'Little Nationalism Turned Chauvinist'[102] is a testimony to it. This debate brought together those who strongly defended the movement on account of its long-term nationality issues and those who found serious undemocratic and chauvinist elements in the movement. However, as the debate moved, there were also changes in the positions by the participants. Notable among them was Hiren Gohain himself, who gradually accepted the fact that the movement carried genuine concerns of the masses which were the 'fall-out of underdevelopment'.[103] During the more than three and half decades of the political trajectory of Assam since the signing of the Assam Accord on 15 August 1985, gradually, almost all political parties and all sections of the society accepted 24 March 1971 as the cut-off year for the detection and deportation of the foreigners. In other words, there was widespread consensus around Section 6A of the Citizenship Act, 1955, as amended and incorporated in 1985.

The NRC is the outcome of a long journey that has passed through the critical trajectory of Assam's nationalist imagination with respect to migration and immigration. It is important to point out that the mobilization and resistance against the influx have always been contentious, and it attracts serious apprehensions and criticisms from different quarters, particularly from the human rights groups. One important reason behind this is the issue of minority rights, particularly the rights of the Muslims, who have been the victims of mobilization against the influx of migrants/immigrants to India. In the case of Assam in particular, and India in general, a mass psyche of reducing illegal migrants to Bangladeshi Muslims and equating East-Bengal-origin Muslims to Bangladeshi illegal migrants cannot entirely be overlooked. However, such a psyche has not been the prime driving force of mobilization against the illegal migrants in Assam. There have been healthy debates about bringing the East-Bengal-origin Muslims into the fold of the greater Assamese society. The colonial schemes of appropriating the resources of the region through tea plantations and jute cultivations were the driving forces of migration to the state. The schemes further received patronage from the Muslim League government led by Syed Muhammad Saadulla, resulting in another wave of huge migration, which eventually created tussles over resources and threatened the security of the language and culture of the indigenous communities. Gross indifference shown by the All India Congress Committee towards Assam's agony over the schemes of Cabinet Mission's Grouping Proposal, 1946, which had proposed to club Assam into the Muslim League-dominated Group C, also implanted fear against the influx of Bengalis, particularly Bengali Muslims, into Assam. Consolidation of the Muslim League in Assam during that period, and constant reference to that period by both by nationalists and right-wing political forces like RSS and Jana Sangh, continues to keep Assam under the shadow of fear over the Bengalis in general and the Bengali Muslims in particular. However, over time, despite the six-year-long Assam agitation, Assam has been struggling to evolve its own accommodative ethos. The armed struggle of the ULFA for *Swadhin Asom* (independent Assam) pushed Assam into a state of agony and repression for almost two decades—from the mid-1980s to the first decade of the present century. The initial euphoria about Assam's ability to fight the mighty Indian State gradually reduced to much despair. The saga of ethnic insurgencies since the late 1980s and a series of violent incidents in the BTAD since its formation in 2003 have also pushed the state into endless miseries and physical and mental trauma. The transition from euphoria to despair has persuaded the larger masses to be pragmatic than emotive on every issue. The introduction of the economic reforms in the early 1990s along with the adoption of the Look East Policy by the Government of India had their implications. These developments facilitated the expansion of the middle classes in Northeast India and opened avenues to get integrated into the Indian consumer market. They also enabled the Indian State to appropriate the resources of the north-east through development agendas like mega hydropower projects, which continue to meet with strong resistance due to the risks they pose to the life and property of millions of people. At the same time, they have also helped the integration of the popular resistance movement of the region with the national resistance movements in the country. With so many issues reining the multi-layered nationalist imagination of Assam and the north-east, consensuses are in short supply. One among them is the gradual realization that the secession of Assam from the Union of India is a distant reality, and Assam's identity lies in a multi-ethnic homeland. This realization has brought another important consensus that the Assam Accord is inviolable, for which it has now been hailed as a public law contract. The near-universal acceptance of the NRC by the greater society in Assam is the logical outcome of this critical journey.

Since the publication of the final list on 30 August 2019, which at the end excluded 1.9 million applicants out of the total 32.9 million, the same concerns continue to reverberate in different corners. The apprehensions were surrounding what India had been passing through under the BJP-led political dispensations, that is, growing violence and hatred against minorities as well as the suppression of intellectual freedom and social justice. The spectre of the Nellie massacre of 1983[104] during the Assam agitation, which led to the brutal killing of thousands of East-Bengal-origin Muslims, continues to haunt the concerned citizens in the country and beyond. Violent elements of the Assam agitation also targeted the tribals, particularly the Bodos, which is often overlooked. The Nellie massacre was preceded by violence and killings in Gohpur,[105] located in the eastern end of the present-day

Sonitpur district of Assam. The East-Bengal-origin Muslims supported the Bodos' demand for self-determination. However, gradually the equations changed, and the community became a target in the Bodo-dominated areas. The violence against the East-Bengal-origin Muslims alleged to be 'Bangladeshis', in the present-day BTC under the pretext of homeland politics, has also created a state of ethnic cleansing.[106] The fate of the D voters[107] in Assam and the plight of those who are languishing in detention camps have also contributed to the growing anxieties over the NRC. The absence of an extradition treaty with Bangladesh[108] and the denial by the Government of Bangladesh of having official evidence of emigration of the country's people to Assam will make the people excluded from the NRC stateless. With as many as 1.9 million people being rendered stateless by the NRC, the matter is bound to create ripples across different quarters. The apprehensions about chauvinism, racial discrimination and violence against minorities haunted the concerned people so much so that a parallel had been drawn between the NRC to that of the Nazi regime's torture of the Jews.

Therefore, warnings from the UN cannot be labelled sectarian. However, without understanding the political dynamics in a longer timeframe, and the polyrhythm of the whole debate on citizenship and immigration in Assam, the rejection of the NRC as a chauvinist or xenophobic design will make such reports one-dimensional and sectarian. The UN has declarations and conventions on the rights of the minorities, refugees and stateless citizens as well as rights of the tribal and indigenous people. It has the 1992 Declaration on the Rights of Persons Belonging to National or Ethnic, Religious and Linguistic Minorities as well as the 1989 convention concerning Indigenous and Tribal Peoples in Independent Countries and the 1994 Draft United Nations Declaration on the Rights of Indigenous People. The UN has a 1951 convention relating to the status of refugees, a 1954 convention relating to the status of stateless persons and the 1961 Convention on the Reduction of Statelessness. Therefore, one cannot overemphasize one and overlook the other. In the context of India, smaller nationalities are a reality, and aspirations of their rights cannot be reduced to xenophobia. Over-centralized federal polity, state's growing nexus with the corporate and their combined drive for appropriation and control over common's resources, among other issues, also need to draw adequate attention.

As pointed out by many critics, there are legitimate concerns over the process followed during the NRC updating exercise as well as the fate of the applicants left out from the final list. However, at the same time, it is important not to equate it with the spelt-out intentions of the government alone and see its significance from political as well as common people's perspectives. For a start, the register was not an instrument designed solely by the government; it was an outcome of long-drawn demands of the people of Assam, and the modalities were developed in consultation with the stakeholders during the Congress-led state government. The actual process started only with the intervention of the Supreme Court. The process received a lot of blows after the BJP-led governments assumed power at the Centre and in the state in 2014 and 2016, respectively. The Supreme Court heavily criticized the Central government and passed several orders to expedite the NRC updating process.[109] The coordinator of Assam NRC was made accountable exclusively to the apex court, relieving him of any obligation to the incumbent governments.[110] The final list disappointed both the incumbent governments and many stakeholders, although the reasons behind the disappointment were different. Most of the stakeholders were disappointed because the number of exclusions irrespective of religious identities turned out to be rather small. The incumbent state government and the ruling party were disappointed because the number of Muslims excluded from the list was too small.

Hiren Gohain, a voice of conscience in Assam, has been one of the consistent defenders of Assam's NRC. In the national and international media, he has been the single voice in this regard. His endorsement of the NRC provoked a lot of criticisms. Indeed, the attack on the NRC from different quarters, particularly from Suraj Gogoi, Angshuman Choudhury and Parag Jyoti Saikia and several others, were the encounters with Hiren Gohain. But that did not deter him from his consistent position on the NRC. In their encounter with Hiren Gohain on his support for the NRC, Angshuman Choudhury and Suraj Gogoi questioned Gohain's shifting position on Assam's nationality question:

> By supporting the NRC process, Gohain gives currency to the political literacy that the caste Assamese middle class routinely espouse. In many ways, the NRC story that Gohain paints is the co-option of his criticism against Assamese chauvinism, which turned him into an intellectual in the backdrop of the Assam Movement.[111]

They have alleged that

> In defending the NRC and discrediting its critics, Gohain hides behind the thick walls of selective history and erases the experiences of the victim. He gives a lesson on the violent churning of 1980s Assam, but only after assuming that 'people outside Assam' know little about its history—a much-favoured tactic amongst Assamese ethno-nationalists to shut down criticism from the outside. Gohain then talks about 'underground saffron brigades' that incited violence during the Assam Movement (1979–85), resulting in 'some grim incidents'.[112]

> Gohain's defence of the NRC comes from a chauvinist understanding of Assamese society that privileges the Assamese-speaking middle class elite over the 'others' within the state's territorial space. For him, the vaguely-defined 'Assamese national culture' and its agents play the role of the large-hearted 'hosts' who tolerate and accommodate, while the Bengal-origin Muslims and Hindus are reduced to 'guests' who 'are tolerated'.[113]

It may be mentioned that Hiren Gohain's position on Assam's nationality question shifted diametrically, but with reasoned convictions. His changed position did not make him close to the chauvinist elements of the state. Gohain's famous essay in *EPW*, 'Cudgels of Chauvinism' (1980), was a scathing indictment of the anti-foreigner agitation that had erupted the previous year. The 'chauvinistic movement' against migrants from Bangladesh, Gohain contended, was built on the back of 'propaganda in the Assam press—skilfully mixing up news about influx of outsiders with stories of Bengali trickery, deceit and treachery'.[114]

But in 2019, Hiren Gohain faced 'charges of sedition—for opposing the settlement in Assam of Hindu migrants from Bangladesh'. He was alleged to have advocated the secession of Assam during a protest against the CAB. He, of course, did not make such statement but reminded those who raised this issue that 'such a demand can have relevance if and when all democratic resources have been exhausted'.[115]

In a series of writings and interviews in both national and international media[116] apart from his regular interventions in local media, Hiren Gohain defended the NRC. His articulation on the register became sharp while responding to his critics. In his interview to Saif Khalid of *Al Jazeera*, Gohain categorically stated,

> If the NRC process is allowed to go in a normal way without any hindrances, without undue haste, with fair consideration to all, it may indeed resolve the imbroglio. Rightly or wrongly the citizenship issue has become a crucial talking point and an issue in Assam politics. Unless it is settled, you cannot go forward.[117]

But what was more important in the interview was his position on the natives of Assam. He suggested that all those who were granted citizenship should also be called the natives of Assam. He said,

> Natives also include children of immigrants. All those who were in Assam prior to 1947 or even 1971—when Bangladesh was born following its independence from Pakistan—should be treated as natives of Assam, irrespective of their religion and language. That has been the democratic consensus. That's why we have accepted 1971 as the cut-off year and the preparation of the NRC as a kind of benchmark to ascertain this.[118]

Gohain's position on natives provoked adverse reactions in Assam, and he was immediately labelled pro-Bangladeshi.

While acknowledging the fact that 'the democratic space for the rights of Muslims has been shrinking in India ever since independence', he has also pointed out that the Muslims today 'may be murdered in broad daylight with impunity'. This political environment in the country may have had some adverse impact on some Muslims during the preparation of the NRC.

> But that does not ipso facto prove the whole exercise bogus and mala fide. Millions of Muslims have found their names in it. Besides, people in Assam are still not hooked to the kind of venomous hatred of Muslims that seems to be thriving in North India. They should be helped to maintain

this attitude and not pushed to the atrocious Hindu–Muslim hostility by misguided concern.[119]

Udayon Misra, while reminding the critics of the NRC with his historical insights 'Why Many in Assam See the National Register of Citizens as a Lifeline'[120] has also cautioned that the parameters of the definition of 'Assamese' should be broadened to include the Bengali-speaking Muslims who have already embraced Assamese as their mother tongue.

> Meanwhile, with the parameters of Assamese nationality having expanded over the years to include all those initially Bengali speaking Muslims who have been returning Assamese as their mother tongue through the different censuses, the question remains as to whether they too would naturally come within the definition of 'Assamese' when it comes to constitutional safeguards relating to land, representation and culture. Now that a great many of them have been enlisted as genuine citizens in the NRC, their demand to be seen and accepted as Assamese is bound to be strengthened.[121]

What is important to note here is that the endorsement of the NRC as the lifeline for Assam did not deter him to talk about the humanitarian crisis embedded into the process as 'neither Delhi nor Dispur has been working on a proper plan for those who will soon be declared stateless'.[122]

Writing just after the publication of the final draft of the NRC, Misra also pointed out that even though after the process of claims and objections,

> The actual number of deletions will substantially come down. But even then, there would be a massive number of stateless persons, necessitating a well-coordinated, nationwide move to work out a solution within humanitarian parameters. But that in itself should not deflect from the ground reality in Assam where immigration and demographic change continue to be a major concern for the indigenes.[123]

The critics, of course, continued to attack the defenders of the NRC. Suraj Gogoi and Parag Jyoti Saikia termed these defenders as proponents of intellectual racism.

> Hiren Gohain, Harekrishna Deka, Sanjib Baruah and Udayon Misra have shown 'limited sympathy' and seek to create a secure environment for the 'Assamese', whose definition itself remains ambiguous. In their narrow

opinion, they propose to consider a certain section of individual's action as reduction of space and rights for others. When they should have written about cultivating equal respect, tolerance and inhibit those that go against them, they stood at the wrong side of history. Through passivity, denial, ignorance, and even outright support for the section of humans whom they call 'autochthons', they have shown the lack of ability and desire to love everyone equally.[124]

Only history will prove whether the critical defenders of the NRC, who have also been the critics of Assamese chauvinism, xenophobic tendencies of whatever kind and the majoritarian communal offensive, are intellectuals of racism. But one thing is certain that these young scholars who have been using all possible abusive languages against critical defenders of the NRC are the obsessive defenders of the minority rights which itself is another form of xenophobia. They appear to be intellectuals of the pure kind who are far away from the multi-layered subjugations and contradictions of smaller nationalities and appear to be in nexus with the global human rights club whose approach to human rights is driven by singular track or one-dimensionality.

But defending the NRC does not mean being indifferent to the plights of those who have been excluded from the final list. Hiren Gohain has asserted,

Now that the NRC has ended, what are we to do with the 19 lakh (1.9 million) people left out? The problem is that their fate will be decided by Foreigners' Tribunals which are short of mature and judicially trained members and who have so far leaned on reports of the Border Police. An option of appeal to the higher echelons of the judiciary does exist for those excluded but that is likely to be expensive and sometimes unaffordable. The government has promised legal aid, but we have to wait and watch if it is dispensed impartially.[125]

BEYOND THE NRC: A PROPOSAL FOR AN INCLUSIVE SOCIETY

The NRC is one step ahead towards resolving the foreigners' issue in Assam; it is not the end. The plight of the 1.9 million excluded applicants is a huge political and humanitarian challenge. The Government of India has ruled out the option of deportation.[126] India cannot afford to deal with the issue of illegal migrants through detention.[127] Indeed, the whole idea of detention must be done away with completely. The state should not be allowed to use those excluded from the NRC as non-recognized labour force either, as this will make way for inhuman exploitation. Therefore, in the long run, the critical defenders must negotiate with both the state and the greater civil society for general amnesty through which the excluded migrants are gradually recognized as full citizens. That amnesty, unlike the CAA, must be universal and secular. But that will be achieved only if the state redefines its character of being the appropriator of resources to that of the guarantor of entitlement of the commons over resources. Both the critical defenders and the opponents of the NRC must understand that resource entitlement is pivotal towards resolving the issue of citizenship in the region of Northeast India. The resurgence of people's movements on land, forest and ecology in the post-liberalization period is a key towards an inclusive society, provided these movements can transcend ethnic and regional obsessions. The struggle in Kaziranga,[128] where the defenders of the NRC sided with the 'suspected' immigrants and fought back the state's vested designs, may be a ray of hope in this regard.

A proposal that may trigger immediate controversies but will be the only feasible way to resolve this crisis is to accept the NRC as the base document. In the long run, all applicants of the NRC including those who have been excluded from the final list will have to be granted citizenship as they will neither be deported nor will be put in the detention camps, and those whose names figure in the final list have to be recognized as 'natives' with full political rights including the right to representation. This will require shifting the base year for constitutional safeguards as envisaged under Clause 6 of the Assam Accord and as proposed by the Justice Biplab K. Sharma Committee (2020)[129] from 1951 to 24 March 1971, the cut-off date of detection, deletion and deportation of foreigners as envisaged in the Assam Accord and Section 6A of the Citizenship Act, 1955. Such a radical proposal will invite public wrath, but after 50 years of citizenship it will not be politically sustainable to deprive any one from the right to representation.

NOTES

1. Samudragupta Kashyap, 'Assam NRC: All Happy with First Part Draft, but What Happens Next?' *Indian Express*, 3 January 2018, http://indianexpress.com/article/beyond-the-news/assam-national-register-of-citizens-nrc-all-happy-with-first-part-draft-but-what-happens-next-5009742/.
2. Hiren Gohain, 'It Is Important to Contextualise the NRC', *The Hindu*, 5 September 2019, https://www.thehindu.com/opinion/op-ed/it-is-important-to-contextualise-the-nrc/article29334764.ece.
3. Ibid.
4. Harsh Mander, 'It's Time We Listened to the Plight of Assam's "Foreigners"', *Al Jazeera*, 4 August 2018, https://www.aljazeera.com/indepth/opinion/time-listened-plight-assam-foreigners-180803143309823.html.
5. Government of Assam, 'White Paper on Foreigners' Issue', October 2012, 6, para 1.2.1, https://cjp.org.in/wp-content/uploads/2018/10/White-Paper-On-Foreigners-Issue-20-10-2012.pdf.
6. Nirode K. Barooah, *Gopinath Bardoloi: Indian Constitution and Centre–Assam Relations* (Guwahati: Publication Board of Assam, 1990), 30.
7. Ibid., 31.
8. Government of India, 'Immigrants (Expulsion from Assam) Act, 1950' (10 of 1950), https://www.indiacode.nic.in/bitstream/123456789/1674/1/A1950-10.pdf, accessed on 29 March 2021.
9. Government of Assam, 'White Paper on Foreigners' Issue', 7, para 1.3.1.
10. Ibid., 7, para 1.4.1.
11. Ibid., 7, para 1.4.2.
12. Ibid., 8, para 1.5.1.
13. Ibid., 9, para 1.5.3.
14. Ibid., 9, para 1.5.4.
15. Ibid., 9–10, para 1.6.1.
16. Ibid., 10–11, para 1.6.2.
17. Ibid., 11, para 1.6.3.
18. Ibid., 12, para 1.7.1.
19. Ibid.
20. Ratnadeep Choudhury, 'Nellie Massacre and "Citizenship": When 1,800 Muslims Were Killed in Assam in Just 6 Hours', *The Print*, 18 February 2019, https://theprint.in/india/governance/nellie-massacre-and-citizenship-when-1800-muslims-were-killed-in-assam-in-just-6-hours/193694/.
21. Sangita Bora, 'Violence and Memory: The Communal Riots at Nagabandha during 1983' (unpublished PhD thesis, Department of Political Science, Gauhati University, 2017), 125–126.
22. Hemen Das, *Asamor Communist Andolanar Chamu Itihas* [A Short History of Communist Movement of Assam] (Guwahati: Navayog Prakashan, 2014), 94–95.
23. Government of Assam, 'White Paper on Foreigners' Issue', 30, para 3.3.1.
24. R. Dutta Choudhury, 'Events Which Made NRC a Reality', *The Assam Tribune*, 1 August 2018, http://www.assamtribune.com/scripts/detailsnew.asp?id=aug0118/at060.

25. Quoted from the Supreme Court of India, *Abdul Kuddus vs Union of India*, on 17 May 2019, para 6 (4), https://indiankanoon.org/doc/34077895/.
26. *The Times of India*, 'We Will Not Accept NRC Update in Assam: Aamsu President', 26 March 2012, https://timesofindia.indiatimes.com/city/guwahati/We-will-not-accept-NRC-update-in-Assam-Aamsu-president/articleshow/12412894.cms.
27. Md Ali, 'A Controversy Might Flare Up over Indian Citizenship in Assam', TwoCircles.net, 17 July 2010, http://twocircles.net/2010jul16/controversy_might_flare_over_indian_citizenship_assam.html.
28. Jatin Anand, 'Pan-India NRC Was Never on the Table, Says PM Modi', *The Hindu*, 22 December 2019, https://www.thehindu.com/news/cities/Delhi/pan-india-nrc-was-never-on-the-table-says-narendra-modi-at-delhi-rally/article30372096.ece.
29. Supreme Court of India, Writ Petition (Civil) No. 562 of 2012, Writ Petition (Civil) No. 274 of 2009 and Writ Petition (Civil) No. 876 of 2014, 17 December 2014, https://indiankanoon.org/doc/50798357/.
30. Ibid., 2, para 1.
31. Ibid., 15, para 12.
32. Ibid., 17, para 15.
33. Ibid.
34. Ibid., para 33.
35. Ibid., para 35.
36. Ibid., 36–47.
37. Ibid., para 47.
38. Ibid., para 48.
39. Gauhati High Court, Writ Petition (Civil) No. 2634 of 2016, *Manowara Bewa vs The Union of India and Others*, 28 February 2017, para 43.1.
40. Ibid.
41. Supreme Court of India, Special Leave Petition (Civil) No. 16441 of 2017, *Rupjan Begum vs Union of India & Others*, 5 December 2017.
42. Supreme Court of India, Writ Petition (Civil) No. 1020 of 2017, *Kamalakhya Dey Pukayastha and Others vs Union of India & Others*, 5 December 2017, 7.
43. *The Assam Tribune*, 'CM Urges People Not to Panic', 1 January 2018, http://www.assamtribune.com/scripts/detailsnew.asp?id=jan0118/at058.
44. *The Assam Tribune*, 'NRC a Tribute to Martyrs of Agitation: AASU', 1 January 2018, http://www.assamtribune.com/scripts/detailsnew.asp?id=jan0118/at059.
45. R. Dutta Choudhury, 'Legacy Data Major Game Changer: Hajela', *The Assam Tribune*, 2 January 2018, http://www.assamtribune.com/scripts/detailsnew.asp?id=jan0218/at056.
46. Ashik Chanda, 'West Bengal CM Mamata Banerjee Terms NRC Conspiracy to Expel Bengalis Out of Assam', *The New India Express*, 3 January 2018, https://www.newindianexpress.com/nation/2018/jan/03/west-bengal-cm-mamata-banerjee-terms-nrc-conspiracy-to-expel-bengalis-out-of-assam-1743518.html.

47. Sanjib Baruah, 'Stateless in Assam', *The Indian Express*, 19 January 2018, https://indianexpress.com/article/opinion/national-register-of-citizens-5030603/.

48. Ibid.

49. Supreme Court of India, Writ Petition (Civil) No. 274 of 2009, 5 February 2018.

50. *The Assam Tribune*, 'Indigenous Bodies Seek Stay on NRC Work Order', 7 February 2018, http://www.assamtribune.com/scripts/detailsnew. asp?id=feb0718/at061.

51. Rajiv Roy, 'UN Special Rapporteurs Dash Off Letter to Sushma Swaraj on NRC', *Northeast Now*, 22 June 2018, https://nenow.in/north-east-news/un-special-rapporteurs-dash-off-letter-on-nrc.html.

52. Ibid.

53. Ibid.

54. http://www.ummid.com/news/2018/July/17.07.2018/over-03-lakh-sign-petition-india-stop-deleting-muslims.html.

55. *The Hindu*, 'Uproar in Parliament over Assam NRC Update', 30 July 2020, https://www.thehindu.com/news/national/uproar-in-parliament-over-assam-nrc-update/article24555843.ece.

56. *The Hindu*, 'Assam Draft NRC Release: Mamata Sees It as Part of Vote Bank Politics by BJP', 30 July 2018, https://www.thehindu.com/news/cities/kolkata/centre-resorting-to-vote-bank-politics-mamata-on-draft-nrc-list/article24553049.ece.

57. Hartosh Singh Bal, 'Is India Creating Its Own Rohingya?' *The New York Times*, 10 August 2018, https://www.nytimes.com/2018/08/10/opinion/india-citizenship-assam-modi-rohingyas.html.

58. Mander, 'It's Time We Listened'.

59. *The Wire*, 'UN Special Rapporteurs Re-emphasise Concern over NRC in Second Letter to Indian Govt', 17 December 2018, https://thewire.in/rights/nrc-assam-united-nations.

60. Sanjib Baruah, 'The Missing 4,007,707', *The Indian Express*, 2 August 2018, https://indianexpress.com/article/opinion/columns/assam-nrc-draft-list-names-citizenship-5287213/.

61. Hiren Gohain, 'Debate: The NRC Is What Will Allow Assam to Escape from the Cauldron of Hate', *The Wire*, 13 August 2018, https://thewire.in/politics/debate-the-nrc-is-what-will-allow-assam-to-escape-from-the-cauldron-of-hate.

62. Ibid.

63. Ibid.

64. Udayon Misra, 'Why Many in Assam See the National Register of Citizens as a Lifeline', The Wire, 24 August 2018, https://thewire.in/history/history-nrc-assam.

65. Ibid.

66. The hearing took place on 31 July, 7 August, 16 August, 28 August, 5 September, 19 September, 23 October, 1 November and 12 December in 2018, and 24 January, 5 February, 13 March, 10 April, 8 May, 23 July and

8 August in 2019, apart from three orders on relevant issues on 17 May, 30 May and 13 August in 2019.

67. Arunabh Saikia, 'Why Was NRC Coordinator Prateek Hajela Transferred Out of Assam?' Scroll.in, 18 October 2019, https://scroll.in/article/940991/ why-was-nrc-coordinator-prateek-hajela-transferred-out-of-assam.

68. Countercurrents.org, 'The Final Draft of State Sponsored Statelessness: NRC and the 4 Million "Stateless People" of India', 1 August 2018, https://countercurrents.org/2018/08/the-final-draft-of-state-sponsored-statelessness-nrc-and-the-4-million-stateless-people-of-india/.

69. *Al Jazeera*, 'What's Next for the 4 Million Stripped of Citizenship in India?' 30 July 2018, https://www.aljazeera.com/news/2018/07/4-millions-stripped-citizenship-india-180730080348753.html.

70. *India Today*, 'Assam Final NRC List Released: 19,06,657 People Excluded, 3.11 Crore Make It to Citizenship List', 31 August 2019, https://www.indiatoday.in/india/story/assam-final-nrc-list-out-over-19-lakh-people-excluded-1593769-2019-08-31.

71. *Firstpost*, 'Assam NRC Final List: Original Petitioner in SC Says Document Is "Flawed" as Apex Court Rejected Reverification Plea', 31 August 2019, https://www.firstpost.com/india/assam-nrc-final-list-original-petitioner-in-sc-says-document-is-flawed-as-apex-court-rejected-reverification-plea-7260851.html.

72. *India Today*, 'Assam NRC Final List: Unhappy with Exclusion Figure, AASU to Move Supreme Court', 31 August 2019, https://www.indiatoday.in/india/story/assam-nrc-final-aasu-move-supreme-court-1593827-2019-08-31.

73. *The Assam Tribune*, 'Unhappy AASU to Move SC', 1 September 2019, http://www.assamtribune.com/scripts/detailsnew.asp?id=sep0119/at057.

74. Ibid.

75. Bharatiya Janata Party, 'Assam Vision Document 2016–2025', 2016, https://mmscmsguy.assam.gov.in/sites/default/files/swf_utility_folder/departments/mmscmsguy_webcomindia_org_oid_2/this_comm/vision-document.pdf.

76. Ibid., 11.

77. Government of Assam, 'Budget Speech 2016–17', 31–32, para 18.1, https://finance.assam.gov.in/sites/default/files/porlets/Budget%20Speech%20%28English%29%202016%20-%202017.pdf.

78. *The Times of India*, '"We Did What Congress Could Not", Says BJP MP Amit Shah in Rajya Sabha about Assam NRC Final Draft', 31 July 2018, https://timesofindia.indiatimes.com/india/we-did-what-congress-could-not-says-bjp-mp-amit-shah-in-rajya-sabha-about-assam-nrc-final-draft/articleshow/65211167.cms.

79. Sangeeta Barooah Pisharoty, 'Why Is BJP Changing Tack on NRC in Assam?' The Wire, 30 August 2019, https://thewire.in/politics/bjp-change-tack-nrc-assam.

80. *India Today*, 'Assam Govt Rejects Present NRC, Wants To Be Part of National NRC: Himanta Biswa Sarma', 20 November 2019, https://www.indiatoday.in/india/story/assam-nrc-national-cut-off-himanta-biswa-sarma-bjp-amit-shah-1620965-2019-11-20.

81. The Wire, 'NRC-excluded Won't Be "Stateless," Will Have All Rights Till They Exhaust Legal Remedies: MEA', 2 September 2019, https://thewire.in/external-affairs/nrc-excluded-wont-be-stateless-will-have-all-rights-till-they-exhaust-legal-remedies-mea.

82. Ibid.

83. Bikash Sing, 'Rejection Process on Pause as Assam's NRC Yet To Be Notified', *The Economic Times*, 1 June 2020, https://economictimes.indiatimes.com/news/politics-and-nation/rejection-process-on-pause-as-assams-nrc-yet-to-be-notified/articleshow/76127526.cms. Read more at https://economictimes.indiatimes.com/news/politics-and-nation/rejection-process-on-pause-as-assams-nrc-yet-to-be-notified/articleshow/76127526.cms?utm_source=contentofinterest&utm_medium=text&utm_campaign=cppst.

84. Deepankar Basu and Debarshi Das, 'Assam's Politics and the NRC', *Economic & Political Weekly* 55, no. 5 (1 February 2020): 61–63.

85. Ibid., 63.

86. Ibid.

87. Ibid.

88. Ibid.

89. Suraj Gogoi, 'Psychology behind NRC Mirrors Narrow, Dominating Side of Assamese Language, and Its Fragile Nationalism, Cultural Identity', *Firstpost*, 20 October 2019, https://www.firstpost.com/india/psychology-behind-nrc-mirrors-narrow-dominating-side-of-assamese-language-and-its-fragile-nationalism-cultural-identity-7526031.html.

90. Angshuman Choudhury and Suraj Gogoi, 'Citizenship Amendment Act and NRC Are Two Sides of Same Coin; Both Seek to Alienate India's Muslims', *Firstpost*, 17 December 2019, https://www.firstpost.com/politics/citizenship-amendment-act-and-nrc-are-two-sides-of-same-coin-both-seek-to-alienate-indias-muslims-7781461.html.

91. Angshuman Choudhury and Suraj Gogoi, 'Re-contextualising the NRC: A Response to Hiren Gohain', Countercurrents.org, 10 September 2019, https://countercurrents.org/2019/09/re-contextualising-the-nrc-a-response-to-hiren-gohain/.

92. Angshuman Choudhury and Suraj Gogoi, 'A Narrow Nationalism Again', *The Hindu*, 12 September 2019, https://www.thehindu.com/opinion/op-ed/a-narrow-nationalism-again/article29394298.ece.

93. Suraj Gogoi and Abhinav P. Borbora, 'Assam's NRC Consensus: Lack of Public Disorder after Draft List Didn't Mean Absence of Violence', Scroll.in, 13 December 2019, https://scroll.in/article/944214/inside-the-nrc-consensus-the-lack-of-public-disorder-does-not-mean-the-absence-of-violence.

94. Eleventh Column, 'Crisis of Citizenship: A Critical Reading List on Assam's NRC and Beyond', 1 March 2020, https://www.eleventhcolumn.com/2020/03/01/crisis-of-citizenship-a-critical-reading-list-on-assams-nrc-and-beyond/.

95. Harsh Mander, 'A Flawed Process That Pleased None', *The Hindu*, 2 September 2019, https://www.thehindu.com/opinion/op-ed/a-flawed-process-that-pleased-none/article29317452.ece.

96. Ditilekha Sharma, 'Determination of Citizenship through Lineage in the Assam NRC Is Inherently Exclusionary', *Economic & Political Weekly* 54, no. 14, 6 April 2019, https://www.epw.in/engage/article/determination-citizenship-through-lineage-assam-nrc-exclusionary.

97. Ibid.

98. *Economic & Political Weekly*, 'Quandary of National Register of Citizens', Editorials 54, no. 37 (14 September 2019), https://www.epw.in/journal/2019/37/editorials/quandary-national-register-citizens.html.

99. The Assam Accord has been called a 'public law contract' by the Forum Against Citizenship Act Amendment Bill led by Hiren Gohain in its memorandum submitted to the JPC on CAB, 2016, dated 7 May 2018. It is the anti-CAB movement in Assam which made the NRC more urgent. What one needs to keep in mind is that the cut-off date of 1971 has already been challenged in the Supreme Court, demanding 1951 as the cut-off date. A public consensus on the NRC, therefore, is a political negation to that proposal. On the other hand, defending the NRC is also a political negation of the CAA, even though it has now been enacted.

100. These arguments were initially developed in the author's article 'Assam and the NRC: A Political Reading', *Economic & Political Weekly* 55, no. 39 (26 September 2020) https://www.epw.in/system/files/pdf/2020_55/39/DI_LV_39_260920_Akhil%20Ranjan%20Dutta.pdf.

101. Hiren Gohain, 'Cudgel of Chauvinism', *Economic & Political Weekly* 15, no. 8 (23 February 1980: 418–420.

102. Amalendu Guha, 'Little Nationalism Turned Chauvinist: Assam's Anti-foreigner Upsurge, 1979–80', *Economic & Political Weekly* 15, no. 41/43 (October 1980, special issue), https://www.epw.in/system/files/pdf/1980_15/41-42-43/national_question_in_assam_little_nationalism_turned_chauvinist.pdf

103. Hiren Gohain, 'Fall-out of Underdevelopment', *Economic & Political Weekly* 15, no. 12 (22 March 1980): 589–590.

104. In a series of investigative writings, Harsh Mander revisited the Nellie massacre, which occurred on 18 February 1983 amid the Assam agitation. In this heinous act of violence, the local tribal community slaughtered 2,191 Muslim settlers, left 370 children orphaned and destroyed their homes in 16 villages. The ghost of the terror continues to haunt the families and relatives of those who had been slaughtered Mander, Harsh. 2008. 'The forgotten Nellie massacres," *The Hindu*, 14 December available at http://www.sacw.net/article423.html. Mander also argued that the violence against the East-Bengal-origin Muslims continued and intensified with the rise of homeland politics pursued through the strategy of ethnic cleansing. Referring to the violence against the East-Bengal-origin Muslims in the present-day BTC, Mander writes,

> Assam has near-fatally imploded with the politics of competing persecutions, as oppressed groups arm and organise themselves to violently drive away other wretched and deprived people, in pursuit

of dangerous, impossible (and unconstitutional) aspirations of ethnically cleansed homelands. Their plight is aggravated by bankrupt and opportunistic politics and State policy, and equivocal rationalisations by civilian observers. In battles between indigenous inhabitants and settlers, many of the region's poorest people are living out their lives in fear, confined to camps, people who no one wants and who have nowhere to go. (Mander, Harsh. 2012. 'Assam's Tragedy'. *The Hindu*. August 25. Available at https://www.thehindu.com/opinion/columns/Harsh_Mander/assams-tragedy/article3820732.ece).

Gupta, Shekhar. 2019. 'Blood, bodies and scars: What I saw after the 1983 Nellie massacre in Assam'. *The Print*, 18 February. Available at https://theprint.in/opinion/blood-bodies-and-scars-what-i-saw-after-the-1983-nellie-massacre-in-assam/194662/. who visited the massacre site on the day it happened, also provided a vivid but ghostly account of it.

105. Sumanta Sen and Jagannath Dubashi in their article titled 'Nellie Massacre: Assam Burns as Ethnic Violence Singes the State', *India Today*, 15 March 1983, provide a broad canvas of the violence in 1983, both before and after the Nellie massacre. The authors point out that rumours played a vital role in spreading the violence. In Gohpur, there were rumours about burning down of Assamese villages and killing of Assamese people by the tribal hoarders belonging to the Bodo community, which was retaliated by burning down of 27 Bodo villages and killing of 30 Bodos. The Bodos became a target, as they supported the pro-election Plain Tribals Council of Assam (PTCA) and thereby opposed the diktat issued by the agitators to boycott the elections.

106. Monirul Hussain, 'Ethnicity, Communalism and State: Barpeta Massacre', *Economic & Political Weekly* 30, no. 20 (20 May 1995), https://www.epw.in/journal/1995/20/commentary/ethnicity-communalism-and-state-barpeta-massacre.html.

107. D voters means disputed or doubtful voters, whose names were de-enfranchised in 1997 by the Election Commission during the comprehensive revision of the electoral rolls in the state due to their failure to produce the valid document of citizenship. Around 0.24 million cases of D voters were referred to the FTs, and out of this around 0.13 million cases have been disposed of. The remaining 0.12 million D voters, whose names were not inserted into the NRC final draft released on 30 July 2018, continue to languish in the detention camps and the FTs. *The Shillong Times*. 2018 "D' voters' plight: 102-year-old Chandradhar Das has to brave age, ailments to shuttle between home and Foreigners' Tribunal to prove citizenship', 18 August. Available at https://theshillongtimes.com/2018/08/18/d-voters-plight-102-year-old-chandradhar-das-has-to-brave-age-ailments-to-shuttle-between-home-and-foreigners-tribunal-to-prove-citizenship/

108. As per Clause 5.8 of the Assam Accord, 'Foreigners who came to Assam on or after March 25, 1971 shall continue to be detected, deleted and expelled in accordance with law. Immediate and practical steps shall be taken to

expel such foreigners.' The phrasing 'in accordance with law' has remained vague, as India has not yet signed an extradition treaty with Bangladesh for the expulsion of foreigners. Pushing such foreigners back to the territory of Bangladesh is not a solution, as those pushed back will not be accepted by Bangladesh as citizens of the country. In January 2013, India and Bangladesh signed an extradition treaty. However, it will not cover illegal migrants. 'The treaty will allow exchange of convicts sentenced for more than a year in prison but will not be applicable to political prisoners and asylum seekers'. Haroon Habib. (2013). 'India-Bangladesh extradition treaty takes effect'. *The Hindu*, 23 October. Available at https://www.thehindu.com/news/national/ indiabangladesh-extradition-treaty-takes-effect/article5265681.ece

109. The Supreme Court's orders are available on the NRC website at http://www. nrcassam.nic.in/court-orders.html.

110. In its order dated 13 July 2017, the Supreme Court objected to the statement of the chief minister of Assam on the date of publication of the draft NRC which contradicted the date set by the Court. The Court gave consent to the new date proposed by the NRC state coordinator which conformed with the date suggested by the chief minister. However, the Court categorically instructed that the coordinator henceforth would report directly to the Court.

111. Choudhury and Gogoi, 'Re-contextualising the NRC'.

112. Ibid.

113. Ibid.

114. Arunabh Saikia, 'Meet Hiren Gohain: Once the Fiercest Critic of Assamese Chauvinism, Now Facing Charges of Sedition', Scroll.in, 12 January 2019, https://scroll.in/article/909122/meet-hiren-gohain-once-the-fiercest-critic-of-assamese-chauvinism-now-facing-charges-of-sedition.

115. Ibid.

116. Important among them are (a) Saif Khalid,'Gohain: If Citizenship Issue Isn't Settled Assam Can't Go Forward', *Al Jazeera*, 20 July 2018, https:// www.aljazeera.com/indepth/features/gohain-citizenship-issue-isn-settled-assam-180717090910612.html; (b) Hiren Gohain, 'It's Important to Know the History of the NRC before Passing Judgment on It', The Wire, 8 August 2018, https://thewire.in/rights/assam-nrc-history-immigration; (c) Hiren Gohain, 'Debate: The NRC Is What Will Allow Assam to Escape from the Cauldron of Hate', The Wire, 13 August 2018, https://thewire.in/politics/debate-the-nrc-is-what-will-allow-assam-to-escape-from-the-cauldron-of-hate; (d) Hiren Gohain, 'Debate: Colonial Policy Created the Northeast's Citizenship Problem', The Wire, 8 February 2019, https://thewire.in/rights/debate-colonial-policy-created-the-northeasts-citizenship-problem; (e) Gohain, 'It Is Important to Contextualise the NRC'; (f) Hiren Gohain, 'Discussion: Linking Excesses in NRC Process to Assamese Xenophobia Is Unwarranted', *Economic & Political Weekly* 55, no. 9 (29 February 2020), https://www.epw.in/engage/article/ discussion-linking-excesses-nrc-process-assamese?0=ip_login_no_cache%3 Dba2f84792dcce0e5abfc1f8be34927de.

117. Khalid, 'Gohain: If Citizenship Issue Isn't Settled'.
118. Ibid.
119. Gohain, 'It's Important to Know the History of the NRC'.
120. Misra, 'Why Many in Assam See the National Register of Citizens'.
121. Ibid.
122. Udayon Misra, 'Assam's Humanitarian Conundrum', *The Hindu*, 15 August 2019, https://www.thehindu.com/opinion/lead/assams-humanitarian-conundrum/article29095073.ece.
123. Udayon Misra, 'National Register of Citizens: Beginnings and Endings', *The Indian Express*, 7 August 2018, https://indianexpress.com/article/opinion/columns/nrc-assam-aasu-bangladesh-assamese-bengali-1971-national-register-of-citizens-beginnings-and-endings-5294784/.
124. Suraj Gogoi and Parag Jyoti Saikia, 'NRC and Intellectual Racism', Sabrang, 29 August 2018, https://sabrangindia.in/article/nrc-and-intellectual-racism.
125. Gohain, 'It Is Important to Contextualise the NRC'.
126. Sanjib Baruah, 'Defining Thousands as Non-citizens Will Create a New Form of Precarious Citizenship—People with Fewer Rights, Entitlements', *The Indian Express*, 31 August 2019, https://indianexpress.com/article/opinion/columns/a-more-precarious-citizenship-assam-nrc-list-jammu-kashmir-5949158/.
127. In an important order, the Gauhati High Court criticized the Assam government 'for operating six detention centres for housing illegal foreigners within jail premises and directed it to submit an action taken report within 10 days regarding hiring of suitable accommodation for the purpose' (*Outlook India*, 'HC Slams Assam Govt for Operating Detention Centres in Jails', 8 October 2020, https://www.outlookindia.com/newsscroll/hc-slams-assam-govt-for-operating-detention-centres-in-jails/1951965).
128. Akhil Ranjan Dutta, 'Conservation vs. Peoples' Entitlements: Contestations in Kaziranga National Park', in *Developmentalism as Strategy: Interrogating Postcolonial Narratives on India's North East*, Sage Studies on India's Northeast, ed. Rakhee Bhattacharya (New Delhi: SAGE Publications, 2019), 280–303.
129. Details of the proposal by the committee are discussed in Chapter 3.

Hindutva at the Core

CAB-turned-CAA and Assam's Political Destiny

3

CAB-turned-CAA exploded into a full-blown crisis in Assam on 11 December 2019—the day the CAB was passed by the Rajya Sabha, the Upper House of the Indian Parliament. The Bill was already passed by the Lower House, that is, Lok Sabha, on 9 December 2019. The act of passing the Bill exhibited complete disrespect to the long-drawn consensus on the cut-off date of 24 March 1971 for the detection, deletion and deportation of foreigners. The date agreed upon by the Assam Accord, 1985, was subsequently entered into the Citizenship Act, 1955, by inserting Section 6A in December 1985. The passage of the Bill, which amid intense debate on the streets as well as in the process of preparing the report on the Bill by the JPC, exhibits serious flaws and weaknesses of the Indian federal system which can override the regional aspirations through brute majority in the Parliament. The report by the JPC presents a gloomy picture about the functioning of the parliamentary system in India as the committee endeavoured to legitimize the Bill rather than suggesting measures through which it could have been improved to accommodate the diverse aspirations of the regions. The Bill's passage also reveals the weaknesses of smaller nationalities that fall prey to dominant political forces and the civil society who refuses to build unity in resistance against the hegemonic forces. More importantly, the passage of the Bill exhibits the disconnect between the social discontent in the greater society and the electoral outcomes.[1] This disconnect helps the incumbent regime to legitimize its political actions in the pretext of electoral consent by the people even if it disrespects the larger social and political aspirations.

This chapter will examine all these issues in detail by undertaking the journey of the incumbent political regime in the passage of the Bill and its encounter with the greater society.

THE CONTESTED MOMENTUM OF CITIZENSHIP

Citizenship is a momentum concept which 'produces contested imaginaries of the political community and corresponding competing notions of the citizen and his/her terms of membership'.[2] Roy has also pointed out that 'citizenship is deeply contested, is experienced and unfolds in specific social fields amidst heterogeneous and often contesting political imaginaries, assumptions and practices, has also become influential in thinking about citizenship'.[3] Citizenship entails two simultaneous processes—encompassment and closure. Roy argues,

> While the logic of encompassment may therefore be envisaged as a progressive opening up of democratic spaces, a paradox inheres in citizenship which is manifest in the closures which come into play immediately when citizenship unfolds in practice. Closure, therefore, is a simultaneous differential experience of citizenship which accompanies each liberating moment of encompassment.[4]

The momentum of citizenship in India has a singular reference, that is, the migrant. Writing in 2008, Roy referred to three moments that brought about the momentums: during 1955 while enacting the Citizenship Act, during 1986 while amending the Constitution to give legality to the provisions of the Assam Accord and in 2003 by incorporating the notion of overseas citizenship. From 2016 to 2019, we witness the fourth and the most contested and lengthiest momentum that finally brought in a new category of citizenship—the non-Muslim minorities from Afghanistan, Pakistan and Bangladesh. In the case of the first three momentums, the issues were settled before legislations. In the case of the fourth momentum, the issues continued to unfold, and it is yet to be settled despite being inserted into the Citizenship Act. The dialectics of 'encompassment' and 'closure' are distinctly manifested in the current momentum, and it created a distinct category of hierarchical citizenship based on religion which was not the case in previous citizenship momentums.

CAB-turned-CAA generated an unprecedented political momentum in the history of Indian democracy. But for Assam, it was both a momentum and a polyrhythm. Assam encountered two momentums: the CAB-turned-CAA and NRC. These two instruments have been contested widely and have generated different layers of dialectics along with hierarchies. It is absolutely difficult to identify the processes of 'encompassments' and 'closures' in both the processes. The NRC, if looked at from human rights' perspective, is a 'closure' as it ousts around 1.9 million people from the legal–constitutional entity of citizenship. For the indigenous people of Assam, however, it is not a closure at all. Rather, it is an encompassment as it gave legal–juridical recognition and thereby rights to a category of migrants who do not enjoy the same status in other parts of the country. The NRC also ended the hierarchies drawn between two streams of immigrants—1951–1966 stream and 1966–1971 stream—who were granted citizenship in two different ways. The first stream was granted citizenship instantly through the amendment to the Citizenship Act, 1955, but for the second stream, conditionalities were imposed towards registering as citizens. The NRC had done away with the hierarchies.[5] The CAB-turned-CAA, in a way, is an encompassment, as it opens up the avenues of citizenship for certain categories but builds its own closure that deprives certain other categories. Therefore, either encompassment or closure is also a much-contested category. The affiliation to this or those imaginary categories is defined by locations—regional, political and ideological.

The contestations over the CAB-turned-CAA did not have a single pattern. It was not only contested between the state and the greater society. The state, of course, had a pattern. It presented the issue with a single orientation. But the greater society had frictions within, not only between the apparently opposite blocks, for example, between the Hindu Bengali migrants and indigenous Assamese people, but also within the Assamese civil society who fought against the Act. The conflicts are embedded into political and ideological differences. As we drive through the trajectory of the Act, those multi-layered contestations will come to the forefront.

The contestations over citizenship in Assam have been conditioned by the contradictions of the regime driven by its monolithic

Hindutva ideology on the one hand and its strategic electoral pursuit of a Rainbow Alliance on the other. The CAA represents the former, and its exemptions in the Act for the indigenous people and the discourses on the constitutional safeguards for the Assamese people represent the latter. In the process, it has also manufactured many closures and 'otherness'. Whereas the CAB/CAA has a distinct frame of 'closure', the exemptions for the Sixth Schedule and the Inner Line Permit (ILP) areas have also manufactured both closures and otherness in Northeast India. Thereby, it has also succeeded in bringing friction within Northeast India, particularly within the civil society forces.

BJP: The Unknown Guest

In 2016, the greater Assamese society almost took BJP's 'Rainbow' campaign for granted. It refused to see its saffron hue. But it was not only the ordinary Assamese people who hailed the new colour of the BJP in Assam, but perceptive political commentators like Pratap Bhanu Mehta also argued that 'Assam is a significant result for many reasons.' The decisiveness in the verdict apart, Mehta credited the BJP for settling the leadership issue so amicably and also building the broad coalition. He also had a sense of satisfaction over the way the issue of immigration was handled during the campaign. He called it a new vista for the BJP, which is often not recognized by many. Mehta wrote,

> But most importantly, though it stuck to its policy message on immigration, the campaign was subtle and sophisticated, and less polarising than many had feared. It piggybacked on the local leadership rather than subverting it. It injected newness by holding out the possibility of a new combination of elements: Sonowal and Sarma and Prafulla Mahanta together. Managing this combination will be a challenge; but it opens up a new vista of possibilities as well. It shows the BJP's extraordinary capacity to think politically rather than merely ideologically, when it sets its mind to it. This is something the BJP's opponents have been underestimating at every stage.[6]

Mehta wrote it on the day the BJP registered a landslide victory in Assam, that is, 20 May 2016. On the same day, Hiren Gohain, an eminent intellectual and political commentator from Assam, warned the people of Assam and argued, 'The Assamese people do not really know the Guests that they have welcomed with open arms.'[7] He acknowledged the fact that the 2016 assembly election is to be 'a watershed moment for Assam' and also 'historic' as has been claimed by BJP's new political strategist, the former Congress veteran Himanta Biswa Sarma. But Gohain reminded the people,

> The effects are not likely to be transient, given the extensive and strong bases the RSS-led Hindutva brigade has built over the years with painstaking, systematic work all over the state, among all communities, and with solid background by local TV channels which virtually ran a prolonged campaign against the Congress.[8]

Gohain, who has been the most consistent and credible intellectual threat to the Hindutva brigades in Assam both inside and outside the BJP, had pointed out even before the BJP assumed power in the state that "to insure itself further from unexpected turns, the BJP assured lakhs of Hindu refugees from Bangladesh that if voted to power in Assam it would guarantee them citizenship as victims of religious persecution."[9] There were a very few takers of Gohain's views at that point. Indeed, Gohain and around 40 intellectuals and educationists of Assam became the immediate target of public wrath for appealing the voters not to vote for the BJP in the 2016 assembly elections. In the appeal issued on 2 April 2016, that is, just two days ahead of the first phase of the elections in Assam scheduled for 4 April 2016, the group said, 'The BJP has been trying to negate real patriotism with insane patriotism. The nation will gradually be in the grip of darkness if this party continues to remain in power.'[10]

The appeal created a political havoc. The local media and the larger sections reacted sharply. In a statement, another group of educationists and concerned citizens led by former vice-chancellor of Gauhati University, Nirmal Kumar Choudhury, and former DGP of Assam, Nishinath Changkakoti, commented,

> Asking people not to vote for a particular party is in itself a threat to democracy. Nobody has the right to issue a fatwa to the people on exercising their democratic rights. They are trying to mislead the voters on the eve of polling day.[11]

On the day the statement was issued, the editor-in-chief of a local television channel Pratidin Time hosted a solo episode by himself to question the moral right of Hiren Gohain and the co-signatories to appeal not to vote for a particular party. Social media was flooded with hostile comments against the group, and they were projected as the true traitors of the *jati*. The BJP remained a silent spectator, knowing well the political dividends that the party will gain out of the emotional outbursts against the statement. For a couple of months thereafter, the issue remained the mostly debated political issue in the state, and the editorial pages of the leading local dailies were filled with sharp commentary about the statement. Hiren Gohain remained the main target. Himanta Biswa Sarma, BJP's core strategist in Northeast India and the most vocal proponent of CAB in Assam, alleged Hiren Gohain to have indulged in intellectual misconduct (*bouddhik byabhichar*).[12] On his part, Gohain continued to criticize the BJP and warned the people of Assam to remain vigilant of the 'guests' that they have welcomed without knowing their true character.

The First Encounter: The 2015 Notifications on Persecuted Minorities

BJP's first fortune in the state was its victory in the 2014 parliamentary elections. With 36.5 per cent votes and 7 out of 14 Lok Sabha seats, the party also registered lead in 69 out of 126 assembly segments.[13] The BJP registered remarkable victory in the constituencies in Upper Assam in the Brahmaputra Valley, where it had no significant electoral presence till these elections. With former AASU President Sarbananda Sonowal as BJP's State President, who was crowned with the title of '*Jatiyo Nayak*' (national hero) for his victory in getting the much controversial IMDT Act, 1983, declared unconstitutional in a landmark Supreme Court verdict in 2005, the party was in a position to build an image of pro-Assamese nationality, keeping its monolithic Hindutva ideology under the surface. The people of Assam reposed faith in the vision and leadership of Narendra Modi, who famously declared, 'You can write it down. After May 16, these Bangladeshis better be prepared with their bags packed,'[14] implying his imminent victory in the elections and his stern action against the illegal migrants. But the people in the state did not pay attention to what he said in February 2014 in Silchar, 'As soon as we come to power at the Centre, detention camps housing Hindu migrants from Bangladesh will be done away with,' and asserted, 'We have a responsibility toward Hindus who are harassed and suffer in other countries. Where will they go? India is the only place for them. Our government cannot continue to harass them. We will have to accommodate them here.'[15]

Betraying the enormous emotional and political trust endowed upon Narendra Modi and Sarbananda Sonowal, the Modi-led Union government issued two notifications on 7 September 2015, triggering immediate reactions in Assam. Through these two notifications that amended the Passport (Entry into India) Rules, 1950, and the Foreigners Order, 1948, the government exempted

> persons belonging to minority communities in Bangladesh and Pakistan, namely, Hindus, Sikhs, Buddhists, Jains, Parsis and Christians who were compelled to seek shelter in India due to religious persecution or fear of religious persecution and entered into India on or before the 31st December, 2014.[16]

from the purview of the definitions of illegal migrants as defined in the Citizenship Act and in relevant rules. The Citizenship Act, 1955, defines an illegal migrant as a person who enters India (i) without valid documents including passport or other travel documents; or (ii) with valid documents including passport or other travel document and the validity of any of such documents has expired. The CAB, 2016, is the result of these two notifications, and the CAA, 2019, is its culmination.

The notifications immediately met with protests in Assam. On 9 September 2015, just after two days of the notification, AASU brought out a protest march against the notification. The organization declared its decision to take out a torchlight procession all over the state the next day to register their protest against the decision of the Union Government to accord citizenship to the post-March 24, 1971 Hindu migrants living in Assam. The members of the student body also burnt copies of the notifications. They also condemned the statement of the governor of Assam who reportedly said, '"There is nothing sacrosanct" so far as the deadline for the acceptance of migrants from Bangladesh is concerned.'[17] The governor was referring to the deadline set by the Assam Accord—that is, 24 March 1971. One of the signatories to the Assam Accord and two times chief minister of Assam, Prafulla Kumar Mahanta, also took a strong exception to the notifications and pointed out that it would only add to the 'woes of the State which is already facing the problem of illegal infiltration from across the border'.[18]

Assam witnessed the first mass protests on 12 September 2015, with AJYCP calling for a state-wide bandh against the notifications. The 12-hour bandh 'crippled life in Assam'. Sporadic violence also took place on that day. The bandh received support from a number of ethnic student outfits such as the All Bodo Students Union (ABSU), All Assam Muttock Yubak Chhatra Sanmilan, All Dimasa Students Union (ADSU), Karbi Students Union, Goria–Moria–Deshi Jatiya Parishad, Sonowal Kachari Students' Union, All Assam Muttock Sanmilan, All Assam Madahi Janjati Students Union, All Assam Manipuri Students Union, Chutia Yuba Sanmilan and Moran Students' Union. The bandh also forced close down of schools, colleges, other educational institutions and commercial establishments in the state. Except for a few buses of the Assam State Transport Corporation that plied in a few areas, the vehicular traffic also remained off the roads in most of the districts in the state.[19]

It would be appropriate to point out that before these notifications had been issued, the government was willing to give a long-term visa rather than citizenship to the refugees. It was reported that the government had a series of meetings with many minority organizations in this regard and also conducted a number of visits to different places. It was also reported that on 23 December 2014, the Home Ministry had convened a meeting 'with representative associations, especially of minority communities from neighbouring countries, to address their grievances related to granting Long Term Visa (LTV) and Indian citizenship'. The meeting, which was chaired by the additional secretary (foreigners) in the MHA, was attended by about 75 representatives from 15 such associations. Some associations from Assam also attended the meeting. It was also reported that the teams of MHA officials visited 24 identified districts[20] for citizenship in 8 states and 14 districts[21] for Long Term Visa (LTV) cases of these applicants. Ironically, Assam was kept out of the purview of these visits.

These discussions and visits culminated in the issuing of the two notifications on 7 September 2015.

The government was unaware of the number of the persecuted people in those countries and also did not have any mechanism to prove who the persecuted people are. It admitted the complexities that may arise out of the existing provisions as laid down in the Assam Accord. Government sources were reported to have said,

> It would be a complex question for the Government to answer and no discussion has yet been held on the issue in the highest level of the Government of India. As per the Assam Accord, the foreigners who came to Assam on or after the midnight of March 24, 1971, would be detected and deported but the recent decision of the Government is against that provision of the Accord.[22]

In September 2015, Assam witnessed a lot of protests against the notifications. Some organizations even threatened to challenge it in the Court. As the protests intensified, the government insisted on the fact that it was a pan-Indian issue and not specific to Assam. Therefore, the resentment in Assam was somewhat misplaced. Stating this position, Union Minister of State for External Affairs V. K. Singh said in Guwahati, 'This is a pan-India notification and not applicable to just a particular area. Hence, this issue should not be politicised.' He also argued that it is only 'natural and pragmatic for people to go to the nearby places when they migrate and so the burden has fallen on Assam after the 1971 war'.[23]

On 3 October 2015, AASU denounced the notifications and urged all the political parties to make their stand clear 'whether they are in favour of protecting the interests of the indigenous people of Assam and the genuine Indian citizens living in the State'.[24] AASU also urged them to clarify their stand on the date for the detection and deportation of foreigners as settled by the Assam Accord, that is, 24 March 1971.

October remained calm as it is a month of festivities, including Durga Puja, which is celebrated widely across the state and with great fervour. By November 2015, the protests against the notifications gradually dried out. In that month, Sarbananda Sonowal, state minister in the Union Council of Ministers, replaced Siddhartha Bhattacharya as the state president of the BJP. The BJP was getting ready for the elections with reconstituting the election management committee for the state, with Sarbananda Sonowal as its chairman and Dr Himanta Biswa Sarma, the Congress veteran who joined the BJP in August 2015, as its convener. The party formally launched its campaign for the forthcoming assembly elections in November 2017 with a huge public rally in Dibrugarh town. The rally was addressed by BJP's National President Amit Shah. While urging the gathering to dislodge the Tarun Gogoi-led Congress government as 'it has failed to uplift the State and protect its borders', Shah said, 'The State must be ruled by patriotic people who can develop the State, alleviate poverty, generate employment, halt infiltration and protect the boundaries for the State's security and dignity.'[25] He also alleged that the state government misused the funds allocated under Central schemes. Shah also claimed that the Congress was having a secret dealing with the AIUDF, and such an alliance can never stop infiltration. What was remarkable is that the issue of citizenship for the persecuted minorities from the neighbouring countries did not figure in the meeting and in the run-up to the elections it gradually disappeared.

In the meantime, the Central government also considered the possibility of delegating powers to select state governments to grant citizenship under the provisions made under the 7 September 2015 notifications. This issue also drew the attention of certain quarters but did not arouse strong resistance.[26]

By January 2016, new political equations started unfolding in the state. The BJP unveiled its agenda of Rainbow Alliance and started bringing in the regional forces into its fold. The first success was its electoral tie-up with BPF, which took a formal shape after Prime Minister Narendra Modi addressed a mega public rally in Kokrajhar, the capital of the BTAD, on 19 January 2016. This meeting can be termed as the foregrounding of BJP's strategies for the ensuing elections. The prime minister played it safe; he did not assure statehood to the Bodos but made a few important announcements, including according ST status of the Bodos in the hill districts of the state. On the other hand, he set the tone of the political strategies of his party, where it targeted the ruling Congress, digging up the report card of Manmohan Singh, the former prime minister who represented Assam in the Rajya Sabha from the mid-1990s, including his tenure as the prime minister. 'I was under the impression there is no problem in Assam. Assam is the State from where the Prime Minister was elected for 10 years. The Congress has ruled the State for the last 15 years,' Modi said. 'But I am shocked to see the problems and issues here. So, what has the Prime Minister, who was elected from the State for 10 years, done?'[27]

A delegation of AASU met the prime minister at the Guwahati airport and demanded the implementation of the Assam Accord in a definite timeframe. He assured them that he would initiate a dialogue at his level about the implementation of the accord. It was reported that the organization made it clear that 'Assam would not accept any more burden of Bangladeshi nationals and the Government of India should exclude the State from the recent notification of providing shelter to the foreigners who came to Assam because of religious perse-cution in their own countries.' Prime Minister said that 'he understood the sentiments of the people of Assam and would discuss the issue.'[28]

In the next two and half months, as has been discussed in Chapter 1, Assam saw a wave of BJP's Rainbow Alliance, leading to the landslide victory of the party in the 2016 assembly elections. The anger and discontent over the notifications had dried up, at least for the time being. As the elections approached, the Rainbow Alliance consolidated and the local media at large also became a goodwill partner of the BJP campaign machine. BJP's penetration could be well understood from the antagonistic reactions to the call by a section of concerned citizens not to vote the BJP in the ensuing elections.

Encompassment vs Closure: CAB and Its Implications for Assam

Assam had already been under scrutiny for its demand and pur-suit of the NRC when the rumbling about the CAB started. For the humanists, and even the UN human rights agency, the NRC was anti-humanitarian, as it creates hierarchical boundaries and pushes the agenda of creating 'otherness' as against the 'self' of the indigenous people. As the NRC was approaching the final stage, the campaign against it became intense in India as well as at the global level. Amid such a charged environment, the CAB also got its momentum, and the government was determined to pass it through in the Parliament. The government adopted several strategies to build legitimacy for the Bill. One way was to get it scrutinized by a JPC, which the government constituted within a month of the introduction of the Bill in the Parliament in August 2016. The committee submitted its 438-page report on 9 January 2019, that is, after almost three and half years of intense debates and deliberations. Assam was the epicentre of protests against the Bill. Therefore, keeping in mind the ensuing Lok Sabha elections, it was important to calm down the protesters in the state. As the parliamentary elections were approaching, the Union government constituted a nine-member, high-level committee for the implementation of Clause 6 of the Assam Accord with retired Union Secretary M. P. Bezbaruah as the chairman.[29] Just three days ahead of the notification of the committee, on 4 January 2019, Prime Minister Narendra Modi declared at a poll rally in Bengali Hindu-dominated Silchar town of Assam:

> Our government is progressing constantly towards accomplishing Citizen Amendment Bill, which is deeply tied to our emotions & lives. It will make sure that no son or daughter of India gets harassed. If they are met with any misfortune, then instead of questioning them on their blood relations or the color of their passport, the bill will take care of every relevant issue and protect their individuality. I am very positive about the bill getting passed and that it shall shield every devotee of Mother India.[30]

The announcement added more fuel to the anti-CAB protests in Assam. By 12 January 2019, six of out the nine members of the committee, including its chairman, refused to be part of it due to the massive protests, and the committee became redundant.[31]

The JPC report is an interesting document to understand the frames of hierarchies, encompassment, closure, self and the others. While the government's proclaimed goals have been to define self and 'positive equality' by opening up the avenues of citizenship for certain categories, critics have primarily focused on the hierarchies that it has created through the proclaimed encompassment and the very particular kind of positive equality. The critics of CAB in Assam also referred to Article 14 of the Constitution while defending the principle of equality enshrined in the Constitution. But, for Assam, it has been both critical and relevant to guard the political consensus that emerged through the Assam Accord. Both Assam and Northeast India spoke for upholding the values of diversity, that is, the right to language and identity of the indigenous people of the region within the fundamental principle of equality that did not have boundaries drawn on the basis of any communal hierarchy as was proposed by the Bill and guarded by the Act. To understand the criticalities, let us analyse the Bill and the JPC report, focusing more specifically on Assam's encounter with the JPC. It should be mentioned that Assam figures prominently in the JPC report, and Northeast India figures prominently in the final version of the Bill and the Act.

JPC primarily encountered two issues: the constitutionality of the Bill in the eyes of Article 14 of the Constitution and the desirability of the Bill in the light of its adverse impact on the settlement reached through the Assam Accord for the detection, deletion and deportation of foreigners. Assam had argued on both the issues intensely, although Assam's stake on the issue of the constitutionality of the Bill in the light of Article 14 has not drawn adequate attention.

But before we delve into all these issues, an exploration of the main features and the contents of the report will help us to understand its contradictions and limitations.

JPC REPORT: A BRIEF SKETCH

The 30-member JPC on the CAB, 2016, was appointed to examine the Bill and to report to the Parliament with modifications if needed at all for consideration by the Parliament. The Bill, introduced in the Lok Sabha on 19 July 2016, was referred to the JPC through a resolution adopted in the Lok Sabha and Rajya Sabha on 11 and 12 August 2016, respectively. The JPC was mandated to submit the report by the first day of the last week of the Winter Session (2016). However, the committee was granted an extension of time on six occasions, starting from the first day of the last week of Budget Session (2017) up to the first day of the last week of the Winter Session (2018). Finally, the report was submitted and laid down in both the houses of the Parliament on

7 January 2019.[32] The report was prepared based on memorandums, witnesses, evidence and hearing of different stakeholders. Important among them are the following:9,000 memorandums received from different organisations, individuals and experts; (pp. 18–21)

1. Views and feedback received through study visits conducted in six places, i.e. Jodhpur (Rajasthan); Ahmadabad and Rajkot (Gujarat); Guwahati and Silchar (Assam) and Shillong (Meghalaya); (pp. 21–32)
2. Oral evidence of the public representatives/experts/organisations/ association (Nonofficial witnesses); (p. 32)
3. Evidence of the representatives of the State Governments of Assam, Bihar, Gujarat, Jharkhand, Maharashtra and West Bengal; (p. 32)
4. Background Note, Written Reply, Post-Evidence Information/ Clarification and other requisite documents from the Ministries of Home Affairs, Law & Justice (Department of Legal Affairs and Legislative Department) and External Affairs. The committee also took oral evidence of the representatives of the aforesaid Ministries/ Departments including that of the Intelligence Bureau (IB) and Research & Analysis Wing (RAW). (pp. 32–33)

The 438-page report is divided into various sections; it starts with the conceptual understanding of the notion of national citizenship and how the idea of citizenship has travelled in India from the constituent assembly debates to the enactment and subsequent amendments to the Citizenship Act, 1955, and how the present Bill for further amendment has been formulated and with what objectives. This section also documents 30 core suggestions/recommendations drawn from the 9,000 memorandums. This is followed by the documentations of the gist of the important points brought to the notice of the committee at six places that it had visited to collect feedback and insights from the ground.

The JPC deliberated on four core issues at length (pp. 35–82). Three of them were concerning the three amendments proposed by the Bill, that is, (a) exempting six minority religious communities from Afghanistan, Pakistan and Bangladesh from the purview of the definition of 'illegal migrants'; (b) reducing the length of years required to be eligible for citizenship through naturalization for these communities; and

(c) making Overseas Citizen of India (OCI) registration more stringent by adding one more ground for cancellation of the OCI registration. The fourth one was 'The Bill vis-à-vis the Assam Accord'. Out of the four, the JPC examined two issues comprehensively—the first one (pp. 35–52) and the last one (pp. 60–82). The core theme of the first issue was centred on Article 14 of the Constitution which guarantees equality before the law or equal protection by law within the territory of India. The debates between the government and the opponents of the Bill centred on the interpretations of the article. Intention to discriminate against Muslims and violation of Article 14 of the Constitution are the two major criticisms that the Narendra Modi government faces over the CAB that aims to recognize non-Muslim migrants from Bangladesh, Pakistan and Afghanistan who are treated as illegal immigrants under the existing laws. Ironically, the government also defended the Bill by upholding this Article, interpreting it under the principle of *intelligible differentia*.

As the objective of this chapter is to understand Assam's responses to the Bill as well as the encounter with the governments in its protests against the Bill-turned-Act, let us examine Assam's take on the Bill first as is evident from the report with special reference to a few memorandums submitted to the JPC.

Assam's take on the Bill can be read in three sections of the Bill:

1. The gist of the memorandums
2. The gist of the study visits
3. Deliberations on the Bill vis-à-vis the Assam Accord

Before we move to Assam's encounter, let us understand the core logic of the government towards guaranteeing citizenship to the six minority communities within the purview of Article 14 of the Constitution.

The Bill and the Intelligible Differentia

As mentioned already, the primary challenge for the Bill has been the allegation that it violates Article 14 of the Indian Constitution, which guarantees equality before the law or equal treatment by law. The government defended the validity of the Bill on the principle of intelligible differentia as permissible within the provisions of the Constitution.

Accordingly, the government defended the Bill on three main arguments:

The parent countries of the illegal immigrants have a state religion,

The illegal immigrants to be benefited were persecuted for their religious belief,

Article 14 allows a classification that is founded on an intelligible differentia provided differentia has a direct nexus to the object sought to be achieved by the statute in question. This simply means a separate class of people can be created (non-Muslim immigrants in this case) by an enabling law.[33]

Interestingly, the JPC expansively dealt with this issue and concurred that the Bill passes the tests of constitutional validity in its scrutiny. The justification given by the committee was exclusively based on the clarifications received from various departments of the government. Even though the committee consulted with a few experts, the report did not document their opinions comprehensively. The committee noted:

Apprehensions have been raised at some quarters that Article 14 and Article 25 of the Constitution would be violated if the six religious communities are continued to be mentioned in the Bill and it will not stand Judicial Scrutiny. Clarifying the position, the Ministry of Home Affairs have stated that the views of the Ministries of Law and Justice, External Affairs and Overseas Indian Affairs, besides Cabinet Secretariat (R&AW) and Intelligence Bureau were obtained and considered while finalising the Cabinet Note proposing the Amendments. The Legislative Department have clarified that the proposed Amendment Bill will not violate the spirit of Article 14 as it upholds the test of reasonable classification as propounded by a seven Judge Bench of the Supreme Court in the State of West Bengal vs. Anwar Ali Sarkar case (AIR 1952 SC-75).[34]

The JPC appears to have overwhelmed by the clarifications given by the Legislative Department on the constitutional validity of Articles 14 and 25. It noted:

The Legislative Department have further submitted that Article 25 will also not be violated because the proposed Amendment Bill does not in any way affect the right of any person to freely profess, practice and propagate any religion in the Country. The Department of Legal Affairs have submitted that differential treatment does not per se constitute violation of Article 14 of the Constitution. It has been very lucidly explained that any legislation may withstand challenge on the ground of discrimination and violation of Article 14 of the Constitution, in case the classification created by it is founded on an intelligible differentia which distinguishes persons or things that are grouped together from others left out of the group, and that differentia has a rational relation to the object sought to be achieved by the statute in question. The Department have further clarified that the positive concept of equality does not postulate equal treatment of all persons without distinction but rather stresses on equality of treatment in equal circumstances as to similarly situated persons and the Bill appears to have the object of facilitating all such members of minority communities without any discrimination.[35]

On every critical issue that the JPC encountered, it wishfully finally found legitimacy in the opinions and clarifications received from the concerned departments. It is pertinent to mention that it is a necessary requirement on the part of the departments to justify the acts of the political executive. But a committee of the Parliament has no such obligation. The vast majority of views expressed in the report are aimed at bringing legitimacy to the Bill as well as adding more provisions to strengthen the objective of the Bill. Therefore, apart from agreeing 'with the proposed Amendment of Clause (b) of sub Section (1) of Section 2 of the Principal Act', the committee became concerned about removing 'any probable ambiguity and reconciling the proposed Amendments with the Assam Accord' and, accordingly, recommended to add the following proviso in the proposed Amendment of Clause (b) of Subsection (1) of Section 2 of the Principal Act:

> Provided further that on and from the date of commencement of the Citizenship (Amendment) Act, 2019, any proceeding pending against any person referred to in the first proviso shall be abated and such person shall be eligible to apply for naturalisation under Section 6.[36]

How reasonable was the JPC in accepting the justifications offered by the concerned departments of the government? Anupama Roy, an expert on Indian citizenship, minutely analysed the arguments offered by the report and pointed out serious gaps in them.

According to Roy, the JPC accorded legitimacy to the Bill by invoking the 'legislative competence of Parliament, drawn from Article 11 of the Constitution', which empowers the Parliament unrestrained power to make laws on issues concerning citizenship. Roy has reminded that this 'assertion of legislative competence and authority is, however, buttressed by a higher order normative claim drawn from the Constituent Assembly'. She has also pointed out,

> While claiming authority from the constitutional text and the deliberative processes in the Constituent Assembly, the JPC prepared the ground for exceeding the scope of Article 11, justifying the fundamental changes that were being sought through the CAB in the principles underlying citizenship in India. In the process, the JPC took recourse to a self-referential process, abrogating upon itself the responsibility of offering administrative and legal support for violation of constitutional norms.[37]

She has also added,

> It disregards, however, the fact that Parliament's powers of regulating citizenship by law were not restrained by anything laid down in Part II of the Constitution, which deals with citizenship. Article 11, however, does not exclude the constraints that other parts of the Constitution would continue to apply on the law-making powers of Parliament, including, but not confined, to the preamble and fundamental rights provisions.[38]

It could be read from the JPC report that it took recourse to the two standards of evaluation—of intelligibility and reasonableness—drawing the seven-judge bench verdict of the Supreme Court in the *State of West Bengal vs Anwar Ali Sarkar* case (AIR 1952 SC-75). Reading this particular judgment closely, Roy has pointed out that the validity accorded by JPC falls short of the critical comments given by the particular judgment. She notes,

> The criteria of intelligibility of the differentia and the reasonableness of classification, foregrounded by the JPC as protection against judicial scrutiny, can still be prised open for constitutional validation, to ask whether they satisfy both grounds of protection guaranteed by Article 14, that is, protection against discrimination (equality before the law) and protection against the arbitrary exercise of state power (equal protection of the law).[39]

Critically reading the said judgment, Roy has also pointed out that the judgment did not endorse positive discrimination the way it has been interpreted by both the government and the JPC report.

The Bill vis-à-vis the Assam Accord: A Fight for Identity, Language and Culture

In opposing the CAB, 2016, Assam also categorically asserted that neither the issue of citizenship nor foreigners could be discriminated on the basis of religion. Religiosity in citizenship will only violate the very foundation of the secular premises of the Indian Constitution. Such an assertion on the part of forerunners of the agitating groups against the CAB helped in forming loose federations consisting of different outfits. A single federation did not of course emerge. Two important federations have been AASU plus 30 ethnic organizations and that of the platform constituted by 70 nationalist organizations led by KMSS and AJYCP. Another important federation has been the Nagarikatwa Aain Songsudhan Bidheyak Birodhi Mancha (the platform against the Citizenship Act Amendment Bill, 2016), led by eminent intellectual Hiren Gohain, which provided representations to democratic, secular and progressive non-party voices. The formation led by AASU helped in mobilizing both the mainstream Assamese nationalist voices and the voices of the ethnic communities. The platform led by KMSS and AJYCP brought together the voices of the grassroots, particularly the peasantry, forest dwellers as well the victims of erosion and evictions, the core constituents of the KMSS as well as the ethno-national groups inclusive of the East-Bengal-origin Muslim communities. While these two formations led by AASU and KMSS–AJYCP respectively failed to coordinate with each other, the third formation led by Hiren Gohain collaborated with those two formations apart from its attempts to reach out to diverse sections and communities. Taking together, all these formations succeeded in raising unprecedented resistance against the agenda of the current regime towards communalizing the secular entity of citizenship. All these three formations met the All India Congress Committee President Rahul Gandhi on 5 February 2019 as a strategy to prevent the CAB in the Rajya Sabha, which indeed had borne fruits as the government was forced to drop its firm resolve of passing it in the last session of the Parliament. These three formations apart, there have also been a number of other organizations, including the Assam State Employees Council (Asom Rajyik Karmachari Parishad), as well as the Ukil Santha (Advocates' Association), who came out strongly against the Bill. Asom Nagarik Samaj (ANS), a civil society initiative, also provided a liberal democratic space to bring together liberal, secular and moderate voices on the issues of both the NRC and CAB. Taking together, all these formations contributed towards sustaining relative peace in the post-NRC final draft and the final list despite the fact that the resistance failed to transform into electoral outcome in the 2019 parliamentary elections. This important dimension has been missed out by most of the critical commentators on the NRC in Assam.

Assam felt let down not only by the Bill but also the way the JPC started functioning. One of the initiatives undertaken by the JPC was to draw feedback, and insights on the Bill were to invite oral evidence from different stakeholders that included eminent persons and organizations. The JPC was certainly aware of the concerns of the Assamese people and the ethno-tribal communities of Northeast India. However, the committee preferred to start the dialogue with the Bengali Hindu organizations and the Hindu Legal Cell from Assam. On 13 October 2016, four organizations were invited for oral evidence: All Assam Bengali Youth Students Federation, Hindu Legal Cell, Citizens Rights Preservation Council and All India Bengali National Council. On 25 October 2016 too, a few more organizations were invited from Assam, but mostly Bengali organizations. They were the Barak Upatyaka Banga Sahitya O Sanskriti Sammelan, Sammilita Sanskrit Mancha, AASU, AGP, Joint Action Committee for Bengali Refugees and North East Citizens Initiative for Peace and Development. It was only on the last day of presenting oral witnesses that most of the tribal organizations were invited to depose their views.[40] All Assam Bengali Youth Students Federation was invited for the second time to present its oral evidence. It can be seen from the list that the highest number of organizations was from Assam, and the majority of them opposed the Bill. The Bengali organizations, naturally, supported the Bill. A total of 49 individuals and organizations also submitted memorandums through other sources like the MHA, PMO and President's Secretariat. KMSS, the organization that had been in the forefront of the ant-CAB movement, submitted its memorandum through these avenues.

Before we discuss the two core issues the JPC deliberated upon, let me refer back to the gist of the 9,000 memorandums (pp. 18–21 of the JPC report) and that of the field visits (pp. 22–32). The gist of the memorandums is framed into 30 points and out of these, 9 are exclusively related to Assam, which oppose the Bill.[41] Three issues figured as far as Assam is concerned: the sanctity of the Assam Accord, sanctity of the NRC and the rights of the indigenous people. While opposing the CAB, the nationalist organizations consistently defended the NRC and asserted,

> If the NRC is updated as directed by the Hon'ble Supreme Court, the problems of infiltration can be solved to a large extent. Now any disruption and dislocation in the process will further aggravate the problem of infiltration in Assam. If any change in the Citizenship Act is required, it must be done in accordance with the provisions of Assam Accord. Assam should be excluded from the purview of the proposed amendments as an exceptional case.[42]

The gist of field visits is divided into three parts: gist of the visit of Jodhpur, gist of the visit to Ahmedabad and Rajkot, and gist of the visit to Guwahati, Silchar and Shillong. Except for Guwahati, Silchar and Shillong, in the three other places, the study team mostly interacted with the migrants from Pakistan. They informed the committee regarding the discrimination that they encountered in Pakistan on the ground of religion, conversion, untouchability, denial of access to state services, etc. Those were mostly personal narratives. Besides, they pointed out the difficulties faced in India while dealing with the authorities. The core issues they raised were long-term visiting visa instead of pilgrim visa, access to facilities such as drinking water, electricity, gas connections, hospital, BPL/caste certificates, ration card, Aadhaar card, bank account, continuous rental facilities, access to education for the migrant children, allowing medical degree holders to pursue practices and relaxation in the process of acquiring citizenship within the given provisions of the Citizenship Act. The biggest demand they made was the following:

> Ministry of Home Affairs (MHA) have issued instructions to State Governments/UT Administrations on 19.8.2016 to grant various facilities to persons belonging to minority communities in Afghanistan, Bangladesh and Pakistan, namely, Hindus, Sikhs, Buddhists, Jains, Parsis and Christians,

staying in India on Long Term Visa (LTV) such as, permission to take up self employment or doing business, allowing free movement within the State/UT. (excluding Protected/Restricted/Cantonment areas) where they are staying instead of restricting their movement within the place of stay, issue of driving license, etc. It should be ensured that these instructions should be made applicable at the earliest by all concerned functionaries including Reserve Bank of India, Ministry of Law & Justice, RTO and other relevant authorities, so that the migrants can avail the benefits at the earliest as announced. Also the State Government should provide robust executive mechanism accordingly.[43]

In Rajkot and Ahmedabad too, the migrants raised the same sort of issues regarding discrimination in Pakistan based on religion and denial of services in India. On the citizenship issue, they raised the procedural lapses and difficulties and demanded better coordination and relaxations within the given Citizenship Act in the country.[44]

The committee, in its report, took note of the issues raised by the migrants in those areas and appreciated the government for undertaking a number of measures to address their grievances and concerns. It particularly noted the facilities made available under LTV that includes issuing of

Driving License, Pan Card and Aadhar number, permission to open NRO Account, take self-employment, purchase dwelling units, allowing SDMs besides District Magistrates for administering the oath of allegiance, reduction in registration fees for minority community people from Pakistan from Rs. 15,000/- to Rs. 100/- only etc.[45]

Apart from all these, the committee also desired that 'such facilities should continue to be given to the migrants on LTVs so as to assure a normal life for them on the Indian soil.'

The gist of the meetings in Guwahati, Silchar and Shillong has been accumulated into 37 points. Out of these, 30 points (i to xxi and xix to xxxii) document the opposition to the Bill and the remaining 7 points (xxii to xxviii) support the Bill directly or indirectly. Only in one place (xxviii), there is mention of religious persecution in Bangladesh which states,

Hindus have been persecuted in Bangladesh and that is why people from there have moved to settle down in this part of Assam. However, there is no specific data regarding the movement of migrants from Bangladesh during the last five years to settle down in Barak Valley.[46]

Quite a large number of issues have been raised by the opponents to the Bill: the threat to the language, culture and heritage of the ethnic people of Assam; sanctity of the Assam Accord; threat to peace in the post-Assam Accord period; interest of the tribal communities; basic structure of the Constitution; NRC; demographic change; linguistic, religious, indigenous congregation of groups; integrity and security of the North-eastern region, etc. The following two issues came up strongly[47]:

> (xx) The reasons for so much of resentment is due to the fact that Assam is the immediate victim if rehabilitation is given to the Hindus as it has the immediate proximity with Bangladesh. No data is available with the government regarding the number of persons who have been persecuted religiously in Bangladesh. There is mention of only few religions and not Muslim. This Bill, therefore, will not last the judicial scrutiny.

> (xxi) The Bill will create two types of polarisation; one is linguistic and the other is religious. It will destroy the cultural and ethnic fabric of the society. The Bill in the present form and even in amended form should be discouraged.

While in the case of other three contentious issues in the Bill, the JPC validated the proposed amendments through witnesses and evidence mostly drawn from the officials of the concerned ministries of the Union government, in the case of the issues concerning Assam, the committee endeavoured to allay the fears of the people of Assam from any possible adverse effect of the Bill on its language, culture, identity and resources and, therefore, recommended a number of administrative and legislative measures to be undertaken by the government. Let us go through the deliberations.

A number of issues emerged through the deliberations concerning Assam in the JPC report. Important among them are the following:

1. The legal and constitutional sanctity of Section 6A of the Citizenship Act
2. The exact provisions of Section 6A and the possible harmful impact of the proposed Bill on it

3. The gap between the settlements through the Assam Accord and the provisions of Section 6A of the Citizenship Act
4. Reconciling the provisions of Section 6A of the Citizenship Act and the objectives of the Bill
5. Provisions of inclusions of the newly naturalized citizens into the NRC
6. Provisions of exemption for the north-east from the purview of the proposed Bill

Let us examine some of those issues as these emerged through the deliberations in the report.

Assam Accord, Section 6A and the Bill

The Supreme Court of India delivered a judgment on 17 December 2014[48] which laid down a definite timeframe to prepare and publish the updated NRC. This was a combined judgment on three writ petitions filed by Assam Sanmilita Mahasangha and Others (2012); APW (2009) and All Assam Ahom Association and Others (2014). The judgment dealt with two fundamental issues: the constitutional validity of incorporating Clause 6A in the Citizenship Act, 1955, through the 1985 Amendment in accordance with the provisions of the Assam Accord which altered the constitutionally mandated (Article 6) dates of giving citizenship to illegal migrants (first petition of 2012) and updating the NRC 1951 for Assam (second petition, 2009). The said judgment refrained itself from giving any verdict on the first question on the ground that the issues associated with this question 'are substantial questions [which] need to be answered by an appropriate Bench as most of them are substantial questions as to the interpretations of the Constitution' and, therefore, referred it to be decided by a constitution bench for which the judgment laid down 13 questions. In the said judgment, the Court, however, took Section 6A of the Citizenship Act 'deemed to be valid' and took a detailed note of the progress in implementing various clauses of Assam Accord and issued directions to the appropriate authorities to undertake necessary measures to expedite the process.

Out of the 13 questions that the said judgment was referred to be examined by the constitution bench, the following 2 are the core issues:

(i) Whether Section 6A violates Article 355? What is the true interpretation of Article 355 of the Constitution? Would an influx of illegal migrants into a State of India constitute 'external aggression' and/or 'internal disturbance'? Does the expression 'State' occurring in this Article refer only to a territorial region or does it also include the people living in the State, which would include their culture and identity?

(ii) Whether Section 6A violates the basic premise of the Constitution and the Citizenship Act in that it permits Citizens who have allegedly not lost their Citizenship of East Pakistan to become deemed Citizens of India, thereby conferring dual Citizenship to such persons?[49]

The constitution bench is yet to give its verdict on it.

The JPC enquired about the response of the government to the 13 queries raised by the Supreme Court regarding Section 6A. In response, the concerned departments of the government pointed out that any Act of the Legislature can be challenged on two grounds, that is, on the lack of legislative competence and the violation of any of the fundamental rights guaranteed in Part-3 of the Constitution. Section 6A of the Citizenship Act has not been challenged on these two grounds, and, therefore, the Court set aside the contention of the petitioner that Section 6A of the Citizenship Act is unconstitutional.

Now, the vital question was whether there are conflicts between Section 6A and the proposed amendment? The report records the opinion received from the legal department which argues that Section 6A of the Citizenship Act and the proposed amendment deal with two different timeframes, and the objectives of one differ from the other. Hence, there is no inherent conflict between the two. Section 6A of the Principal Act only deals with foreigners who entered India, from Bangladesh into Assam between 1 January 1966 and 24 March 1971. It does not provide for any form of detection, deletion or expulsion of foreigners beyond the said date. The proposed proviso to exempt persons belonging to certain minority communities coming from

Afghanistan, Bangladesh and Pakistan has general application beyond the Assam Accord and is intended to apply to the whole of India. The other issue that drew the attention of the committee was regarding the possible implications for those against whom proceedings have been opened under relevant provisions of the Foreigners Act as per the Assam Accord. On this issue, the government proposed to bring reconciliation by adding appropriate provisions in the proposed amendment. It was argued that

> To remove any probable ambiguity, we may reconcile the stipulations of the notifications with the Assam Accord by incorporating a provision that where any proceeding pending against any person referred to in the proposed proviso to clause (b) of sub Section (1) of Section 2 shall be abated and such persons shall be entitled to apply for citizenship by naturalisation under Section 6 of the Citizenship Act.[50]

While endorsing the views of the various ministries and departments, the committee suggested that the anxieties of the people and communities need to be addressed for which it suggested that 'the State and Central Governments should formulate rules and regulations under this Clause (6A) to ensure that the identities of indigenous peoples are not threatened in any way by unintended consequences of the Citizenship Bill.'[51] There were questions regarding how to bring reconciliation between the updated NRC and the migrants who are to be awarded citizenship beyond the cut-off date through the amendment. Government suggested that 'amendment may also include a special provision that the names of persons who are naturalised may automatically find place in NRC of Assam or in the respective registers of respective States.'[52]

The committee, while rejecting the MHA contention that there had been/will be no impact on Assam's demographic composition due to the influx from Bangladesh as well as due to the granting of citizenship under the proposed amendment, suggested that the

> Re-settlement packages and compensation to the State Governments, as provided by the Central Government for accommodating the migrants should motivate and encourage the State Government to help settle such migrants especially in places which are not densely populated, thus, causing

lesser impact on the demographic changes and providing succour to the indigenous Assamese people.[53]

The government, while enacting the Bill into Act, has finally added Section 6B (1–4) to ensure that any proceeding standing against the identified migrants stands abated and certain exceptions are accorded to certain communities and areas of Northeast India. The exemptions have been accorded under Section 6B (4) which reads: 'Nothing in this section shall apply to the tribal area of Assam, Meghalaya, Mizoram or Tripura as included in the Sixth Schedule to the Constitution and the area covered under "The Inner Line" notified under the Bengal Eastern Frontier Regulation, 1873.'[54] The home minister declared in the Rajya Sabha on 11 December that Manipur has been added in ILP system along with Arunachal Pradesh, Nagaland and Mizoram, where the CAB will not be applicable.

PROTESTS AFTER THE ENACTMENT OF THE ACT

The discontent of the people in Assam was already building up just before the Bill was passed in the Parliament. More than four years of protests against the Bill had fallen on deaf ears. The composition of the anti-CAB movement had also transformed. Two outfits—AASU and KMSS—were spearheading the anti-CAB protests in the state, and they continued to be in the forefront. However, towards building up the wave of protests just ahead of the passing of the Bill, the movements almost took a spontaneous turn. This time the initial lead was taken by the students' communities. The students' unions of three state universities—Cotton University, Dibrugarh University and Gauhati University—registered unprecedented protests which had also been joined by the students of Tezpur University, a central university in the state. Writers and artists also came out on the street, forcing many artists affiliated to the BJP to resign and join back in the people's protests. Protesting against the CAB, Jahnu Barua, the National Award-winning filmmaker, withdrew his film from the 8th Assam State Film Awards and the year's film festival scheduled to be held in Guwahati.[55] The Gauhati University Teachers' Association

(GUTA) brought out a protest march on 6 December 2019 against CAB. Dibrugarh University Teachers' Association (DUTA) also did the same. Protesting against the silence of the Assam College Teachers' Association (ACTA) over CAB, many college units declared their withdrawal of membership from the association. The outrage forced ACTA to take an anti-CAB stand. On 10 December 2019, the day after the CAB was passed in Lok Sabha, AASU and NESO called for an 11-hour bandh which almost paralysed the entire Brahmaputra Valley and many other parts of Northeast India. On 11 December 2019, the day Bill was debated and passed in the Rajya Sabha, Assam witnessed vigorous protests throughout the state, particularly in the Guwahati city. Paramilitary forces were deployed in the city, but the protestors stopped the regular lives in the city. Assam Secretariat was blocked by the protesters, forcing all ministers and officials to remain absent in their offices. Sporadic violence also erupted. In the evening, curfew was imposed in the city and other places of the state, which was subsequently extended for an indefinite period. Internet services were withdrawn from the evening on 11 December in 10 districts in the pretext 'to prevent "misuse" of social media to disturb peace and tranquillity and to maintain law and order'.[56] But the real objective was to prevent publicity of the protesters through social media. Amid curfew, on 12 December, thousands of people gathered in Latashil Field at the centre of the city to register the protests against the CAB-turned-CAA. The seriousness of the situation forced the Government of India to postpone the India–Japan summit, which was scheduled to take place in Guwahati on 15–17 December and to be attended by Indian Prime Minister Narendra Modi and Japanese Prime Minister Shinzo Abe. The visit of Indian Home Minister to the North Eastern Police Academy in Shillong was cancelled due to the ongoing protests. There had been attacks on police and destruction of public properties. Five persons were succumbed to death in police firing amid the anti-CAA protests.[57] There were reports of lathi charges and the use of tear gas from different places. Casting doubts on the ability of the Assam Police to deal with the law and order situation, the Union government deputed a non-Assamese police official in the rank of ADGP to the state.

Meanwhile, the government tried to bring division in the ongoing resistance by targeting select organizations, particularly the KMSS. Its rank and file, including main leader Akhil Gogoi, were arrested. Akhil Gogoi, initially arrested in Jorhat by Assam Police, was arrested by National Investigation Agency (NIA) on 17 December allegedly for having Maoist links. The agency failed to file the charge sheet against Akhil Gogoi within the permissible timeframe of 90 days, and he was granted bail by the special NIA court.[58] The agency appealed for the stay of the order in Gauhati High Court which was not immediately entertained. But Assam Police arrested him immediately after the bail. Altogether, 13 cases have been slapped on him. Apart from the Jorhat and NIA cases, The FIRs were filed between 11 and 13 December for his anti-CAB-turned-CAA protests. Apart from the two cases cited above, he was arrested in a crime branch case in Guwahati, a case in Teok thana in the Jorhat district in which he got anticipatory bail, two cases in the Sivasagar district, total six cases in Chabua thana alone in which he got anticipatory bail in one case, and one case in Dibrugarh. His three colleagues Dhaoirjya Konwar, Manas Konwar and Bitu Sonowal were arrested on a number of cases mostly in Guwahati. Akhil Gogoi was granted bail in most of the cases except for the case by NIA on which he was granted bail by NIA special court but subsequently the order of the NIA special court was stayed by the Gauhati High Court.[59] The cases against him were overlapping. For example, on 28 March, he was granted bail in a case registered in Sivasagar. On the very day, he was shown arrest in a case registered in Chabua thana in Dibrugarh district. The shown arrest practice serves to seek custody of persons without physically producing them before courts. Immediately after he was granted bail in a case registered in Dibrugarh thana on 31 March, he was arrested again in the case registered in Chabua thana for which he was shown arrest on 28 March 2020. On 11 July 2020, Mr Gogoi was tested positive for COVID-19 while in the Guwahati Central Jail and was subsequently shifted to Gauhati Medical College and Hospital (GMCH) for treatment. An interesting aspect of the situation is that whereas most of the nationalist organizations in Assam, including AASU and AJYCP, came out to the street and mobilized people against CAB-turned-CAA, the government targeted only the

KMMS for the act of resistance. In a very comprehensive interview to The Wire,[60] the then General Secretary of AASU Mr Lurinjyoti Gogoi pointed out that Akhil Gogoi was arrested to scare the resistance forces in the state, including the AASU.

CHALLENGING THE ACT IN THE COURT

The Supreme Court was flooded with petitions against CAA immediately after its enactment. Among the petitioners included Rashtriya Janata Dal (RJD) leader Manoj Jha, TMC MP Mahua Moitra, All India Majlis-e-Ittehadul Muslimeen (AIMIM) leader Asaduddin Owaisi, Muslim body Jamiat Ulama-i-Hind, AASU, Peace Party, CPI, NGOs Rihai Manch and Citizens Against Hate, advocate M. L. Sharma, Indian Union Muslim League (IUML) and Congress leader Jairam Ramesh and the opposition Congress leaders of Assam. On 18 December 2019, a bench headed by Chief Justice S. A. Bobde heard a batch of 143 petitions and issued notice to the Centre for its response.[61]

The IUML sought an interim stay on the operation of CAA and the Foreigners Amendment (Order), 2015, and Passport (Entry into India) Amendment Rules, 2015. The petition by the organization had alleged that the government's CAA was against the basic structure of the Constitution and intended to explicitly discriminate against Muslims, as the Act extended benefits only to Hindus, Sikhs, Buddhists, Jains, Parsis and Christians. The petition filed by Congress leader Jairam Ramesh termed the Act a 'brazen attack' on core fundamental rights envisaged under the Constitution and treats 'equals as unequal'. His plea also alleged that

> The impugned Act creates two classifications, viz, classification on basis of religion and the classification on the basis of geography and both the classifications are completely unreasonable and share no rational nexus to the object of the impugned Act i.e., to provide shelter, safety and citizenship to communities who in their native country are facing persecution on grounds of religion.[62]

The Supreme Court bifurcated the petitions against CAA into two groups—one concerning Assam and Tripura and another concerning the Act in general—and gave the Centre four weeks to reply. 'The Supreme Court also restrained High Courts from passing any order on the Citizenship (Amendment) Act. The Supreme Court said it may refer pleas challenging the validity of the Citizenship Amendment Act to a larger Constitution bench, consisting of five justices.'[63]

In its preliminary affidavit, the Union government asserted that 'only parliament has got sovereign powers to legislate on citizenship.' The affidavit also pointed out that 'under Article 246 of the Constitution, the parliament has got the exclusive power to make laws with respect to any matters listed in the list One in 7th schedule, in that, item 17 is to do with citizenship and naturalisation of aliens.' The affidavit further asserted, 'The CAA does not impinge upon any existing rights of a citizen. It won't affect the legal, democratic or secular rights of people.'[64]

By mid-March 2020, India plunged into the COVID-19 epidemic. With the series of lockdowns and containment measures, the street protests had gradually disappeared. The focus of the media also shifted to the epidemic. This helped the government to regain popular legitimacy to an extent. But ironically, the government missed the deadline of finalizing the rules of CAA for its implementation. There are confusions regarding the date of expiry; some reports suggested that it expired on 18 June 2020, and some sources say that it expired on 10 July 2020. However, what is certain is that the time has expired. Under these circumstances, the government will have to seek permission from the presiding officer of the Lok Sabha for an extension for the notifications. After the finalization of the rules, those will be placed before both the houses of the Parliament. But there are critical issues.

> According to the parliamentary system, the subordinate legislation committee of the Parliament will scrutinise the rules to vet whether these were framed in conformity with the Act notified in the (official) gazette. There were instances in the past of subordinate legislation committee objecting to the rules and the government complying with the recommendations.[65]

In early August 2020, it was reported that the Home Ministry sought three months' extension to frame the rules while responding to the query from the parliamentary committee on subordinate legislation.[66]

Fragmenting the Resistance: Drifting Away of ABSU

The Act, in the pretext of protecting the rights of the indigenous people, exempted the Sixth Schedule areas and the states under ILP in Northeast India from the purview of the Act. However, the Brahmaputra Valley, epicentre of the anti-CAB-turned-anti-CAA resistance remained under the purview of the Act. The Act brought divisions among the federating units of the civic resistance forces as many ethno-tribal organizations, particularly ABSU, immediately drifted away from this resistance. The Government of India signed a tripartite agreement with the Bodo civil society groups and all factions of the NDFB and the state government on 27 January 2020 in New Delhi in the presence of the Union home minister and Assam chief minister. Through the agreement, the government promised to upgrade the BTC to BTR with added provisions, including the increase of members of the present council. After three days of the signing of the accord, the grand ceremony of the surrender of arms by the NDFB factions took place in the GMCH auditorium. It was the first brave public show in the aftermath of the violence in Guwahati around the anti-CAA resistance. It was also attended by the chief minister of Assam. This was followed by the huge rally addressed by the prime minister of India in Kokrajhar on 7 February 2020 to celebrate the signing of the accord. The prime minister called the day as 'a new beginning in the 21st century, a new dawn, a new inspiration'. He also said that a foundation had been laid down to 'welcome a peaceful Assam, a New Resolute India'.[67] This was a significant development as the scheduled summit between the prime minister of India and his Japanese counterpart in Guwahati in December 2019 had to be cancelled due to the anti-CAA protests. All these signified a gradual grip of the government over the law and order situation in the state.

CONSTITUTIONAL SAFEGUARDS FOR ASSAMESE PEOPLE: ANOTHER BETRAYAL?

While taking part in the debate on CAB in the Rajya Sabha on 11 December 2019, Union Home Minister Amit Shah stated, 'Clause Six will take care of all your concerns. I would like to urge the

Clause Six Committee; please send the report as soon as possible.' He also said, 'I want to assure all the original residents of Assam that this BJP government will ensure that all your rights are protected. There should not be even an iota of doubt on this.'[68] It may be mentioned that the Home Ministry formed a 9-member high-level committee on 7 January 2019 under the chairmanship of retired Union Secretary M. P. Bezbaruah. However, due to the vehement protests, most of the members, including the chairman, Mr Bezbaruah, refused to be part of the committee and, therefore, the committee automatically got dissolved. The Union Home Ministry formed a 13-member new committee on 15 July 2019 under the chairmanship of a retired judge of Gauhati High Court, Biplab Kumar Sharma, with the joint secretary of the MHA (North-East Division) as its member secretary. The committee was given six months to submit the report.[69] Through another notification of the MHA dated 30 July 2019, Professor Mrinal Miri was included as the 14th member of the committee. Through another notification issued on 14 January 2020, the committee was given one-month extension for submitting the report. Total six terms of references (ToRs; 2a to f) were laid down for the committee towards suggesting measures on the implementation of Clause 6. The said clause of the Assam Accord mandates that the 'Assamese people' would be granted 'constitutional, legislative and administrative safeguards, as may be appropriate' to 'protect, preserve and promote the cultural, social, linguistic identity and heritage'.[70] The committee was also asked to consult a slew of stakeholders 'including social organisations, legal and constitutional experts, eminent persons from the fields of art, culture and literature, conservationists, economists, linguists and sociologists' to determine the appropriate level of reservation of seats in the state assembly and local bodies for the 'Assamese people'.[71]

The 141-page report was finalized and signed by the chairman and the members on 10 February 2020 and was supposed to be submitted to the home minister on 11 February 2020. The member secretary, Satyendra K. Garg, whose name was placed on the left side of the first row of the signatories and opposite to the Chairman Justice Sharma's name, did not sign the report. One of the members revealed that the chairman wrote to the Home Ministry three times asking about the procedure of submission to which no reply was received. Under these circumstances, the committee was compelled to submit the report to the chief minister of Assam on 25 February 2020. Three AASU members of the committee refrained from taking part in the delega- tion that submitted the report. The committee remained unaware of whether the report was received by the Home Ministry or not. The member, while expressing disappointment over these developments, suggested that the report should now be made available to public institutions like universities so that they may be the custodian of the report and make it available for research. Otherwise, he feared, the report may even go missing.[72] Samujjwal Bhattacharya, AASU adviser and a member of the committee, said on 25 July that it was not yet clear whether the chief minister handed over the report to the Home Ministry or not even after the elapse of five months after receiving the report.[73] It was under these circumstances that on 11 August 2020 the AASU released the report through a press meet and elaborated the important recommendations of the committee.[74] The AASU leadership claimed that the people of Assam have every right to know the details of the report of the committee constituted by the Union Home Ministry on the implementation of Clause 6 of the Assam Accord. After a few hours of the release of the report, the chief minister stated that his government was committed towards the implementation of Clause 6 of the accord, but termed the action of AASU as 'very unfortunate'.[75]

The report is divided into nine chapters and includes five annex- ures. The discussion on the core ToRs laid down by the notification of the MHA dated 15 July 2019 covers 75 pages of the report—from pages 5 to 79.[76]

The most contentious issue for the constitutional safeguards as mandated by Clause 6 of the Assam Accord has been the definition of the 'Assamese people'. In 2015, the issue generated widespread debates when the then speaker of the Assam Legislative Assembly, Pranab Gogoi, took an initiative to define it for Clause 6. However, in the process of exploring the definition, the very terminology of 'Assamese people' got transformed into 'indigenous people of Assam'.

It happened so in the context of gross discontent among the ethnic tribal communities refusing to accept the tag 'Assamese', as 'Assamese' is a distinct linguistic entity, and insistence on the terminology would only deprive them of enjoying the benefits of the constitutional safeguards provided under Clause 6. After a series of discussions with the AASU, AJYCP, leading ethnic organizations and literary outfits, Gogoi offered the following definition in a report submitted to the Assam Legislative Assembly on 31 March 2015: 'Indigenous person of Assam means a person belonging to the state of Assam and speaking the Assamese language or any tribal dialect of Assam or, in case of Cachar, the language of the region.' The report by the speaker suggested that the year 1951 be considered as the cut-off date and the NRC, 1951, be taken as the basis for defining Assamese people 'for the purpose of reservation of seats and constitutional safeguards as required by the Assam Accord.'[77] The ruling Congress and the opposition AIUDF opposed the definition, while the BJP and nationalist organizations, including the AASU, hailed it.

The committee headed by Justice Sharma also pursued the issue and, drawing from the suggestions and feedback received from the stakeholders, proffered that 'Assamese people' for the specific purpose of Clause 6 of the Assam Accord

> shall be construed as including (1) All citizens of India who are part of (i) *Assamese Community* or (ii) Any *Indigenous Tribal Community of Assam* or (iii) *Any other indigenous community of Assam* or (iv) *All other citizens of India* 'residing in the Territory of Assam on or before 01.01.1951'. *and* (v) *Descendants of the above categories.*[78]

The pertinent question here is: Why 1951? On what grounds two categories of citizens have been created—one with the constitutional safeguards and the other without those safeguards? The committee has provided the following explanation:

> It needs to mention that the underlying philosophy of the Assam Accord seeks to provide a fine balance between the interests of the Assamese people and of regularization of the migrants from erstwhile East Pakistan until *March 24, 1971 vide Clauses 5.1 to 5.3 of the Accord.* It would only be fair therefore that *Clause 6* in striking the balance would be applicable only to

the 'Assamese people' so as to maintain the demographic integrity of the State of Assam and preserve, promote and protect the cultural, social, economic and political rights of its indigenous people. Following this rationale, the Committee is of the view that the safeguards envisaged under Clause 6 of the Assam Accord shall not be applicable for any future categories *post March 24, 1971*, who are to be deported.[79]

It may be noted that in ToR 2(c), the committee was asked 'to assess the appropriate level of reservation of seats in Assam Legislative Assembly and local bodies for the Assamese people'. But the committee exceeded this mandate and suggested reservations in the Parliament and jobs under different agencies. While doing this, it took recourse to ToR 2(f), which mandates that 'the Committee may suggest any other measures as may be necessary to protect, preserve and promote cultural, social, linguistic identity and heritage of the Assamese people.' Accordingly, the committee identified and recommended the following:

(i) Reservation of seats in the Parliament; (ii) reservation in employment in Central Government, Semi-central government, Central PSUs and Private Sector jobs and (iii) protection of land rights of 'Assamese People'. During discussion, the Committee was of the view that without these rights, other rights and protections traceable to the main *Terms of Reference and Clause 6* will remain woefully under articulated.[80]

Notably, while the committee recommended reserving 80 per cent seats in the Assam Legislative Assembly and local bodies for the 'Assamese people' including the already existing reservations, the members of AASU in the committee demanded the reservation of 100 per cent seats for the Assamese people in those bodies excluding the seats already reserved for the ST/SC communities. The committee 'unequivocally' recorded the view.[81]

The committee justifies its recommendation on the ground that 'had there not been large scale immigration to the state of Assam over the years, 100 per cent seats in Assam Legislative Assembly would have been occupied by the representatives of the 'Assamese People' for all time to come.'[82] It also points out that as immigrants from Bangladesh (erstwhile Pakistan) have been granted citizenship as per the provisions of the Assam Accord, causing demographic changes at the cost of the 'Assamese people', therefore,

> The quantum of seats in Assam Legislative Assembly represented by *'Assamese people'* should be such that those representatives will have the final and controlling say in the Assembly in respect of the major decisions pertaining to the State and the *'Assamese People'* in the areas of their culture, language and identity.[83]

Concerning ToR 2(f) that asks for 'other measures to protect, preserve and promote the cultural, social, linguistic identity and heritage of the Assamese people', the committee recommended that at least 80 per cent of seats in the Parliament allotted to the state, including the constituencies reserved for scheduled categories, be reserved for the 'Assamese people'.[84] It also called for reserving 80 per cent of Group C- and Group D-level posts under Central/semi-Central government/ Central PSUs/private sector, including establishments under PPP mode that are located in Assam.[85] The most critical recommendation under the said ToR is about the implementation of the Assam Accord of 1985. The report categorically states,

> The Assam Accord is yet to be fully and effectively implemented even after 35 years of its signing. It is felt that complete implementation of all Clauses of Assam Accord especially Clauses 5.1 to 5.9, Clauses 7, 10 and 11 are essential for the safeguards to be provided under Clause 6 of the Assam Accord.[86]

It may be mentioned that Clause 5.8 of the Assam Accord states, 'Foreigners who came to Assam on or after March 25, 1971 shall continue to be detected, deleted and practical steps shall be taken to expel such foreigners.'

While recommending to strengthen measures to detect foreigners in the state as per the provisions of the Assam Accord as well as to undertake diplomatic initiatives with the Government of Bangladesh for the deportation of all 'declared foreigners post 1971 stream to Bangladesh', the committee also suggested that 'till such deportation is completed, as an interim measure, the post 1971 stream should be resettled in areas outside the State of Assam' as Assam has already taken the burden of the foreigners of the 1951–1971 stream.[87] These recommendations challenge the fundamental objectives of the CAA, 2019.

Exceptions may be there for industrialization, construction of highways and other such activities to be undertaken by the Central and state governments. But without land rights along with political rights, the full implementation of Clause 6 of the Assam Accord will only be a futile exercise. The committee believes that Section 8 of the Assam Agricultural Land (Regulation of Reclassification and Transfer for Non-agricultural Purpose) Act, 2015, negates the objectives sought to be achieved by the Act and allows the conversion of agricultural land for non-agricultural purposes. The committee suggested for necessary amendments to the said section and adding penalty provision for violating the basic spirit of the Act. The committee also recommended a few more suggestions, including a time-bound programme for granting *patta* to the 'Assamese people' who are in occupation of land for decades but without land documents. Freeing wetlands, professional grazing reserve (PGR) and village grazing reserve (VGR) from encroachment and protecting them from further encroachment; surveying of *char* areas and treating newly created *char* areas as government land for the rehabilitation of erosion-affected people or for agriculture and other activities; and statutory provisions towards prohibiting the transfer of tea plantation land for any other use without the permission of the state government are some other recommendations of the committee. The committee also concurred its approval to the recommendation of the Brahma Committee[88] to exempt the tribal belt and block land from the provisions of Assam State Capital Region Development Authority Act, 2017.[89]

In Annexure V (pp. 127–141), the committee lays down the detailed suggestions for appropriate constitutional/legislative amendments to provide the constitutional safeguards for 'Assamese people'. Most important among them is the suggestion for amending Article 371 of the Constitution of India to insert special provisions, that is, Article 371B 'with respect to the state of Assam in matters connected with the Assam Accord' to guarantee constitutional safeguards. A detailed structure of the proposed amendment has been framed, which includes the definition of 'Assamese people'; provisions for the reservation of seats in the Parliament, Assam Legislative Assembly and local bodies; and reservations of employment in Central, state and private sectors and the structure of the Legislative Council. The related Articles that will necessitate amendments have also been mentioned. Under legislative safeguards, the necessary amendments to various sections of the Representation of the People (RoP) Act, 1950; Section 11 of the Assam Municipal Act, 1956; and Amendment to the Assam Panchayat Act, 1994 have been recommended in detail. The committee also recommended the introduction of ILP for Assam. Full details of a chapter titled 'Protected Areas and Protected Antiquities' to be incorporated by amending the Assam Ancient Monuments and Records Act, 1959, have been laid down in the report.

Taking together, it is a comprehensive report that addresses the aspirations of the 'Assamese people'. But the recommendations are too strong for the incumbent governments. The implementation of its core recommendations will mean exempting Assam from the purview of the CAA. Besides, whereas the Union government sought to dilute Clause 5 of the Assam Accord by offering benefits through Clause 6, the committee asserted the primacy of Clause 5 and even suggested making Assam free from the burden of the post-1971 streams of immigrants from Bangladesh. Its definition of what constitutes 'Assamese people', if accepted, will only undo the political objectives behind CAA.

After the report was made public by the AASU, Assam's Finance Minister and NEDA Convener Himanta Biswa Sarma reacted along an expected line. He appeared to have taken AASU's act lightly and said that the organization was now a political party.[90] "'They are going to form a new political party. So they would definitely say that the government has a lack of goodwill in the implementation of Clause 6 of the Assam Accord,'" he stated.[91] He pointed out that only the Legislative Assembly can fix the definition of 'Assamese people': 'The Assam Assembly only can fix the definition of Assamese. There is no role of the Centre. Until the definition of Assamese is determined in the Assam Assembly, the Centre has nothing to do over Clause 6 of the Assam Accord.'[92] Sarma also indicated that the definition provided by the 12 members of the committee could not be final. In other words, he asserted the primacy of the legislature over the Union government on implementing the recommendations of the high-powered committee constituted by the Union home minister.

He casually stated, 'The state government will take recommendations of the high-level committee in someday. After the debates or in the later phases after determination of the definition of Assamese, the Centre will be able to enter it.'[93] Sarma also questioned the procedure of identifying the 'Assamese people' as defined by the committee, as there is no mention of the documents to be used to determine whether a person came to Assam before or after 1951. These reactions and the casual attitude of the state and Central governments towards the report signal that they have no intention of taking the report seriously even for consideration. The Chief Minister of Assam Sarbananda Sonowal accompanied by Finance Minister Dr Himanta Biswa Sarma finally submitted the report to the Union home minister on 20 September 2020 after it had been reported in the Rajya Sabha by Union home minister (State) that the report was under the consideration of the state government. The home minister reportedly asked the chief minister to get the report 'examined by legal experts and determine if there is any need for amendments'.[94] Reacting to this statement, one of the members of the expert committee of the report said that rather than being examined by legal experts it is important to get it examined by social science experts as to understand the greater social implications of the report. He, of course, personally suggested names of three former Supreme Court judges from Assam if the report needed to be examined by legal experts at all.[95]

However, there are larger issues for critical debates. The debates on the CAB and NRC have generated consensus among the 'Assamese people'. They have defended the NRC while consistently opposing the CAB. In the case of the NRC, Assam confronted both the incumbent governments and the human rights advocates and networks from across the globe. For defending the NRC, Assamese people were alleged to be chauvinists. Nonetheless, Assam continued to defend it as a larger political consensus evolved around it across communities and political parties and organizations in the state except for the sections from within the government. But facing criticisms from the international community, the Ministry of External Affairs also unequivocally defended the NRC. There are reservations even within the organizations who steered the movements for the NRC regarding the conspicuously small number of people who have been made ineligible to get registered in the NRC. The original petitioner of the NRC—the APW—called the NRC final document a flawed one. The organization also doubted the credibility of the software used for updating the NRC data.[96] But nobody challenged the NRC as an instrument for political resolutions to the issue of immigrants beyond 24 March 1971. Resistance against CAB contributed towards the larger consensus around the Assam Accord and the NRC.

What will be the reactions on the recommendations on the constitutional safeguards? The human rights networks will be critical about the new hierarchies being drawn within the citizens in the state in this report. It has added new closures rather than facilitating a process to accommodate the 1951–1971 streams of immigrants into the greater Assamese society who have been guaranteed citizenship through the tripartite settlements in the form of the Assam Accord and subsequent amendments to the Citizenship Act, 1955, in 1985. The central logic behind the constitutional safeguards has always been in lieu of accepting the 1951–1971 streams of the immigrants. Otherwise, there was no reason for inserting a clause on constitutional safeguards in the Assam Accord. But the demand for reservations in all domains— from representation to employment opportunities exclusively for the Assamese people as defined in the report—may lead to frictions within the larger society in Assam. By 2021, the immigrants who came to Assam between 1951 and 1971 will complete a period between 70 and 50 years. If a person is deprived of job opportunities even in the private sector despite living in the state for such a long time, the process of assimilation of the 1951–1971 streams of immigrants-turned-citizens into the fabrics of the Assamese society will get hindered. The greater Assamese society must debate it. Constitutional safeguards must incorporate provisions of both closures and encompassments. Political representation and ownership over land reservations for original inhabitants/indigenous communities are acceptable within the purview of the UN guidelines. However, the demands for up to 80 per cent (AASU has demanded reservations up to 100 per cent) reservations of employment opportunities in both public and private institutions exclusively for Assamese people may, in the long run, pose a challenge to the process of building a peaceful, tolerant and accommodative society in Assam.

Besides, too much faith in the political class belonging to the 'Assamese people' as the true custodian of the greater Assamese community or the state of Assam is also too naïve. The political class who defended CAB and CAA and unsettled the political consensus around NRC in the state is also from within the 'Assamese people'. Therefore, while advocating for the constitutional safeguards we should not take every class from within the 'Assamese people' granted. It involves larger political issues including political ideology which we tend to ignore.

CONCLUSION

The debates on and the resistance against the CAB-turned-CAA raise several issues regarding the overall health and the future of the federal democratic polity of India. The way the amendment has been carried through itself signifies the dark side of the parliamentary practices in India. The JPC, which was entrusted with the responsibility of examining and suggesting measures for modifications amid criticisms regarding the move to amend the Citizenship Act, made visits to different parts of the country and conducted public hearings. It also received memorandums from the stakeholders. Although the Assam Accord, 1985, drew due attention from the committee, its final recommendations have primarily been drawn from the suggestions received from the concerned departments of the Union government. Instead of proposing measures to address the apprehensions of the indigenous people of Northeast India, in general, and Assam, in particular, the JPC took recourse to bring divisions within the greater society by suggesting exemptions for certain communities and regions, compromising the federal question in the process. The 1985 amendment to the Citizenship Act, 1955, was based on a tripartite consensus, that is, the Assam Accord which involved the Union government, state government and the leadership of the anti-foreigner movement. In the case of the present amendment, which undermines the consensus arrived through the Assam Accord to grant citizenship to only the 1951–1971 stream of illegal migrants, neither the state government nor the greater civil society was taken into confidence. The state government was reduced to an entity to deal with only the law and order situation. The continuous campaign for the CAB-turned-CAA has its long-term implications on the social and communal harmony in the greater society. The way the Union government handled the report on Clause 6 of the Assam Accord prepared by a committee appointed by the MHA is a glaring example of gross indifference and insensitivity of the over-centralized federal polity. These attitudes will deepen the sense of deprivations of the people in Northeast India and may give rise to more obsessive tendencies. All these will drive away people's attention from the substantive issues concerning life and livelihoods and help the incumbent governments to consolidate its Hindutva agenda at the cost of a possible peaceful, harmonious and prosperous society.

NOTES

1. The unprecedented wave of resistance against CAB in Assam before the 2019 Parliamentary elections had no negative impact on the electoral fortunes of the BJP in Assam.
2. Anupama Roy, 'Between Encompassment and Closure: The "Migrant" and the Citizen in India', *Contributions to Indian Sociology* 42, no. 2 (2008): 219.
3. Ibid., 220.
4. Ibid., 221.
5. Sangeeta Barooah Pisharoty, 'Citizenship and Assam: An Explainer on the Legal Questions That Still Loom Large', The Wire, 25 November 2019, https://thewire.in/rights/citizenship-and-assam-the-legal-questions-that-still-loom-large.
6. Pratap Bhanu Mehta, 'A BJP-dominant System', *Indian Express*, 20 May 2016, https://indianexpress.com/article/opinion/columns/bjp-assam-elections-sarbananda-sonowal-tarun-gogoi-kerala-elections-2809631/.
7. Hiren Gohain, 'The Assamese People Do Not Really Know the Guests That They Have Welcomed with Open Arms', The Wire, 20 May 2016, https://thewire.in/politics/the-assamese-do-not-really-know-the-guests-they-have-welcomed-with-open-arms.
8. Ibid.
9. Ibid.
10. *The Indian Express*, 'Assam: Intellectuals Appeal to Vote against BJP Kicks Up Row', 3 April 2016, https://indianexpress.com/article/elections-2016/india/india-news-india/assam-intellectuals-appeal-against-bjp-kicks-up-row/.
11. Ibid.
12. Himanta Biswa Sarma, *Bhinna Samay Abhinna Mat* (Guwahati: Saraswati Printers, 2019), 51.

13. Akhil Ranjan Dutta, 'BJP's Consolidation, AIUDF's Polarization, and Congress Defeat in Assam', in *India's 2014 Elections: A Modi-led BJP Sweep*, ed. Paul Wallace (New Delhi: SAGE Publications, 2015), 381–403.

14. This was the statement that echoed the sentiments of the Assamese people and made him dear to their hearts. He repeated the statement in both Assam and West Bengal. Source: NDTV, 'Come May 16, Bangladeshi Immigrants Must Pack Up: Narendra Modi', 22 September 2015, https://www.ndtv.com/elections-news/come-may-16-bangladeshi-immigrants-must-pack-up-narendra-modi-559164.

15. NDTV, 'Hindu Migrants from Bangladesh Must Be Accommodated: Narendra Modi', 22 January 2014, https://www.ndtv.com/india-news/hindu-migrants-from-bangladesh-must-be-accommodated-narendra-modi-551611.

16. Ministry of Home Affairs, Government of India, *The Gazette of India*, Extraordinary (2015) F. No. 25022/50/2015-F.I & [F. No. 25022/50/2015-F.I], https://indianfrro.gov.in/frro/Notifications_dated_7.9.2015.pdf.

17. *The Assam Tribune*, 'AASU Flays Governor's Comment on Assam Accord', 10 September 2015, http://www.assamtribune.com/scripts/detailsnew.asp?id=sep1015/at052.

18. *The Assam Tribune*, 'AGP against Staying Rights to Hindu Migrants', 11 September 2015, http://www.assamtribune.com/scripts/detailsnew.asp?id=sep1115/at053.

19. *The Assam Tribune*, '12-hour Bandh Cripples Life in Assam, Hundreds Arrested', 12 September 2015, http://www.assamtribune.com/scripts/details-new.asp?id=sep1215/at042.

20. The 24 districts visited by the MHA officials on the issue of citizenship were Indore and Bhopal in Madhya Pradesh; Nagpur, Thane, Mumbai, Pune, Amravati and Jalgaon in Maharashtra; Ahmedabad, Surat, Kutch, Rajkot, Patan, Banskantha and Gandhinagar in Gujarat; Raipur in Chhattisgarh; Lucknow in Uttar Pradesh; Jodhpur, Jaisalmer and Barmer in Rajasthan; Sirsa in Haryana; and Bangalore, Krishna and Karwar in Karnataka. Source: *The Assam Tribune*, 'Long-term Visas for Hindu Bengalis Likely', 12 September 2015, http://www.assamtribune.com/scripts/detailsnew.asp?id=sep1215/at052.

21. The 14 districts visited by the MHA officials concerning LTV were Indore and Bhopal in Madhya Pradesh; Mumbai, Pune and Nagpur in Maharashtra; Ahmedabad and Gandhinagar in Gujarat; Jodhpur, Jaisalmer and Barmer in Rajasthan; Lucknow in Uttar Pradesh; and Bangalore, Krishna and Karwar in Karnataka. Source: Ibid.

22. *The Assam Tribune*, 'Centre Yet to Formulate Plans on Settlement', 14 September 2015, http://www.assamtribune.com/scripts/detailsnew.asp?id=sep1415/at050.

23. *The Assam Tribune*, 'VK Singh Calls for End to Controversy', 17 September 2015, http://www.assamtribune.com/scripts/detailsnew.asp?id=sep1715/at052.

24. *The Assam Tribune*, 'AASU Asks Parties to Clarify Stand', 4 October 2015, www.http://www.assamtribune.com/scripts/detailsnew.asp?id=oct0415/at050.

25. *The Assam Tribune*, 'Amit Shah Kicks Off BJP Poll Campaign', 28 November 2015, http://www.assamtribune.com/scripts/detailsnew.asp?id=nov2815/at051.

26. *The Assam Tribune*, 'Centre May Delegate Power to States', 3 December 2015, http://www.assamtribune.com/scripts/detailsnew.asp?id=dec0315/at053.

27. *The Assam Tribune*, 'PM Assures Bodos Development, Avoids Statehood', 19 January 2016, http://www.assamtribune.com/scripts/detailsnew.asp?id=jan1916/at044.

28. *The Assam Tribune*, 'AASU Moves Modi for Constitutional Safeguards', 20 January 2016, http://www.assamtribune.com/scripts/detailsnew.asp?id=jan2016/at053.

29. *The Economic Times*, 'Government Sets Up Panel to Implement Clause 6 of Assam Accord', 7 January 2019, https://economictimes.indiatimes.com/news/politics-and-nation/government-sets-up-panel-to-implement-clause-6-of-assam-accord/articleshow/67414320.cms.

30. Narendra Modi, 'PM Modi Addresses a Public Rally in Silchar Assam', 4 January 2019, https://www.narendramodi.in/pm-modi-addresses-public-meeting-at-silchar-assam-542897.

31. The Wire, 'Six of Nine Members Refuse To Be Part of Centre's Committee on Assam Accord', 11 January 2019, https://thewire.in/government/five-of-nine-members-refuse-to-be-part-of-centres-committee-on-assam-accord.

32. Lok Sabha Secretariat, 'Report of the Joint Committee on the Citizenship (Amendment) Bill, 2016', 7 January 2019, https://www.prsindia.org/sites/default/files/bill_files/Joint%20committee%20report%20on%20citizenship%20%28A%29%20bill.pdf.

33. Ibid.

34. Lok Sabha Secretariat, 'Report of the Joint Committee', 50–51.

35. Ibid., 51.

36. Ibid., 52.

37. Anupama Roy, 'The Citizenship (Amendment) Bill, 2016 and the Aporia of Citizenship', *Economic & Political Weekly* 54, no. 49 (14 December 2019): 30, https://www.epw.in/system/files/pdf/2019_54/49/PE_LIV_49_141219_Anupama_Roy.pdf.

38. Ibid., 31.

39. Ibid., 32.

40. On the day ADSU, All Assam Moran Students' Union (AAMSU), All Assam Sonowal Kachari Students' Union (AASKSU), All Adivasi Students' Association (AASA), Karbi Students Union (KSU), All Assam Karbi Students' Association (AAKSA), Sadou Asom Goria–Moria–Deshi Jatiya Parishad (SAGMDJP), All Assam Hajong Student Union (AAHSU), All Tiwa Students'

Union, All Rabha Students' Union, Takam Mising Porin Kebang, All Assam Tribal Youth League (AATYL), All Assam Tribal Sangha (AATS), All Assam Deori Students Union (AADSU), ABSU and All Gorkha Students Union (AGSU) deposed before the JPC.

41. The points are ix, x, xi, xii, xiii, xiv, xv, xvi and xxx, pp. 18–21.
42. Point xi, p. 19.
43. Lok Sabha Secretariat, 'Report of the Joint Committee', 24–25.
44. Ibid., 27.
45. Ibid., 81.
46. Ibid., 31.
47. Ibid., 30.
48. Supreme Court of India, *Assam Sanmilita Mahasangha & Ors vs Union Of India & Ors*, Writ Petition (Civil) No. 562 of 2012; Writ Petition (Civil) No. 274 of 2009 and Writ Petition (Civil) No. 876 of 2014, 17 December 2014, https://indiankanoon.org/doc/50798357/.
49. Ibid.
50. Lok Sabha Secretariat, 'Report of the Joint Committee', 66–67.
51. Ibid., 79.
52. Ibid., 69.
53. Ibid., 80.
54. The Citizenship (Amendment) Act, 2019, No. 47 of 2019, Gazette Notification (Extraordinary), Ministry of Law and Justice, Government of India, http://egazette.nic.in/WriteReadData/2019/214646.pdf.
55. Scroll.in, 'Citizenship Bill Protests: Filmmaker Jahnu Barua Withdraws His Film from Assam Film Festival', 12 December 2019, https://scroll.in/latest/946585/citizenship-bill-protests-filmmaker-jahnu-barua-withdraws-his-film-from-assam-film-festival.
56. *The Times of India*, 'Suspension of Internet in 10 Assam Districts Extended for 48 Hours', 12 December 2019, https://timesofindia.indiatimes.com/india/suspension-of-internet-in-10-assam-districts-extended-for-48-hrs/articleshow/72489742.cms.
57. Anupam Chakravarty, 'How Five People in Assam Were Killed During Anti-Citizenship Amendment Protests', The Wire, 16 December 2019, https://thewire.in/rights/assam-anti-citizenship-amendment-act-protest-deaths.
58. News 18, 'Akhil Gogoi Gets Bail as NIA Fails to File Charge Sheet within 90 Days, but Will Remain in Jail', 17 March 2020, https://www.news18.com/news/india/akhil-gogoi-gets-bail-as-nia-fails-to-file-charge-sheet-within-90-days-but-will-remain-in-jail-2540209.html.
59. Information received from Krishna Gogoi, the advocate hired by Akhil Gogoi, on 25 July 2020.
60. Sangeeta Barooah Pisharoty, 'Akhil Gogoi Was Arrested to Scare Us, Says AASU's General Secretary', The Wire, 23 January 2020, https://thewire.in/politics/aasu-lurinjyoti-gogoi-caa-protest-political-alternative.

61. The Wire, 'Supreme Court Gives Centre 4 Weeks to Respond on CAA Petitions, No Stay on Law', 22 January 2020, https://thewire.in/law/supreme-court-citizenship-amendment-act-hearing.
62. Ibid.
63. The Week, 'CAA: SC "Delinks" Assam, Tripura Pleas from Rest, Gives Centre 4 Weeks to Reply', 22 January 2020, https://www.theweek.in/news/india/2020/01/22/sc-caa-pleas-bench.html.
64. NDTV, 'CAA "Legal, Can't Be Questioned before Court": Centre to Supreme Court', 17 March 2020, https://www.ndtv.com/india-news/citizenship-amendment-act-caa-perfectly-legal-constitutional-cant-be-questioned-before-the-court-gov-2196141.
65. The Wire, 'CAA: Home Ministry Misses Deadline to Finalise Rules, Implementation Likely To Be Delayed', 17 July 2020, https://thewire.in/government/citizenship-amendment-act-caa-mha-deadline-rules.
66. The Hindu, 'Citizenship Amendment Act | Home Ministry Seeks Three More Months to Frame Rules', 2 August 2020, https://www.thehindu.com/news/national/citizenship-amendment-act-home-ministry-seeks-three-additional-months-to-frame-caa-rules/article32253089.ece.
67. Narendra Modi, 'PM Attends Celebrations on Signing of Bodo Accord at Kokrajhar in Assam', 7 February 2020, https://www.narendramodi.in/prime-minister-narendra-modi-participates-in-historic-bodo-agreement-ceremony-in-assam-548324.
68. The Assam Tribune, 'Govt Will Implement Clause 6 Report: Shah', 12 December 2020, http://www.assamtribune.com/scripts/detailsnew.asp?id=dec1219/at059.
69. The other members of the committee are: Dr Romesh Borpatra Gohain, Advocate General, Assam; Subhash Chandra Das, IAS, (Rtd)—both of them were members of the earlier committee too; Shri Nilay Dutta, Advocate General, Arunachal Pradesh; Shri Pallav Bhattacharyya, IPS (Rtd); Dr Srishtidhar Dutta, Professor (Rtd); Shri Sumanta Chaliha, author and columnist; Dr Jaikanta Sharma, professor and columnist; Mr Wasbir Hussain, senior journalist; Dr Samujjwal Bhattacharya, Chief Adviser, AASU; Shri Dipanka Nath, President, AASU; and Shri Lurinjyoti Gogoi, General Secretary, AASU. Joint Secretary, North-East (MHA), was the member secretary of the committee. Source: Ministry of Home Affairs (North-East Division), Notification, New Delhi, 15 July 2019 (No. 11012/04/2019-NE. VI), https://www.mha.gov.in/sites/default/files/filefield_paths/HLC_Clause_6AssamAccord.PDF?fbclid=IwAR1sUOj9A4GOB6kmuLyO9ZOVpKEg6SQCu0EJLrNCxavd8WeehHbyUUHUaDA.
70. Sangeeta Barooah Pisharoty, 'Centre's "High Level" Committee on Assam Accord Meets Amit Shah', 25 July 2019, https://thewire.in/government/committee-clause-6-assam-accord-amit-shah.
71. Ibid.

72. In a personal conversation with Nilay Dutta, Advocate General of Arunachal Pradesh and member of the committee, he revealed these issues. The conversation took place on 26 July 2020. He personally tweeted about the severe apathy of the government.

73. *The Assam Tribune*, 'Centre Yet to Spell Out Measures on Clause 6 Report', 26 July 2020, Guwahati.

74. R. Dutta Choudhury, 'AASU Releases Report on Clause 6 of Assam Accord', 12 August 2020, *The Assam Tribune*, http://www.assamtribune.com/scripts/detailsnew.asp?id=aug1220/at056.

75. *The Assam Tribune*, 'Govt Committed to Implement Clause 6, Says Sonowal', 12 August 2020, http://www.assamtribune.com/scripts/detailsnew.asp?id=aug1220/at057.

76. Report of the Committee on Implementation of Clause 6 of the Assam Accord (Constituted by the Government of India, Ministry of Home Affairs), 10 February 2020, Guwahati (a copy is with the author).

77. Bikash Singh, 'Congress, AIUDF Prevent Speaker from Tabling the Report on Definition of Assamese', *The Economic Times*, 1 April 2015, https://economictimes.indiatimes.com/news/politics-and-nation/congress-aiudf-prevent-speaker-from-tabling-the-report-on-definition-of-assamese/articleshow/46772373.cms?from=mdr.

78. Report of the Committee on Implementation of Clause 6 of the Assam Accord (Constituted by the Government of India, Ministry of Home Affairs), 10 February 2020, Guwahati (a copy is with the author), 43 (para 6.9).

79. Ibid., 43, para 6.11.

80. Ibid., 44, para 6.12.

81. Ibid., 50, para 7.3.2.

82. Ibid., 51, para 7.3.7.

83. Ibid.

84. Ibid., 56, para 7.6.2.

85. Ibid., 56, para 7.6.3.

86. Ibid., 56, para 7.6.1.

87. Ibid., 62, para 7.6.6-m.

88. Through an order issued by the Governor of Assam, the Committee for Protection of Land Rights of the Indigenous People of Assam headed by former Chief Election Commissioner (CEC) Hari Shankar Brahma was constituted on 6 February 2017. The committee submitted its report in January 2018. The 190-page report suggested strict measures for the protection of the land rights of the indigenous people. However, neither substantive discussion happened in the public domain regarding the recommendations in the report nor concrete measures were undertaken by the government in this regard. (The report is with the author.)

89. Report of the Committee on Implementation of Clause 6 of the Assam Accord, 57, para 7.6.4.

90. AASU has made it public that it will form a regional political party and will contest 2021 assembly elections.

91. Kalpa Jyoti Saikia, 'AASU Is Now a Political Party, Says Assam Minister Himanta Biswa Sarma', North East Now, 12 August 2020, https://nenow.in/north-east-news/assam/aasu-is-now-a-political-party-says-assam-minister-himanta-biswa-sarma.html.

92. Ibid.

93. Ibid.

94. *The Assam Tribune*, 'Centre Wants Clause 6 Report Examined by Legal Experts', 21 September 2020.

95. Nilay Dutta, Advocate General of Government of Arunachal Pradesh and member of the Clause 6 Expert Committee, pointed out these points in a personal conversation over the phone on 22 September 2020.

96. The Wire, 'Original Petitioner APW Unhappy with "Flawed NRC"', 31 August 2019, https://thewire.in/rights/original-petitioner-apw-unhappy-with-flawed-nrc.

Dream Seller's Economy

Promises and Populism

The BJP promised a qualitative transformation of Assam's development trajectory in its 'Assam Vision Document 2016–2025' released on the eve of the assembly elections 2016. It laid down a road map for this transformation to be achieved in a time-bound manner. Acknowledging that the state's economy was encircled by sea of challenges, the government, nevertheless, promised that it will 'innovate, experiment, struggle, learn and cross the sea with the support and inspiration from three crores of people of Assam. The goal is to strengthen the State's economy from within'.[1] However, throughout its tenure, the BJP-led regime in Assam made hyper-nationalism, populism and dream selling through both budgets and other economic measures a core state agenda. With its first government in Assam, the BJP launched a relentless campaign to squarely put the blame for the economic woes of the state on the previous Congress-led governments, projecting itself as the true guardian of the interests of the state. Its self-proclaimed commitment to the interests of the indigenous people has also been accompanied by uncompromising allegiance to a strong India, leaving no scope to raise questions about the over-centralized federal polity. Rather, the appeasement of the Centre and the Central leadership has been its principled position. As is the case with both the NRC and CAB-turned-CAA, the state government remained subdued to the policies of the BJP-led Union government in pursuing its development agenda. Assam, which took pride in being the first state to implement the GST, organized the first-ever Global Investors' Summit in the state, continued to project Prime Minister Narendra Modi as the saviour of the state's interests and, during the pandemic of the COVID-19, unquestionably adhered to the advisories issued by the Union government. The regime succeeded in increasing its internal revenues to an extent but registered no benchmark in terms of qualitative change in budget-making and budget implementing. In the 'Assam Vision Document 2016–2025', the BJP identified a few core areas to be prioritized in its overall development pursuit. Agriculture and irrigation were two of those important areas. But during its tenure, these sectors failed to receive due attention. The state failed to climb up in the ladder of the state's ranking in both the GSDP and per capita income (PCI). The much-publicized glory of the economy got extremely exposed once the pandemic of the COVID-19 invaded the state. The healthcare sector, which has been a priority in both policy pursuits and allocations of funds, invited very poor score towards achieving the Sustainable Development Goals (SDGs). Contrary to the claims and perceptions, a comprehensive analysis of the development agenda and the achievements reveals broader similarity between the Congress-led and the BJP-led regimes with the exception that the latter was more populist than the former.

ASSAM'S ECONOMY: A BRIEF SKETCH

Before we embark upon the analysis of the achievements and short-comings of the BJP-led government concerning the development of the state, it is pertinent to understand the overall size and nature of the economy. Both GSDP and government expenditure rose almost three times from 2011–2012 to 2020–2021 (see Table 4.1). The GSDP has grown in the range between 2.9 per cent (2012–2013) and 15.67 per cent (2015–2016) in current prices, but during the period the average growth has been about 6 per cent. The contribution of government expenditure to GSDP has been in the range between 21 (2011–2012) and 29 per cent (2021–2022), although the contribution of government expenditure showed an upward movement.

The sectoral contributions to the GSDP revealed higher shares of the service sector compared to agriculture and industry (see Table 4.2). The agriculture and allied sectors showed a consistent decline in terms of their contribution to the GSDP (see Table 4.3). This decline also

Table 4.1 GSDP and Government Expenditure in Assam

Year	GSDP (Current Prices; in ₹ Crore	GSDP (Constant Prices 2011–2012; in ₹ Crore)	Government Expenditure Actual (in ₹ Crore)	Government Expenditure as % of GSDP (Constant Prices)
2011–2012	143,175	143,175	30,268	21.14
2012–2013	156,864	147,342	33,747	22.90
2013–2014	177,745	154,525	37,178	24.05
2014–2015	195,723	165,212	46,811	28.33
2015–2016	227,959	191,109	36,142	18.91
2016–2017	254,382	20,2081	57,407	28.40
2017–2018	288,691	228,714	65,436	28.61
2018–2019	324,038	246,938	71,851	29.09
2019–2020	374,096 (BE)	NA	99,419 (BE)	26.57 (current prices)
2020–2021	408,627 (BE)	NA	103,762 (BE)	25.39 (current prices)

Sources: Compiled from the Economic Survey, Assam (2019–2020); White Paper on Assam Finances (2016); Budget Speeches of the Finance Minister of Assam 2016–2017 to 2020–2021.

Note: BE = budgeted estimate.

Table 4.2 *Sectoral Composition of GSDP at Current and Constant Prices*

Year	2011–2012		2017–2018 (PE)		2018–2019 (QE)	
	Current Prices (%)	Constant Prices (%)	Current Prices (%)	Constant Prices (%)	Current Prices (%)	Constant Prices (%)
Agriculture and Allied	19.89	19.89	16.76	16.39	15.80	15.76
Industry	30.63	30.63	32.71	36.80	33.51	36.36
Service	43.97	43.97	45.36	41.10	45.63	41.24
Taxes and Subsidies	5.51	5.51	5.16	5.70	5.06	6.65

Source: Economic Survey, Assam 2019–2020, Tables 3.3 and 3.4, pp. 31–32.
Note: PE = provisional estimate; QE = quick estimate.

Table 4.3 *Contribution of Agriculture and Allied Sectors to GSDP at Current and Constant Prices (%)*

Sectors	2016–2017		2017–2018 (PE)		2018–2019 (QE)	
	Current Prices	Constant Prices	Current Prices	Constant Prices	Current Prices	Constant Prices
Crops	13.44	12.96	12.27	12.13	11.33	11.54
Livestock	0.98	0.92	1.14	0.93	1.15	0.92
Forestry and Logging	1.06	0.83	0.99	0.80	0.95	0.79
Fishing and Aquaculture	2.50	2.57	2.36	2.53	2.36	2.51
Total	**17.98**	**17.27**	**16.76**	**16.39**	**15.80**	**15.76**

Source: Economic Survey, Assam 2019–2020, Table 5.1, p. 65.
Note: PE = provisional estimate; QE = quick estimate.

stems from the fact that the total area of farm cultivation declined over the years. There has been a marginal increase in farm production, which is attributable to a variety of factors. *ASHDR, 2014*, comprehensively investigated these issues and identified that poor access to assets, including financial assets, halted the growth of the agriculture sector. Minuscule coverage of irrigation and landholding patterns fettered the economy. The government expenditure in agriculture and allied sectors as well as in rural development has been lower than most of the states in India. Recurring floods and a lower rate of mechanization coupled with moribund credit facilities contribute to the decline of the share of agriculture in GSDP. It has a bearing on the outmigration of rural youths to other states, although no authentic data is available on such migrants. During COVID-19, the government registered around seven lakh such migrants under the Assam Cares programme.

Assam has a total of 40.87 lakh hectares of gross cropped area, of which only 10.07 lakh hectares (24.64%) are covered under irrigation facilities. Out of the total potential irrigation facilities created so far, 2.47 lakh hectares (27.15%) have been created through major and medium irrigation projects and schemes, and the remaining 7.33 lakh hectares (72.85%) have been created under minor irrigation projects.[2]

Assam produces 51 per cent of India's tea, followed by West Bengal (29%) and Tamil Nadu (12.4%). It has around 11 per cent share in the world tea market. Tea contributes 3 per cent to India's GDP, and Assam's share is more than 1.5 per cent.[3] The tea industry employs an average of 6.86 lakh people in the state. What is remarkable is that 1.01 lakh small tea growers occupy less than one-third of the total cultivated land for tea, but per hectare production of tea by them is much higher than by big tea growers (see Table 4.4).[4] The small tea growers face severe challenges as they do not have access to the market and manufacturing facilities. They primarily produce tea leaves and are vulnerable to the price fluctuations of the product. What is ironic is that even though the state government spends a considerable amount of money to improve the lives of the tea labourers, they continue to live on the fringe, and they have become a rallying point in deciding the destiny of the political parties. Insecurity in tenure, poor housing and living conditions, low wages and unhealthy working conditions, breach of maternity rights and exposure to pesticides are the chronic problems of the tea labourers in the state.[5]

The state's economy, which was ruined by perennial conflicts and other social and natural disasters, including floods during the 1980s

Table 4.4 *Land Occupied by Small and Big Tea Growers in Assam and Their Respective Shares in Production*

Entities	Total Numbers	Land Holding Patterns	Total Land Occupied (in Hectares)	Per Grower Average Landholding	Total Production (kg)	Per Hectare Production (kg)
Small Tea Growers	101,085	Up to 10.12 hectares per grower	105,291	1.04 hectares	304,490,000	2,891.89 kg
Big Tea Growers	765	More than 10.12 hectares per grower	232,400	303.79	387,420,000	1,667.03 kg

Source: Compiled from Economic Survey, Assam 2019–2020, p. 165.

and 1990s, witnessed a recovery since the middle of the first decade of the new century. Beginning with several accords with ethnic militant groups in the state, including the one signed with the Bodos in 2003, ushered in an atmosphere of calm and peace. The UPA government at the Centre, which came to power in 2004, introduced several policies and schemes such as NREGA, 2005, and NRHM, 2005, which ensured a flow of funds to the states. These funds relieved the state government to use its internal revenue for its expenses, especially to pay salaries and other parks to the state government employees. However, the structural imbalance in the economy sustained with gradual decline of agriculture and the allied sectors in terms of their contribution to the GSDP. It has enormous bearing on the overall well-being of the state's population as agriculture absorbs the highest percentage of the working population.

ECONOMY INHERITED BY THE BJP-LED GOVERNMENT: A SHORT OVERVIEW

By the late 1990s, Assam's economy was in tatters. The government even failed to pay the salaries to its employees on time. The state finance was in overdraft, and the overall development activities were stalled. In an interview to *The Telegraph* on 21 November 1999,[6] the then Chief Minister of Assam Prafulla Kumar Mahanta, revealed the dire financial situation in the state. He confessed that counter-insurgency operations took a toll on the finances, and the Centre was yet to reimburse the security-related expenditures to the Assam government. He further informed that his government was still deliberating about signing the MoU with the Centre on fiscal reforms, acknowledging that signing the memorandum 'would necessitate harsh steps like freezing employment, hiking electricity tariff and transferring the state transport corporation to the private sector'. Mahanta said that his government had already frozen employment except in some departments like education. In the same interview Mahanta also said,

> The monthly receipts of the state amount to Rs. 391 crore at present, while the monthly expenditure is Rs. 451 crore. As a result of this monthly deficit, the overdraft figures for every month have been increasing. This has led to a situation where we are unable to liquidate the overdraft....

The economy had deteriorated to a level that one of his ministerial colleagues suggested declaring a financial emergency in the state.[7] The second half of the 1990s was marked by atrocities by insurgents and security forces deployed to counter them. The situation deteriorated further in the later years of the decade with a series of secret killings allegedly engineered by the state with the help of surrendered ULFA members. Operations Bajrang and Rhino—launched by the Army against the separatists—brought immense misery to the common people.[8]

All these events had a disastrous impact on the economy. It took almost a decade to overcome the situation. By the end of the first decade of the new century, the economy showed signs of recovery and peace and tranquillity also returned to the state. By the middle of the second decade of the present century, the state economy was stable.

ASHDR, 2014, pointed out that during the decade of 2004–2014, the state's growth rate increased from 3.74 to 5.87 per cent. The agriculture sector was beginning to do well, and industrial and service sectors were growing steadily. The agricultural growth was a mere 1.92 per cent at the beginning of 2005; it rose to 4.45 per cent in 2013–2014. The industrial growth rate was negative (−3.53%) in 2005 but improved to 4.28 per cent in 2013–2014. The services sector also maintained its steady growth—estimated at 6.95 per cent in 2013–2014, which was 7.93 per cent in 2005.[9]

The report also elaborates the challenges associated with the core concerns of livelihood of the common people. It disaggregates achievements in human development into geospatial and social categories. Based on a large primary data, which was 10 times larger than the NSSO rounds and 8 times larger than the National Family Health Survey (NFHS) in the state, the report highlights the primary human development challenges in the state, which include inequality across diverse categories, deprivations of many forms, unemployment as well as low achievements in health and education.[10] Inequalities and unemployment figure prominently in the report. On inequality, the report asserts,

> It is estimated that about one-third (30 per cent) of the potential aggregate human development is lost due to the prevailing inequalities underlying

achievements in education, health and income dimensions. The loss due to inequality is the highest in the income dimension (about 44 per cent) followed by health (32 per cent) and then education (9 per cent). Moreover, it was found that, district wise, dimensional inequalities vary distinctly.[11]

The report points out that the overall human development of women was lower than that of men by about 14 per cent. Focusing on multidimensionally poor people in the state, it suggests that the issue of poverty needed to be addressed beyond income poverty. The report highlights that inequalities in access to productive resources and basic amenities were manifested in landholding. It argues,

> The extent of inequality in land holding, for example, is evident from the fact that the top 20 per cent of the people holds about 70 per cent of the total cultivable land while 80 per cent share 30 per cent of the remaining land. Consequently, the top 20 per cent shares 45 per cent of the total consumption expenditure while the bottom 20 per cent shares only 8 per cent.

Unemployment was taking an alarming turn. The total unemployment rate (percentage of people within the age of 15–59 years finding no employment) was estimated at 13.4 per cent in the age group of 15–59. The female unemployment rate was as high as 33.9 per cent compared to 8.0 per cent in the case of males. The youth unemployment rate in the age group of 15–24 was as high as 37.7 per cent.[12]

The report stresses that gainful employment, quality and universal education, and healthcare are the three important means to achieve sustainable human development. The report also asserts that 'redressal of inequalities is fundamental in achieving human development and making it inclusive as well as sustainable'.[13]

It may be pointed out that although the report was initiated and completed during the Congress-led government in the state, it refused to release it, sensing a negative impact on electoral outcomes. The report was finally released by the new government on 3 October 2016. The Chief Minister Sarbananda Sonowal noted on the release of the report, 'While public expectations from the government have increased tremendously over the years, their level of satisfaction with the service delivery has gone down drastically.' He particularly emphasized the improvement of the farm economy to come out of the cycles of poverty and deprivations. He said, 'Keeping this in mind, the government has already launched the Chief Minister's Samagra Gramya Unnayan Yojana (CMSGUY) to improve farm economy of the state in sync with Garib Kalyan Yojana launched by the Govt. of India.'[14]

It is important to point out that the chief minister also released the state government's 'Vision & Strategic Architecture Document—Assam 2030: Our dream, Our Commitment'. The document intended to cover a 'wide range of activities like employment generation, poverty alleviation, development in youth affairs, infrastructure, industrial sector, agriculture, rural and urban development'.[15]

BALLOONING THE BUDGETS: THE BLACK SIDE OF THE WHITE PAPER

Immediately after assuming power, the BJP-led government in Assam published a white paper on the overall health of finances of the state. It was a well-articulated document which talks about the poor financial health inherited by the new government. Filled with statistics, the paper attempted to expose the mismanagement of the economy by the previous regime. Prepared under the guidance of the new finance minister, it was an insider's narrative, as he happened to be one of the most powerful ministers in all of the three tenures of the previous government. Titled 'White Paper on Assam State Finances (As on 24th May 2016)',[16] it was presented to the Assam Legislative Assembly on 3 June 2016, and quickly the document generated a heated debate inside and outside the assembly. Bound by its commitment to pursue the model of good governance, the new government also immediately

realised that the very fulcrum of governance and means for development, namely the state finances, is in gloom, despair and doldrums. The State Cabinet also felt that its primary duty is to inform each and every citizen of the State about the actual reality of the public finances as the new Government assumed the office. Such attempt would also be in accordance with the highest ideals and great standards that the new Government would like to set for itself to maintain transparency, accountability and 'citizen-first' approach.[17]

The white paper articulated the poor health of the finances left behind by the previous Congress regime, which saddled the new regime with a huge liability. The paper also exposed the earlier regime on many counts—from ballooning the budgets without adequate financing to the insignificant growth in internal revenue for which the Congress-led regime failed to keep its promises to the people. However, a critical investigation and analysis reveal that there are several black spots in the white paper.

₹10,000 Crore + Liability?

A more than ₹10,000 crore liability from the previous government was the main highlight of the paper in the media.[18] The white paper laid down the figures which became the talking points inside and outside the assembly. It showed that ₹4,800 crore out of the total liability was due to the implications of the pay revision of 2016–2017, which was yet to be announced and implemented. ₹900 crore was attributed to the payment of dearness allowances (DA) with effect from 1 January 2016. Analysts doubted whether these amounts could be considered as liability. Biswas (2016) pointed out that the payment of the 6 per cent DA since 1 January 2016 had to be put on hold 'due to the election model code of conduct. Now the moot question is—can this expenditure to be incurred for the payment of DA to be considered a "liability" handed down by the previous regime?'[19] He also pointed that 'the issue of "liability" would certainly have surfaced had the earlier government defaulted in paying the DA up to 31 December 2015. But that has not been the case.' The Congress government led by Tarun Gogoi was among a handful of states in the country which had been paying the DA regularly since the implementation of the Sixth Pay Revision in 2009.

The amount also could not be called a liability as the government was yet to accept and implement the recommendations of the new pay revision commission. However, the Congress party ill-prepared to refute those allegations in the assembly. Consequently, the document created an impression among the people that its government indeed left behind a massive liability for the new government.

More importantly, the exaggeration of the liability continued beyond the white paper, as the budget speech of 2016–2017 revised the estimated amount to ₹14,276.97 crore.

Budgets without Finance

The new finance minister attacked the previous government on its huge budgetary layouts, which he called ballooning of the budgets without clear provisioning of financing. This was read from the budget estimates and actual expenditures of the last five financial years of the previous government. According to the minister, the budget almost doubled from ₹38,562.88 crore in the financial year 2011–2012 to ₹72,572.88 crore in 2015–2016, amounting to an increase of 88 per cent. However, the actual expenditure had never been 80 per cent. For example, it was 78.49 per cent in 2011–2012, 69.93 per cent in 2012–2013 and 2013–2014, 71.98 per cent in 2014–2015 and only 49.80 per cent in 2015–2016. The white paper argued, the 'whole budget making process was reduced to non-serious exercise and just to show that the budget size is very huge'. It also argued, 'The main reason for the above state of utterly low expenditure has been lack of proper financing of the budget. It appears that the previous Government for a very long period has completely forgotten the necessity to finance the budget.'[20] In other words, the government did not have resources in hand to meet its budget promises. An important reason behind it was low internal revenue generation.

In his first budget speech, the finance minister expressed confidence in his government's capacity to overcome the trend of the ballooning of budgets and liabilities. He said,

> Above state of lagging economy, improper budgeting and mounting liabilities are the realities that this Government will take on its stride to explore opportunities for every challenge because we believe in Parivartan and we will change the scenario by involving every stake-holder in the process.[21]

However, the BJP-led government performed no better than the Congress governments. Contrary to its wishful rhetoric, it failed to cross 70 per cent of its revised expenditure target. The revised estimate of expenditure was inflated, but the actual expenditure was much below than the budgeted expenditure.

Table 4.5 *Expenditure Estimates and Actual Expenditure from 2016–2017 to 2020–2021 (in ₹ Crore)*

Year	BE	RE	AE	% of AE Out of BE	% of AE Out of RE	Growth of AE (%)
2016–2017	78,253.36	83,017	57,407	73.36	69.10	–
2017–2018	85,923	99,453	65,436	76.15	65.79	13.98
2018–2019	90,270	108,490	71,851	79.59	66.22	9.80
2019–2020	99,419	119,716	–	–	–	–
2020–2021	103,762	–	–	–	–	–

Source: PRS Legislative Research, Assam Budget Analysis (2016–2017 to 2020–2021), https://www.prsindia.org/parliamenttrack/budgets/assam-budget-analysis.
Note: BE = budgeted estimate; RE = revised estimate; AE = actual expenditure.

Table 4.5 shows that the actual expenditure had been much lower compared to both budgeted and revised estimates. The actual expenditure, of course, was calculated against the revised expenditure.

The finance minister, in his last (i.e., 2020–2021) budget presentation, justified the actual expenditure in the following words, tactfully quoting the absolute figures and hiding the percentage of the actual expenditure:

[The] spending under our Government has set new benchmarks each year, crossing Rs. 50,000 Crore mark for the first time in 2016–17, then Rs. 60,000 Crore mark in 2017–18 and crossing the Rs. 70,000 Crore mark in 2018–19 (Provisional Estimates). During the last three years of our Government, we have increased the state's expenditure by almost 70% compared to expenditure growth achieved in 2015–16. Further, the YoY expenditure growth has been increasing rapidly under our Government and grew at over 36.9% in 2016–17 over the expenditure in 2015–16 (on a smaller base). The expenditure growth in 2018–19, over a much larger base of 2017–18, has still witnessed a highly impressive growth.[22]

The speech reveals that the actual expenditure of the incumbent BJP-led government has not crossed 70 per cent of the revised estimates. From 2015–16 to 2018–19, the percentage of expenditure was 56, 69, 66 and 67 per cent. The claim of the finance minister that the spending under the government had surpassed the ₹50,000 crore mark for the first time in 2016–2017 was not true for the fact that his criticism of the previous budgets was not based on the absolute amount of expenditure but the percentage of the expenditure out of the total budgetary outlay. What he argued was that even 78 per cent of the actual expenditure of the budgetary layouts meant 'ballooning' of the budgets without proper provisioning of the finances. Going by the same logic, the incumbent government indulged in more ballooning as it had not even exceeded 70 per cent in spending of its budgetary allocations.

Permanent Assets: A Continuing Failure

In his white paper, Dr Himanta Biswa Sarma disaggregated the expenditure into non-plan and plan expenditures. He also criticized that capital expenditure was too low; saying that it only indicated that the government failed in terms of creating permanent assets. Ironically, his government also did do no better in this regard. Table 4.6 reveals that capital expenditure has not even reached 15 per cent of the revised estimate.

In crucial departments such as agriculture, rural development and irrigation, and flood control, the allocation had been deplorably low— lower than the average of most of the states in the country—and capital expenditure had been absolutely meagre. These statistics indicate that the government was not committed to creating permanent assets in the rural economy.

Internal Revenue

The finance minister alleged in the white paper that the ballooning of the budget did not match with the collection of revenue. Therefore, the actual expenditure was much lower than both the budgeted and revised estimates. But his government is no saint on this front because his budget estimates got substantially reduced in actual expenditure due to low receipts compared to its estimates. In 2016–2017 and 2017–2018, the actual receipts were even lower than actual expenditure. What is important to point out here is that the revised estimates of receipts were

Table 4.6 *Capital Expenditure and Revenue Expenditure (in ₹ Crore)*

Year	Total Expenditure			Capital Expenditure			Revenue Expenditure		
	BE	RE	AE	BE	RE	AE	BE	RE	AE
2016–2017	78,253.36	83,017	57,407	15,794	17,340	8,044	62,459	65,676	49,363
2017–2018	85,923	99,453	65,436	17,603	20,197	9,956	68,319	79,257	55,481
2018–2019	90,270	108,490	71,851	18,941	26,486	14,952	71,329	82,005	56,899
2019–2020	99,419	119,716	–	19,677	27,502	–	79,742	92,214	–
2020–2021	103,762	–	–	20,985	–	–	82,772	–	–

Source: PRS Legislative Research, Assam Budget Analysis (2016–2017 to 2020–2021), https://www.prsindia.org/parliamenttrack/budgets/assam-budget-analysis.

Note: BE = budgeted estimate; RE = revised estimate; AE = actual expenditure.

lower than estimated receipts in both years. The government failed to earn the revised receipts too. In 2018–2019, the revised estimated receipts were higher than the estimated receipts, but the government collected revenue which was substantially lower than the estimated receipts. The figures in Table 4.7 explain these discrepancies.

The failure of the state government also lies in the low capital expenditure for which the infrastructure capacity of the state could not develop. The budgets were mostly spent on revenue expenses such as salary and pension. The white paper blamed the previous government for the near-stagnation in internal revenue collection.

> The notable components of State Own Resources are VAT and other taxes administered by Taxation Department, Excise, Motor Vehicle Tax, Forest and Minor minerals apart from Oil Royalty ... during the last five years, the growth in internal revenue flow into the state exchequer has virtually stagnated.[23]

However, the data presented in the paper itself speaks the opposite: The state government did remarkably well in internal revenue collection, which increased 26.52 per cent between 2002–2003 and 2011–2012. In 2002–2003 and 2004–2005, the increase was above 25 per cent and in 2005–2006 and 2009–2010, it was above 20 per cent. On average, the internal revenue collection was, therefore, good. The sharp fall from 2012–2013 was due to the internal conflicts in the government, apart from other factors.

Table 4.8 in the white paper reveals that the ratio of the state's revenue to the total revenue increased during almost throughout the three tenures. In 2000–2001, the state share of the revenue was 34.35 per cent, from 2001–2002 to 2013–2014 it was above 35 per cent, and in 7 years it was more than 38 per cent. Therefore, the allegation of a fall in internal revenue does not hold ground.

It is pertinent to point out that the revised estimate of revenue receipts for the financial year 2018–2019 was increased by 21.2 per cent, but the actual receipt from the BE was 14.14 per cent less (see Table 4.8) and the actual receipt from the RE was lesser by 29.36 per cent. The government increased the revised estimate of revenue in the state's tax by 60.61 per cent and grants-in-aid from

Table 4.7 Receipts and Expenditure (*in* ₹ Crore)

Year	Receipts					Expenditure			
	ER	RER	AR	% of Receipts of the ER	% of Receipts of the RER	BE	RE	AE	% of Expenditure Out of RE
2016–2017	77,423	70,146	53,140	68.63	75.75	78,253.36	83,017	57,407	69
2017–2018	84,732	70,401	62,583	73.85	88.89	85,923.00	99,453	65,436	66
2018–2019	90,673	106,442	75,237	82.97	70.68	90,270.00	106,442	71,851	67
2019–2020	98,339	109,806	–	–	–	99,419.00	119,716	–	–
2020–2021	105,246	–	–	–	–	103,762.00	–	–	–

Source: PRS Legislative Research, Assam Budget Analysis (2016–2017 to 2020–2021), https://www.prsindia.org/parliamenttrack/budgets/assam-budget-analysis.

Note: ER = estimated receipt; RER = revised estimated receipt; AR = actual receipt; RE = revised estimate.

Table 4.8 *Revenue Receipts of the State Government from 2016–2017 to 2020–2021 (in ₹ Crore)*

Financial Year	BE	RE	% Change from BE to RE	Actual	% Change from BE to AE
2016–2017 (Total receipts)	77,423	70,146	–9.4	53,140	–
2016–2017 (Revenue receipts)	66,180	59,008	–10.8	49,220	–25.63
2017–2018 (Total receipts)	84,732	70,401	–16.9	62,583	–
2017–2018 (Revenue receipts)	70,719	55,905	–20.9	54,131	–23.46
2018–2019 (Total receipts)	90,673	106,442	17.4	75,237	–
2018–2019 (Revenue receipts)	74,188	89,854	21.2	63,479	–14.44
2019–2020 (Total receipts)	98,339	109,806	11.7	–	–
2019–2020 (Revenue receipts)	83,148	93,026	11.9	–	–
2020–2021 (Total receipts)	105,246	–	–	–	–
2020–2021 (Revenue receipts)	91,931	–	–	–	–

Source: PRS Legislative Research, Assam Budget Analysis (2016–2017 to 2020–2021), https://www.prsindia.org/parliamenttrack/budgets/assam-budget-analysis.
Note: BE = budgeted estimate; RE = revised estimate; AE = actual expenditure.

the Centre were increased by 47.3 per cent. But the actual receipt in state's own non-tax revenue was 37.54 per cent less than the revised estimate. In the case of the grant-in-aid, it was lesser by 57.12 per cent. The state government kept on claiming unprecedented patronage of the central government towards the state's finances. However, the annual growth rate of the transfer of the revenue from the state to the centre does not hold ground to that claim (see Table 4.9).

Table 4.9 *Revenue Shares of the State and Central Governments and the Revenue Growth*

Year	State's Own Revenue	Share of the Total Revenue %	Annual Growth %	Transfer from the Centre	Share of the Total Revenue %	Annual Growth %	Total Revenue	Annual Growth %
2015–2016	12,265	–	–	29,609	–	–	42,458	–
2016–2017	16,433	33.39	34.98	32,787	66.61	10.37	49,220	15.92
2017–2018	17,288	31.93	5.20	36,844	68.03	12.37	54,131	9.97
2018–2019	24,146	38.03	39.66	39,333	61.96	6.32	63,479	17.26
2019–2020	–	–	–	–	–	–	–	–

Source: PRS Legislative Research, Assam Budget Analysis (2016–2017 to 2020–2021), https://www.prsindia.org/parliamenttrack/budgets/assam-budget-analysis.

PCI: Maintaining the Status Quo

The finance minister also commented in the white paper that the growth of PCI of Assam from 2011–2012 to 2015–2016 did not correspond to the announced budget sizes. In his 2016–2017 budget speech, the minister lamented,

> Even in 1950–51, per capita income in Assam was 4 per cent above the national average (Planning Commission, 2002). Now, after about 68 years of Independence, we are the fourth poorest state of India. All social and economic indicators are failing the State and pushing down its position to lower levels.[24]

Has the state really improved under the BJP-led regime?

From the year 2011–2012 to 2014–2015, Assam ranked 19th among the 21 major states and 30th among the states and union territories in PCI at current prices. Since 2015–2016, Assam improved its position by one rank, that is, 18th among the major states and 29th among the states and union territories. Three major states are behind Assam—Uttar Pradesh, Bihar and Jharkhand. All small states except Manipur are ahead of Assam in PCI. Within the states of Northeast India, Assam is the second-lowest developed state after Manipur in terms of PCI.

Haryana topped during this whole period in PCI among the major states. Uttarakhand, Kerala and Karnataka variably have held the second position. In the last few years, Karnataka retained this position. Kerala, Karnataka and Maharashtra usually fight for the third, but, lately, Telangana has occupied that position. Gujarat has been moving between 6th and 7th ranks among the major states. Punjab has all along occupied the 10th position during this period. West Bengal has improved its position from 15th to 13th. Odisha has moved between 15th and 16th, and J&K had started with the 14th but slipped to 17th. Major and small states, as well as the union territories combined, Goa has topped all along. In 2011–2012, the PCI of Goa at current prices stood at ₹225,944, which increased to ₹458,304 in 2018–2019, that is, a growth of 76.4 per cent in eight years. Haryana stood at ₹106,085 in 2011–2012, which rose to ₹236,147 in 2018–2019—an increase of 122.6 per cent. During the same period, all-India average increased from ₹63,462 to ₹126,521—an increase of 99.36 per cent. Assam stood at ₹41,142 in 2011–2012, and it increased to ₹82,078 by 2018–2019. The state registered a 99.49 per cent PCI growth in eight years.[25]

As almost all states grew at the same pace with some exceptions like Haryana, the state could not move up in the PCI ranking. There have been assertions that Assam would be one of the best five states in the coming days. However, the real performance shows that it is not only a distant dream but also quite unreachable unless some miracles happen.

As per GSDP PCI in 2018–2019, the ranking of the above-mentioned states among all states and union territories are Haryana: 5, Karnataka: 7, Kerala: 8, Uttarakhand: 9, Gujarat: 10, Telangana: 11 and Maharashtra: 12. The states of Northeast India did not figure in the ranking for 2018–2019 as recorded by the Ministry of Statistics and Programme Implementation as on 28 September 2019. Sikkim, which is a member of North Eastern Council, figured in the list and occupied the 3rd rank. The ranks of the states of Northeast India for the year 2017–2018 are as follows: Mizoram: 18, Arunachal Pradesh: 19, Tripura: 20, Nagaland: 21, Meghalaya: 28, Assam: 29 and Manipur: 31.[26]

The claim that the Congress-led governments' performance has been poor, and the misrule of the party was responsible for the slow growth of Assam's economy, holds no ground. Table 4.10 reveals that there is no radical change in the BJP-led government's performance in

Table 4.10 *Assam's Per Capita Income at Current Prices and Its Rank among the Major States/States and Union Territories since 2011–2012 (as on 28 February 2020; in ₹)*

Year	Assam's PCI	India's PCI	Assam's PCI as % of India's PCI	Assam's Rank among the Major States	Assam's Rank among the States and Union Territories
2011–2012	41,142	63,462	64.82	18	29
2012–2013	44,599	70,983	62.83	19	30
2013–2014	49,734	79,118	62.86	19	30
2014–2015	52,895	86,647	61.04	19	30
2015–2016	60,817	94,797	64.15	18	29
2016–2017	66,330	104,880	63.24	18	29
2017–2018	74,184	115,293	64.34	18	29
2018–2019	82,078	126,521	64.87	18	29

Source: Central Statistical Organisation, Government of India, New Delhi, https://esopb.gov.in/static/PDF/GSDP/Statewise-Data/statewisedata.pdf.

improving growth in terms of either GSDP or PCI. During the Congress regime, the value addition to PCI per year was between ₹7,000 and ₹9,000. It has increased to ₹11,000 during BJP's rule.

NEW MODEL OF GOVERNANCE AND ENDLESS POPULISM

Two striking features of the BJP-led government in Assam are self-glorification and hyper-populism. The statistics above show that the government could not achieve something remarkable which can distinguish it from the earlier Congress-led governments. The information made available through economic surveys in various years is a testimony to it.

The budget speeches of the new government took a new turn. A budget speech primarily focuses on the state of the economy, challenges confronted by the government and initiatives taken to overcome the challenges. No finance minister in the past used the speeches to talk about the paradigm of governance so extensively or to indulge in appeasement of the Central leadership as was done by Himanta Biswa Sarma. Let me give a summary of it. Until the 1970s, the state governments used to be critical on institutional arrangements of allocation/distribution of funds under the federal structure, irrespective of whether the same or the opposition party was in power at the Centre. Let me refer to Sarat Chandra Singha, who was the chief minister of Assam from 1972 to 1978, including the Emergency period. The Congress government under Indira Gandhi at the Centre enjoyed an overwhelming majority. Presenting his budget for the year 1972–1973, the chief minister pointed out that the Finance Commission did not have empathy with the financial difficulties of the state. He said,

> In fairness to the Finance Commission it has to be admitted that it is difficult for the Commission to prescribe different standards for different States. Still we cannot help feeling that the Fifth Finance Commission have not given due recognition to the unique problems of Assam and have not done full justice to us as they have recommended devolution of only Rs. 195 crores to Assam as against our estimated requirement of Rs. 321 crores.[27]

He also pointed out the following:

> [A] scheme was also started for adjustment of accumulated over-draft on extremely difficult terms and conditions. In the case of Assam, it has been contemplated that out of the accumulated over-draft of Rs. 45.50 crores as much as Rs. 17 crores would be straightway deducted from the receipts payable to the State on account of its share of Central taxes and duties and plan assistance. Fifteen per cent of the balance amount of Rs. 28 crores would also be similarly deducted in addition. This would mean that the State Government will not only not have the facilities of drawing money from the R.B.I. to meet their immediate pressing requirements due to any imbalance between receipts and expenditure specially during the first few months of the financial year but also that the amount payable by the Central Government to the State would stand reduced additionally to the extent of about Rs. 21.50 crores.[28]

There was a critical review of the Centre–state financial relationship, and the finance ministers restrained themselves from appeasing the Central leadership. The budget speeches started with the state of the economy. That had been the trend almost till 2015–2016, although by that time hyper-populism had emerged as a trend in budget speeches.

The year 1986 was a significant year in Assam's history. The new AGP government came to power after six-year-long Assam agitation (1979–1985). The popular enthusiasm was very high. But while presenting the first budget, the new Chief Minister and Finance Minister of the State Prafulla Kumar Mahanta, the youngest chief minister of his time, devoted only one paragraph thanking the people for the mandate. He immediately shifted to the state income, followed by the state of affairs in different departments. The main text of his budget speech was of 4,400 words long. The length of the speeches increased over the years but did not indulge in glorification of any kind. Hiteswar Saikia also followed the same principles in his budget speeches. Tarun Gogoi's budget speeches had become longer, but he also continued the same trend. For example, the first three sections of his budget speech in 2003–2004 were about the state economy, prices and employment. Reflecting on prices was an important component of budget speeches. When presenting the 2012–2013 budget after his party came back to power with a landslide victory in 2011 assembly elections, Tarun Gogoi immediately delved into the economic environment, finances and debt position of the state. He did not use his budget speech to thank the people for the overwhelming support.

The BJP-led regime brought a shift to budget speeches. For example, the first budget speech of the Finance Minister Himanta Biswa Sarma, which contained a magnanimous 39,500 words, started with *Asato Maa Sad-Gamaya/Tamaso Maa Jyotir-Gamaya/Mrytonmamritang – Gamayeti*, (Oh God, give me the power to move from the illusion to the reality that is, eternal self; help me to transcend the darkness and to journey to the light i.e. spiritual knowledge; give me the power to move from the world of mortality to that of immortality i.e. self-realization). and ended with a poem by Lakshminath Bezbarua, and chanting of *Bharat Mata ki Jay*. He devoted around 2,500 words to define the new philosophy and the model of his government.[29] His subsequent budget speeches had been filled with similar rhetoric and poetics. He, of course, provided every detail of the schemes and other initiatives of the government. Interestingly though, he had never discussed critical issues concerning the economy. He converted budget speeches into popular essays with a lot of citations, poems and *shlokas*. Initially, he expressed his apprehensions over the populist policies and assured to address more fundamental issues of the economy but, gradually, indulged in hyper-populism.

In his first budget speech, the finance minister declared,

> But our Government, under the leadership of Shri Sarbananda Sonowal, follows the words of Noble Laurite and Kavi Guru Shri Rabindra Nath Tagore: 'You can't cross the sea merely by standing and staring at the water.' We need alternatives. We will innovate, experiment, struggle, learn and cross the sea with the support and inspiration from three crores of people of Assam. The goal is to strengthen the State's economy from within. We need to be self-reliant with a long-term agenda to develop internal resources. At least by the 75th anniversary of India's Independence, the State should be able to finance the total salary and pension burden from its internal resources so that funds from the Centre can be fully put to capital expenditure which will help constructing the steel frame of the resilient economy of Assam.[30]

In the last budget speech, the finance minister asserted,

> [On] May 24, 2016, a new era dawned in Assam; an era of hope, of aspiration, of development and of a promise of a future that embraces everyone. Today, I stand before you in all humility, to proudly state that we have done our utmost to keep that promise.[31]

He also asserted,

> In my Budget Speech 2019–20, I reminded this August House that we are at the cusp—*xondhikhyon*—of a momentous journey and we cannot now afford to step back. I reiterate the same today, but with a greater urgency and an even greater conviction! We cannot, and should not squander this golden opportunity to take our destiny in our own hands and carve out a prosperous Assam, an Assam that is progressive and developed, with each and every citizen achieving the pinnacle of health, wealth and happiness.[32]

Invoking new paradigms was one of the salient features of the government. The government declared a new architecture of governance on the eve of assuming power. 'The architecture of New Model of Governance will be erected on four pillars, namely (1) Personal Integrity, (2) Political Inclusivity, (3) Governance Legitimacy and (4) People Participation. As such, these four themes are recurrent in this budget.'[33]

> The four themes of this New Model of Governance are drawn from the life message of Pandit Deen Dayal ji who gave us the concept of 'Integral Humanism'. This is the guiding principle for us in Governance. This Mantra of 'Integral Humanism' stands out as a clear way of thought firmly rooted in the Indian tradition.[34]

The self-glorification was accompanied by an equal measure of hyper-populism. Populism has been one of the fundamental features of the neoliberal state in India since the early 21st century. It has numerous contradictions. On the one hand, the governments across party lines followed the dictates of the neoliberal orthodoxies, pushing privatization and liberalization of the economy in a consistent manner; on the other hand, manufactures multi-layered dependent beneficiaries through the populist policies. These policies, which have implications on people's economic and social being, are aimed at keeping the social and economic hierarchies intact and contribute towards intensification of social and economic inequalities. The objective of the populist policies has been to address poverty, not inequality. Poverty is addressed through the parameters of income rather than larger issues of freedom and capability as insisted by the human development approach. These policies and schemes are fragmented in nature and ensure relief rather than structural changes in the economy through which sustainable livelihood sources may be ascertained. In the case of Assam in general and the BJP-led regime in Assam in particular, these populist policies have larger electoral designs. The incumbent government has targeted certain communities while designing and developing these policies/ schemes. Tea tribe communities have been the main target for this government in terms of providing state patronage.

ACHIEVEMENTS

The *ASHDR, 2014,* critically investigated into the core concerns of livelihood of the people and human dignity. Inequality and unemployment were two issues that the report focused on comprehensibly. These two are linked to the issues concerning the sources of livelihoods. But the government did not pay due attention to this critical and comprehensive report in pursuing the development agenda.

As stated, the government achieved some notable success in generating more internal revenue compared to the previous governments. The contribution of government expenditure to the GSDP also increased, reaching 28 per cent, which was around 21 per cent in 2011–2012. The government implemented the revised pay scale almost on time and without facing any agitation from its employees. The arrear accrued due to the revised pay scale was also paid almost on time. The government launched a series of individual-oriented beneficiary schemes and paid them on time. But the ambitious objectives as having been laid down from time to time could not be achieved. Rural development has been one of the important objectives of the government, and agriculture was its highest priority. The new government launched a mega mission titled Chief Minister Samagra Gramya Unnayan Yojana (CMSGUY)[35] to be implemented in five years, with the primary objective to 'double the farm income, in unison with the vision of Hon'ble Prime Minister of India'. It was proposed to be culminated in the year 2021–2022, coinciding with 75 years of India's independence. It also declared its aim of generating employment opportunities to curb social discontent.

A critical analysis, however, reveals that the government did not achieve anything which could distinguish it from the previous government. The report on the state's economy published by the government in the backdrop of COVID-19 is a testimony to it. Let us examine a few issues.

Let us start with growth. In his last full budget speech (2020–2021), the finance minister claimed: 'Despite sluggish growth across the globe and slowdown of the Indian Economy, the state of Assam achieved an impressive rate of growth.'[36] He also asserted that the average annual growth rate with respect to GSDP at current prices during the period 2016–2017 to 2019–2020 (BE) was 12.38 per cent. It was 11.63 per cent in 2016–2017, 13.37 per cent in 2017–2018, 12.15 per cent in 2018–2019 and 12.38 per cent (BE) in 2019–2020. The economy has, however, been pushed to the brink by COVID-19, which has brought an immediate halt to the economic activities since mid-March 2020.

But the *Report on Economy of Assam in the Backdrop of COVID-19 Pandemic*, prepared by State Innovation and Transformation Aayog (SITA), Government of Assam, in collaboration with OKD Institute of Social Change and Development, Guwahati, pointed out that even before COVID-19, India's economy was witnessing a visible slowdown, and the growth rate for 2019–2020 had been estimated to be 5 per cent, which was the lowest in the last 11 years, marking about 27 per cent fall over the previous year's (i.e., 2018–2019) rate of 6.8 per cent.[37] Assam's economy was also passing through the same trajectory. Quoting the Directorate of Economics and Statistics, Government of Assam, the report pointed out that since 2017–2018, the rate of growth of the state's GDP had been declining. 'For the year 2019–20, the rate of growth of the Gross State Domestic Product has been estimated at 5.8 per cent which is 16 percent lower than the previous year.'[38]

The slowdown had negatively impacted the overall employment scenario in the country. Quoting the Periodic Labour Force Survey (PLFS) of 2017–2018 (NSSO, Government of India), the report pointed out that the unemployment rate in the country had gone up to 6.1 per cent, which was the highest in last four decades. This had also been accompanied by a fall in the absolute number of workers compared to the previous survey in 2011–2012. 'It has also been estimated that some 62 lakh employment has been lost during 2011–12 and 2017–18. Worsening employment scenario in the country, naturally, resulted in reduction in levels of income of people.' In the case of Assam, the PLFS 2017–2018 estimated the unemployment rate at 7.9 per cent. It was just 2.9 per cent in 2013–2014.[39]

Reflecting on the possible impact of COVID-19 on the economy, the report had also pointed out that unlike the country, the state did not have an officially projected growth rate. But depending on the downward trends over the last three years, the report stated that the projected growth rate would be 3.7 per cent for the financial year 2020–2021. The pandemic, the report suggested, would lower the state growth rate by 1.3 to 5.2 per cent. The cumulative loss in GSDP for the year 2020–2021 due to the epidemic was estimated at ₹3,219 crore to ₹12,877 crore at 2011–2012 prices. The loss was equivalent to ₹4,442 crore to ₹17,770 crore at the current prices. This was only an early estimate as the report was submitted in May 2020 itself.[40] The report documented the probable loss of jobs and the increases in poverty due to the impact of COVID-19. The rate of unemployment, which stands at 8 per cent, may go up to 27 per cent. On the other hand, the poverty ratio, currently at 32 per cent, is likely to be as much as 50.8 per cent. In the case of rural Assam, the poverty ratio, which stands at 33.9 per cent, may go up to 54 per cent.[41]

The report has closely looked at the worsening employment scenario in the state. The report has pointed out that the majority of the labour forces in the state are 'self-employed'. As per the estimates of the PLFS 2017–2018, the worker population ratio in Assam was 43.7 per cent. It is around one crore workers altogether. Nearly 56.5 per cent of them were engaged as self-employed; only 25.1 per cent were regular salary/wage earners and the remaining 18.5 per cent were casual workers. The report had pointed out that in rural areas 'these proportions are 57.5, 22.9 and 19.6 percent respectively. In urban areas 47.8, 43.4 and 8.8 percent are engaged as self-employed, regular wage earner and casual labour respectively.'[42]

As per the estimates drawn from the PLFS, out of the almost 56 lakh people who were engaged as self-employed, 20 lakh were engaged in agriculture. The number of people self-employed in non-agricultural activities was 36 lakh.

It will be relevant to mention that agriculture has been one of the proclaimed priorities of the BJP-led government. In his 2016–2017 budget speech, Sarma claimed that at the current pace of development of the state, it would take '79.34 years to double the farm income in Assam against 13.56 years in the country'.[43] This is the backdrop of the CMSGUY 'Mega Mission'. The government promised that there would be massive investments in rural areas to usher in a complete transformation in the rural economy, assuring empowerment of the rural folk 'in a period of 5 years in a focused and concerted manner to realize the dream of doubling the farm income.'[44] Reflecting on the strategies to be adopted for the said objective, it was declared that about ₹1.20 crore of investment per revenue village was on the works. The total requirement for the mission was ₹30,000 crore over a period of five years. Ten per cent of the total proposed investment would be in the form of community resources such as land and man-days, and the remaining 90 per cent would be from the state resources.[45] However, other schemes and departments apart, in the core departments of agriculture and allied sectors as well as in the Department of Rural Development, the allocations have been meagre.

The actual expenditure in these two departments has been worryingly poor even in proportion to the budgeted expenditure. Table 4.11 is explanatory in this regard. This failure owes to the fact that neither the internal revenue nor the capital expenditure grew as was envisaged by the government while assuming power. The overall growth rate of the GSDP was also not up to the level of expectations. Too much emphasis on the populist schemes also drifted away the resources from the critical domains like agriculture.

Higher allocations in both health and education did not, however, yield in qualitative achievements. For example, the achievement of the state in health and well-being under the SDGs had been worryingly poor. One of the important reasons behind this failure had been government's obsession with building physical infrastructure rather

Table 4.11 Budgetary Allocations in Key Departments: A Comparison

Sectors	2018–2019	2019–2020	2020–2021
Education	17.9 per cent, which is higher than the average expenditure allocated to the department by 18 other states in 2017–2018	21.5 per cent, which is higher than the average expenditure allocated to the department (15.9%) by other states in 2018–2019	19.2 per cent, which is significantly higher than the average budget allocation (15.9%) for education by other states in 2019–2020
Health	5.6 per cent, which is higher than the average expenditure of 18 other states	7.4 per cent, which is higher than the average allocation (5.2%) by other states in 2018–2019	6.4 per cent, which is higher than the average allocation by other states (5.3%)
Agriculture and Allied Departments	1.9 per cent, which is significantly lower than the allocations of 18 other states (6.4%)	5.9 per cent, which is marginally lower than the allocations by other states (6.4%) in 2018–2019	5 per cent, which is lower than the average allocations by other states (7.1%)
Rural Development	4.1 per cent, which is lower than the average (5.6%) of 18 other states	5.4 per cent, which is marginally lower than the average (6.1%) for other states in 2018–2019	3.8 per cent, which is lower than the average allocation for rural development by other states (6.2%)

Source: PRS Legislative Research, Assam Budget Analysis (2016–2017 to 2020–2021), https://www.prsindia.org/parliamenttrack/budgets/assam-budget-analysis.

than quality human structure. Expenditure in populist schemes also took away the higher portions out of the total allocations.

The rural economy, particularly the agriculture sector, was constrained by a lack of access to necessary assets. *ASHDR, 2014,* documents that as whole the percentage of households reporting lack of agricultural asset was as high as 69.6 per cent. It was 64.5 per cent in rural areas. Nearly 36 per cent households also suffered from a lack of financial assets.[46] A series of government schemes had certainly contributed in meeting those requirements. However, the rural people had also relied on the remittances received from the out-migrants of the state to meet needs. In one study conducted by Ratul Mahanta titled 'Out-migration, Remittance and Its Socio-economic Consequences in Assam' and another by K. Das (2020) titled 'Unemployment and Outmigration for Work from Northeast India: How Does It Ensure Economic Wellbeing', it has been indicated that

> Presently some 15 to 18 lakh people of the state are working outside the state. Government of Kerala (2013) estimates that in Kerala alone has some 4.32 lakh workers from Assam whose average annual per capita remittance stands at Rs. 64,000 (i.e. a little over 5,000 per month).[47]

The report also shows that close to 16.5 per cent of the remittance received are used for agricultural investment and operations. Giving an estimate, the report says, 'The total amount invested in the agricultural sector of Assam from the money remitted by the out-migrants could be ₹175 crore from the intra-state migrants alone.' But the potential investment in agriculture from the remittances received from the inter-state out-migrants can be within the range of ₹670 crore to ₹1,900 crore annually.[48]

The above-mentioned factors marginally increased farm production in the state, but a decline of the contribution of agriculture and allied sectors to GSDP is evident. The area under crops in Assam declined during the period from 2015–2016 to 2018–2019. The total area used for the production of total food grains reduced from 26.83 lakh hectares to 26.30 lakh hectares. Areas under winter rice and summer rice also showed a marginal decrease (from 18.89 lakh hectares to 18.80 lakh hectares and from 4.05 lakh hectares to 4.01 lakh hectares, respectively). Areas for autumn rice production declined from 1.91 lakh hectares to 1.45 lakh hectares and areas under wheat production contracted from 0.21 lakh hectares to 0.17 lakh hectares during the same period. There was also a decrease in areas under oil production (excluding coconut) from 3.11 lakh hectares of land to 3.09 lakh hectares.[49] It may be mentioned that there has been an overall decline in areas under crops production since 2011–2012 onwards, and there were also ups and down from year to year.

The yield rates of principal crops showed a marginal increase between 2015–2016 and 2018–2019. For example, the yield rate of winter rice increased from 2,003 kg to 2,205 kg per hectare, autumn rice from 1,364 kg to 1,468 kg and summer rice from 2,818 to 2,858 kg. Yield rates for total pulses remained almost the same, hovering between 755 and 757 kg per hectare during the same period.[50]

The government acknowledges that 'lack of organized marketing facility, lack of storage infrastructure near the filed, poverty and need of money after harvest for repayment of agricultural debt and other contingencies forced the farmers to dispose off their hard earned produces at the earliest and throwaway prices.'[51] Therefore, it insisted on increasing the storage capacity as one of the strategies to help the farmers. However, the government data shows that rather than improving, the storage capacity declined from 759,739 MT to 721,868 MT from 2016–2017 to 2018–2019 (see Table 4.12).

The underwhelming achievements may also be read from the record of the state's performance in meeting the SDGs.

Table 4.12 *Storage Capacity Created by Different Organizations (in MT)*

Organization	2016–2017	2017–2018	2018–2019
Food Corporation of India	389,976	385,913	379,969
Central Warehousing Corporation	72,150	72,983	73,713
State Warehousing Corporation	250,838	242,910	221,407
Assam State Agricultural Marketing Board	46,775	46,775	46,775
Total	**759,739**	**748,581**	**721,868**

Source: Economic Survey, Assam 2019–2020, Table 5.92, p. 82.

SUSTAINABLE DEVELOPMENT GOALS

Along with the *ASHDR, 2014,* Assam's Chief Minister Sarbananda Sonowal released the blueprint of the state government towards achieving the SDGs. However, the achievements of the governments in this regard have been miserably poor. The five-page report enumerated in the Economic Survey, Assam (2019–2020),[52] drawn from the *SDG Baseline Report, 2018,* is a testimony to the very disappointing picture of Assam's performance in this regard. SDGs index value is divided into four categories, assigning a range of values against each category. The lowest is the aspirational category with values in the range of 0–49, performer and front runner are the middle categories with the range of values between 50 and 64 and 65 and 99, respectively and achiever is the highest category with the highest value of 100.

Assam has been placed in the lowest category of composite SDG India (CSI) score, that is, aspirational category in the bottom third rank. Assam's CSI score is 49. Uttar Pradesh is in the bottom, and Bihar occupies the second rank from the bottom. It should be pointed out that this goes along the PCI, where Assam occupies almost the same rank among the large states in the country. No state in the country achieved the achiever rank; three states, namely Himachal Pradesh, Kerala and Tamil Nadu, are in the front runner category; and all the remaining states are in the category of performer.

A total of 13 indicators of SDGs are taken into consideration while calculating the SDG value for the states. Assam has performed worst in SDG 3, that is, health and well-being, with a very poor value of 30, whereas the national value for this indicator is 52. SDG takes into account the successful interventions to reduce maternal mortality rate, under-five mortality rate, maternal and child health on nutrition, universal immunization for children below two years, etc.[53] It may be mentioned that the Department of Health and Family Welfare has been in the limelight for the last 15 years or so, as the current health and family welfare and the finance minister have been holding the department for almost 15 years except for a brief period. In the recent period, the Department of Health received more allocation compared to the average budgetary allocations of most of the states of India. Quoting the NFHS-4, Saswati Choudhury has pointed out,

> Approximately 36% of women in Assam had a Body mass index (BMI) that was below normal and 8% were obese. Anaemia was prevalent in 72% of pregnant women and 69% of women who were not pregnant. In addition, teenage pregnancy (15–19 years age group) was at 61.4% and 13.6% of them were already mothers. Then came COVID-19.[54]

Along with health and well-being, Assam also performed poorly in the other five SDGs. Those are gender equality (SDG 5), clean water and sanitation (SDG 6), affordable and clean energy (SDG 7), industry, innovation and infrastructure (SDG 9) and sustainable cities and communities (SDG 11).

In certain areas of SDG, Assam has done well, and the best has been in SDG 15, which deals with forest cover, water bodies and population of wild elephants. Assam has been placed in the achiever's category in this goal, with the highest score of 100. In case of reduced inequality (SDG 10) and peace, justice and strong institutions (SDG 16), Assam has scored well—71 in each category—and therefore placed in the front runner category. In four categories, Assam has been placed in the performance category: no poverty (SDG 1), zero hunger (SDG 2), quality education (SDG 4) and decent work and growth (SDG 8).

All these indicate that Assam is in a poor state of human development, and the dream seller's economy has not contributed towards overcoming the challenges of human development.

GLOBAL INVESTORS' SUMMIT

On 3–4 February 2018, the Government of Assam hosted the 'Advantage Assam'—the Assam Global Investors' Summit in Guwahati. It has been termed as 'the largest-ever investment promotion and facilitation initiative by the Government of Assam.' The primary aim of the summit was 'highlighting the state's geostrategic advantages offered to investors by Assam'.[55] Inaugurated by the prime minister of India, the summit was attended by 213 representatives from 23 foreign countries, including the prime minister and minister of economic affairs of the

Royal Government of Bhutan, Cambodian minister of tourism, minister of industries of Bangladesh and the minister of commerce of Myanmar. Top business houses, including Reliance, Medanta, Patanjali Ayurved, SpiceJet, McLeod Russel India Ltd and Sun Pharmaceutical Industries Ltd also participated. Representatives of various agencies such as Asian Development Bank, ONGC and NITI Aayog were also in attendance.

On the first day of the summit, as many as 176 initial pacts worth ₹65,186 crore with 160 firms were signed. Interestingly, the highest amount of investment was promised by public sector oil agencies.

> Public sector oil behemoth ONGC committed Rs. 13,000 crore investment in the state, while another oil public sector unit (PSU) Oil India Ltd pledged an investment of Rs. 10,000 crore.... Indian Oil Corporation (IOC) and Numaligarh Refinery Ltd also evinced interest to invest Rs. 3,432 crore and Rs. 3,410 crore.[56]

Reliance Industries promised an investment of ₹2,500 crore in various sectors, including retail, petroleum, telecom, tourism and sports, creating jobs for at least 80,000 people over the next three years'. Tata Trusts promised to join hands with the Assam government to establish a cancer care programme in 17 centres across 15 districts of the state from next year with an investment of around ₹2,000 crore. Indo UK Institute of Health promised to invest ₹2,700 crore. Among others, Century Ply assured ₹2,100 crore and SpiceJet outlined plans of a ₹1,250 crore investment.[57] With another 25 MoUs signed on the final day of the summit with a potential investment of ₹35,000 crore, the summit attracted a combined investment of ₹100,000 crore.[58]

The summit generated enormous publicity and media attention, and roadshows were organized to attract investors. In December 2017, Chief Minister Sarbananda Sonowal kick-started a roadshow of 'Advantage Assam'—the Assam Global Investors' Summit, 2018, at a hotel in Bengaluru.

> As a part of the roadshow, Chief Minister Sonowal in a move to woo investors presented the business landscape of the State especially 'ease of doing business', 'single window clearance system', 'skilled work force' and state's verdant natural resources before a galaxy of as many as 300 business leaders.[59]

State finance minister attended a roadshow in Singapore on 1 December 2017. He was accompanied by his cabinet colleague, Rihon Daimari.[60]

Has Assam really gained from the investment summit? Till September 2018, the government managed to attract investment worth ₹8,020.21 crore and claimed that around ₹39,951.65 crore investment was on the pipeline.[61] After September 2018, the issue of global investment suddenly disappeared. As politics in the state was gradually overtaken by anti-CAB movement, and the government indulged in hyper-populism for electoral gains, it put its own highly proclaimed global investments under the carpet. Throughout its tenure, the BJP-led regime had to face public wrath due to its failure in reviving the sick industries like the two Hindustan Paper Corporation Limited (HPCL) mills in Nagaon and Cachar. The Nagaon Paper Mill is closed (without notice) from 13 March 2017. The Cachar Mill is also closed (also without notice) from 20 October 2015. It was reported that the workers have not been paid for 37 and 39 months, respectively, till April 2020.[62] Failing to receive its due, the employees approached the Delhi High Court. The court in its order directed the HPCL liquidator and the Employees' Provident Fund Organisation (EPFO) to disburse ₹160 crore, the remaining PF amount, at the earliest.[63]

CORPORATE DRIVE

On 12 August 2016, Assam became the first state to ratify the CAB for the Goods and Services Tax (GST).[64] While the country as a whole was debating the merits of the tax initiative, which created havoc for the middle and small sector industries, the state government's prime concern was to occupy the first position among the states in the country in appeasing the move. However, all these have not helped the state in achieving anything substantive, in either improving the state's rank in PCI or consolidating its SDG value. On 25 June 2016, the Union government declared its decision of international bidding of 67 underdeveloped oilfields of the country which included 12 oil fields of Assam. These 12 fields hold a combined estimated reserve of 21 million MT of oil and oil equivalent gas.[65] The decision was welcomed by public protests across the state. Oil has been at the core of Assam's nationalist sentiments, and it had generated strong reaction during the period of Assam agitation too. 'We shall spill our blood but shall never part with the oil which we own.' The Numaligarh and Guwahati oil refineries are the products of the sentiments this slogan evoked in the 1980s.[66] In April 2020, the Standing Committee of the National Board of Wild Life (NBWL) under the Union Ministry of Environment, Forest and Climate Change recommended approving Coal India Limited's (CIL) proposal for legalizing the illegal mining at Dehing Patkai forest. The decision again met with a strong backlash. Social media was filled with people's anger. A composer, Rahul Rajkhowa, called it the killing of lungs of Northeast: 'Enough Covid-19 talk/My Assam is burning for real/Another set of ministers desperate to steal/causing damage to our forest/to the point it cannot heal/killing the lungs of Northeast/ how the hell cannot you feel....'[67] This forced the state government to constitute a committee for a judicial enquiry to be headed by a retired judge of the Gauhati High Court. While the public wrath against the Dehing Patkai illegal coal mining issue was already in the air, the draft Environment Impact Assessment (EIA) notification, 2020, issued on 12 March by the Union Ministry of Environment, Forest and Climate Change set off another round of huge protests in Assam and Northeast India. The notification has been termed as 'the next flashpoint in Assam after the National Register of Citizens (NRC) and Citizenship (Amendment) Act (CAA), 2019, with several prominent groups and parties opposing it by terming it anti-north-east.'[68] EIA has been an issue in contention in Assam in particular and in Northeast India in general for more than a decade now around the construction of large river dams in Northeast India. The proposed provision of post facto clearance of projects elicited anger and dismay in the state.

CONCLUSION

The new regime that came to power endowed with popular support, expectations and enthusiasm disappointed the state not only on political issues but also on almost all substantive issues concerning development. But the rhetoric of extraordinary performance at the development front continued, and the absence of strong research scrutiny on achievements on development helped the government to sustain its image as the saviour of the destiny of the commons to an extent. The endless populism that manufactured multi-layered individual beneficiaries helped the government to divert the attention of the common masses from the larger and crucial issues of development as mandated by SDGs and brought to the forefront by the *ASHDR, 2014*. The government indeed succeeded in sustaining the new incarnation of neoliberalism, blending religion in politics and populism in pursuing the agenda of transferring the resources of the commons to the private and corporate forces.

NOTES

1. Dr Himanta Biswa Sarma, *Budget Speech 2016–17*, para 12.1, Government of Assam.
2. Government of Assam, Economic Survey, Assam (2019–2020), p 91.
3. BASIC, Study of Assam Tea Value Chains, October 2019, p 13.
4. Government of Assam, Economic Survey 2019–20 p 165.
5. BASIC, *Study of Assam Tea Value Chains* (October 2019), 20, https://lebasic. com/wp-content/uploads/2019/10/BASIC_Assam-tea-Value-Chain-Study_ October-2019.pdf.
6. *The Telegraph Online*, 'Mahanta Hedges on Reforms', 21 November 1999, Guwahati, https://www.telegraphindia.com/india/mahanta-hedges-on-reforms/ cid/910537.
7. Ibid.
8. Akhil Ranjan Dutta, 'The ULFA and the Indian State', in *Unheeded Hinterland: Identity and Sovereignty in Northeast India*, ed. Dilip Gogoi (Abingdon: Routledge, 2016), 195.
9. Government of Assam, *Assam State Human Development Report* (Managing Diversities, Achieving Human Development; 2014), 5–6, https://sita.assam. gov.in/portlets/assam-human-development-report-0.
10. Ibid.
11. Ibid., xxix.
12. Ibid., xxx.
13. Ibid., xxxi.
14. India Blooms, 'Sonowal Releases Assam Human Development Report 2014', 3 October 2016, https://www.indiablooms.com/news-details/N/24765/sonowal-releases-assam-human-development-report-2014.html
15. Ibid.
16. Government of Assam, 'White Paper on Assam State Finances (As on 24th May 2016)', https://finance.assam.gov.in/sites/default/files/A%20White%20 Paper%20On%20Assam%20State%20Finances%20%28English%29.pdf.
17. Ibid., para 1.4.
18. Ibid., para 4.13.
19. Joydeep Biswas, 'OPINION: White Paper Blues', NewsMen,12 June 2016, https://newsmen.in/news/opinion-white-paper-blues/.
20. Government of Assam, 'White Paper on Assam State Finances', para 2.1.3.

21. Government of Assam, *Budget Speech 2016–17*, para 10.13.
22. Government of Assam, *Budget Speech 2020–21*, para 13.
23. Government of Assam, 'White Paper on Assam State Finances', 2016, para 2.3.
24. Government of Assam, *Budget Speech 2016–17*, para 13.2
25. StatisticsTimes, 'Indian States by GDP per Capita', 2019, http://statisticstimes. com/economy/gdp-capita-of-indian-states.php.
26. Ibid.
27. Government of Assam, *Budget Speech 1972–73*, 3.
28. Ibid., 6.
29. Government of Assam, *Budget Speech 2016–17*, para 11–13.
30. Ibid.
31. Government of Assam, *Budget Speech 2020–21*.
32. Ibid., 1, para 2.
33. Government of Assam, *Budget speech 2016–17*, 15, para 12.3.
34. Ibid., 15, para 12.4.
35. Ibid., 36, para 23.4.
36. Government of Assam, *Budget Speech 2020–21*, para 9.
37. Government of Assam, *Report on Economy of Assam in the Backdrop of COVID-19 Pandemic* (Guwahati: Prepared by Innovation and Transformation Aayog (SITA), Government of Assam, in collaboration with OKD Institute of Social Change and Development, 2020), 4.
38. The rates are at 2011–2012 constant prices. Ibid., 4.
39. Ibid., 4–5.
40. Ibid., 6
41. Ibid., 11–12.
42. Ibid.
43. Government of Assam, *Budget Speech 2016–17*, 4, para 9.4.
44. Ibid., 37–38, para 23.6.
45. Ibid., 39, para 23.16.
46. Government of Assam, *Assam State Human Development Report, 2016*, 59.
47. Quoted from the Government of Assam, *Report on Economy of Assam*, 14–15.
48. Ibid.
49. Government of Assam, Economic Survey, Assam (2019–20), 68.
50. Ibid., 69.
51. Ibid., 82.
52. Ibid., 280–284.
53. Ibid., 281.
54. Saswati Choudhury, 'Healthcare and Nutrition for Women in Assam Was Already Inadequate. Then Came COVID-19', The Wire, 4 June 2020, https:// thewire.in/women/assam-women-nutrition-health.
55. Government of Assam, 'Advantage Assam', https://advantageassam.com/.
56. LiveMint, 'Assam Investors' Meet: 176 MoUs of Rs. 65,186 Crore Signed on Day 1', 3 February 2018, https://www.livemint.com/Companies/ KxrkuSNdeQnlcKOl7q899J/Assam-investors-meet-176-MoUs-of-Rs65186-crore-signed-on.html.

57. Ibid.
58. News18 Business, 'Assam Gets Investment Commitments of Rs. 1 Lakh Crore', 4 February 2018, https://www.news18.com/news/business/assam-gets-investment-commitments-of-rs-1-lakh-crore-1650513.html#:~:text=Guwahati%3A%20 Assam%20has%20received%20investment,of%20the%20summit%20on%20 Sunday.
59. GPlus, 'Roadshow of Advantage Assam to Attract Investors', 20 December 2017, https://www.guwahatiplus.com/daily-news/roadshow-of-advantage-assam-to-attract-investors.
60. Himanta Biswa Sarma's tweet, 1 December 2017, https://twitter.com/himantabiswa/status/936579675865808896?lang=en.
61. Bikash Singh, 'Advantage Assam: Global Investors' Summit Has attracted Rs. 8,020.21 Crore till Now Says Chandra Mohan Patwary', *The Economic Times,* 27 September 2018, https://economictimes.indiatimes.com/news/politics-and-nation/advantage-assam-global-investors-summit-has-attracted-rs-8020-21-crore-till-now-says-chandra-mohan-patwary/articleshow/65983301.cms.
62. Gaurav Das, 'Delhi HC Orders State-owned Paper Mill in Assam to Release Money Owed to Workers Immediately', The Wire, 25 April 2020, https://thewire.in/labour/delhi-hc-orders-state-owned-paper-mill-in-assam-to-release-money-owed-to-workers-immediately.
63. Ibid.
64. LiveMint, 'Assam Becomes First State to Ratify GST Bill', 12 August 2016, https://www.livemint.com/Politics/gMqghJdOgThPvQ4muqRhiN/Assam-becomes-first-state-to-ratify-Constitution-amendment-b.html.
65. *Business Standard,* 'Centre's Small Oil Fields Auction to Include 12 from Assam', 25 June 2016, https://www.business-standard.com/article/economy-policy/centre-s-small-oil-fields-auction-to-include-12-from-assam-116062500607_1.html.
66. Sangeeta Barooah Pisharoty, 'Oil and "Outsiders": Outrage in Assam over the BJP's Decision to Privatise Oil Fields', The Wire, 10 July 2016, https://thewire.in/politics/bjp-assam-oil-privatisation.
67. Abdul Gani, 'Killing Lungs of Northeast': Rapper Sings on Coal Mining in Assam's Dehing-Patkai Forest', Outlook, 6 June 2020, https://www.outlookindia.com/website/story/india-news-killing-lungs-of-northeast-rapper-sings-on-coal-mining-in-assams-dehing-patkai-forest/354274.
68. Utpal Parashar, 'Terming It Anti-northeast, Assam Groups and Parties Up Ante against Draft EIA 2020', *Hindustan Times,* 18 July 2020, https://www.hindustantimes.com/india-news/terming-it-anti-northeast-assam-groups-and-parties-up-ante-against-draft-eia-2020/story-973anIqcppVby9lDtcN6WP.html.

Conservation, People's Entitlements and National Security

This chapter brings together two important judgments and orders of the Gauhati High Court—one on *Kaziranga National Park vs Union of India & Others*[1] and the other on *Akhil Gogoi vs State of Assam & 2 Others*[2] to illustrate the interface between the executive and the judiciary during the BJP-led regime in Assam. Both judgments have implications on people's entitlements. The first judgment, which was delivered in October 2015, that is, during the Congress-led regime in Assam, was executed after the BJP-led regime had assumed power in Assam in May 2016. These two judgments and orders illustrate two different kinds of interfaces between two institutions: the executive and the judiciary. The first judgment represents an apparent convergence, and the other presents a case of confrontation. The convergence in the first case, however, is very problematic and not driven by the same objective. Therefore, the convergence has also inherent contradictions. The first case is about encroachment in the KNP and the directive of the Gauhati High Court to evict the encroachers. It was a suo moto case registered by the court based on newspaper reports about the killing of Assam's pride—one-horned rhinos—in the park. For the court, the 'encroachers' were a secular entity irrespective of their religious affiliations. However, the state's drive to evict them took a communal turn, as it sought to label them as 'illegal Bangladeshis' who were supposedly Muslims. The court's order was based on Assam's nationalist sentiments about the killing of the prized animal and the concerns about the conservation of the national park—the home to the animal. The secular concerns of the court, however, opened up a course of confrontation between the executive (I am interchangeably using both the state and the executive) and the victims of the eviction. The two sides represent two radically different perspectives on forest and conservation. The state-driven discourse on conservation manufactures an antagonistic relationship between the people and the forest or a national park. The forces that fuel the concerns of the commons both inside and around the forest or a national park pursue an alternative discourse on conservation, where the relationship is based on mutually reinforcing co-existence. The judiciary, in its overriding concerns over conservation of the one-horned rhinos, overlooked these two mutually antagonistic narratives on conservation and thereby facilitated the state to drive a course of evictions with coercions.

The other case is about undermining the constitutionally and legally guaranteed procedures in driving actions by the state in enforcing extraordinary laws related to national security. In this verdict, the procedures got prominence over the substance of a case registered by the state. The case brings a different side of the interface between the executive and the judiciary to the forefront. Akhil Gogoi, the leader of the KMSS, was arrested on the ground of his alleged statements, which caused a threat to national security and integrity, and, therefore, he was detained and jailed under the NSA. The court, while issuing the order to grant him bail, did not have to look into the substance of the allegations. It examined the procedural lapses at different stages of the case and granted him bail with a note of warning to the executive to be careful in enforcing the extraordinary laws.

Both cases have an interesting linkage. The first verdict led to the arrest of Akhil Gogoi, who steered the resistance against the eviction drives in KNP. He was charged with inciting the resistance. In the second case, the same person was granted bail by the high court for the alleged mishandling of procedures while invoking the NSA.

CONSERVATIONS VS PEOPLE'S ENTITLEMENTS: CONTESTATIONS IN KNP

KNP in Assam, located in India's north-east, is one of the incredible success stories of preserving the one-horned rhinos. The park hosts almost two-thirds of the entire global population of the animal.

Kaziranga is also a national pride for Assam, and it echoes the rhythms of the nationalist imagination of its people. A UNESCO World Heritage Centre, KNP represents

> [O]ne of the last unmodified natural areas in the north-eastern region of India. Covering 42,996 ha, and located in the State of Assam it is the single largest undisturbed and representative area in the Brahmaputra Valley floodplain. The fluctuations of the Brahmaputra River result in spectacular examples of riverine and fluvial processes in this vast area of wet alluvial tall grassland interspersed with numerous broad shallow pools fringed with reeds and patches of deciduous to semi-evergreen woodlands. Kaziranga is regarded as one of the finest wildlife refuges in the world. The park's contribution in saving the Indian one-horned rhinoceros from the brink of extinction at the turn of the 20th century to harbouring the single largest population of this species is a spectacular conservation achievement. The property also harbours significant populations of other threatened species including tigers, elephants, wild water buffalo and bears as well as aquatic species including the Ganges River dolphin. It is an important area for migratory birds.[3]

The ecology of the park is very complex and dynamic. River fluctuations of the Brahmaputra have gifted KNP a uniquely diverse bio-space.

> River fluctuations by the Brahmaputra river system result in spectacular examples of riverine and fluvial processes. River bank erosion, sedimentation and formation of new lands as well as new water-bodies, plus succession between grasslands and woodlands represents outstanding examples of significant and ongoing, dynamic ecological and biological processes. Wet alluvial grasslands occupy nearly two-thirds of the park area and are maintained by annual flooding and burning. These natural processes create complexes of habitats which are also responsible for a diverse range of predator/prey relationships.[4]

The park is composed of wetlands, foothills and floodplains, and it regularly witnesses the succession between grasslands and woodlands. It has changed its form, substance and size since the beginning of the 20th century. The colonial imagination of the park was associated with the political economy of tea plantation which required secure landscapes which used to be the habitat of a variety of wild animals. Kaziranga, therefore, is also testimony to the fragmentation of the landscape of Brahmaputra Valley in Assam under the necessity of colonial plantation economy.[5] Declared as a forest reserve in 1908, Kaziranga was redesignated as a game sanctuary in 1916. It was declared as a wildlife sanctuary in 1950. In 1974, the Government of India accorded the official status of a national park to Kaziranga after the Government of Assam had enacted the National Park Act in 1968 and declared it as a designated national park. In 1985, UNESCO recognized it as a World Heritage Centre. As the protection of wildlife and conservation of forests have emerged as new milestones for national imagination, Kaziranga continues to expand by adding the neighbouring human habitations to the park, which, in turn, has brewed conflicts between the park and its neighbourhood.

In recent times, the park has emerged as an epitome of controversies which mark conflict between the state-driven discourse of conservation and communities in its vicinity. The expansion of the park by attaching six adjacent areas (officially called additions), which was done through bureaucratic exercises without taking the communities into confidence, triggered conflict and tension in the neighbourhood human habitations. The verdict of the Gauhati High Court[6] which resulted in the ruthless eviction drives in September 2016 and the documentary prepared by the British Broadcasting Corporation (BBC) titled 'Our World: Killing for Conservation'[7] generated intense debate in India and abroad on the conservation model and the brutality in the name of conservation in Kaziranga.

The origin of the conflict may be traced back to the enactment of the Wild Life (Protection) Act, 1972, and Forest (Conservation) Act, 1980. These Acts fused the initiatives of wildlife protection and forest conservation with the nationalist sentiment of the state. Such conservation nationalism, which is mostly elitist, fails to recognize the interrelationships between the forest and its animal habitats with the surrounding human settlements. The mainstream discourse of conservation manufactures animosity between the forests and the communities in their vicinity. This conflict has immense significance in understanding the limits of the development paradigm and the conservationist models in India in general and Northeast India in particular.

The following section briefly reflects on the contestations around the development and conservation paradigms.

Three Cultures: Growing Antagonism

At the heart of the intense global debate surrounding development discourse is whether it only involves two 'cultures'—developmentalism and environmentalism—or there are more, which may also include the culture of people's entitlements which confront both. This is a pertinent and politically provoking question which encounters the state- and corporate-driven development and conservationist agenda in India in general and Northeast India in particular. Jairam Ramesh, former Environment and Forest Minister of India under the UPA government, argues that there are two mutually antagonistic approaches to development, which he terms 'two different cultures'. Referring to the British physicist-author C. P. Snow, who spoke of 'breakdown of communications between the "two cultures" of modern society—the culture of science and that of humanities', Mr Ramesh explores 'a later-day facet of the "two cultures" syndrome'.[8] Here, he outlines the mutually incompatible approaches of faster economic growth and protection of the environment. Ramesh argues,

> [O]n the face of it, there should be no gap at all—who can argue against faster economic growth since that alone will generate more jobs and at the same time who can argue against the preservation of our rivers, lakes, mountains and wonderful biodiversity in its myriad forms since that alone will make sustainable development.[9]

Ramesh, however, laments that both these approaches stick to their exclusive concerns and look at each other, rather than explore the possibility of convergence and dialogue. He also points out that both the approaches talk of a balance, but with contrary articulations. The proponents of growth talk of a 'fetish which is being made of the environment' and the environmentalists talk of the fetish which is 'being made of economic growth'. Ramesh's primary concern, as a minister of environment and forest, was to explore the possibility of bringing these two contrary approaches to dialogue. In his judgement, there are three approaches to development or, for that matter, faster economic growth. They are 'yes', 'yes, but' and 'no'. While the growth constituency primarily stands for 'yes' but concedes to 'yes, but' and cries foul with 'no', the environmentalists believe in the reverse sequence: 'no', 'yes, but' and they denounce 'yes'. Ramesh's mission had been to enhance and expand the category of 'yes, but'. He found a lot of shortcomings in understanding growth itself and, therefore, reiterated a lot of innovations undertaken by different thinkers and agencies. He mentions the transition of GDP from gross domestic product to green domestic product, and GNP from gross national product to green nature product. Ramesh argues that such innovations will adequately and properly reflect 'the consumption of precious depletable natural resources in the process of generating national income'.[10] He also argues that environmental concerns cannot be reduced to elitist concerns for clean air and protection of tigers alone. These should be able to address the larger public health issues arising out of faster economic growth. Finally, Ramesh looks for a solution and argues,

> Having said this, I want to return to the very formulation of this modern-day 'two cultures'. Is the debate really environment *versus* development or is it one of adhering to rules, regulations and laws *versus* taking the rules, regulations and laws for granted? I think the latter is a more accurate representation and a better way to formulate the choice.[11]

Ramesh thinks that the Indian Parliament enacted several progressive laws to address the concerns of these two cultures. Important among them are the Wild Life (Protection) Act of 1972, Water (Prevention and Control of Pollution) Act of 1974, Forest (Conservation) Act of 1980, Air (Prevention and Control of Pollution) Act of 1981, Environment (Protection) Act of 1986 and the most recent FRA of 2006. For Ramesh,

> The question before the country is very, very simple: are these laws to be enforced or are they to just adorn the statute books, honoured more in their breach than in their observance. This is the intellectually honest way of formulating C P Snow's dialectic in the Indian context today.[12]

While appreciating environmental concerns, Ramesh would also make a difference within the environmentalist approach: 'Livelihood environmentalism as I would term it as opposed to lifestyle environmentalism of the privileged sections.'[13] In other words, environmentalism is also a class question, which invites serious attention. This empirical study of KNP seeks to analyse the issue, which has emerged as a centre stage of debate in the recent years due to the growing conflicts between the state-driven conservationist model and the communities living in its vicinity.

In a rejoinder to Jairam Ramesh, Hiren Gohain, eminent intellectual and activist on issues around people's entitlements of Northeast India, argues that there are indeed three cultures, not two, in Ramesh's formulations, and they are in 'opposition to each other: the corporate-driven campaign for economic development at any cost, the elitist concerns articulated by non-governmental organisations, and the desperate struggle of indigenous people who are under the threat of extinction'.[14]

Gohain points out that Ramesh, through his proposition of a dialogue between two antagonistic cultures, introduces and legitimizes the hegemonic logic of development. He also finds it problematic to accept Ramesh's proposition of equating development-generated employment with that of livelihood. Livelihood is a larger issue and encompasses concerns beyond employment. Gohain argues that under the present hegemonic order, the balance that Ramesh proposes is bound to break down. With empirical evidence from Northeast India, particularly concerning the ongoing struggles of the indigenous people in the region against the hydropower projects, Gohain suggests that policy structures and priorities of the Government of India themselves are anti people, and, therefore, the balance explored by Ramesh is unachievable and unsustainable.

This debate encourages us to explore the political economy and the limitations of not only developmentalism but also environmentalism in addressing the concerns of the commons in Northeast India. Environmentalism may also arise as a mask of the developmental state in pursuing its vested interests. India's legislation concerning wildlife, environment and forest rights and other issues have common concerns, but there are fundamental differences in addressing the relationship between the forest/environment/wildlife and the common people. The local inhabitants' oppositions to these Acts came to the forefront in Assam in the recent years with the Gauhati High Court verdict on KNP in October 2015[15] and the subsequent eviction drives undertaken by the Government of Assam in September 2016. The debate got intensified after BBC telecast a documentary on Kaziranga on 11 February 2017 titled 'Our World: Killing for Conservation'.[16] The basic argument of the documentary is that in KNP, the forest guards have been granted extrajudicial power with impunity and the guards have indulged in killing suspected poachers for the protection of the one-horned rhinos. It argues that the number of people killed in the park has been higher than the number of rhinos being killed. The documentary provoked widespread controversies, forcing BBC to stop its circulation. Subsequently, the broadcasting company came under severe scrutiny and faced a five-year ban on documenting/filming tiger reserves in the country. Ironically, both the government and the conservationists objected to misrepresentation of facts on Kaziranga in the documentary, but the local communities came out in support for the bold documentation. While BBC refrained from broadcasting the documentary again, the report prepared by Justin Rowlatt, its South Asia correspondent, titled 'Kaziranga: The Park That Shoots People to Protect Rhinos',[17] which first appeared on the BBC News website on 10 February 2017, is still available to read.

Gauhati High Court Verdict on KNP and the Evictions

The Gauhati High Court verdict on KNP and the evictions brought to the forefront a larger question on the very model of conservation, which draws wall distrust between the human entitlements and forest and animal conservation. Fanari and Doley aptly capture this antagonism:

> The question that arises is, whether the warped issue of eviction is actually linked to the danger of poaching, or is it related to an ever-expanding lexicon of neo-conservation policies that always find a reason to dispossess the most marginalised? The policies of Kaziranga National Park, that plans to double its own territory in the name of additions and corridors, continuously feed the need of displacement, exacerbating into an environment of conflict.[18]

The Gauhati High Court delivered a combined judgment and an order on 9 October 2015 on two public interest litigations (PILs) and two writ petitions on KNP. Whereas the PILs were concerned with the illegal poaching of rhinoceros and killings of wild animals in the park which required evictions of human habitations in and around the park, the two writ petitions were concerned with restraining evictions. The illegal poaching of rhinos in the park has been in the media for quite a long time, and it has been a widely contested political issue in the state as well. In 2014, on the eve of the general elections, the issue of poaching the rhinoceros became a contention among competing political forces. BJP's prime ministerial candidate, Narendra Modi, alleged the Congress of indulging in the killing of rhinos to clear jungles and resettle illegal Bangladeshis there.[19] The Congress regime in Assam became a target from different quarters for its inability to stop the killings of the rhinos. The park emerged as a determining political dynamic in both 2014 general elections and 2016 state assembly elections.

The Gauhati High Court suo moto registered a PIL (66/2012) 'to inquire into the news report regarding illegal poaching and killing of wild animals in the KNP'.[20] The suo moto registration was provoked by reports of killing of rhinos and wild animals in three leading news dailies—*The Telegraph, The Indian Express* and *The Hindu* in September 2012.[21] Along with the suo moto registration, the high court also admitted another PIL (67/2012) filed by Mrinal Saikia, the BJP MLA of the Khumtai constituency, which, apart from petitioning to enquire into the killing of rhinos and wild animals, sought 'an additional relief of removal of human habitation and encroachment in the animal corridors in and around the KNP'.[22]

The writ petitions [WP(C) 648/2013 and 4860/2013] were concerned with protecting human habitations and ensuring measures against any drive of evictions without compliance to the provisions of the FRA of 2006 as well as past decisions of the successive governments in settling the habitations. The petitions also proposed certain models of cohabitation between human and wildlife, which, however, did not draw attention in the final judgment. There were two intervening applications (IA 1261/2015 and 1262/2015), filed by the applicants to be impleaded in PIL 66/2012. The IAs asserted that the contested habitations were indeed revenue villages with the habitants holding pattas and, therefore, could not be evicted. The verdict delivered on 9 October 2015 entirely rejected both the writ petitions and the IAs with the following remark:

> The individual claims for a handful of persons is in conflict with the public and national interest. There have been persistent and repeated reports of poaching of rhinoceros, elephants and other wild animals. It is irresistible inference that the habitants in KKP area would fall in suspect group and they would be well-acquainted with the areas and animal movements, therefore they would alone be in a position to do poaching successfully or abet poaching by others. The concept of national park in the Wildlife Act contemplates that there should be no human habitation.[23]

In its judgment and the order, the court invoked the Directive Principles of the State Policy (Article 48A) and the Fundamental Duties of Citizens (Article 51A(g)) enumerated in the Constitution of India, concerning the responsibility of the state towards protecting the environment and wildlife and that of the responsibility of the citizens in this regard.[24]

The court, from the very beginning of the hearing, was seriously concerned about the illegal poaching and kept directing the appropriate authority from time to time to stop the killings of rhinos at any cost. In its order dated 4 March 2014, the court, while directing the director of KNP 'to submit the detail report on or before the next date of hearing suggesting therein the effective and remedial steps for implementation to curb poaching of rhinos in the Kaziranga National Park', said,

> We express our serious concern about the incidences of poaching in Kaziranga National Park which have recently taken place and are taking place from time to time, we view it seriously. At any cost, in our view, the same must be stopped at the earliest to save the nature's most priceless and precious endangered species 'Rhino'. Indeed, it is our duty to preserve this God's gift to this world at any cost.[25]

A critical reading of the judgment and the order reveals that the court got trapped into one-dimensionality due to its overriding concern over illegal poaching of the rhinos. Its genuine concern is evident from the fact that it suo moto registered the PIL. However, the one-dimensionality forced it to prioritize the Acts concerning the protection of the wildlife and the conservation of forests over the FRA, which provides entitlements of the forest dwellers. The possibility of co-habitation of the wildlife and human beings was completely ruled out in the process. The legal technicalities got precedence over the substantive issues. As a result, the court legitimized the state's language regarding the protection of wildlife and conservation of forests. The court had the opportunity of balancing between wildlife protection and the protection of human habitation, as the FRA, 2006, was already available for them to lean on. When we argue that the court indeed validated the state's language, we draw the evidence from the fact that the court relied on the reports of the state officials alone—either Kaziranga's director's or the high-powered committee's—in arriving at the conclusions over its (court's) concerns.

A chronological reading of the judgment, which passed through a series of hearings and orders, will be relevant in understanding the one-dimensionality in the judgment and the order.

In one of its order dated 4 March 2014, granting two months, the Chief Justice of the Gauhati High Court issued directions to the director of KNP 'to submit a detailed report about the geographical features, the flora and fauna, the animal life, the contributory reasons, which is aiding the poaching and illegal activities and also to give long-term solutions to remedy the ills affecting the Park'.[26] The director documented the multidimensional issues associated with the killing of rhinoceros in KNP in a 402-page-long report. He stated,

> The factors identified as threat to the survival of the rhinos, other than poaching, are loss and fragmentation of habitat, lack to technology and strategic advantage over poachers, certain lacuna in policy and law and their implementation, challenges of growth and development on the fringes of the park and possible impacts of climate change and climate variations. The approach to mitigate the threats and ensure long term survival of Kaziranga is multi-pronged and multi-disciplinary with a series of immediate, short term, medium term and long term measures to be undertaken. Some of the suggested measures include erosion control, habitat improvement, extension of habitat, corridors retrofitting, upscaling of anti-poaching infrastructure, security and surveillance in and around the Park, adopting a landscape based approach and constitution of a landscape authority for conservation and development of the areas, adopting a green growth approach for development in the landscape, adopting better management strategies such as organizational restructuring, increased staff strength,

staff welfare and creating some key and necessary infrastructure, adopting better policies and strengthening further the legal provisions, and above all creating several secure habitats outside Kaziranga for the rhinos.[27]

The director further noted,

> The actual implementation of the recommendations would require a series of ground surveys, in depth study, execution of Proof of Concepts, preparation of DPRs and Technical Feasibility Reports. The implementation would largely depend upon how strong is the institutional framework, availability of funds, support of the stakeholders, especially the local stakeholders, and the monitoring and feedback mechanisms put in place.[28]

The report indicated that the issue of poaching could not be reduced to one or the other factor. It also could not be reduced to a nexus of the local people with the poachers. There were larger issues, which he suggested in his report required ground surveys and validation and execution of existing concepts and impression surrounding illegal poaching in KNP.

None of these matters figured in the court's final judgment and order dated 9 October 2015; instead, it was reduced to invasion by the encroachers, and the local inhabitants were put into the shadow of suspected facilitators of poaching of rhinos in the park.

A high-powered committee was constituted by the court, and the committee was

> [T]old to do the counting of residences in the Kaziranga National Park area, which would include the first Addition to sixth Addition, and also to survey the population in the residential buildings, huts, etc. The committee shall also take biometrics of the people residing in the area and submit the report by 26th June, 2015.[29]

The committee constituted was not an independent committee; it was composed of the commissioner (Home), Government of Assam; revenue secretary, Government of Assam; inspector-general of police (Border), Assam; director (NE-II), MHA; and inspector-general (Forest), NTCA Regional Office.[30] The court could have appointed an independent committee, but that was not the case.

This committee visited the additions to KNP, the core national park areas and the vicinity, and interacted with the people. It primarily investigated the nature of habitation, probable duration of stay, pattern of houses, land entitlements, etc., and directed the deputy commissioners of the three districts which KNP falls in and other appropriate authorities to document 'encroachers/settlers on the government land in the vicinity of Kaziranga National Park'. There is a fundamental difference between the report submitted by the director of the park and the approach adopted by the committee. While the director approached the problem from a wide range of issues, including lacunae in the existing laws and lapses in security, etc., the committee was asked only to document encroachment and illegal settlement near the national park. The committee, while doing so, gave its abstract observations without a comprehensive enquiry. In the case of the second addition to KNP, the committee report suggested the following:

> The Committee observed that the general impression after the field visit, in the 2nd Addition areas, was that most of the constructions were new dating back from last one to ten years and temporary and semi-permanent in nature, which have been erected with an apparent intention of bargaining for land elsewhere.[31]

In the case of the sixth addition, the committee observed,

> In the 6th Addition, the semi-permanent, make-shift bamboo structures called khutis were observed to have been put up recently. It could be sensed on talking to the encroachers that many of them had mischievously been planted by some vested interests.[32]

Are not these very casual statements? Have the entitlement documents been examined carefully to arrive at such conclusions? In the case of Bandardubi and Deuchur, the two most contentious habitations in Kaziranga, the committee informed, 'A detailed in-depth survey of individuals/families occupying Government land along with land status report is to be prepared by the concerned DC/SDO (Civil) and it should be provided to police within one month for taking further action.'[33]

The Bandardubi and Deuchur Chang villages, which are outside the additions to KNP, have become key battlegrounds of contestations after the high court verdict. The counsel for the suo moto PIL asserted that in the Bandardubi village, 183 families lived as encroachers, and in Deuchur Chang village, 122 families lived as encroachers; thus, total 305 families lived as encroachers. Curiously though, those families had received building materials under Indira Awas Yojana, a government scheme for building houses. It was also said that lower primary schools, madrasas, idgahs and masjids were constructed in villages. Arguments were also made that the government was encouraging encroachers and facilitating their permanent settlement. Many residents of these villages, as was reported by independent reporters, settled much before Kaziranga was declared as a national park. The residents of the villages were also not illegal migrants or 'Bangladeshis'. The villages had a composite demographic character, and there were not only East-Bengal-origin Muslims but also of different indigenous communities of Assam. Indeed, many Muslim families had settled in those villages much before the indigenous Assamese people started inhabiting there. Bandardubi is a very old village. The government constructed a *pucca* masjid and a *naamghar* in 1951. The first primary school was established in 1960, which was provincialized in 1966. There are a total of 1,735 bighas of government land in the village, and after survey in 1963, Bandardubi was recognized as a village in 1963 by the revenue department of the Government of Assam.[34] However, the authorities appointed by the court did not consider these issues comprehensively. These villagers were simply dubbed as encroachers, and in its order dated 15 July 2015, the court directed: 'In so far as the Bandardubi and Deuchur Chang villages are concerned, the Deputy Commissioner, Nagaon shall evict the encroachment of Government land from the said two villages on or before 12-08-2015, if necessary with effective police assistance.'[35]

The verdict cited government data, information and report to substantiate its concerns over illegal poaching of rhinoceros and killing of the wild animal in Kaziranga. The counsel on behalf of the suo moto PIL leaned on the provisions of the Wild Life (Protection) Act, 1972, and Forest (Conservation) Act, 1980, as well as referred to relevant verdicts by the Supreme Court to substantiate the concerns of the PIL. The FRA, 2006, did not figure much. The dominant popular perception that the poaching is an act of illegal migrants and that the communities living around the park are illegal encroachers almost got validated through the verdict. One can reasonably argue that the case was fought between two unequal parties. On the one hand, there were the court and the government officials, and on the other, there were the alleged 'encroachers', who were already under the imminent threat of eviction.

The writ petitioners had come up with internationally recognized models of co-existence between animal and human habitations. The court could have examined these models through an independent committee. It could have also directed to experiment the models for a certain period before ordering for eviction. It, however, did not consider these steps to be appropriate and relevant and ordered for eviction. Therefore, the verdict, rather than bringing a resolution, legitimized the state's coercion. Not only that, it also helped the dominant forces to play the communal card.

It is pertinent to ask an important question here: What came first—the proposal for the expansion of KNP through new additions to the park or the habitations in the contested additions? It is in this context that a report published in The Wire, titled 'As Kaziranga Expands, the Fate of Grazing Communities Hangs in the Balance',[36] is worth mentioning. Fanari and Doley traced the history of habitation in the additions to understand the conflict between the wildlife in Kaziranga and the local community. The contested territories had been used by the cattle-rearing families prior to independence. The government permitted that. The conflict between the state and these families started since the mid-1980s, 'when Kaziranga decided to expand its boundaries to the northern bank of the Brahmaputra river'.[37] But the local people reported that there were rumours of expansion of Kaziranga since the early 1970s, just after the enactment of the Wild Life (Protection) Act, 1972.

The notification to include the north bank of Brahmaputra under the KNP came out only in 1986, and it comprised the sand bar islands (*chapori*) and the banks, the mobile stretch of land that gets repeatedly reshaped by the endless movement of the river. These fertile green areas represent an integral part of the rural economy for grazers, farmers and fishing communities, and are considered vital for the survival of more than 10,000 families.[38]

The local communities filed a petition in the Gauhati High Court and challenged the decision to include the areas into KNP in 1994. The court took more than a decade to decide the fate of the petition. After examining the claims and counter-claims on the issue, it finally gave its verdict on 21–22 November 2002 and announced a state of hold with a direction to 'determine the rights of occupants (petitioners) in the notified area and till such determination is made the authorities were directed not to disturb the possession of such lands'.[39] When the court was still hearing the matter, the government issued a notification in 1999 and declared an area of 37,600 hectares under the sixth addition. After that, violence and harassment escalated, and the grazers filed another petition in the Gauhati High Court in 2006. The court gave its verdict in 2013 and declared, 'No illegality has been committed in proposing to evict the encroachers of forest land.'[40]

Amid these developments, in 2012, the Gauhati High Court registered the suo moto PIL on the issue of poaching of one-horned rhinos and killing of wild animals in Kaziranga. The verdict delivered on 9 October 2015 categorically stated the following:

> Keeping in view the larger interests of the public and the Constitution mandates, the claim of the petitioners in WP(C) 4860/2013 is held to be untenable and accordingly the writ petition is dismissed. Similarly the claim of the applicants in IA 1261/2015 and 1262/2015 for the reasons stated above are dismissed. The claim of the petitioners in WP(C) 648/2013 is rejected. The Deputy Commissioners of Golaghat, Sonitpur and Nagaon are directed to take expeditious steps to evict the inhabitants in the second, third, fifth and as well the six additions of the Kaziranga National Park, including Deurchur Chang, Banderdubi and Palkhowa, within one month.[41]

The Congress-led government did not implement the court order even though the court ordered to take expeditious steps to evict the inhabitants in the identified additions of the park. The BJP took up encroachments in Kaziranga as one of its important poll issues in both 2014 and 2016. For the party, the Congress government's inaction towards the killing of one-horned rhinos in Kaziranga had the objective of settling illegal migrants in the park through deforestation. In 2014, while campaigning in Assam, Narendra Modi said,

> Aren't rhinos the pride of Assam? These days there is a conspiracy to kill it. I am making the allegation very seriously. People sitting in the government ... to save Bangladeshis ... they are doing this conspiracy to kill rhinos so that the area becomes empty and Bangladeshis can be settled there.[42]

Therefore, the drive of eviction was indeed the culmination of its poll promises. The eviction in Kaziranga was violent: 'A dozen bulldozers and as many elephants entered three villages that encroachers had set up on government and forest land in Kaziranga—Banderdubi, Deuchur-chang and Palkhowa—police used force to quell their resistance, leading to the death of two persons including a woman.'[43] The evictions instantly evoked the nationalist sentiments and received support from the conservationists. AASU welcomed the move. BJP president, who was in Kozhikode at that time, not only endorsed the eviction drive of the state government but also termed those against whom eviction was undertaken as 'infiltrators'.[44]

The Gauhati High Court verdict drew national attention when the Government of Assam undertook the eviction drive in September 2016 as per the court order. It received strong resistance from the local inhabitants. It is important to point out that the eviction was selective; it did not cover the habitations in the second, third, fifth and sixth additions of the park but targeted the villages of Deuchur Chang, Banderdubi and Palkhowa.[45] The confrontation led to police firing against a peaceful demonstration under the banner of KMSS, Assam, and killed two persons on 19 September 2016. The opinion of the state also got polarized, with the elite sections in the greater society dubbing the protestors as illegal migrants. The polarization was so high that there was not enough scope to know the identity of the protestors. The government was praised for its bold decision, and it justified the eviction drive referring to the court order.

Before the incident had happened, the Finance and Health Minister Himanta Biswa Sarma met the protesting villagers at the SDC office in Koliabor, where KMSS leader Akhil Gogoi was also present. Dr Sarma asserted that the government was bound by the court order to evict the people of the three villages by 21 September. The people present in the meeting asked for compensation and rehabilitation before the eviction drive, as they had been living there for 40–50 years and also had the land documents with them. In reply, Dr Sarma reportedly said, 'The state government will announce a compensation as per the Land Acquisition, Rehabilitation and Resettlement Act, 2013, within 30–40 days.' It was alleged that to the surprise of the people present in the meeting, the minister asked

> the DC to give in writing to seven Assamese Hindu families that they will be given four times compensation for the loss of their land and told the rest of us, who are of Bengali Muslim origin, that he will see what he can do for us, may be those with proper documents will get compensation.[46]

The firing on 19 September 2016 brought several other issues into focus. First of all, it only exposed the hollowness of the elitist conservationism. However, it could not entirely be rejected as elitist conservationism, because the whole issue of poaching of rhinos provoked huge condemnation too. Here lies the question of media trial too. The local media had been reporting that there had been encroachments in and around Kaziranga, and the encroachers were illegal migrants, mostly Bangladeshis. Therefore, along with the conservationists, nationalist organizations, such as AASU, not only supported the eviction drive but also 'voted for the BJP on the plank of eviction of Bangladeshi settlers'.[47] Using all coercive means, including heavy equipment like bulldozers, the eviction team removed 331 houses and cleared over 2,400 bighas of land. There was a resistance against the move in Banderdubi village on 19 September 2016 under the banner of KMSS. The police fired on the protestors, which led to the killing of two persons. On 2 October 2016, KMMS leader Akhil Gogoi was arrested on the ground of inciting violence during the period of eviction, which led to the death of two persons on 19 September 2016.[48]

There were many controversies about the identity of the villagers and their rights over the settlements.

> Some groups have debated claims that the encroachers had rights over the land. The court order, however, states that Deuchur-chung was notified as

a reserved forest in 1916, Banderdubi is not only social forestry land but also a tiger resort and animal corridor, and Palkhowa too is forest land.[49]

But there are counter-narratives to it. Fanari and Doley argue,

> The violation perpetuated in the name of these additions, today considered under Kaziranga by the official documents, is questionable. First, its own notification, as observed above, has ignored the important judgment of 2002 and indiscriminately encroached upon the revenue land of people. Second, after Kaziranga was declared a Tiger Reserve in 2007, the sixth addition was categorised under the buffer area, a land territory 'which aims at promoting co-existence between wildlife and human activity with due recognition of the livelihood, developmental, social and cultural rights of the local people'.[50]

Moreover, according to the FRA, 2006, land tenure and customary rights should be recognized to all the STs and forest dwellers traditionally inhabiting these lands.

BBC Documentary on Kaziranga: The Contestations

Before the controversy around the evictions in the vicinity of KNP in September 2016 faded away, BBC created a storm by telecasting a documentary on the park on 11 February 2017, titled 'Our World: Killing for Conservation', which was prepared by BBC South Asia correspondent Justin Rowlatt. BBC also published a detailed account of Kaziranga prepared by the same correspondent on its website just one day ahead of broadcasting the documentary, that is, on 10 February 2017, titled 'Kaziranga: The Park That Shoots People to Protect Rhinos'.[51] While the documentary has now been banned, the original article, as well as the radio version of the documentary, is still available. The documentary has been alleged to have done 'irreparable damage ... to India's reputation', and therefore, BBC has been banned for five years from filming national parks and sanctuaries in India.[52] Just after the broadcasting of the documentary, the National Tiger Conservation Authority (NTCA) issued a show-cause notice to BBC for grossly erroneous reporting and recommended 'the blacklisting of the BBC's South Asia correspondent Justin Rowlatt for a documentary that highlighted the government's "ruthless anti-poaching strategy" for Kaziranga tiger reserve in Assam'.[53] NTCA, in its memorandum dated 27 February, directed the chief wildlife wardens of all tiger range states and field directors of tiger reserves not to grant permission for filming to BBC for five years. The Ministry of Environment and Forests extended the ban to all national parks and sanctuaries through its order dated 10 April 2017.[54] It was alleged that the documentary deviated from the original script submitted to the Ministry of External Affairs, Government of India, and NTCA, and 'projected a negative, malicious and sensational portrayal of India's conservation success story at Kaziranga Tiger Reserve'.[55] The controversy related to the documentary lies on the contention that the forest guards had been given almost impunity for shooting a suspected poacher by the Government of Assam under Section 197(2) of Criminal Procedure Code (CrPC), 1973, which reads,

> Only if it is held by an Executive Magistrate through an enquiry that use of firearms have been unnecessary, unwarranted and excessive and such a report has been examined and accepted by the Government, then alone any proceeding including institution of a criminal case of any nature or affecting an arrest can be initiated by police.[56]

The BBC documentary reveals that in the 11 years before the impunity was provided to the forest guards, that is, during 2000–2011, 17 poachers were shot dead inside Kaziranga, while 68 rhinos were killed. However, after the impunity was provided to the forest guards, between 2011 and 2016 alone, a total of 59 poachers were killed, while 103 rhinos were poached.

The documentary and the detailed reporting by Justin Rowlatt reveal the coercive approach of conservation, which creates a violent relationship between the park and its neighbourhood. The state's regimented approach to conservation is revealed through this relationship, which was also evident in the Gauhati High Court verdict of September 2015.

Justin Rowlatt explores and exposes a certain kind of narratives and relationships in the conservation discourse and culture in India. One dominant narrative is nationalism. Conservation is also about how we perceive nationalism, where tigers and wild animals are projected as the pride of the nation and the communities near the conservation centres become perpetrators or infiltrators or encroachers. In the

Assamese nationalist discourse, Kaziranga has appeared as one of the reference points.

The public discourse, directed by the sense and sensibilities of the Assamese nationalists, has over the years pushed KNP into a place whose management is beyond public criticism. The desire to preserve KNP, well pronounced in the Assamese public life, is not essentially driven by a sense of recovery of a natural space but more specifically due to its embodied cultural value. This cultural value is further reinforced by the fact that unlike in the 19th century, the Brahmaputra Valley has lost its importance as an undisturbed natural space. It is because of both these reasons that the protection of the prized species became an important agenda in the Assamese public imagination.[57]

The second one is tourism, particularly foreign tourists. Kaziranga hosts around 170,000 tourists annually. Conservation centres are also like showcases of the nation to the outsiders. People living in the vicinity, who are poor, malnourished, illiterate and unsophisticated, may look like a shame of the nation. With such a strong perception in the conservation culture, the nation builders create an unbreakable boundary between the conservation centres and communities around them. The expansion of the conservation centres becomes important and necessary, even at the cost of the neighbouring communities. Such a culture gives the state and other authorities much impunity, including impunity for shooting under suspicion. In other words, the impunity granted under Armed Forces (Special Powers) Act, 1958, for the protection of the nation from insurgency is expanded in kind to the conservation authorities. In an interview with Justin Rowlatt, a forest guard said, 'The instruction is whenever you see the poachers or hunters, we should start our guns and hunt them…. Fully ordered to shoot them. Whenever you see the poachers or any people during night-time we are ordered to shoot them.' They have no fear of consequences. Using the language of the critics, Justin Rowlatt calls it 'extrajudicial executions'. The impunity granted to the forest guards under CrPC cannot theoretically be blanket. Because, if proved guilty of using firearms without being necessary, one can be booked for criminal offences. However, proving such an offence is very difficult, because it can be proved only if a magisterial enquiry takes place and comes up with a report that 'firearms have been unnecessary, unwarranted and excessive and such a report has been examined and accepted by the Government....' Therefore, Survival International, a London-based charity, has argued, 'The park is being run with utmost brutality.... There's no jury, there's no judge, there's no questioning. And the terrifying thing is that there are plans to roll [out] the shoot at sight policy across [the] whole India.'[58]

The bigger issue which has emerged from the Kaziranga episode is that the brutality operates in an environment of the interdependent relationship between the park and the communities around. Where is the boundary and how is that boundary drawn and maintained in KNP? Is that boundary settled? Rowlatt mentions, 'There are no fences or signs marking the edge of the park, it just merges seamlessly into the surrounding countryside and fields.' He documented the stories of the disabled boy Gaonburah and the school-going boy Akash Orang, who survived the firing by the forest guards, and now live miserable lives. The incidents of this kind only expose the brutality committed by the forest guards in the un-demarcated boundaries of the park.

Human rights activists have been arguing that this brutality will be of no help. Justin Rowlatt quotes Pranab Doley, a tribal rights campaigner, who asserts that 'the park is in collision with the local people.' And he firmly believes: 'Without the people taking care of the forest, no forest department will be able to protect Kaziranga. It's the human shield which is protecting Kaziranga.'[59]

Trishant Simlai and Raza Kazmi, both conservationists by profession, published two articles in The Wire on 23 and 24 February 2017, titled 'Grasslands of Grey: How the BBC's Flawed Kaziranga Muckraker Has Done Harm'[60] and 'Grasslands of Grey: The Kaziranga Model Isn't Perfect—But Not in the Ways You Think',[61] respectively. The first article is a critique of the BBC's film. The authors pointed out that apart from its procedural lapses, the film is under-researched and partisan in nature. But it acknowledges that the documentary has also 'opened up a long-due debate on the alleged excesses of conservation policies in Kaziranga national park'.

The BBC team's investigation has faltered on multiple fronts, not the least of which is hoodwinking the authorities by submitting a false synopsis of the planned documentary. According to the Ministry of Environment, Forest and Climate Change, the BBC approached them for permission to film night patrols of forest guards in Kaziranga. The synopsis provided was that the video would be about a 'story on challenges and expertise of India's conservation drive. We would like to report on and feature what we consider the most exciting aspect of conservation in India—the elite rangers of Kaziranga as they go on night patrol and show our viewers the efforts being taken to protect wildlife in India'.[62]

The documentary was aired without showing it to a representative of the Government of India, although it was a part of the undertaking while seeking permission by BBC to do the documentary. But there was also an ulterior motive on the part of the BBC team behind filming Kaziranga. The authors allege,

> However, the documentary that was telecast deviated from the script and suggested an ulterior motive behind the exercise. While it is true that the BBC team was looking to highlight a very important issue—the complex conservation model used to administer Kaziranga by equipping the forest guards with punitive powers—the way they went about dealing with this issue seemed partisan in nature. The product seemed to lack in research and nuance.[63]

Despite being critical about the BBC's procedural lapses and ulterior motives, the authors acknowledge that the BBC team had 'brought out issues that are pertinent to the global discourse on conservation militarisation'.[64] The authors have strongly asserted that the Kaziranga conservation model has a lot of limitations.

> Clearly, all is not well with the Kaziranga model. It needs to be revised while outstanding issues with the local communities need engagement through widespread consultation. It is also time that conservation organisations and conservationists stop referring to allegations of excesses by the department as 'unfortunate but acceptable', 'collateral damage' or dismissing all such cases as accidents. Doing so legitimises the use of illegal force on marginalised people, who bear the largest costs of conservation. Such discourse shows an attitude of indifference towards local people, adding fuel to the fire and gives more ammunition to anti-conservation groups.[65]

Terming government's decision to ban the BBC's filming across India as immature, the authors have also asserted that 'While armed protection of Kaziranga is necessary since threats to rhinos are very real, and will only increase with the rising prices of the rhino horn in the black market', the future of 'the region's wildlife can only be ensured by active support of the local communities'.[66] The approach of militarization for conservation is both unethical and unsustainable.

Arupjyoti Saikia, a researcher on forest and ecological history of Assam, argues that fault lines lie in the conservation discourse and its implications for KNP.

> A conservation discourse which identifies people as a powerful enemy of nature is bound to have unwelcome repercussions. Without taking the neighbourhood social milieu into account, conservation would have a long way to go before it can achieve its goal. That the rural non-industrial world in Assam has created mechanisms to ensure its means of livelihood, i.e., ecological landscape, needs to be recognised. This will not only ensure adequate community participation but will also integrate local ecological understanding with macro-conservation science, and hopefully hold a better future for the KNP and other protected areas of the Valley.[67]

The Gauhati High Court verdict of 2015 could not appreciate these wider dimensions of challenges to KNP and, therefore, the crisis in the park was reduced to a mere matter of illegal poaching. It also did not consider the challenges posed by the polluting industries, such as stone quarries, oil refinery and parasitic rubber plantations in the Kaziranga-Karbi Anglong Landscape.[68] Therefore, the verdict has failed to bring any new insight into the ongoing conflict between the state-driven culture of conservation and the people's entitlements for life and livelihood.

JUDICIAL SCRUTINY OVER PREVENTIVE DETENTION: AKHIL GOGOI VS THE STATE OF ASSAM

The Gauhati High Court's verdict on 21 December 2017 on the writ petition filed by Assam's political activist and farmers' leader Akhil Gogoi[69] presents a different interface between the executive and the judiciary. Through this verdict, the court reaffirmed the primacy of the constitutional rights regarding preventive detention as ensured by Article 22(5) of the Constitution of India. The judgment also exposed the laxity and casualness of the state authorities in exercising power under the NSA, 1980. The 76-page verdict extensively referred to a number of prior significant verdicts pronounced by both the Supreme Court and the Gauhati High Court, which reiterate the need for constitutional validity for preventive detention, irrespective of the circumstances and pretexts of the detention. The said verdict assumed immense significance because the grounds on which Gogoi was detained did not at all figure in the process of adjudication; the procedural lapses in applying the NSA were enough to quash the detention order. The judgment, apart from disposing of the writ petition, directed the chief secretary of the Government of Assam to enquire and analyse the serious procedural shortcomings which led to the preventive detention order against Gogoi under the NSA and to ensure that corrective measures were adopted to preclude such lapses and lacunas in future.

Background of the Case

Gogoi, who is also the adviser of KMSS, was detained in custody under Section 3(3) of the NSA by an order of detention on 24 September 2017, in the pretext that he 'has been actively abetting/instigating/provoking/motivating and conspiring to wage war against the state on certain grounds'.[70] Gogoi has been a force of resistance in Assam for more than a decade. The Wire has listed him as one of the top 10 voices of defiance against the BJP-led governments and right-wing forces in the country in 2017.[71] His organization—KMSS—which was formed in 2005, has been building resistance against both the Central and state governments on several issues, including large river dams, land policies, CAB-turned-CAA to grant citizenship to Hindu Bangladeshis and lack of constitutional safeguards for indigenous people in Assam. Gogoi comprehensively used RTI Act, 2005 to unearth corruption in different departments of the state government. Using the FRA, 2006, he and his organization have been demanding rights for forest dwellers to settle in reserved forests. For his acts of defiance, he was arrested and detained by the Congress government during 2005–2016 and by the BJP-led government after 2016. Several cases have been registered against him[72]; therefore, if he gets bail in one case, he may be arrested in another. While he has been arrested a total of 14 times so far, only the September 2017 detention was under the NSA.[73] He was booked on sedition charges on 13 September 2017 and subsequently was detained into custody under the NSA for the statements which he allegedly made in a public rally in Moran Town in the Dibrugarh district of Assam on 12 September 2017. The Wire reported,

> Opposing the Modi government's decision to grant citizenship to Hindu Bangladeshis residing in the state, non-implementation of the 1985 Assam Accord by the central government and dearth of constitutional safeguards to protect the rights of the indigenous people, Gogoi is reported to have said in the public rally that perhaps the time has come to take up AK 47s against the government instead of the *hengdang*, a traditional Assamese sword used by the Ahom army for defence.[74]

Gogoi was booked under Sections 124A (sedition), 120B (criminal conspiracy), 121 (waging or attempting to wage war against the Government of India), 109 (abetment of an offence), 153 (causing communal disharmony) and 153A (hate speech) of the IPC for making the statement.[75] The district magistrate of Nagaon issued an order of detention on 24 September 2017 against Gogoi under Section 3(3) of the NSA. The Gauhati High Court quashed the preventive detention order in its 21 December 2017 judgment on the writ petition filed by Gogoi.

The Verdict

The striking dimension of the judgment is that the Gauhati High Court disposed of the writ petition by exposing the discrepancies in the process of transacting the detention order at different levels. The court did not even have to address the very grounds of detention under the NSA being cited by the detaining authorities, that is, the accusation that 'the petitioner had been actively abetting/instigating/provoking/motivating and conspiring to wage war against the State....'[76]

Reminding the detaining authorities about their responsibilities in handling preventive detentions, the court's strongly worded order states,

> [I]t is also a matter of concern that the detenues under the preventive detention are required to be released as because the detaining authority while

making the order of detention either does not provide all that are required to be provided in a detention order under the law or that in the subsequent follow up procedure of the requirements of law are not being scrupulously followed. The object and reason of the National Security Act is that in a preventive situation of communal disharmony, social tensions, extremist activities, industrial unrest etc., it was considered necessary that the law and order situation in the country be tackled in the most determined and effective way.... Any laxity or casualness on the part of the authorities who are involved in the process of making and sustaining an order of preventive detention, which would result in the release of the detenue, would therefore, have to be termed to be a factor, which contributes to such anti-social and anti-national activity.[77]

The vital issues of contention in the case wherein the 'laxity and casualness' of the detaining authorities were exposed both in the arguments of the counsel for the petitioner and in the analytical and rebuttal part of the judgment have been as follows: (a) the petitioner's right to representation against preventive detention as guaranteed under Article 22(5) of the Constitution of India; (b) the unexplained delay in disposing of the representation of the petitioner both by the state and central governments; (c) the failure to communicate all the grounds of detention to the detenu; and (d) the serious discrepancies in the process of transacting the detention order. The issue of the right of the detenu to legal assistance has also figured as an important issue of concern in the judgment. The primary reference point of the judgment has been Article 22(5) of the Constitution. The court, with no ambiguity, asserts that 'taking a person into custody under the laws of preventive detention would have to be strictly scrutinized within the cornerstone of right to life under Article 21 and 22(5) of the Constitution'.[78] Here is a brief survey of the issues enumerated in the judgment.

Petitioner's Right to Representation against the Detention Order

In the communication dated 24 September 2017, which contained the grounds of Gogoi's detention, the petitioner was informed that

[I]f he desires to submit representation against the order of detention, the petitioner may send his representation to the Principal Secretary to Govt. of

Assam in the Home and Political Department and that he may also make a representation to the Chairperson of the Advisory Board, Assam for the National Security Act.[79]

Accordingly, the petitioner submitted a representation on 27 September 2017 to the aforementioned authorities. A serious lapse in the communication, as has been argued by the counsel for the petitioner and which was endorsed by the judgment, was that the petitioner was not informed about his right to make a representation before the detaining authority itself as well as to the Central government. The counsel argued that lapse in the detention order was a violation of the rights enshrined in Article 22(5) of the Constitution of India; therefore, the order of detention 'is liable to be set aside on this ground alone'.[80] The counsel's assertion was based on a series of judgments of the Supreme Court as well as the Gauhati High Court, particularly the decision of the Constitution Bench of the Supreme Court in the *Kamaleskumar Ishwardas Patel vs Union of India* (reported in 1995 4 SSC) and the directions of the Gauhati High Court in *Konsam Brojen Singh vs State of Manipur and Others* (reported in 2006 (1) GLT 375). The counsel representing the detaining authority attempted to counter this argument by referring to the representation made by the detenu on 27 September 2017, where the 'detenue on his own volition had requested that the said representation be placed before the Advisory Board and/or any other competent authority under National Security Act for their consideration and appropriate orders'.[81] Through this request, the counsel for the detaining authority argued that 'the detenue has waived his right to be informed that he has also a right to make the representation before the aforesaid two authorities.'[82] Referring to a number of verdicts by the Supreme Court, the counsel for the petitioner asserted that the

[R]ight to submit a representation is a fundamental right under Article 22(5) of the Constitution of India ... [and] can a breach of obligation imposed on the State be waived by any person and is it open to the State to disobey the Constitutional mandate merely because a person tells the State that it may do so....[83]

It may be mentioned that the secretary to the Government of Assam in the home and political department issued an order on 5 December

2017 in which the detenu was informed that he might submit a representation against the order of detention of 24 September 2017 before the detaining authority and also before the Central government. However, it was pointed out by the petitioner's counsel that

> [T]he order of detention having been made on 24.09.2017, the opportunity given on 05.12.2017 to make the representation to the detaining authority and the Central government does not constitute an earliest possible opportunity given to the detenue and hence, there is an aberration of Article 22(5) of the Constitution of India.[84]

The court considered the argument in length, analysed a number of decisions/mandates of the Supreme Court of India and the Gauhati High Court on relevant cases[85] and declared that 'the order of detention of 24.09.2017 stands vitiated'.[86]

Delay in Disposing of Representation

The second issue that came up for comprehensive scrutiny by the court was the unexplained and extraordinary delay in disposing of the representation of the detenu dated 27 September 2017 submitted before the state government and the chairman of the Advisory Board of the NSA. The state government disposed of the representation on 25 October 2017, after an unexplained delay of 28 days. Although the detenu was not informed in the original order of detention about his right to representation before the Central government, the state government on its own transmitted the representation to the Central government, which was disposed of on 14 November 2017, 48 days after the date of representation made by the detenu.

By referring to the chronology of the events from the date of submission of the representation by the detenu on 27 September 2017 to its rejection by the state government on 25 October 2017, as submitted by the respondent authorities in the court, the counsel for the detenu exposed the laxity and casualness in transacting and transmitting the representation from one level of the government to the next. The counsel for the petitioner presented a number of decisions of the Supreme Court,[87] wherein a delay of 17–22 days in disposing of the representation submitted by a detenu was considered fatal. Therefore, the delay of 28 days in disposing of the representation in Gogoi's case was an appropriate example to be considered fatal.

The court minutely analysed and scrutinized the unexplained delay in the transaction of the representation and its disposal by both the state government and the Central government.[88] For example, according to the records presented by the respondent authorities, the state government purportedly sent the representation which was made by the petitioner on 27 September 2017 to the Central government on 16 October 2017. However, scrutiny of the postal receipts indicated that it was sent only on 25 October 2017 through speed post. There was, however, no explanation about why it took nine days to do the simple task. The court did not take the inexplicable delay kindly, terming it a violation of principles laid down by the Apex Court in that regard. Based on those principles too, the order of detention was declared unsustainable and therefore stood vitiated.

Detenu's Right to Know Every Single Ground of Detention

Article 22(5) of the Constitution of India mandates that the right of a person detained under preventive detention to know the ground or grounds on which he or she is being detained is a fundamental right. Can a detaining authority afford not to inform the person detained under preventive detention about the reason or reasons for detention, which apparently is/are supposed to be known by the detenu?

Gogoi was informed about the grounds of his detention on the very day the detention order was served, that is, 24 September 2017; however, soon the issue of an alleged 'CD' emerged. The detention order mentions the disc, but it was not provided to the detenu while serving the order of detention and communicating the grounds thereof. The dossier provided to the petitioner referred to certain video clippings and video footage, which allegedly established that the petitioner had instigated people to take up 'AK 47s' against the nation. The counsel for the petitioner contemplated that the said CD might have contained the alleged obnoxious statements made by the petitioner which were considered by the detaining authority in issuing the detention order; not providing it to the petitioner amounted to not informing all the grounds of detention, which, in turn, would vitiate the order of detention. To validate the arguments, the counsel for the petitioner referred to a number of decisions of the Supreme Court.[89] Endorsing the argument, the court categorically stated that having access to all grounds and materials based on which the decision of preventive detention is arrived at is a constitutional right of the detenu under Article 22(5) of the Constitution of India. While quashing the order of detention in Gogoi's case, the Gauhati High Court observed: '[T]his Court is of the considered view that the grounds for which the concerned CD also constitutes a material for arriving at the satisfaction regarding the existence of the ground, stands vitiated, for not being provided with the CD under reference.'[90]

There was a further omission in the detention order. While framing the grounds for detention, the detaining authority referred to a police case which resulted in a charge sheet against the petitioner for an incident which occurred on 22 June 2011, in which supporters of the petitioner allegedly set a police vehicle on fire, causing injuries to four persons who were inside the vehicle. This particular information was a half-truth, as it did not mention the fact that a competent criminal court subsequently acquitted the petitioner in the case. While the half-truth might have been a satisfactory ground for the detaining authority in issuing the order of detention, the court found that the failure to mention the order of acquittal was an aberration of the principles laid down by the Supreme Court, and therefore the information provided by the detaining authority stood vitiated.

Detenu's Right to Avail Legal Assistance in the Proceedings before the Advisory Council

In the instant case, the detenu made a specific request through an application on 4 October 2017 that he be allowed to be represented by a legal counsel before the Advisory Board. The application was rejected by the Advisory Board in an order on 22 October 2017. The counsel for the petitioner argued that such a denial violated Article 14 of the Constitution, which guarantees the right to equality before the law. The counsel argued, referring to the mandate of the Supreme

Court in *A K Roy Etc. vs Union of India* (1982 AIR SC 710), where it has been held that

> The officer who assists the Advisory Board, although are not legal practitioners or legal advisers, but such officers who assist or advises on facts or law must be deemed to be in a position of a legal adviser and therefore, permitting the detaining authority or the Government to appear before the Advisory Board with the aid of such legal adviser would violate Article 14, if a similar facility is denied to the detenue.[91]

In the instant judgment, the court recorded the mandate of the Supreme Court in paragraph 76 but refrained from giving any conclusive view on the issue. The judge argued that from the records available before him, it could not be ascertained as to whether any officer of the government having experience of advising the government on facts of law had appeared before the Advisory Board to justify the order of detention, or whether such officers merely carried records.

Non-compliance with Laws on Preventive Detention: Directions to the State Government

In the instant case, as evident from the discussion above, the state authorities indulged in laxity and casualness, which invited strictures of the court. The court, accordingly, directed the chief secretary to the Government of Assam to conduct a detailed enquiry regarding the lapses in the process leading to the order of preventive detention dated 24 September 2017 and all subsequent actions. Such an enquiry had to involve all the persons who had played either a constructive or an advisory role in the process. The court directed to make a proper analysis to find out how such serious lapses had occurred and to take corrective measures so that these are not repeated in future. The court further directed that it is a constitutional requirement for the state government to educate all authorities connected with the process of making and sustaining an order of preventive detention about the principles as enshrined in Article 22(5) of the Constitution. The Government of Assam has also been asked to set up an effective monitoring mechanism to ensure due compliance with the constitutional requirements in the process of preventive detention.

CONCLUSION

The interface between the executive and judiciary in the two cases does not represent a definite pattern. However, the actions of the executive while undertaking the eviction drive in September 2016 in compliance to the high court order of October 2015 on KNP and the arrest of Akhil Gogoi under NSA in 2017 reveal the approach of the state towards the forces which trigger resistance against the state on crucial issues related to the lives and livelihoods of the commons. There is no dispute that protecting Assam's national pride, the one-horned rhinos, is an inviolable responsibility of the state. That responsibility entrusts upon the state to protect and preserve KNP. However, the protection of the rhinos cannot be at the cost of human habitations in and around the park. In the context of Assam, this debate also exposes the inherent limitations of the dominant nationalist forces like the AASU towards scrutinizing the conflicts between the conservationist paradigm of development and that of the entitlements of the commons to the sources of lives and livelihoods. The BJP-led regime in Assam took the maximum advantage of the nationalist imaginations of the dominant civil society forces to drive its own agenda of Hindutva.

NOTES

1. *Kaziranga National Park vs Union of India & Others,* PIL (suo moto) 66/2012, 67/2012; and WP(C) 648/2013 and 4860/2013, the Gauhati High Court, judgment and order dated 9 October 2015, 34, http://ghconline.gov.in/Judgment/PIL662012.pdf.
2. *Akhil Gogoi vs State of Assam & 2 Ors*, WP (Crl) 14 of 2017, the Gauhati High Court judgment and order dated 21 December 2017, http://ghconline.gov.in/Judgment/WPCrl142017.pdf.
3. UNESCO, 'Kaziranga National Park' (n.d.), https://whc.unesco.org/en/list/337/.
4. Ibid.
5. Arupjyoti Saikia, 'Kaziranga National Park: History, Landscape and Conservation Practices', *Economic & Political Weekly* (6 August 2011): 12–13, https://www.epw.in/journal/2011/32/states-columns/kaziranga-national-park-history-landscape-and-conservation-practices.
6. *Kaziranga National Park vs Union of India & Others,* PIL (suo moto) 66/2012, 67/2012; and WP(C) 648/2013 and 4860/2013, the Gauhati High Court, judgment and order dated 9 October 2015.

7. BBC, 'Our World: Killing for Conservation', 11 February 2017, https://www.bbc.co.uk/programmes/n3ct0by7. (Note: The video was withdrawn by BBC after the controversy.)

8. Jairam Ramesh, 'The Two Cultures Revisited: The Environment–Development Debate in India', *Economic & Political Weekly* (16 October 2010): 13, https://www.epw.in/journal/2010/42/commentary/two-cultures-revisited-environment-development-debate-india.html.

9. Ibid., 13.

10. Ibid., 14.

11. Ibid., 15.

12. Ibid., 15.

13. Ibid., 16.

14. Hiren Gohain, 'Livelihood Losses and National Gains', *Economic & Political Weekly* (18 December 2010): 79, https://www.epw.in/journal/2010/51/discussion/livelihood-losses-and-national-gains.html.

15. *Kaziranga National Park vs Union of India & Others,* PIL (suo moto) 66/2012, 67/2012; and WP(C) 648/2013 and 4860/2013, the Gauhati High Court, judgment and order dated 9 October 2015.

16. BBC, 'Our World: Killing for Conservation'. There were three broadcasts of the documentary on the day, but subsequently, it was withdrawn. The film is not available on the BBC website now.

17. Justin Rowlatt, 'Kaziranga: The Park That Shoots People to Protect Rhinos', BBC News India, 10 February 2017, https://www.bbc.com/news/world-south-asia-38909512.

18. Eleonora Fanari and Pranab Doley, 'As Kaziranga Expands, the Fate of Grazing Communities Hangs in the Balance', The Wire, 26 February 2018, https://thewire.in/environment/contested-boundaries-eviction-in-the-sixth-addition-of-kaziranga-national-park.

19. *India Today*, 'Rhinos Being Killed to Make Room for Bangladeshi Settlers: Modi in Assam' (31 March 2014), https://www.indiatoday.in/elections/story/narendra-modi-bjp-assam-government-congress-poaching-of-rhinos-bangladeshi-settlers-187001-2014-03-31.

20. *Kaziranga National Park vs Union of India & Others,* PIL (suo moto) 66/2012, 67/2012; and WP(C) 648/2013 and 4860/2013, the Gauhati High Court, judgment and order dated 9 October 2015, 6, para 2.

21. Ibid., 6, para 1.

22. Ibid., para 2.

23. Ibid., 34, para 39.

24. Ibid., 34–35, para 40.

25. Ibid., 8, para 4.

26. Ibid., 7, para 4.

27. Ibid., 9, para 5.

28. Ibid.

29. Ibid., 11, para 7.

30. Ibid., 10.
31. Ibid., 12, para 8(4).
32. Ibid., 13, para 8(8).
33. Ibid., 12, para 8(3).
34. Tridib Nilim Dutta, 'Kajirangar Tinikhon Ucchedit Gaon' [three Displaced Villages of Kaziranga], *Natun Padatik*, October 2016, Guwahati, 60–63.
35. *Kaziranga National Park vs Union of India & Others*, PIL (suo moto) 66/2012, 67/2012; and WP(C) 648/2013 and 4860/2013, the Gauhati High Court, judgment and order dated 9 October 2015, 14, para 10.
36. Fanari and Doley, 'As Kaziranga Expands'.
37. Ibid.
38. Ibid.
39. Ibid.
40. Ibid.
41. *Kaziranga National Park vs Union of India & Others*, PIL (suo moto) 66/2012, 67/2012; and WP(C) 648/2013 and 4860/2013, the Gauhati High Court, judgment and order dated 9 October 2015, 36–37, para 44.
42. *India Today*, 'Rhinos Being Killed'.
43. Samudra Gupta Kashyap, 'The Politics of Cleaning Up Kaziranga', *The Indian Express*, 26 September 2016, https://indianexpress.com/article/india/india-news-india/kaziranga-eviction-drive-assam-elections-bjp-sonowal-government-politics-dead-3051774/.
44. Ibid.
45. Dutta, 'Kajirangar Tinikhon Ucchedit Gaon', 62.
46. The Wire, 'Two Killed in Police Firing Near Kaziranga, Eyewitnesses Say', 19 September 2016, https://thewire.in/rights/kaziranga-firing-two-killed.
47. Kashyap, 'The Politics of Cleaning Up Kaziranga'.
48. Bikash Singh, 'Akhil Gogoi Arrested for Allegedly Inciting Violence in Kaziranga Eviction', *The Economic Times*, 2 October 2016, https://economictimes.indiatimes.com/news/politics-and-nation/akhil-gogoi-arrested-for-allegedly-inciting-violence-in-kaziranga-eviction/articleshow/54643796.cms.
49. Kashyap, 'The Politics of Cleaning Up Kaziranga'.
50. Fanari and Doley, 'As Kaziranga Expands'.
51. Rowlatt, 'Kaziranga: The Park That Shoots People'.
52. Jay Mazoomdaar, 'Kaziranga Film: BBC Banned for 5 Years from All National Parks, Sanctuaries', *The Indian Express*, 15 April 2017, https://indianexpress.com/article/india/kaziranga-film-bbc-banned-for-5-years-from-all-national-parks-sanctuaries-4613758/.
53. Ibid.
54. Ibid.
55. Ibid.
56. Ibid.
57. Saikia, 'Kaziranga National Park', 13.
58. Rowlatt, 'Kaziranga: The Park That Shoots People'.

59. Ibid.
60. Trishant Simlai and Raza Kazmi, 'Grasslands of Grey: How the BBC's Flawed Kaziranga Muckraker Has Done Harm', The Wire, 23 February 2017, https://thewire.in/culture/kaziranga-bbc-rhino-survival.
61. Trishant Simlai and Raza Kazmi, 'Grasslands of Grey: The Kaziranga Model Isn't Perfect—But Not in the Ways You Think', The Wire, 24 February 2017, https://thewire.in/environment/kaziranga-bbc-shoot-poaching.
62. Simlai and Kazmi, 'Grasslands of Grey: How the BBC's Flawed Kaziranga Muckraker Has Done Harm'.
63. Ibid.
64. Simlai and Kazmi, 'Grasslands of Grey: The Kaziranga Model Isn't Perfect'.
65. Ibid.
66. Ibid.
67. Saikia, 'Kaziranga National Park', 12–13.
68. Mayuri Gogoi, 'Kaziranga under Threat: Biodiversity Loss and Encroachment of Forest Land', *Economic & Political Weekly* (11 July 2015), https://www.epw.in/journal/2015/28/reports-states-web-exclusives/kaziranga-under-threat.html.
69. The three respondents to Gogoi's writ petition (Crl) 14 of 2017 are the state of Assam; the district magistrate cum deputy commissioner, Nagaon, Assam; and the chairman, Advisory Board (constituted under the NSA, 1980).
70. *Akhil Gogoi vs State of Assam & 2 Ors*, WP (Crl) 14 of 2017, the Gauhati High Court judgment and order dated 21 December 2017, para 2.
71. The Wire, 'Watch: Ten Acts of Defiance in 2017', 1 January 2018, https://thewire.in/209582/watch-ten-acts-defiance-2017/.
72. In an interview with Pratidin Time, a local television channel, on 26 December 2017, Gogoi said that the total number of cases registered against him was 119, which is the highest number of cases registered against any political activist, or an insurgent, in the state of Assam. More and more cases have been registered against him in the subsequent time. He was arrested again on 12 December 2019 for leading the resistance against CAA and was later booked under the UAPA.
73. In the interview with Pratidin Time, Gogoi also asserted that it was one of the very few instances in the history of India that the NSA had been used against a political activist, who was leading a non-violent mass movement in the state. Since 2005, he has been arrested 14 times under various sections of Indian Penal Code (IPC), 1874. Gogoi has been booked under Sections 120A and 120B (criminal conspiracy); 124A (sedition) and 125 (waging war against any Asiatic power in alliance with the Government of India); 353 (assault or criminal force to deter public servant from discharge of his duty), etc. (Source: This author's conversation with Gogoi on 30 December 2017).
74. The Wire, 'Farmers' Rights Activist Akhil Gogoi Arrested under National Security Act', 26 September 2017, https://thewire.in/181523/assam-farmers-rights-activist-akhil-gogoi-arrested-under-national-security-act/.

75. The Wire, 'Assam Farmers' Rights Leader Akhil Gogoi Arrested on Sedition Charges', 14 September 2017, https://thewire.in/177373/assam-farmers-rights-leader-akhil-gogoi-arrested-sedition-charges/.
76. *Akhil Gogoi vs State of Assam & 2 Ors*, WP (Crl) 14 of 2017, the Gauhati High Court judgment and order dated 21 December 2017, para 2.
77. Ibid., para 81.
78. Ibid., para 82.
79. Ibid., para 2.
80. Ibid., para 9.
81. Ibid., para 27.
82. Ibid.
83. Ibid., para 33.
84. Ibid., para 37.
85. Ibid., 24–41, para 35–58.
86. Ibid., para 59.
87. *Pabitra N. Rana vs Union of India and Others*, reported in (1980) 2 SSC 38; *Narinder Singh Suri vs Union of India and Others*, reported in (1980) 2 SCC 357; *Sri Saleh Mohammad vs Union of India and Others*, reported in (1980) 4 SCCC 428; *Sardar Kasmir Singh vs Union of India and Others*, reported in 1981 (Supp) SCC 55; etc.
88. *Akhil Gogoi vs State of Assam & 2 Ors*, WP (Crl) 14 of 2017, the Gauhati High Court judgment and order dated 21 December 2017, 53–59, para 60–65.
89. The counsel referred to the decisions of the Supreme Court in the cases of *Kamla Kanyalal Khushalani vs State of Maharashtra and Others*, reported in (1981) 1 SSC 748; *Icchu Devi Choraria vs Union of India and Others*, reported in (1980) 4 SSC 53; and *Pritam Nath Hoon vs Union of India and Others*, reported in (1980) 4 SCC 525.
90. *Akhil Gogoi vs State of Assam & 2 Ors*, WP (Crl) 14 of 2017, the Gauhati High Court judgment and order dated 21 December 2017, para 69.
91. Ibid., para 26.

Pandemic and Politics

BJP's Electoral Prospects

6

Assam's fight against the pandemic of COVID-19 revealed interesting political dynamics. The state government, which had been at logger-heads with the civic resistance forces on the issue of CAB and CAA till February 2020, suddenly witnessed a wave of regime legitimacy through its strategic moves while fighting the pandemic. The initial legitimacy was derived from the ethno-religious composition of the COVID-19 posi-tive cases in the period of the outbreak. Except 1, all of the 35 persons tested positive for the virus between 31 March and 24 April 2020 were Muslims and had direct or indirect connections with the Tablighi Markaz of Nizamuddin.[1] Such a composition of the patients added impetus to the already-polarized society in Assam. The government played safe by apparently refusing to indulge in the language of religious polarization but also refrained from intervening to stop the polarization. However, by constantly focusing on the names of the COVID positive patients and also referring to the Nizamuddin Markaz as the epicentre of the virus, the government also contributed towards the anti-Jamaat bandwagon. The government concentrated on the strategies of fighting the virus and invited the greater society to be its trusted companion. In an unprec-edented manner, the greater society, particularly the employees of the state government, went as far as contributing more than ₹100 crore to the 'Assam Arogya Nidhi' (AAN) to help the government.

The suddenness of the pandemic dealt a severe blow to the anti-CAA mobilizations and sentiments. A series of lockdowns which fol-lowed brought in new challenges for the government, and the single focus on hospitalization of all COVID positive cases also created public wrath. The handling of the inter-state migrant returnees was one of the worst times for the government.

However, as the lockdowns were gradually relaxed and finally withdrawn, the government slowly regained legitimacy despite the surge of the cases. There has also been an erosion of the vibrant democratic space in the state, as is the case in the whole country. While in the run-up to the 2021 elections the BJP attempted to consolidate its position through state resources and aggressive campaign strategies, the anti-CAA forces became fragmented and formed independent regional political outfits with the avowed objective of defeating saffron brigade in the elections. While doing so, these forces have refused either to come together to form a unified regional force or to align with other anti-CAA mainstream political parties like the Congress or AIUDF. The Congress and AIUDF were yet to declare a pre-poll alliance for the ensuing elections despite hinting at that by the state leadership. However, a possible alliance between the Congress and AIUDF came under severe attack with the BJP constantly targeting the AIUDF as the core enemy of the greater Assamese society and projecting the Congress as a co-conspirator in this regard. After the signing of the BTR agreement on 27 January 2020, the United People's Party Liberal (UPPL) came to the forefront as a core challenger to the ruling BPF in the present-day BTC. Differences have surfaced between the BJP and BPF—BJP's ally in BTAD—in the aftermath of the BTR agreement. In the council elections in BTC held in December 2020, the BJP took the ruling BPF as its core electoral enemy. These developments present a complex and competitive electoral battleground for the ensuing assembly elections in early 2021.

OUTBREAK OF THE PANDEMIC: THE POLITICAL CONTEXT

For the incumbent government, coming in terms with the citizens was a challenging task in the post-CAA moments. The unprecedented resistance built up by the civic-political forces both in the run-up to the enactment of the CAA, 2019, and in the immediate aftermath of it created a huge legitimacy deficit for the government. The resistance continued, although the government arrested the most vocal voice against the Bill and the Act—Akhil Gogoi—adviser of the KMSS, and detained him under the UAPA on 12 December 2019. Subsequently,

he was handed over to the NIA. The main functionaries of the organization were also put behind the bar. But other organizations, particularly the AASU, intensified their resistance. The Act, in the pretext
of protecting the rights of the indigenous people, exempted the Sixth
Schedule areas and the states under the ILP from its purview. However,
the Act remained applicable in the Brahmaputra Valley, the epicentre
of the anti-CAB-turned-anti-CAA resistance. The CAA brought divisions among the federating units of the civic resistance forces, as many
ethnic–tribal organizations, particularly the ABSU, immediately drifted
away from the resistance. The Government of India signed a tripartite
agreement with the Bodo civil society groups and all factions of the
NDFB and the state government. The signing-in ceremony took place
on 27 January 2020 in New Delhi in the presence of the Union home
minister, Assam's chief minister, BTC Chief Hagrama Mohilary and the
leaders of all factions of the NDFB as well as representatives of Bodo
civil society forces. Apart from the insurgent factions, civil society
forces like ABSU also signed the agreement.[2] Apparently, the accord
was all-inclusive, but frictions started soon after the signing. Three
days after the signing of the accord, a grand ceremony of the surrender
of arms by the NDFB factions took place in the GMCH auditorium. It
was attended by the chief minister, finance minister, BTC chief, chief
secretary and the director general of police, and other representatives
of the Bodo civil society, including the ABSU president.[3] It was the
first brave public show in the aftermath of the violence in Guwahati
during the anti-CAA protests. The event was followed by a huge rally
which was addressed by the prime minister of India in Kokrajhar on
7 February 2020 to celebrate the signing of the accord, where he said,

> Today is the day for the entire Northeast including Assam to welcome a
> new beginning in the 21st century, a new dawn, a new inspiration. Today
> is the day to take a pledge that development and trust would continue to
> be our mainstay and that they would be further strengthened. Let us not be
> engulfed by the darkness of violence ever again. Let us welcome a peaceful
> Assam, a New Resolute India.[4]

This was a significant development as the summit between the prime
minister of India and his Japanese counterpart in Guwahati scheduled for December 2019 had to be cancelled due to the anti-CAA

protests. Therefore, the signing of the accord with the Bodos signified a gradual grip of the government over the law and order situation in the state.

The accord brought the various factions of the NDFB to the negotiating table and thereby settled the groups of deadly insurgents in the region. However, the accord also 'unsettled another set of extremists who signed the second accord in February 2003 and went on to rule the Bodoland Territorial Council (BTC)'.[5] The BTC Chief Hagrama Mohilary reportedly said that the new accord merely changed the name of BTC to BTR. It did not have anything substantive to offer. Therefore, Mohilary and his ruling BPF refused to accept it and asserted that they would not even use BTR as part of their vocabulary.[6]

Amid these developments, COVID-19 overpowered the country and the political dynamics started changing. The politics of Assam immediately transformed, and the vocal and vibrant civic forces became silent abider of the government directives. The pandemic brought an unprecedented wave of people's loyalty to the government. This was so equivocally spelt out by Dr Himanta Biswa Sarma, who has been at the forefront of the fight against the COVID-19 in the state. Dr Sarma is a regular feature in the media for his provocative and accusing voices against his political rivals, critics in the civil society domain and also the government employees. But when his appeal for public contributions towards the AAN received remarkable responses, he became so overwhelmed that he acknowledged: 'Never before in my long political/govt career I have come across a moment like this when people so overwhelmingly came out to join a cause. We have 97.92 crores under Assam Arogya Nidi as a donation for # Covid_19. Gratitude 45367 donors.'[7]

WAR AGAINST THE PANDEMIC

No COVID-19 positive case was reported in Assam till 31 March 2020. Still, on 27 March 2020, the Government of Assam declared its war against the virus. It announced that three out of seven medical colleges would be converted into COVID-19 treatment hospitals with a capacity of 5,000 beds in total. It also laid down a modality for a tie-up with private hospitals for the treatment of non-COVID patients along with converting the national stadium at Sarusajai, Guwahati, into a 700-bed quarantine centre. In Guwahati, 36 private hospitals came forward to help the government in its drive against the virus and to treat patients under various schemes of the government.[8] The same modality was also put in place in Dibrugarh and Silchar, where the two medical colleges were converted into COVID-19 treatment hospitals. The state health department also laid down the road map for huge infrastructural overhauling, including a proposal to establish five prefabricated COVID-19 treatment hospitals with a combined capacity of 1,500 beds, which were to be made functional within 2 months. 'Each hospital will cost around ₹40–45 crore. We should be able to construct four of them with contributions made by MPs from the state, state government employees and donations received from the public,'[9] Health Minister Dr Sarma said. The first COVID-19 case in Assam was detected on 31 March 2020 at Silchar Medical College. By 16 April, total cases went up to 34. Then after a gap of 7 days, the 35th case was reported on 23 April 2020. Out of the 35 cases, all except 1 person were Muslims and had direct or indirect linkages with the Tablighi Jamaat, which added fuel to the aggressive campaign against the community. Electronic and social media were filled with hate campaigns against the community and termed them as virus bearers. The government issued a warning against them as if they were terrorists. On 6 April 2020, the Health Minister of Assam Himanta Biswa Sarma asserted that his government had the names of 831 people from Assam who attended Tablighi Jamaat event in Delhi. Out of it, only about 500 people were traced so far 'despite repeated appeals by ministers in the state'. The government was fed up with the low turnout. Therefore, he issued a final warning that 'if people from Assam, who had attended the Tablighi Jamaat event in Delhi, do not report by today evening, then legal action will be taken against them starting tomorrow.'[10] The government also declared, 'It will start filing cases against all those who attended the Tablighi Jamaat event in Delhi, who test positive for Coronavirus (COVID-19).'[11] The only non-Muslim COVID-19 positive case was reported from a very rich apartment named Spanish Garden in Guwahati. The patient, a Marwari businessman, spoke of his infection in social media and he became a celebrity. Social media was filled with prayers for his health and immediate recovery—a sharp contrast compared to the hate heaped on the other patents.

The government on its part, particularly the health minister, avoided making any communal remarks. Rather, he succeeded in projecting himself as the most credible non-partisan entity in the fight against the epidemic. The government, under his initiative, took a series of innovative measures and transformed the COVID-19 unit in the National Health Mission (NHM) office as a 24×7 centre. However, gradually, the picture changed, and the new cases of infection were beginning to be reported from across religious identities. As the cases piled up, it became just impossible to name them. Overenthusiasm on the part of the health minister also provoked controversies over importing personal protective equipment (PPE) kits from China. Assam government reportedly imported 50,000 PPE kits from China for the frontline healthcare workers combating the COVID-19 pandemic in the state on 15 April 2020. After receiving the kits at the Guwahati airport, the state health minister tweeted, 'Keeping life first as the motive, we are glad to have imported, 50,000 PPE kits from Guangzhou, China … A big reassurance for our doctors & nurses.'[12] It was reported that Assam was the first state to import PPE kits from China directly, and it was attributed to the personal initiatives of the health minister. Amid controversy regarding the quality of the kits, initially, the use of them was suspended. Ironically, it also came to light that the kits were purchased through private agencies and not by the government directly.[13]

The initial success gained against the epidemic gradually diminished as the cases started rising from mid-June 2020. By September 2020, it took a very serious turn. In mid-June, Assam reported around 5,000 cases with less than 10 reported deaths. By mid-July, the reported infected cases crossed 18,000 and death toll touched 50. By mid-August, the total reported cases jumped to 75,000 with more than 180 reported deaths. By mid-September, the reported cases touched almost 1.5 lakh, and the death toll was around 500. By mid-October, the cases increased to almost 2.0 lakh, and the reported death cases were around 850.[14] Guwahati, the capital city of the state, became one of the epicentres of COVID-19 infection in the country. In early September 2020, the health minister acknowledged that Assam had been passing through a critical phase. He said, 'Coronavirus situation in Assam is "worrying". Last month, on an average, Assam had been reporting 2,000 cases a day, but now the average is nearly 3,000, which could lead to close to 1 lakh a month.'[15] However, he asserted that Assam's COVID-19 fatality rate was much lower. 'The state has a recovery rate of 78.3% and a fatality rate of 0.31%.'[16] Nevertheless, the minister also acknowledged that there had been confusion regarding COVID-19 deaths data. 'For example, if a coronavirus-infected person was treated and later he turned negative but died after developing complications, then that person won't be added to the deaths' list. So there are technicalities.'[17]

Scroll.in reported that Assam had been undercounting the deaths by misinterpreting the ICMR norms. Assam's COVID deaths were confirmed by the Death Audit Board. According to the version of the Board, 'If a patient suffering from chronic kidney disease dies of end-stage renal failure and incidentally he was COVID positive, that is not a COVID death.'[18] However, ICMR took objection to their claims. ICMR guidelines provide a much wider range of options for counting COVID deaths.[19] As per the ICMR guidelines,

> Patients may present with other pre-existing co-morbid conditions.... These conditions increase the risk of developing respiratory infections and may lead to complications and severe disease in a COVID-19 positive individual. These conditions are not considered as UCOD [underlying cause of death] as they have directly not caused death due to COVID-19.[20]

To meet the challenges, Assam gradually increased dedicated COVID hospitals, COVID health centres and dedicated COVID centres during the period of the epidemic. By the end of September 2020, Assam had 23 dedicated COVID hospitals, 283 COVID health centres and 550 dedicated COVID centres.[21] A well-equipped COVID-19 super-speciality hospital was inaugurated at the GMCH on 28 May 2020. This has emerged as one of the best and reliable COVID care hospitals in the public eyes.

Along with the infrastructure, the government intensified testing. The government claimed to have achieved a milestone in terms of

COVID tests, with the number of tests performed reaching 30 lakh by 23 September 2020. The state had only one test laboratory in the last part of May 2020, which, however, increased to seven by 30 May 2020. It increased to 11 by 13 June, and on 28 July, other 6 laboratories were added. The laboratories needed 7–10 days to conduct 1 lakh tests until June, but with the added centres the time required to conduct the same number of tests came down to 2–3 days.[22]

The shortage of health personnel has been one of the challenges. The government had remained reluctant to accept home quarantine and isolation for the infected patients until early July 2020. Hospitalization has been its priority. The government continued to insist on it, but, with the growing number of cases and pressure from the public, the government decided to permit home isolation for infected persons with many conditions. It did so with reluctance, which is evident in its order dated 11 July 2020, which clearly stated, 'The policy of the Health and Family Welfare Department is that all COVID patients will be kept under close medical observation in COVID hospitals or COVID care centres ... and home isolation of COVID-19 patients is not preferred by the Department'.[23]

Acknowledging that 'forced hospitalization and forced home isolation of a person is against the principles of liberty and freedom of choice', and

> [A]fter careful consideration of the circumstances, Health and Family Welfare Department have, with great reluctance, decided that COVID-19 patients who insist on remaining in home isolation will be allowed to do so without burdening the public healthcare system and subject to compliance with the following conditions.[24]

The conditions made the patients solely responsible for their care and treatment and the state burdening themselves off such home isolation cases.

Exclusive focus on hospitalization had also put pressure on the health personnel. As the COVID-19 cases suddenly rose, the government decided to engage the 'health workers and doctors in 11 days' continuous service in the COVID wards and thereafter, only three days of quarantine before re-engaging them in COVID-19 duties subject to testing negative for the disease'.[25] The Assam chapter of the Indian Medical Association strongly protested the decision, arguing that working 11 days at a stretch wearing PPE kits in the 'torrid summer and without air-conditioning in most centres would be exhausting for the COVID-19 warriors'.[26] Finally, the government had to withdraw the decision and restore the ICMR norm of seven days of duty followed by seven days of quarantine.

On 29 April 2020, the Government of India decided to allow migrant workers, pilgrims, students, tourists and other persons stranded at different places to travel. With the return of the migrants, there was a gush in infection in Assam. It was the second wave of cases, the first one being the Tablighi Jamaatees. From 31 March to 16 May 2020, Assam had 91 positive cases, which, within a fortnight, increased to 1,216 by 30 May 2020. The government resorted to 'ruthless quarantine with a human face' to deal with the situation. After the Jamaatees, the migrant returnees were also projected as the virus bearers. 'Large number of cases are imported ones basically from people coming from West and South India and some percentage from West Bengal. However, as the people are coming from outside cases will increase in the future.'[27] On 22 May 2020, the health minister informed, 'Till now 25,693 person by road and 11,724 people by railways has come to Assam since May 4.' He also added, 'We are expecting the return of another 12 lakh people, the number of cases which we got now is just tip of the iceberg.'[28] Therefore, he said, the government adopted a policy of 'ruthless quarantine with a human face'. The government said that per person quarantine cost would be ₹20,000. As the cases increased, the quarantine norms were gradually relaxed.[29]

AAN: The Popular Support

One of the schemes that allowed the government the opportunity to earn respect and claim legitimacy is AAN, which was launched to receive public donations for COVID-19 infrastructure development.

Ironically, there is already a scheme with the same name, which was set up to help the below poverty line (BPL) families for the treatment of critical diseases and injuries. The scheme provides

> financial assistance up to Rs. 1,50,000/- to BPL families and families having a monthly income of less than Rs. 10,000/- (Rupees Ten Thousand) for general and specialized treatment of (i) life-threatening diseases, (ii) of injuries caused by natural and manmade disasters, such as industrial/farm/ road/rail accidents, bomb blasts, etc.[30]

The health department relaunched the same *nidhi* (fund), of which the health minister is the chairperson, for collecting donations. The response to the nidhi has been overwhelming. The state government employees were at the forefront in donating to the nidhi. On 9 April 2020, that is, the day the salary of the employees was released, the donation amount was the highest, that is, ₹42.17 crore. The number of donors stood at 19,039 on the day. By 24 March 2020, the total contribution stood at ₹1.06 crore and the total contributors at 48,242.[31]

The government proposed to establish new hospitals using the fund. However, later, the government abandoned the idea of creating new pre-fabricated hospitals. A committee was formed with eminent doctors from public and private hospitals to advise on the use of the fund.[32] A detailed plan was supposed to be made public. That has not yet happened. The government has also maintained complete silence over the use of the fund collected through the nidhi.

Assam Cares

Another important initiative of the Assam government is the Assam Cares Migrant Outreach Programme. Initially, the programme aimed to create a database of the people stranded outside the state to help them return home and to ensure their health safety. But the scheme was expanded with three important segments: internationally stranded people, people suffering from critical diseases and injuries, and migrant people stranded in different parts of the country. As per statistics, by 24 April 2020, the government reached out to 49 persons stranded in different countries, and they had been given $1,000 each, amounting to a total of ₹3,717,690. Under the category of a critical illness like cancer, heart, kidney and liver diseases, the government has identified 829 people and offered ₹25,000 each, amounting to ₹20,725,000. But the more ambitious part has been to reach out to the migrant workers and students stranded in different parts of the country. The government created a dedicated team to contact them by involving a non-profit organization called Piramal Swasthya and around 800 student volunteers from higher education institutions of Guwahati. This was an online helping mechanism, and a helpline number was created, asking all those who needed the financial assistance to give missed calls to the number. Once the missed call was received, a web link was sent back, asking them to fill up the information such as name, local address in Assam, bank account number with the IFSC and a self-declaration on family income, which needed to be below ₹5 lakh per annum. Once the data was received, it was sent to the respective districts for verification and after successful verification, the government released ex gratia amount of ₹2,000 to the account as the first instalment. As of 24 April 2020, a total of 570,000 missed calls were received. By 22 May 2020, the government transferred the second instalment of ₹2,000 to 3.61 lakh citizens stranded outside the state which cost ₹72.23 crore on the public exchequer. The state finance minister assured that the third instalment for the next month would also be deposited.[33]

ECONOMY UNDER THE COVID-19

SITA, Government of Assam, published a report titled *Report on Economy of Assam in the Backdrop of COVID-19 Pandemic,* which was prepared in collaboration with OKD Institute of Social Change and Development, Guwahati.[34] The report was prepared in May 2020, during the initial phase of the pandemic and the ensuing lockdown. The 37-page document enumerated the overall potential impact on macroeconomic growth and GSDP, on employment and income, on poverty and on the state's finances. It also documented the potential impact on all key sectors of the economy and the overarching impact on inequality, women, critical infrastructure and disaster management. Finally, it offered a set of policy recommendations for the government.

The report also presented the overall state of the economy before COVID-19, which witnessed a slowdown in terms of GSDP growth as well as generating employment. The state was already facing an acute unemployment crisis. The inequality graph was also on the rise. The report stated that since 2017–2018, the rate of growth of the state's GDP had been declining and for the year 2019–2020, the rate of growth of the GSDP was 16 per cent lower than the previous year. Likewise, the state's unemployment rate as estimated by PLFS in 2017–2018 was 7.9 per cent, which was just 2.9 per cent in 2013–2014.[35]

Based on the data available from different sources, and its assessments, the report projected that the cumulative loss in GSDP for the year 2020–2021 due to COVID-19 can be in the range between ₹3,219 crore and ₹12,877 crore at 2011–2012 prices. The loss is equivalent to ₹4,442 crore–₹17,770 crore at the current prices.[36]

The report showed that the current unemployment rate in the state is 8 per cent, which may go up to 16–27 per cent, if the job loss due to lockdown and other adversity of COVID-19 ranges from 10 per cent to 30 per cent, respectively.[37] The pandemic had also resulted in huge return migration to the state, which was estimated to be between 6 and 10 lakh. The report pointed out that they were unlikely to migrate again at least soon, putting further strain on the overall unemployment situation in the state.[38] The poverty ratio, which stood at 32 per cent at 2011–2012 rate before the pandemic, might shoot up to 37.7–50.8 per cent if income fell to 5 per cent and 15 per cent, respectively.[39]

The report suggested for immediate, limited and well-targeted measures to address the challenges, which should especially target the most vulnerable groups. The report pointed out that there were around 25 lakh BPL households/families in the state. As an immediate relief, the report suggested that these BPL households/families should be given a cash transfer of ₹3,000 per household/family per month for at least three months as special COVID-19 relief. As per the estimate of the report, it would require an estimated amount of ₹2,250 crore.[40]

On 4 May 2020, the governor of Assam constituted an eight-member advisory committee for revitalization of state's economy in the backdrop of the situation arising out of COVID-19 pandemic and consequent lockdown. Headed by Subhash Chandra Das, IAS (Retd), the committee was mandated to assess and suggest measures in seven areas altogether through the ToRs. The prime objective of the committee as mandated through the ToRs was to suggest short- and medium-term measures for the revitalization of the state's economy while continuing the efforts to contain the COVID-19 pandemic. The committee was also asked to suggest both fiscal and non-fiscal stimulus to different sectors of the economy.[41] It consulted with various stakeholders, drew feedback from the public and gathered required information and plan of action from various departments of the state government apart from having a special interaction with the chief minister. Based on all these, the committee made a detailed analysis of the macroeconomic, socioeconomic and sector-specific impacts of COVID-19 and lockdown. It also analysed the strengths, weaknesses, opportunities and impending threats emanating from the situation arising out of the pandemic. It critically examined the possibilities of making the state's economy self-reliant and also laid down a road map for action.[42] It submitted its 121-page report on 29 May 2020, that is, within the timeframe stipulated by the notification issued on 4 May 2020. It did a remarkable work by looking into all critical dimensions of the challenges arising out of the COVID-19 pandemic and suggesting short-, medium- and long-term measures to revitalize the economy. It particularly looked into the agriculture and the allied sectors, which is the backbone of the Assam's economy, which absorbs the highest percentage of the working population.

The committee calculated the overall loss in GSDP during the first two phases of lockdown, that is, from 24 March 2020 to 3 May 2020. During these two phases, very limited relaxations were provided, and therefore, the economic activities were completely halted. During these 40 days, the committee estimated the total direct loss in potential contribution to the GSDP including taxes at ₹32,167 crore. It constitutes around 9.5 per cent of the GSDP. The potential loss estimated by the committee in the primary, secondary and tertiary sectors was ₹8,175 crore, ₹7,546 crore and ₹14,787 crore, respectively.[43] However, there was also a huge loss in employment, particularly in the unorganized sector and also a drastic decline in collection of taxes including GST.

Adding these indirect losses in addition to the direct loss cited above, the total potential loss was estimated at ₹51,870 crore, that is, 15 per cent of the GSDP.[44]

The report comprehensively looked into the magnitude of loss in employment due to the pandemic. It pointed out that the state has around 1 crore worker population (population above 15 years of age). The PLFS data reveals that 56.5 per cent of the total workers are engaged as 'self-employed', while 25.1 per cent are regular salary/wage earners and 18.5 per cent are casual workers, the report argued. It also reveals that in Assam, out of 56 lakh people who are engaged as self-employed, 20 lakh are self-employed in agriculture. The remaining 36 lakh self-employed are engaged in non-agricultural activities. However, out of this 36 lakh, close to 20 lakh self-employed are in the unorganized sector and are vulnerable to any external shock. On the other hand, Assam has around 19 lakh casual workers, 18 lakh of which are in rural areas. They work on 'as and when basis' and lack any social security. Added to all these, Assam has around 15 lakh out-migrant labourers, out of which 10 lakh are supposed to have returned to the state. There is a lesser possibility of the majority of them going back in the immediate future. Based on these figures, the report estimated altogether 110 lakh worker population in the state.[45] Out of this, 67 lakh are considered to be highly vulnerable. In the pre-COVID period, the unemployment rate in the state was 8 per cent. However, depending on the probable job loss at the minimum of 10 per cent to the maximum of 30 per cent, the unemployment is estimated to have grown from minimum 15.7 lakh (16%) to 27.1 lakh (27%), respectively.

The committee critically looked into all possible measures including the resources available in the hands of the government and accordingly placed before the government a number of strategies to deal with the challenges emanated from COVID-19 to revitalize the economy. It particularly suggested a few short-term strategies to be implemented within six months and also identified the resources available to do so. The basic objective of those strategies was to help in generating demand and thereby to stimulate economic activities. Agriculture and employment generation received due attention in this regard. For example, in Chapter 7 titled 'Providing Employment: Post COVID 19', the committee has given some concrete and doable suggestions. It has set targets for employment generation in the short, medium and long terms, that is, by April 2021 in various sectors—government, private and self-employment. In the short term, the proposed targets are 3 lakh, 8 lakh and 11 lakh in the short, medium and long terms, respectively. Highest target has been set in the agriculture and allied sectors, that is, 1 lakh, 4 lakh and 5 lakh in the short, medium and long terms, respectively.[46]

To boost the rural economy, the committee proposed a rural market programme called Aamar Bazaar and suggested that it needed to be started immediately. 'The rural markets under this programme are envisaged as local aggregators of village products located conveniently within a cluster of about 10 villages well connected to national or state highways,' the committee suggested. These markets need to be equipped with a large infrastructure 'under which buyers and sellers can do business in all types of commodities produced locally'. The committee also calculated the financial requirement and the possible sources and suggested that the initiative could be taken up under CMSGUY or by panchayats. It has been pointed out that construction of a market infrastructure under the Aamar Bazaar programme would require ₹25 lakh each. Construction of 2,000 such markets would need ₹500 crore. The committee also pointed out that fund already was lying with the panchayats under 14th and 15th Finance Commission Grants, which could be utilized for the programme. It also recommended that preferably the works related to construction and development should be given to the local people.[47]

By November 2020, the stipulated timeframe, that is, six months for short-term measures, already elapsed. The government had not implemented any suggestion laid down by the committee. The chairman of the committee was also not aware of any action taken so far on the report, except for the information that an empowered committee had been constituted to study the report and to develop the action plans by various departments.[48] One member of the committee remarked that constituting such committees had been a strategy only to generate social legitimacy and not to implement them.[49]

Re-energizing the Populist Schemes

The BJP-led government indulged in competitive populism throughout its tenure. The budget speech for the financial year 2020–2021 featured a number of schemes which aimed at individual beneficiaries from almost all sections of the society. COVID-19 had slowed down its implementation in the initial phase of the pandemic. However, as the 2021 assembly election approached, the government revived its populism. The government has been very selective in this regard. It particularly targets the poor sections in general and tea garden communities in particular, who now constitute one of BJP's strong vote banks. Under Anna Yojana, the government made provisions 'to supply rice free of cost for the Tea Garden Workers under the Affordable Nutrition and Nourishment Assistance (ANNA) Yojana. This scheme has benefitted 6.46 Lakh tea workers and Adivasi families so far'.[50] For the year 2020–2021, the government proposed to provide free rice to 'all the beneficiaries under the National Food Security Act. This gesture of the Government will immediately benefit an additional 51.39 Lakh families'.[51] Chah Bagicha Dhan Puraskar Mela launched in 2018 is one of the ambitious schemes of the government for the tea garden workers. This initiative was undertaken 'to address the issues of the "weekly cash cycle" that the tea garden workers were trapped in and provide a safety net to the tea garden employees'. During the financial year 2018–2019, the government had already transferred ₹5,000 through direct benefit transfer (DBT) to 721,485 bank accounts of tea garden workers across 752 tea gardens spread over 26 districts of Assam, in 2 equal instalments of ₹2,500 each.[52] Not meeting the 'know your customer' (KYC) norms by some of these bank accounts created hindrances towards the direct transfer to certain accounts. With the intervention of the Union finance minister, the issue had been settled and the government declared that it would release the third tranche of ₹3,000 to 721,485 bank accounts.[53] The government earmarked ₹220 crore in the 2020–2021 budget for the scheme. It also introduced a special scheme to assist the students belonging to the tea tribes and Adivasi communities and offered ₹10,000 as one-time support to those who pass HSLC and HSC exams. In 2019–2020, more than 1,200 students were assured to be benefited from the scheme and they would continue to receive the same benefit in the financial year 2020–2021 as well. The government declared that the new beneficiaries would be added to the list in 2020–2021.[54]

Orunodoi is the most ambitious and, for the government the 'foremost bead', scheme among the Ashtadash Mukutar Unnoyonee Mala (18 flagship programmes) which the government has been pursuing. In his 2020–2021 budget speech, the finance minister declared, 'Launching hundreds of small schemes each aimed at solving hunger and poverty is like shooting in the dark and hoping for bulls-eye. Most will miss the target, and the families will not escape the poverty trap.' In his opinion, 'The most effective way of lifting millions of our people out of poverty is by making substantial income transfers at one time.'[55] Under this scheme, the government will provide a monthly support of ₹830 per month to a family, effectively meaning an additional income of ₹10,000 to the poor households per annum.[56]

On 17 August 2020, the government announced the launching of the scheme and issued the guidelines scheduled for execution from 2 October 2020. It promised to cover 19 lakh economically backward households. The official notification stated that the scheme aimed 'to empower the women of the State and to provide financial support to the economically vulnerable families'.[57] On 1 September 2020, the government declared that the scheme shall give priority 'to the families with widows, unmarried women, families with a specially-abled member, and families having a divorced woman'.[58] On 2 December 2020, Assam's Chief Minister Sarbananda Sonowal launched the scheme. The scheme will now cover 22 lakh families, with annual budgetary expenses of ₹2,400 crore. Orunudoi has been termed as the biggest DBT scheme.[59]

Another important and in a way unique scheme of this government is the Arundhati scheme. The government states that whereas 'many parts of our country are plagued with social evils surrounding the girl child, like child marriage, female foeticide, dowry, etc., the Assamese society is fortunate to be free from such evils.' But the government is of the view that during the marriage of a girl, the parents desire to 'bestow their child with love, blessings, and gifts…. Gold is always considered auspicious and an asset. The parents believe that a gift of gold ornament would enhance their daughter's social and economic status'.[60] Interestingly, for the government, this is not to be equated with a dowry, which is prevalent in many parts of the world. Accordingly, the government declared the Arundhati Gold Scheme in the budget of 2019–2020. Under this scheme,

> Financial assistance of Rs. 30,000 is being provided to the newly married girls for purchasing gold for her marriage as financial security and to start a new life. The benefit under this scheme has been extended to all brides coming from families which have less than Rs. 5 Lakh annual income and who opt for formal registration of marriages under the Special Marriages Act, 1954.[61]

Marriages solemnized on or after 1 December 2019, and marriages registered on or after 1 January 2020, will be eligible for the scheme, provided the bride and groom should have attained the legal age of 18 years and 21 years respectively at the time of registration of the marriage. On 25 September 2020, the chief minister and the finance minister of the state launched the scheme and distributed ₹40,000 under the scheme (which is ₹10,000 more than the amount declared in the budget speech) to a group of newly married and registered couples.[62]

With assembly polls only a few months away, the state government relaunched the Swami Vivekananda Assam Youth Empowerment (SVAYEM) scheme worth ₹1,000 crore. The scheme was announced in the 2017–2018 budget but could not achieve the target. It aims to provide ₹50,000 each as seed money to 2 lakh selected youths to start business ventures. The government claims that the scheme is the 'biggest self-employment programme launched by any government in Assam since Independence. The ₹1000 cr would come from our revenue without any banking linkage'.[63]

More ambitious are the schemes announced by the government for the tea gardens and tea garden labourers. Declared on 25 September 2020, there are four schemes altogether: (a) For any tea garden which has taken a working capital loan from a commercial bank, the state government will pay 3 per cent of the interest on the borrowed sum. The condition set is that the maximum cap on the subsidy will be ₹20 lakh for each tea garden per year; (b) The tea gardens will also be provided a subsidy of ₹7 per kg to grow orthodox tea 'in a bid to promote production and export of this variant of the hot beverage. This incentive will be over and above the ₹3 per kg of tea to be paid by the Tea Board of India (TBI)'; (c) The state government has also declared that it will provide a 25 per cent subsidy to procure plants and machinery to grow orthodox tea; and (d) An agriculture income tax holiday to tea gardens for three years.[64] Explaining the expectation from the tea gardens from the schemes, Finance Minister Himanta Biswa Sarma said,

> We hope tea gardens will give a 20% bonus for the upcoming Durga Puja to all their workers following the state government's announcements of the new schemes. Employees of gardens under the Assam Tea Corporation, a state government undertaking, have been assured of a 20% bonus.[65]

On 7 October 2020, the state cabinet also decided to provide day-boarding facilities and a free uniform for children in 428 tea garden-managed schools of Assam.[66] Most importantly, it also decided to accord associate official language status to the Bodo language and to constitute a Bodo Kachari Welfare Autonomous Council for the Bodo community outside the Sixth Schedule area.[67]

These are a few examples of the preparation of the government for the ensuing elections. What is evident is that the government completely ignored the core concerns of the economy as had been suggested by the Subhash Chandra Das committee and endlessly pursued the hyper-populist model.

FROM ANTI-CAA RESISTANCE TO THE BIRTH OF NEW POLITICAL PARTIES

Although the anti-CAB and anti-CAA resistance garnered unprecedented popular support, it did not bring in solidarity in resistance. While the AASU-led front brought together almost all tribal ethnic groups into its fold, KMSS steered the efforts to bring around 70 ethnic groups together. The Hiren Gohain-led Nagarikatwa Aain Songsudhan Bidheyak Birodhi Mancha provided with a platform for the liberal–secular–progressive intellectuals and civil–political forces to register their voices against the Bill and the subsequent Act. Both AASU and KMSS have different support constituencies defined by respective ideological orientations. During the peak of anti-CAB and anti-CAA resistance, AJYCP should have been with AASU rather than with KMSS due to its ideological orientation. However, eventually, AJYCP left KMSS and joined AASU to form a new regional political party. AASU's support base is among the middle-class Assamese-speaking population, and it sustains an anti-Bengali Muslim approach in its political pursuits. On the other hand, KMSS represents the poor farmers and marginalized communities like the forest dwellers. It has expanded its base to the Bengali Muslim-dominated areas in western Assam. Both forces have an alliance with the ethnic tribal communities. But the ASSU has an alliance with the leading entities from within the tribal–ethnic communities. It has always been critical of the left parties and intellectuals; KMSS has been close to the non-party left intellectuals, although critical about the mainstream left parties. During anti-CAB-turned-anti-CAA protests too, these differences continued. The government had been eyeing on KMMS because of its radical political agenda, and, therefore, the organization had to withstand the worst of the state anger against the resistance. Its advisor Akhil Gogoi was arrested on 12 December 2019, the day after the enactment of the CAA. Subsequently, a few more leaders were arrested, and several cases were imposed on them. Akhil Gogoi, against whom more than a dozen cases were registered, had also been booked under the UAPA. He has been granted bail on several cases but bails on cases registered by NIA for his alleged link with Maoists and for 'waging a war against the nation' continue to be denied. Mr Gogoi was granted bail by a special NIA court on 17 March 2020 after the investigating agency had failed to file a charge sheet against him within the stipulated period of 90 days. He was again arrested just after two days.[68] On 17 July 2020, the Gauhati High Court granted bail to him in three cases filed by the police in connection with the CAA protests.[69] The NIA special court, however, rejected his bail on 7 August 2020. Subsequently, on 1 October 2020, the NIA special court granted bail to him in another case related to the alleged threat to life to a police official on duty on 9 December 2019 at Chabua in the Dibrugarh district. However, he is yet to get bail in another case registered in Chandmari, Guwahati.

The anti-CAB and anti-CAA resistance brought people to the street from all levels of society. A good number of artists joined the protests and helped instil popular enthusiasm into it. Among those who came to the forefront was Zubin Garg, a popular artist of the state. Several artists, who had been in the BJP, also resigned and joined in the popular resistance. However, as COVID-19 brought about new dynamics and the anti-CAA resistance gradually faded away, many of them sided with the government. Zubeen Garg was reportedly considered to be appointed as a brand ambassador of the agriculture and allied departments of the Assam government.[70] 'Garg wishes to bring a green revolution in the state and sought government help for the project.... The Assam government, assuring necessary help and support, instead appointed Zubeen Garg as the brand ambassador.'[71] Zubeen later asserted that he was not a brand ambassador of the department, saying the 'agriculture department approached me to promote the departmental schemes. I will help them. Our young people are not aware of these schemes. They should avail the benefits.'[72]

Amid these developments, Assam witnessed the formation of several regional political outfits. Important among them are the AASU–AJYCP led Asom Jatiya Parishad (AJP) and KMSS-led Raijor Dal (RD). Both the formations have taken almost the same ideological position—fighting against the BJP and equidistance from communal and national political parties. Anti-CAA is the main rallying point of these formations. While both the formations vow to dethrone the BJP from power, however, they refuse to align with the mainstream political parties like the Congress or the left parties on the ground that they are national parties. The AIUDF is almost untouchable for both the formations on the ground that the party is communal like the BJP. AASU President Dipanka Nath provides the rationale behind the formation of the new party: 'The State government surrendered before the Centre on the Citizenship (Amendment) Act (CAA). We had to step in because the people want a political entity that will not cave into Delhi's demands at the cost of Assam's future.'[73] In the Duliajan conference of the AASU held in November 2020, the general secretary and the core anti-CAA voice of the organization, Lurinjyoti Gogoi resigned to lead the newly formed AJP. On 2 October 2020, KMSS formed RD 'to defeat the fascist Bharatiya Janata Party and Rashtriya Swayamsevak Sangh in the 2021 elections besides keeping the communal combine of the Congress and the All India United Democratic Front (AIUDF) at bay'.[74] Ajit Bhuyan, who was elected to Rajya Sabha with support from the Congress and AIUDF in March 2020, formed a new platform, Anchalik Gana Morcha, in June 2020 to conquer power in the state in 2021.[75]

Bhuyan had tried to bring together the regional forces to a single front but failed. Regarding AASU–AJYCP's new party, he said that it would only help the BJP to win.[76] Critiquing Akhil Gogoi, Bhuyan said, 'We must know who our political enemy is right at this moment. Without supporting the Congress, regional political parties of the state alone cannot defeat the ruling BJP…. Akhil Gogoi's appeal for the unification of the regional forces excluding the Congress is impractical.'[77] The other important development is the possible alliance of the Congress with AIUDF and a few other parties, particularly the left parties. The AIUDF made its mind clear by stating that the alliance with the Congress was certain.[78] The Congress leadership remained indecisive till BTC elections held in December 2020. Tarun Gogoi, the Congress stalwart in Assam and three times chief minister of the state was a strong advocate of the opposition unity at this critical juncture. His demise on 24 November 2020 has been seen as a blow to this unity. Ajit Bhuyan's Anchalik Gana Morcha, which initially pursued a regional unity, gradually shifted towards a Congress-led alliance. This is indeed a very important development. Both the Congress and AIUDF have maintained a certain percentage of votes throughout all the elections. The Congress registered almost equal votes with that of BJP's in the state. However, its votes were spread across the states as it contested in almost all seats. The AIDUF contested in many seats where the party did not have much electoral presence. It also helped the BJP win comfortably. The new alliance, therefore, is seen as a formidable challenge to the BJP.

It is amid these developments that the BJP-led regime revived the issue of granting ST status to six OBC communities, a promise that the BJP gave in 2014 general elections.

CONCLUSION: BJP'S ELECTORAL PROSPECTS IN 2021

The BJP is much ahead of all other political parties in terms of mobility, organization, campaign strategies, control over resources as well as influence over social media. Unlike other parties like the Congress, the BJP does not have many issues concerning leadership either at the national or at the state level. COVID-19 has been a blessing in disguise for the party and the government to regain popular legitimacy which had eroded substantially during the anti-CAB and anti-CAA movements. As election approaches, the government has whipped up its populist agenda. Despite the economic slowdown, the government has not failed to pay salaries to its employees. These indicate a bright prospect for the BJP for the 2021 assembly elections.

However, there are arduous challenges from different quarters. The most important challenge will come from the Congress's alliance with the AIUDF. This will particularly help the alliance in three electoral belts –Barak, Lower Assam and central Assam, with 54 assembly segments. Both in the 2016 assembly elections and 2019 general elections, the BJP and its allies had registered victory/lead in more than 30 constituencies in these belts. In Upper Assam, there are 47 assembly segments spread over five PCs. BJP's political fortunes were determined by these constituencies in all three elections—2014, 2016 and 2019. It had registered victory/lead in 34–35 assembly segments in all the three elections. Tea gardens played an important role in BJP's consolidation in this belt. Will the Congress–AIUDF alliance have any negative impact on BJP's fortunes? Poll analysts argue that the BJP will be benefited due to this alliance as this belt is the epicentre of the mainstream Assamese identity. This belt has strong sentiments against the Bengali Muslims. The indigenous Muslims, who have a substantial presence in this belt, are also averse to the Bengali Muslims due to the latter's growing political clout. BJP's biggest advantage in this belt is the tea gardens. Therefore, this government always is on overdrive to provide benefits to the gardens and tea labourers. Its main challenge in this belt may come from AJP—the new party that the AASU has floated. In the 2019 general elections, a substantial percentage of the anti-CAB votes had gone to the BJP, as they did not have an alternative. The AJP may take away a percentage of those votes. But the loss may be compensated by the RD formed by the KMSS. Apart from consolidating its votes among the poor farmers and other marginalized communities like the forest dwellers, the party may intrude into the Congress hold. These calculations may help sustain BJP's strong electoral advantage in this belt. In the hill districts, the BJP is already in an advantageous position. In the BTAD (now BTR), its fortunes will be determined by how it accommodates the rival political groups from within the Bodos. In the council elections held in December 2020, the BJP projected BPF as the core enemy of the people in BTAD and alleged that the ruling dispensation indulged in corruption and siphoned off public money for personal pursuits. The UPPL, now headed by former ABSU President Promod Boro, also rallied its electoral strategy on attacking the BPF chief Hagrama Mohilary. Both the BJP and UPPL projected the BTR, a gift of the Modi government to the Bodo community through the tripartite agreement signed in January 2020, as the game changer of Bodos future in the coming days. BPF chief Hagrama Mohilary termed the BTR as a betrayal to the community. Taking together, the 2021 assembly elections are all set to witness several political dynamics and equations. The fortunes of the ruling BJP will be determined to a great extent by how the Congress–AIUDF alliance unfolds and works until elections are over and also how political equations and fortunes emerge in the post-BTC elections.

NOTES

1. Tablighi Jamaat was a religious congregation which took place in Nizamuddin in Delhi in mid-March 2020. Around 3,400 people gathered for the event including Jamaatees from different countries on 13 March 2020. It was alleged that the Jamaat defied the Delhi government order on public gathering issued on 16 March 2020. On 20 March 2020, 10 Indonesian Jamaatees were tested COVID positive. A few people in Telangana were reported to have died after attending the Jamaat in Delhi. With all these, the Nizamuddin Jamaat was identified as the epicentre of COVID infections in the country. (Source: Tanseem Haider, 'Timeline of How Nizamuddin Markaz Defied Lockdown with 3400 People at Tablighi Jamaat Event', *India Today* (31 March 2020), https://www.indiatoday.in/india/story/timeline-of-nizamuddin-markaz-event-of-tablighi-jamaat-in-delhi-1661726-2020-03-31.)
2. *India Today*, 'Govt Signs Historic Bodo Peace Accord, Amit Shah says Golden Future Awaits Assam' (27 January 2020), https://www.indiatoday.in/india/story/amit-shah-historic-bodo-peace-accord-sign-assam-1640584-2020-01-27.

3. Hemanta Kumar Nath, '1,615 NDFB Cadres Lay Down arms at Surrender Ceremony in Guwahati, Deposit 178 Weapons', *India Today* (30 January 2020), https://www.indiatoday.in/india/story/1615-ndfb-cadres-lay-down-arms-surrender-ceremony-guwahati-deposit-178-weapons-1641639-2020-01-30.

4. Narendra Modi, 'PM Attends Celebrations on Signing of Bodo Peace Accord at Kokrajhar in Assam', 7 February 2020, https://www.narendramodi.in/prime-minister-narendra-modi-participates-in-historic-bodo-agreement-ceremony-in-assam-548324.

5. *The Hindu*, 'Accord Drives Divide in Assam's Bodo Domain', 17 February 2020, https://www.thehindu.com/news/cities/kolkata/accord-drives-divide-in-assams-bodo-domain/article30837645.ece.

6. Ibid.

7. News Live, Covid 19: Assam Arogya Nidhi Receives Rs. 97.92 Cr Donation', 18 April 2020, https://newslivetv.com/covid19-assam-arogya-nidhi-receives-rs-97-92-cr-donations/.

8. Ratnadip Choudhury, 'Private, Public Hospital Model, 2,000 Bed Quarantine: Virus-free Assam Is Ready for a War', NDTV, 27 March 2020, https://www.ndtv.com/india-news/assam-coronavirus-fight-private-public-hospital-model-2-000-beds-2201919.

9. Utpal Parashar, 'Coronavirus Update: Assam to Set Up Hospitals with 1500 Beds within 2 Months', *The Hindustan Times*, 28 March 2020, https://www.hindustantimes.com/india-news/coronavirus-update-assam-to-set-up-hospitals-with-1500-beds-within-2-months/story-ctWXDzfGH32qnyhSIAkmFO.html.

10. *The Financial Express*, '"Declare or Face Legal Action!" Patience Wearing Thin, Assam Sounds Ultimatum to Tablighi Jamaat', 6 April 2020, https://www.financialexpress.com/india-news/declare-or-face-murder-charge-patience-wearing-thin-assam-sounds-ultimatum-to-tablighi-jamaat/1920385/.

11. Suchitra Karthikeyan, 'Assam Police Nab 12 Markaz Attendees Hiding in Different Mosques; Sent to Quarantine', Republicworld.com, 13 April 2020, https://www.republicworld.com/india-news/general-news/assam-police-nab-12-markaz-attendees-hiding-in-different-mosques.html.

12. News18, 'Assam Imports 50,000 PPE Kits from China; Health Minister Himanta Biswa Sarma Receives Consignment', 15 April 2020, https://www.news18.com/news/india/assam-receives-50000-ppe-kits-from-china-health-minister-himanta-biswa-sarma-receives-consignment-2579321.html.

13. India TV, 'Assam Not to Use 50,000 PPE Kits Imported from China', 18 April 2020, https://www.indiatvnews.com/news/india/assam-not-to-use-ppe-kits-imported-from-china-608971.

14. The health minister updated the cases on everyday basis through his Facebook account and also Twitter. The media also became dependent on his Twitter messages for reporting. (Source: https://www.facebook.com/himantabiswasarma/.)

15. Ratnadip Choudhury, 'Post-Covid Deaths Rising in Assam Is Worrying Sign: Health Minister', NDTV, 4 September 2020, https://www.ndtv.com/india-news/coronavirus-post-covid-19-deaths-rising-in-assam-in-worrying-sign-says-himanta-biswa-sarma-2290547.

16. Utpal Parashar, 'Assam Likely to Have Nearly 90,000 New Covid-19 cases in Sept: Himanta Biswa Sarma', *Hindustan Times*, 12 September 2020, https://www.hindustantimes.com/india-news/assam-likely-to-have-nearly-90-000-new-covid-19-cases-in-sept-himanta-biswa-sarma/story-DI4MZweyh-db9859Yz3ihDO.html.

17. Ibid.

18. Arunabh Saikia, 'Why Assam's Covid Fatality Rate Is Lowest in India—60% of Deaths in Confirmed Cases Not Counted', Scroll.in, 9 September 2020, https://scroll.in/article/972578/why-assams-covid-fatality-rate-is-lowest-in-india-60-of-deaths-in-confirmed-cases-not-counted.

19. Ibid.

20. Ibid.

21. National Health Mission, Government of Assam, 'Dedicated Covid Hospitals', https://nhm.assam.gov.in/portlet-innerpage/dedicated-covid-hospitals.

22. Himanta Biswa Sarma, Facebook post, dated 24 September 2020. Available at https://www.facebook.com/himantabiswasarma/

23. Health and Family Welfare Department, Government of Assam, Order No. HLA 269/2020/25, dated 11 July 2020, https://covid19.assam.gov.in/covid_asm_advisory/home-quarantine-guidelines-for-covid-19-positive-persons/.

24. Ibid.

25. *The Hindu*, 'IMA Calls Out Assam's Handling of Pandemic', 8 July 2020, https://www.thehindu.com/news/national/other-states/ima-calls-out-assams-handling-of-pandemic/article32017338.ece.

26. Ibid.

27. Bikash Singh, '14-day Quarantine a Must: Assam Health Minister Himanta Biswa Sarma', *The Economic Times*, 22 May 2020, https://economictimes.indiatimes.com/news/politics-and-nation/14-days-quarantine-a-must-assam-health-minister-himanta-biswa-sarma/articleshow/75877011.cms.

28. Ibid.

29. Bikash Singh, 'Assam Relaxes Quarantine Rules for Air Travellers coming from Other States', *The Economic Times*, 26 September 2020, https://economictimes.indiatimes.com/news/politics-and-nation/assams-new-quarantine-rules/articleshow/78325125.cms.

30. Government of Assam, 'Assam Arogya Nidhi', https://hfw.assam.gov.in/schemes/assam-arogya-nidhi-aan.

31. Deposited in the bank account no. 32124810101 for Assam Arogya Nidhi maintained by SBI, Assam Secretariat Branch, IFSC SBIN0010755.

32. *G Plus*, 'Committee Formed to Discuss Spending of Arogya Nidhi Funds', 29 April 2020, https://www.guwahatiplus.com/daily-news/committee-formed-to-discuss-spending-of-arogya-nidhi-funds.

33. *The Times of India*, 'Cost of Quarantine in Assam: 20,000 per Head', 22 May 2020, https://timesofindia.indiatimes.com/city/guwahati/cost-of-quarantine-in-assam-20000-per-head/articleshow/75891563.cms.

34. State Innovation and Transformation Aayog, Government of Assam, '*Report on Economy of Assam in the Backdrop of COVID-19 Pandemic*' (Guwahati: Prepared by Innovation and Transformation Aayog (SITA), Government of Assam, in collaboration with OKD Institute of Social Change and Development, 2020).

35. Ibid., 4, para 2.2.

36. Ibid., 5, para 2.8.

37. Ibid., 10, Table 3.

38. Ibid., 10–11, para 2.24.

39. Ibid., 12, Table 4.

40. Ibid., 33–34, para 5.10.

41. Report of the Advisory Committee for Revitalisation of Economy of Assam, 2020 (committee constituted by the Governor of Assam through a notification issued on 4 May 2020 by the Department of Transformation and Development, Government of Assam.), 105, para 9.1.

42. Ibid., para 9.2.

43. Ibid., 15, Table 3.1.

44. Ibid., 17, para 3.13.

45. Ibid., 21, Table 3.2.

46. Ibid., 95, Table 7.1.

47. Ibid., 100.

48. Personal conversation with the chairman on 7 December 2020.

49. Personal conversation with Joydeep Baruah, who was also associated with the report titled *Report on Economy of Assam in the Backdrop of COVID-19 Pandemic*. Ibid.

50. Government of Assam, *Budget Speech 2020–21*, 15, para 55.

51. Ibid., para 56.

52. Ibid., 18, para 73.

53. Ibid., para 74.

54. Ibid., 19–20, para 80.

55. Ibid., 36, para 152.

56. Ibid., 36–37, para 159.

57. *The Sentinel*, 'Assam Govt Announces Guidelines for "Orunodoi" Scheme; Check Details Here', 17 August 2020, https://www.sentinelassam.com/north-east-india-news/assam-news/assam-govt-announces-guidelines-for-orunodoi-scheme-check-details-here-495687.

58. *The Sentinel*, 'Who Will Get Priority in "Orunodoi" Scheme? Himanta Biswa Sarma Reveals Details', 1 September 2020, https://www.sentinelassam.com/north-east-india-news/assam-news/who-will-get-priority-in-orunodoi-scheme-himanta-biswa-sarma-reveals-details-498743.

59. Hemanta Kumar Nath, 'Assam Govt Launches Biggest Direct Benefit Transfer Scheme, Aims to Cover 22 Lakh Families', *India Today* (2 December 2020),

https://www.indiatoday.in/india/story/assam-govt-launches-biggest-direct-benefit-transfer-scheme-orunodoi-lakh-families-1745867-2020-12-02.

60. Government of Assam, 'Arundhati Gold Scheme', n.d., https://charaideo.gov.in/schemes/detail/arundhati-gold-scheme.

61. Government of Assam, *Budget Speech 2020–21*, 22, para 89.

62. *Business World*, 'Assam CM Distributes Financial Assistance under "Arundhati Gold Scheme"', 25 September 2020, http://www.businessworld.in/article/Assam-CM-distributes-financial-assistance-under-Arundhati-Gold-Scheme-/25-09-2020-324481/.

63. Utpal Parashar, 'Assam Re-launches Self-employment Scheme Worth Rs. 1,000 Crore', *The Hindustan Times*, 4 September 2020, https://www.hindustantimes.com/india-news/assam-re-launches-self-employment-scheme-worth-rs-1-000-crore/story-Qzz1iYbGHFakg7noiB7aIL.html.

64. Utpal Parashar, 'Assam Launches 4 Schemes to Boost Covid-hit Tea Industry', *The Hindustan Times,* 25 September 2020, https://www.hindustantimes.com/cities/assam-launches-4-schemes-to-boost-covid-hit-tea-industry/story-UIubxPoOmIF57zP9QjbMDJ.html.

65. Ibid.

66. *The Assam Tribune*, 'Bodo To Be Associate Official Language', 8 October 2020, http://www.assamtribune.com/scripts/detailsnew.asp?id=oct0820/at057.

67. Ibid.

68. Scroll.in, 'CAA Protests: Assam Activist Akhil Gogoi Denied Bail by NIA Court in Guwahati', 7 August 2020, https://scroll.in/latest/969702/caa-protests-assam-activist-akhil-gogoi-denied-bail-by-nia-court-in-guwahati.

69. Ibid.

70. *G Plus*, 'Assam Govt to Appoint Zubeen Garg as Brand Ambassador for Agriculture Sector', 10 August 2020, https://www.guwahatiplus.com/daily-news/assam-govt-to-appoint-zubeen-garg-as-brand-ambassador-for-agriculture-sector.

71. Ibid.

72. News Live, 'I Am Not a Brand Ambassador of Assam Govt: Zubeen Garg', 3 September 2020, https://newslivetv.com/i-am-not-brand-ambassador-of-assam-govt-zubeen-garg/.

73. Rahul Karmakar, 'Assam Students' Unions Float New Political Party', *The Hindu*, 14 September 2020, https://www.thehindu.com/news/national/other-states/assam-students-unions-float-new-political-party/article32604321.ece.

74. *The Hindu*, 'Akhil Gogoi's Group Forms Political Party', 2 October 2020, https://www.thehindu.com/news/national/other-states/akhil-gogois-group-forms-political-party/article32752134.ece.

75. *The Sentinel*, 'Regional Forces Team Up to Defeat BJP in Assam General Election, 2021', 15 June 2020, https://www.sentinelassam.com/guwahati-city/regional-forces-team-up-to-defeat-bjp-in-assam-general-election-2021-482834.

76. Time8, 'AASU Will Help BJP Returning to Power in 2021 Assembly Elections: Ajit Bhuyan', 10 August 2020, https://www.time8.in/aasu-will-help-bjp-returning-to-power-in-2021-assembly-elections-ajit-bhuyan/.

77. Debananda Medak, 'Akhil Gogoi's Appeal Is Impractical; Regional Parties Alone Cannot Oust the BJP: Ajit Bhuyan', *The Sentinel*, 10 September 2020, https://www.time8.in/as/akhil-gogois-appeal-is-impractical-regional-parties-alone-cannot-oust-the-bjp-ajit-bhuyan/.

78. *The Times of India*, 'Alliance with Congress Certain: AIUDF', 5 October 2020, https://timesofindia.indiatimes.com/city/guwahati/alliance-with-congress-certain-aiudf/articleshow/78487678.cms.

Epilogue
The Tough Innings— BJP's Victory in 2021

The BJP has had the upper hand in every election in Assam since the party won big in the state in the 2014 Lok Sabha elections. It won 7 and 9 (out of 14) Lok Sabha seats in 2014 and 2019, respectively, while registering leads in 69 assembly segments in both the elections. In the 2016 assembly elections, the BJP won 60 seats, while the 'Rainbow Alliance' it led succeeded in 86 constituencies. In the 2019 general elections, the NDA led in 82 assembly segments. The alliance has repeated the victory in the 2021 polls, too, although with a reduced majority. This time, the BJP has won 60 seats—the same number of seats that it had won in 2016—but the number of seats for the alliance reduced from 86 to 75. The BJP's vote share increased from 29.5 per cent to 33.21 per cent (Table E.1). The party has achieved this victory through multiple strategies. It manufactured social perceptions, implemented competitive populist schemes and brought almost all mainstream tribal ethnic political outfits into its fold. During the first wave of the COVID-19 pandemic, the BJP regained the political legitimacy to a large extent which it had lost during the period of the CAA enactment through initiatives like the Arogya Nidhi. By exempting the three Sixth Schedule council areas—the BTC, the Karbi Anglong Autonomous Council and the Dima Hasao—from the purview of the CAA, the BJP government succeeded in luring away many ethnic nationalist organizations from the anti-CAA movement. Although two new regional political parties—the AJP and the RD—were formed centred on the anti-CAA sentiments, the BJP limited the anti-CAA fervour to a section of the Assamese-speaking non-tribal population.[1] The victory of Akhil Gogoi, president of the RD, is more a reflection of the peoples' wrath against his extended imprisonment than the anti-CAA sentiments that he symbolizes.

Meanwhile, the grand alliance forged by the Congress with the AIUDF, the Left, the BPF and a few other smaller regional parties had the potential to challenge the ruling alliance. But it failed due to the inter and intra fighting among the parties. The alliance failed both in producing a common minimum programme and executing coordinated electoral strategies. The detailed results show that in around a dozen constituencies, the margin of victory was very low and both the grand alliance and the regional alliance would have performed better by joining hands together.[2] BJP's systematic attack on the East Bengal origin Muslims, particularly on the AIUDF that primarily represents the interest of the community, got intensified after the Congress had allied with the party. The BJP projected both the AIUDF and the grand alliance as a civilizational threat to the indigenous people of Assam and gained political mileage in upper Assam, the epicentre of the anti-CAA resistance. RD's refusal to join the Congress-led grand alliance on the pretext that AIUDF is equally communal like the BJP also had its impact on the voters' psyche in the constituencies inhabited by the indigenous people.[3]

The BJP consolidated its base by foregrounding developmentalism, accompanied by hyper populism. The decades-long work by

Table E.1 *Performance of Political Parties in Assam Legislative Elections 2021*

Parties	Seats Contested	Seats Won	Votes Polled (%)	Striking Rate (%)
BJP	92	60	33.21	65.2
INC	94	29	29.67	31.0
AGP	26	9	7.91	35.0
AIUDF	20	16	9.29	80.0
UPPL	8	6	NA	75.0
BPF	12	4	3.39	33.0
Left	4	1	NA	25.0
RD	38	1	NA	2.6

Source: Prasanta Mazumdar, 'Assam Elections: At 80%, AIUDF Had the Best Strike Rate', *The New Indian Express*, 5 May 2021, https://www.newindianexpress.com/nation/2021/may/05/assam-elections-at–80-aiudf-had-the-best-strike-rate-2298817.html

the RSS had turned the tea tribes, particularly in upper Assam, to BJP supporters. The community received the highest patronage from the incumbent government. The number of beneficiaries under various schemes like the 'Orunodoi' under the National Food Security Act also increased substantially. It also launched new and innovative schemes for different segments of society. Not a single segment of society remained untouched by the populist beneficiary schemes, including girls and women belonging to the minority Muslim community. BJP's *Sankalp Patra 2021* is a case in point. The BJP also successfully engineered the perception that Narendra Modi stands for an all-inclusive development.[4] The RSS mobilized the Sangh Parivar outfits at the grassroots and engaged the socially conscious sections to ensure maximum polling, which also helped the BJP in gaining electoral mileage.[5]

A TOUGH BATTLE

Compared to the past victories, the BJP had to wage a tough electoral battle in the 2021 elections. The Congress-led grand alliance—the *Mahajont*—comprising the AIUDF, BPF, the Left political parties and a few small regional parties, posed a formidable challenge to the BJP-led alliance—the *Mitrajont* (the alliance of friends)—in the majority of the constituencies in the state. The third alliance forged by the two newly formed regional parties, the AJP and the RD, too, created trouble for the BJP-led alliance by snatching away the substantive portions of the mainstream Assamese nationalist votes that continue to oppose the contentious CAA from the BJP. In 2019, a large percentage of the anti-CAB votes had gone in favour of the BJP due to the absence of a credible alternative to the BJP. In 2021, both the AJP and the RD supposedly provided an alternative to the BJP on the issue of CAA. Amidst these challenges, BJP's fourth successive victory in Assam in the 2021 state assembly elections, although with a reduced majority, may be considered remarkable in the context of BJP's humiliating defeat in West Bengal assembly elections. Both Prime Minister Narendra Modi and Union Home Minister Amit Shah massively campaigned in the state and reduced the electoral battle to a personality cult between Prime Minister Modi and West Bengal Chief Minister, Mamata Banerjee.

BJP's victory in 2016 was orchestrated through the 'Rainbow Alliance' with the AGP, the BPF and other ethnic parties of the Assam plains. In 2021 too, the BJP continued with the 'Rainbow Alliance' except for BPF which was replaced by the UPPL. Notably, the BPF was a formidable political force for the BJP in 2016. Several factors contributed to the snapping of ties with the BPF, particularly contestations around the BTR Accord signed in February 2020. The tripartite BTR Accord, the third accord with the Bodos, was signed primarily with the four factions of the NDFB. The other signatories included BTC Chief Hagrama Mohilary, ABSU and the United Bodo People's Organization. The agreement was considered a new milestone in the peace process in the BTAD. However, immediately after the signing of the accord, conflicts and disputes surfaced between the BTC Chief Hagrama Mohilary and the ABSU President-turned- UPPL-President Pramod Boro about the content of the accord. Mohilary alleged that the BTR Accord is unacceptable as it has no content except for changing the name from BTC to BTR. Pointing fingers at the ABSU President Pramod Boro, Mohilary said:

> The BTR Accord was signed only as per the draft of demands prepared by the ABSU and NDFB(P), keeping the intellectuals and the BPF in the dark. Had there been discussions over the draft of the charter of demands, the effectiveness would certainly have been better.[6]

The wrangling finally led to the new political equations in the Bodo politics with the BJP joining hands with the UPPL and snapping ties with the BPF. In the elections held in December 2020 to the 40-member Council, voters returned a fragmented verdict, with ruling BPF winning the highest number of seats (17) but falling short of an absolute majority. The UPPL won 12 seats, the BJP won 9, and the Congress and the Kokrajhar Member of Parliament Naba Kumar Sarania led Gana Shakti Party (GSP) won 1 seat each. In a turnaround of events, the GSP allied with the UPPL–BJP alliance and the only member of the Congress defected to the BJP. With these numbers, the UPPL–BJP alliance formed the Council government. UPPL President Pramod Boro was sworn in as the chief executive member on 16 December 2016. The BPF had, however, challenged the constitutional validity of the appointment of Mr Boro and four others as heads of the council on 15 December, citing rules to argue that the governor, who is the constitutional head of the BTC, should have invited it first to prove majority in the council. Hearing BPF's petition on 22 December, the Gauhati High Court sought a floor test on or before 26 December. The floor test was held on 24 December 2020 and the BJP–UPPL–GSP combine won the composite floor test in the BTC.[7]

These developments led to the snapping of ties with the BPF in the run-up to the assembly elections of 2021. The BJP contested in 92 seats; offered 26 seats to the AGP and 8 to the UPPL. Interestingly, the state BJP President Ranjeet Kumar Dass, who had won the Sorbhog constituency twice consecutively, had left it and contested from the Patacharkuchi constituency. While the BJP replaced 11 of its seating MLAs by new faces,[8] the AGP too denied tickets to 4 of its sitting MLAs, including 2 former presidents—the founder president of the party and two-time chief minister, Prafulla Kumar Mahanta, and former education minister and the leader of the opposition, Brindaban Goswami.

A POLARIZED VERDICT: CSDS DATA

Before we move towards the campaign and electoral strategies, let us have an overall pulse of the people towards the achievements and setbacks of the government in core developmental parameters and also peoples' opinion on contested political issues such as the NRC and CAA, and the AIUDF–Congress alliance. These issues are critical because the incumbent regime foregrounded development as its main campaign plank but invoked the civilizational threat from the East Bengal origin Muslims as a core electoral mobilization. The Congress-led grand alliance fought the elections primarily on the Congress–AIUDF alliance and the regional front foregrounded the CAA and the NRC as its core electoral strategy. It may be mentioned that while both the Congress and the regional alliance pledged to scrap the CAA if voted to power, the BJP maintained silence over the issue. On NRC, the BJP pledged for a corrected one, the Congress promised to complete the process. This background will be pertinent to understand peoples' pulse over the issues at play and their decision to vote on religious lines.

The Centre for the Study of Developing Societies (CSDS) 'Assam Assembly Election Study,2021: Post Poll Survey'[9] provides interesting insights in this regard. The survey reveals that 'Hindu consolidation pays off for BJP'[10] in the elections. The study argues:

> ...[T]he Congress's tie-up with the 'Muslim party' AIUDF seems to have helped the National Democratic Alliance's (NDA) cause, helping them keep Hindu voters firmly on their side and wean away a small but sizeable chunk of Assamese Muslim voters. The two local parties, the Assam Jatiya Parishad (AJP) and the Raijor Dal (RD), had a limited impact, and the latter could win just one seat in Upper Assam. Their influence remained confined to Upper Assam.[11]

There was indeed complete polarization of votes on religious lines. The CSDS data reveals that as high as 67 per cent of Hindus rallied behind the NDA, which is 10 per cent higher than the 2016 elections. The Congress-led alliance was backed by only 19 per cent of the Hindu votes, which was 13 per cent lower than 2016. The data also reveals that the BJP gained support from the Hindus cutting across linguistic-ethnic differences.[12] Among the Hindu voters, 58 per cent also opposed the Congress–AIUDF alliance, while 81 per cent of Muslims rallied behind the alliance.

Although the incumbent regime glorified its developmental achievements, people at large put them only in the average category. On crucial issues such as the creation of job opportunities and improving the farmers' conditions, people gave them a very low score. For example, only 15.7 per cent of people said that there was an improvement in job opportunities as against 30.2 per cent reporting that there was deterioration at this front. As high as 43.4 per cent believed that overall job opportunities remained the same during the last five years. Only 13.5 per cent reported that there was an improvement in the conditions of farmers, while 29.2 per cent reported that the conditions of the farmers had indeed deteriorated. As high as 46.5 per cent of responders believed that the conditions of the farmers remained almost the same. Concerning law and order and the creation of medical opportunities, 28.2 per cent and 34.2 per cent of the survey participants, respectively, reported improvements. But 45.1 per cent and 40.0 per cent, respectively, reported that no change had happened in this regard. More than half of the respondents (52.6%), however, reported improvements in road conditions and the same number of people also said electricity supply had improved.[13]

Despite the lower achievements in critical areas such as job creations and farmers' conditions, the level of satisfaction both with the BJP-led state and central governments was quite high. The CSDS post-poll survey found that as high as 58 per cent of the voters reported satisfaction with the Sonowal-led BJP–AGP government in the state and 56 per cent of voters also expressed satisfaction with the NDA-led government at the centre. Disaggregating the data on religious lines, the survey reveals that 72 per cent of Hindus reported satisfaction with the state government as against 36 per cent of Muslims. More importantly, 62.4 per cent of the voters viewed that governments of the same party, both at the centre and in the state, were conducive for the development of the state.

On NRC, as high as 74.4 per cent favoured it as a concept and 72.3 per cent believed that updating the NRC process would solve the foreigners' issue in Assam and 58.3 per cent expressed satisfaction over the way the NRC updating process was carried out. Disaggregating the data between fully satisfied/fully favoured and somewhat satisfied/somewhat favoured also revealed that a higher percentage of the voters were in favour of the NRC. Only 9.8 per cent of the voters reported that they fully supported the CAA and as high as 46.7 per cent fully opposed the law. The critical question that needs to be asked then is why both the Congress-led grand alliance and the regional alliance, particularly the grand alliance, failed to capitalize the anti-CAA resistance, particularly in upper Assam, its epicentre. This needs to be cross-examined through peoples' perception of the Congress–AIUDF alliance.

As has been pointed out, the voting in the elections took a religious line with a higher percentage of the Hindus voting for the NDA and opposing the Congress–AIUDF alliance. However, although an important one, this is not the only factor. The populist policies, organizational strength and meticulous campaign strategies also helped the BJP-led alliance. Remarkably, under the Congress-led grand alliance, the AIUDF won 16 out of the 20 constituencies that the party contested. Interestingly, it won all 14 constituencies where the party fought under the grand alliance and won 2 out of the 6 constituencies where the party encountered the Congress in friendly contests.[14] The striking rate for the AIUDF was 80 per cent. The Congress won 29 seats of the 94 that the party contested and out of the 29 winners, around a dozen were elected from East Bengal origin Muslim dominated constituencies of lower and central Assam.

Therefore, despite the lower level of satisfaction over development and stiff opposition to CAA, the BJP-led alliance succeeded in gaining political mileage from peoples' disapproval of the Congress–AIUDF alliance at large.

CAMPAIGN AND ELECTORAL STRATEGIES

The BJP had deployed multiple political strategies to win over the hearts of voters. Hindutva and developmentalism are the two core strategies for the party. However, under Modi and Shah, the electoral strategies have extended far beyond these two core ideological orientations. In the specific context of Assam, BJP's electoral strategies have two other important dimensions: (a) postulating the East Bengal origin Muslims as a threat to Assam's civilization and (b) providing political space to the indigenous tribal and other backward communities.

Himanta Biswa Sarma, state finance minister in the Sonowal Cabinet and one of the key campaigners in the present elections, asserts,

> Prime Minister Narendra Modi has made the Northeast the centre of development in the country…There are policies towards the development of infrastructure, roads, railway, universities etc. The state government too took a number of initiatives. People have also appreciated the state government's fight against Covid…and have voted against the divisive politics and unholy alliances of the Opposition.[15]

Taking advantage of being in power, the BJP launched its campaign much ahead of the other parties through various government programmes which also brought the prime minister and other key central ministers to the state in the run-up to the elections. Both the prime minister and the home minister visited Assam several times in the wake of the elections. The election campaign was formally launched by the home minister on 26 December 2020 in a huge government rally held in Amingaon where he laid down the foundation stone of several schemes, including a new medical college in Guwahati and 10 law colleges. Amit Shah also met religious leaders of 8,000 naamghars and distributed financial aid to them.[16]

On 23 January, Prime Minister Narendra Modi addressed a packed rally in Jerenga Pathar in Sivsagar district and distributed land patta to 1.06 lakh indigenous people. Addressing the crowd, he asserted that before the Sarbananda Sonowal led government had assumed power in Assam in 2016, Assam had more than six lakh landless indigenous families. Claiming that during the last few years, more than two lakh families had been allotted land entitlement certificates, the prime minister stated: 'With more than one lakh families added today, the government has shown its commitment to protecting the rights of the indigenous people.' He also said that the ownership certificates would guarantee their *swabhiman* (pride), *swadheenta* (freedom) and *suraksha* (protection).[17] The prime minister again visited Assam on 7 February 2021 and addressed a rally in Dhekiajuli. He laid the foundation stone of two medical colleges, launched various schemes under Asom Mala and spelt out his dream of imparting medical and technical education in the mother tongue in every state through at least one such institution.[18]

The Union Finance Minister, Nirmala Sitharaman, distributed ₹3,000 each to 7.47 lakh tea garden workers in the state, totalling ₹224 crore on 6 February 2021. This was the third tranche of financial assistance for the tea workers under the Assam Chah Bagichar Dhan Puraskar Mela Scheme. Each tea worker had already received ₹5,000 in two phases. It may be mentioned that the incentive was made through DBT mode to 633,411 bank accounts of workers in 2017–2018 and 715,979 accounts in 2018–2019 across 752 tea gardens.[19]

In his last election rally held in Tamulpur in Assam on 3 April 2021, Prime Minister Narendra Modi said:

To continue this momentum of growth and development, it is very important to bring back NDA government to power. We believe in *sabka saath, sabka vikas, sabka vishwas* (with all, development for all, with the trust of all). We do not discriminate in our schemes and everyone is equally benefitted….[20]

On 23 March 2021, the BJP published its *Sankalp Patra*, the Vision Document, with 10 pledges, and one of them was a corrected NRC for the state. It declared that 30 lakh deserving families would be covered under the Orunodoi scheme and the monthly assistance under the scheme would be increased from ₹830 to ₹3,000. A total of 10 lakh jobs—2 lakh in the government sector and another 8 lakh under the private sector—in the coming five years, was one of the important highlights of the document. The party also promised to create 2 lakh entrepreneurs every year and 10 lakh in 5 years. It pledged to speed up the delimitation process to protect the political rights of the Assamese people. Land entitlement to all landless people in the state was an important highlight of the vision document. The foremost promise of the BJP, however, was the Mission Brahmaputra that aims to bring an end to the floods caused by the river by dredging it as well as managing its tributaries and constructing reservoirs.[21]

BJP's campaign strategies, however, took many twists and turns in the run-up to the elections. Initially, it started with the pro-incumbency card highlighting the achievements of the incumbent ruling alliance. However, gradually, the focus shifted from the developmental achievements towards 'civilizational threat'.

The BJP has dubbed this election as 'a conflict of two civilisations'—civilisation represented by 35% population and the civilisation represented by the rest 65% population to strengthen the religion binary. (According to Census 2011, Muslims account for 34.22%, while Hindus and other religions account for the rest of the population in Assam.)[22]

Talukdar has also pointed out that 'The electoral narrative around the AIUDF and Maulana Badruddin Ajmal has been pushed to shape the perception that instead of language, religion should be the basis of identities of the majority Assamese and other ethnic nationalities'.[23]

Among the state leadership, Dr Himanta Biswa Sarma campaigned extensively and aggressively during the elections. Two theme songs in the elections became very popular: one is the 2019 Lok Sabha elections theme song *Akou Ebar Modi Sarkar* (once more the Modi government) and the second one is *Ahise Ahise, Himanta Ahise, Aashaare Botora Loi* (here comes Himanta, with a message of hope). Indeed, the second theme song became more popular than the song around Modi. Dr Sarma campaigned almost in all constituencies of the state, and the theme song was 'the background music to the rallies and padayatras of Himanta Biswa Sarma'.[24] 'From firefighting to accompanying party candidates during nomination filing process to addressing rallies and padayatras and mobilising workers Himanta has been at the forefront of all activities.'[25] As an aggressive Hindutva ideologue and as the architect of competitive populism, Himanta Biswa Sarma helped the BJP to retain Assam. It finally culminated in Dr Sarma replacing the incumbent chief minister, Sarbananda Sonowal, as the chief minister of Assam.

WHAT WENT WRONG WITH THE GRAND ALLIANCE AND THE REGIONAL ALLIANCE?

The Congress-led grand alliance that for the first time allied both with the AIUDF and the Left parties in the present elections posed a formidable challenge to the ruling alliance. The alliance, particularly the Congress, laid down its electoral strategies in a careful manner. The management of the election strategies was almost taken over by the central leadership under the stewardship of the AICC general secretary and the Congress incharge in Assam, Jitendra Singh, and the Chhattisgarh Chief Minister Bhupesh Baghel. While Jitendra Singh endeavoured to revamp the organization of the party in the state, Baghel, the poll observer in the state, played a key role in deciding the electoral strategies. The party also engaged DesignBoxed, a Mohali-based political campaign management company, from January 2021.[26]

Congress's core electoral plank anchored on five guarantees: scrapping CAA through new legislation, providing five lakh government jobs in five years, raising the daily wage of tea plantation workers to ₹365, free electricity up to 200 units per household and ₹2,000 as monthly income support to all homemakers.[27] The Party's *Jan*

Manifesto, 2021, released on 22 March 2021 by Rahul Gandhi, also promised to

> waive off debt for women who have taken loans from micro finance banks, to provide free of cost of yarn, loom and other equipment to weavers, free of cost state transport for all women, agricultural debt will be waived-off for farmers, to revice two paper mills again, a pension will be extended to the families of freedom fighters and martyrs of the Assam agitation, language movement and the CAA movement, land pattas to the landless who currently inhabit state-owned land, to resolve the D voter (doubtful voter) problems for minority groups like Gorkhas, religious minorities, Koch-Rajbangshi, linguistic minorities and other ethnic communities.[28]

The Congress also promised to accord ST status to the six communities: Tai Ahom, Moran, Matak, Chutia, tea tribes and Koch-Rajbongshi. The manifesto also promised to give financial aid to all religious institutions in the state, that is, naamghars, mandirs, mosques and churches. Another important promise made by the Congress was to set up *gaushalas* (cowshed) in each district.

The alliance altogether registered victory in 50 seats with the Congress alone winning 29 seats, 3 seats more than that the Party had won in 2016. The vote percentage dropped from 31.0 to 29.5. AIUDF's tally increased by three seats from 2016, even though its poll percentage dropped from 13.0 to 9.29. BPF's seats, however, dropped from 12 to 4 although its vote percentage dropped only marginally, from 3.9 to 3.39. CPI (M), which won one seat, secured less than 1 per cent of votes. All other small regional parties that formed an alliance with the Congress failed to secure any seat.

Even though the Congress-led grand alliance came under mounting attack from the BJP-led alliance, primarily due to the Congress–AIUDF alliance, it was supported by the secular progressive sections in the greater society. The inner fight of the Congress along with its reluctance to facilitate coordination among the allied partners reduced its potential.

But many have argued that the failure on the part of the opposition to dislodge the ruling alliance primarily lies in the split of votes between the Congress-led grand alliance and that of the regional alliance. The regional alliance from the very beginning categorically refused to be a part of any alliance with the nationalist and the communal parties. As early as 3 January 2021, the AJP President, Lurinjyoti Gogoi, had declared,

> Since the beginning, our stand is clear: we will try to unite all regional forces and maintain distance from the national parties. We are firm on this and so we have decided to form an alliance with Raijor Dal. An agreement in this regards will be signed very soon.[29]

The alliance was sealed on 4 February 2021 with a pledge that it 'will fight together against the national and communal parties to form the next government....'[30]

While the RD too insisted on distancing both from the nationalist and the communal parties, it kept on shifting its position. In an open letter written by the RD President, Akhil Gogoi, from the jail in early March 2021 appealed all political parties to unite against the BJP but keep the AIUDF away from such a united front. Gogoi insisted,

> We do not desire to take along a communal party with fundamentalist ideology to oppose a communal and fascist party...We think the BJP and the AIUDF are two sides of the same coin...If we take them along with us, we will be weakened ethically, ideologically and politically.[31]

The statement invited strong reactions not only from the AIUDF and the other partners of the grand alliance but also from a section of RD's supporters and sympathizers. Hiren Gohain, the chief advisor of the RD, resigned from the post in protest against the position of the RD. Akhil's remark painting the AIUDF and the BJP with the same brush came at a point when the BJP was projecting the East Bengal origin Muslims, at large, and the AIUDF, in particular, as threats to Assam's culture and civilization. Gohain, while resigning from the post of chief advisor of the RD, stated that the BJP is the

> [B]iggest enemy of our democratic country, and Akhil's comments on the AIUDF [are] baseless as I have not heard its leader Badruddin Ajmal making any anti-Assamese or anti-Hindu statements. He has opposed the Citizenship Amendment Act and accepted the Assam Accord.[32]

To further fuel the controversy, the BJP stated that it encouraged forming the two new regional outfits (i.e., the AJP and the RD) to gain political mileage by splitting the anti-CAA votes in the state. Dr Himanta Biswa Sarma argued that even if CAA was no longer a substantive political issue in the state, 'the idea behind creating the new regional parties was to split the votes of those against the law between them and the Congress and its allies'.[33] The statement, of course, was strongly refuted both by the AJP and the RD.

After the results of the elections were declared, the tug of war between the grand alliance and the AJP and the RD intensified, one blaming the other for the victory of the BJP-led alliance. However, minute analysis of the margin of victory by the BJP-led alliance reveals that the split of votes between the grand alliance and the regional alliance helped the BJP to master victory in around a dozen constituencies. Gohain has pointed out that by rejecting the offer for alliance, the regional parties even caused electoral harm to themselves too.

> Actually the dour rejection by AJP of offers of alliance by Congress and the scathing attacks by Akhil Gogoi did not help them at all. AJP came a cropper in all seats it contested, with its president losing heavily in both the seats it contested and Raijor Dal of Akhil Gogoi drawing in only up to three thousand votes in all seats except Sivasagar where Akhil Gogoi won partly because people of good will thought the shining image of militant popular Assamese nationalism which was also secular must not be allowed to be darkened by defeat, and volunteers flocked to campaign for him.[34]

CHANGE OF GUARD: REPLACING THE INCUMBENT CHIEF MINISTER

Assam's incumbent chief minister, Sarbananda Sonowal, enjoyed a clean political image and maintained his cool even during political storms in the state. However, in the public eye, he was a non-performer. For his regionalist background, Mr Sonowal also invited public wrath for his silence and indifference on core political issues such as the CAA, NRC and Clause 6 of the Assam Accord. In the present elections, it was Dr Sarma who was in the forefront, both in formulating electoral strategies and leading the campaign. No wonder, after a week-long dilly-dallying, the BJP has finally pinned its choice on Dr

Himanta Biswa Sarma, the finance, health and education minister, to replace the incumbent chief minister.

Three factors appear to have worked in Dr Sarma's favour: (a) his open and aggressive effort to polarize the electorate around religion through his much-publicized statement that the East Bengal origin Muslims are a civilizational threat to the Assamese paid political dividends, (b) aggressive pursuit of the neoliberal populist policies that brought in almost every section of the society into the fold of beneficiary schemes and (c) third, and most importantly, his organizational skills and meticulous electoral strategies must have convinced the BJP about his inevitability in the next elections, particularly in 2024 Lok Sabha elections. Dr Sarma's ability to take head on the opposition, both inside and outside the assembly, and the resistance forces on the street made him close to the Hindutva forces, particularly during the anti-CAB and anti-CAA days in the state.

Starting with his leadership exercise in Cotton College where he was general secretary of the college union body for three tenures, Himanta Biswa Sarma has journeyed through a long political trajectory. His initial political training from the former chief minister of Assam, Hiteswar Saikia, the politician who handled the most troubled period of the Assam Agitation, taught him to swim through the stormy political winds. Saikia, who earned the title of *ganashatru*, that is, people's enemy, for steering the most infamous 1983 assembly elections, had to resign from the post of the chief minister to facilitate the early elections in Assam as a political arrangement after the signing of the Assam Accord in 1985. Mr Saikia, however, stormed back to power in 1991. Dr Sarma publicly acknowledges his debt to late Mr Saikia for moulding in him a determined leadership quality.

During Tarun Gogoi's three tenures as the chief minister of Assam (2001–2016), Himanta Biswa Sarma was not only the most powerful minister and the trusted colleague of the chief minister but was also the architect of the populist schemes that were in line with the neoliberal policies. He proved his credibility as one of the most imaginative politicians to capture peoples' pulse, and accordingly, to formulate and implement electoral strategies. In his indomitable desire to be the chief minister of Assam, Himanta Biswa Sarma launched the revolt against the incumbent chief minister, Mr Gogoi, in the post-2011 victory of the Congress, which finally showed him the door from the party. Joining the BJP in August 2015, Dr Sarma secured the position of convener of BJP's state campaign committee for the 2016 assembly elections. Sarma played a critical role in framing the 'Rainbow Alliance' that helped to form the first-ever BJP-led government in the state. He was also made the convener of the NEDA.

During the tenure in the BJP for the last five years and so, Himanta Biswa Sarma also became the most aggressive political voice of Hindutva. His constant attack on the Left intellectuals and the secular nationalists made him a blue-eyed boy of the Hindutva forces. He systematically dismantled the consensus around the Assam Accord by raising several uncomfortable questions for the signatories to the accord like on what ground 1971 was accepted as the cut-off date for the detection and deletion of foreigners at the cost of the long-drawn demand of 1951. Compared with the sustained silence of Sarbananda Sonowal, Himanta Biswa Sarma's constant attack on the NRC and aggressive pursuit of the CAA also made him dear to the Hindutva forces and the incumbent union government. With the 2021 assembly elections at the doorstep, Himanta Biswa Sarma manufactured and invoked the narrative on the civilizational threat from the East Bengal origin Muslims. To confront the formidable challenge from the Congress-led grand alliance, he intensified the campaign against the Congress–AIUDF alliance and projected it as an enemy to the interests of the indigenous people. This campaign paid huge political dividends. CSDS Assam assembly elections post-poll survey reveals that as high as 67 per cent of Hindus rallied behind the NDA, which was 10 per cent higher than the 2016 elections.

Under the NDA regime too, Mr Sarma emerged as the core architect of the competitive populist policies. As the finance minister of the state, he introduced several schemes targeting almost all sections of the society and expanded the number of beneficiaries under existing schemes like the National Food Security Act. He has been quite imaginative in this regard. Apart from increasing the coverage under universal schemes like the 'Orunodoi', he introduced different schemes for different categories, like scooters (commonly known as 'scooty') for college-going meritorious girls and promised to give Royal Enfield Bullet motorcycles to the meritorious college-going boys if the BJP is returned to power. Promises of fee waiver in government educational institutions from the primary to the postgraduate level, free textbooks up to higher secondary level and cash transfer schemes for the tea tribes had their electoral impact in BJP's favour.

The BJP is also keeping an eye on future elections, particularly the 2024 Lok Sabha elections. As the convener of NEDA, he played a crucial role in installing the BJP governments in the states of Arunachal Pradesh, Manipur and Tripura. The BJP is also a partner of the coalition governments in Nagaland and Meghalaya. He also shares a close rapport with all the chief ministers and senior politicians of the ruling parties in the region.[35]

By snapping ties with the BPF, Dr Sarma played a critical role in framing the new alliance with the UPPL in the BTAD. He tirelessly campaigned throughout the state and steered efforts to pacify the dissent of those who were deprived of the party tickets in the elections.

All these paved the way for Dr Sarma to replace the incumbent chief minister, Mr Sonowal. He was unanimously elected as the leader of the BJP and the NDA legislative parties on 9 May 2021. He was sworn in as the chief minister of the state along with his cabinet colleagues the following day.

CONCLUSION: THE NEW REGIME AND ASSAM'S FUTURE

Assam has been passing through the critical second phase of the COVID-19 pandemic. Before being sworn in, the new chief minister also apprehended the possibility of the extreme vulnerability of Assam during the current wave of the pandemic. The shortage of hospital beds and ICUs made the situation more alarming. Even though the healthcare sector received quite a substantive amount of allocations during the last five years, which was higher than the all-India average, the state, however, did not do much better in the domain of health and well-being. Although the populist policies allowed the government to successfully reach out to almost all segments of the society, bringing in enormous political and electoral dividends to the BJP, the fundamentals of the economy are not in a good shape. This is evident from the reports of the government like the economic surveys as well as the reports published during the first wave of the COVID-19 pandemic. If neoliberal populism remains the parameters of development in the coming years too, then Assam's economy does not promise a sustainable future.

The Hindutva campaign has taken a centre stage in Assam's politics. Preventing land jihad and love jihad are the promises of the new government. These steps may take a serious communal turn as the 'civilizational threat' has already created a divide along religious lines. The East Bengal origin Muslims constitute more than 30 per cent of the total population in the state. The younger and educated section from within the community is becoming more assertive about their identity. The Miya poetry is a testimony to it. This assertion has also created strong reactions in the greater society. The greater civil society needs to remain very alert to deter any conflict arising out of the assertions either on religious or linguistic lines.

NRC, CAA and Clause 6 of the Assam Accord remain core contentious political issues in the state. The anti-CAA resistance did not have much political impact on the electoral process. However, these issues, if not handled through appropriate political approaches, may storm back to the mainstream of Assam's politics. The writ petition of the state's NRC authority in the Supreme Court for comprehensive re-verification in the pretext of 'major irregularities' for which 'while ineligible names were included, many eligible names have also been excluded' may invite new tensions.

Political stability, communal harmony and sustainable development will be dependent on how these issues are addressed by the new regime.

NOTES

1. Akhil Ranjan Dutta, 'How BJP Retained Assam', *Indian Express*, 3 May 2021, https://indianexpress.com/article/opinion/columns/assam-bjp-win-assembly-election-results-7299593/

2. Hiren Gohain, 'Assam Election Review', 4 May 2021, personal mail dated 5 May 2021.

3. The open letter by Akhil Gogoi, the president of the RD, from the Gauhati Medical College Hospital, where he has been languishing an imprisoned life. Find the details in Abhishek Saha, 'Explained: The Significance of Akhil Gogoi's Letter to Political Parties of Assam', *Indian Express*, 5 March 2021, https://indianexpress.com/article/explained/explained-significance-of-akhil-gogois-letter-to-political-parties-of-assam-7214441/

4. Dutta, 'How BJP Retained Assam'.

5. The RSS steers the state-level coordination network of 36 organizations, including the BJP, Vishva Hindu Parishad and Akhil Bharatiya Vidyarthi Parishad, that pursue the core ideology of Hindutva. The RSS appoints an unmarried *karyakarta* as a general secretary for all those organizations. The Coordination Committee usually meets in *samanya baithak* at the state level once every two months. To prepare for the 2021 assembly elections, this committee, however, had met at the district levels too since October 2020. Many issues, including the selection of candidates, were discussed at these meetings. Under the RSS initiative, around 2,000 citizens' meets were held in the run-up to the elections that brought in the leading citizens at the local levels. One of the issues discussed in those meetings was how to ensure 100 per cent polling in the ensuing elections. Information regarding the Coordination Committee and the citizens' meeting was provided by Ranjib Kumar Sharma, an RSS *karyakarta* based in Guwahati, in a telephonic conversation on 21 April 2021.

6. *Deccan Herald*, 'New Bodo Accord Is a Non-entity: BJP's Ally in Assam', 18 March 2020, https://www.deccanherald.com/national/east-and-northeast/new-bodo-accord-is-a-non-entity-bjps-ally-in-assam-815008.html

7. Prasanta Mazumdar, 'Bodo Council: BJP-UPPL-GSP Combine Wins Floor Test, Opposition BPF to Move Court', *The New Indian Express*, 24 December 2020, https://www.newindianexpress.com/nation/2020/dec/24/bodo-council-bjp-uppl-gsp-combine-wins-floor-test-opposition-bpf-to-move-court-2240565.html

8. Rahul Karmakar, 'Assam Assembly Elections | BJP Denies Ticket to 11 Sitting MLAs', *The Hindu*, 6 March 2021, https://www.thehindu.com/news/national/other-states/bjp-denies-ticket-to-11-sitting-mlas-in-assam/article34001130.ece

9. This survey in Assam was coordinated by the Department of Political Science, Gauhati University, with Dr Dhruba Pratim Sharma, associate professor in the Department as its coordinator. I gratefully acknowledge Sanjay Kumar, a fellow at CSDS, New Delhi, and a key person in the election studies for sharing the important database with me.

10. Suhas Palshikar et al., 'Assam Assembly Elections | Hindu Consolidation Pays Off for BJP', *The Hindu*, 8 May 2021, https://www.thehindu.com/elections/assam-assembly/hindu-consolidation-pays-off-for-bjp/article34509288.ece

11. Ibid.

12. Ibid.

13. CSDS, *Assam Assembly Election Study 2021: Post Poll Survey* (Delhi: CSDS, 2021).

14. Mazumdar, 'Assam Elections: At 80%, AIUDF Had the Best Strike Rate', *The New Indian Express*, 5 May 2021, https://www.newindianexpress.com/nation/2021/may/05/assam-elections-at-80-aiudf-had-the-best-strike-rate-2298817.html

15. Liz Mathew, 'On CAA… I Feel We Must Protect Genuine Refugees': Himanta Biswa Sarma', *Indian Express*, 3 May 2021, https://indianexpress.com/article/india/caa-refugees-illegal-migrants-himanta-biswa-sarma-assam-election-7299751/

16. Manoj Anand, 'Amit Shah Sounds 2021 Poll Bugle in Assam, Says only a BJP Govt Can Stop Infiltration', *Deccan Chronicle*, 27 December 2020, https://www.deccanchronicle.com/nation/politics/261220/amit-shah-sounds-2021-poll-bugle-in-assam-says-only-a-bjp-govt-can-st.html

17. Scroll.in, 'Assam: Modi Criticises Previous Governments, Says They Deprived Indigenous People of Land Rights', 23 January 2021, https://scroll.in/latest/984901/assam-modi-criticises-previous-governments-says-they-deprived-indigenous-people-of-land-rights

18. Umanand Jaiswal, 'Narendra Modi Lays Stress on Teaching in Local Language', *The Telegraph*, 8 February 2021, https://www.telegraphindia.com/north-east/narendra-modi-lays-stress-on-teaching-in-local-language/cid/1805973

19. *The Print*, 'Ahead of State Elections, FM Sitharaman Distributes Rs. 3000 Each to 7.47 lakh Assam Tea Workers', 6 February 2021, https://theprint.in/india/ahead-of-state-elections-fm-sitharaman-distributes-rs-3000-each-to-7-47-lakh-assam-tea-workers/600175/

20. Utpal Parashar, 'Bring NDA Back to Power, Modi Tells Voters at His Last Poll Rally in Assam', *Hindustan Times*, 3 April 2021, https://www.hindustantimes.com/india-news/bring-nda-back-to-power-modi-tells-voters-at-his-last-poll-rally-in-assam-101617436267306.html

21. India TV, 'Assam: BJP Manifesto Promises "Corrected" NRC, Rs. 3,000 Allowance to 30 Lakh Families', 23 March 2021, https://www.indiatvnews.com/elections/news-bjp-manifesto-assam-assembly-polls-2021-highlights-692844

22. Sushanta Talukdar, 'The Ground Report in the Assam Duel', *The Hindu*, 22 March 2021, https://www.thehindu.com/opinion/lead/the-ground-report-in-the-assam-duel/article34125761.ece

23. Ibid.

24. Hemanta Kumar Nath, 'Assam Polls: Decoding Himanta Biswa Sarma's Campaign Strategies', *India Today*, 18 March 2021, https://www.indiatoday.in/elections/assam-assembly-polls-2021/story/decoding-himanta-biswa-sarma-campaign-strategy-in-assam-1780808-2021-03-18

25. Ibid.

26. Utpal Parashar, 'From No Contest to Likely Winners, How Congress Turned around Its Assam Campaign', *Hindustan Times*, 9 April 2021, https://www.hindustantimes.com/elections/assam-assembly-election/from-no-contest-to-likely-winners-how-congress-turned-around-its-assam-campaign-101617882815122.html

27. *The Hindu*, 'Priyanka Gandhi Launches 5-Guarantee Campaign in Assam', 2 March 2021, https://www.thehindu.com/news/national/other-states/elections-priyanka-launches-5-guarantee-campaign-in-assam/article33971589.ece

28. Anand Patel and Hemanta Kumar Nath, 'Rahul Gandhi Releases Congress Manifesto for Assam Polls, Promises to Nullify CAA, Give 5 Lakh Govt Jobs', *India Today*, 22 March 2021, https://www.indiatoday.in/elections/assam-assembly-polls-2021/story/congress-manifesto-assam-scrap-caa-5-lakh-jobs-rahul-gandhi-1781621-2021-03-20

29. Sumir Karmakar, 'Setback for Congress as Assam Regional Parties Reject Grand Alliance Offer', *Deccan Herald*, 3 January 2021, https://www.deccanherald.com/national/setback-for-congress-as-assam-regional-parties-reject-grand-alliance-offer-934741.html

30. *The Hindu*, 'AJP, Jailed Activist Akhil Gogoi's Party Seal Pre-poll Pact', 4 February 2021, https://www.thehindu.com/news/national/other-states/ajp-ties-up-with-raijor-dal-for-assam-assembly-polls/article33748373.ece

31. Abhishek Saha, 'Explained: The Significance of Akhil Gogoi's Letter to Political Parties of Assam', *The Hindu*, 5 March 2021, https://indianexpress.com/article/explained/explained-significance-of-akhil-gogois-letter-to-political-parties-of-assam-7214441/

32. *The Wire*, 'Author Hiren Gohain Resigns as Raijor Dal Advisor after Party President Calls AIUDF "Communal"', 4 March 2021, https://thewire.in/politics/author-hiren-gohain-resigns-as-raijor-dal-advisor-after-party-president-calls-aiudf-communal

33. *The Hindu*, 'BJP Planned Creation of AJP, Raijor Dal to Split Anti-CAA Votes: Himanta Biswa Sarma', 2 April 2021, https://www.thehindu.com/elections/assam-assembly/bjp-planned-creation-of-ajp-raijor-dal-to-split-anti-caa-votes-himanta-biswa-sarma/article34224858.ece

34. Gohain, 'Assam Election Review'.

35. Utpal Parashar, 'Himanta Biswa Sarma: From BJP's Key Strategist in Northeast to Assam CM', 10 May 2021, https://www.hindustantimes.com/india-news/himanta-biswa-sarma-from-bjp-s-key-strategist-in-northeast-to-assam-cm-101620586214553.html

SELECT BIBLIOGRAPHY

Ahmed, A. N. S., ed. *Nationality Question in Assam: The EPW 1980–81 Debate*. New Delhi: Akansha Publishing House, 2006.

Ahmed, Farhana. 'Rhinos Killed to Settle Bangladeshis'. *The Assam Tribune* (1 April 2014).

Al Jazeera. 'What's Next for the 4 Million Stripped of Citizenship in India?' (30 July 2018). https://www.aljazeera.com/news/2018/07/4-millions-stripped-citizenship-india-180730080348753.html.

All Assam Lawyers' Association. 'Memorandum from All Assam Lawyers' Association (AALA) Regarding the Introduction of the Citizenship (Amendment) Bill, 2016'. 7 May 2018. Guwahati.

Alternative Economic Survey Group. *Two Decades of Neoliberalism*. Delhi: Daanish Books, 2010.

Asam Sahitya Sabha. 'Submission on Behalf of Asam Sahitya Sabha in the Matter of Citizenship (Amendment) Bill, 2016 before the Hon'ble Joint Parliamentary Committee'. 7 May 2018. Guwahati.

Asom Gana Parishad. 'Memorandum to the Chairman, Joint Parliamentary Committee, Citizenship (Amendment), Bill, 2016'. 7 May 2018. Guwahati.

Assam Pradesh Congress Committee. 'Views of Assam Pradesh Congress Committee on the Citizenship (Amendment) Bill, 2016, Bill No 172 of 2016'. 7 May 2018. Guwahati.

Azad, Abdul Kalam. 'Definition of Assamese People: NRC Updation and Recent Political Developments in Assam'. 2 April 2015. https://abdulkazad.wordpress.com/tag/definition-of-assamese/.

Azad, Abdul Kalam. 'Assam NRC: A History of Violence and Persecution'. The Wire (15 August 2018). https://thewire.in/rights/assam-nrc-a-history-of-violence-and-persecution.

Azad, Abdul Kalam. 'The Tragic Demise of a "Declared Foreigner" at Goalpara Detention Centre'. The Wire (12 January 2020). https://thewire.in/rights/goalpara-detention-death-assam.

Bal, Hartosh Singh. 'Is India Creating Its Own Rohingya?' *The New York Times* (10 August 2018). https://www.nytimes.com/2018/08/10/opinion/india-citizenship-assam-modi-rohingyas.html.

Barooah, Nirode K. *Gopinath Bardaloi, Indian Constitution and Centre-Assam Relations*. Guwahati: Publication Board of Assam, 1990.

Baruah, Sanjib. 'ASSAM-Cudgel of Chauvinism or Tangled Nationality Question?' *Economic & Political Weekly* 15, no. 11 (15 March 1980): 543–545. https://www.epw.in/system/files/pdf/1980_15/11/assam_cudgel_of_chauvinism_or_tangled.pdf.

Baruah, Sanjib. 'Beyond Patriots and Traitors Sanjib Kumar Baruah'. *Economic & Political Weekly* 15, no. 20 (17 May 1980): 876–878. https://www.epw.in/system/files/pdf/1980_15/20/assam_i_beyond_patriots_and_traitors_0.pdf.

Baruah, Sanjib. 'Little Nationalism Turned Chauvinist: A Comment'. *Economic & Political Weekly* 16, no. 15 (11 April 1981): 676–681. https://www.epw.in/system/files/pdf/1981_16/15/discussion_little_nationalism_turned_chauvinist.pdf.

Baruah, Sanjib. 'Immigration, Ethnic Conflict, and Political Turmoil: Assam, 1979–85'. *Asian Survey* 26, no. 11 (1986): 1184–1206.

Baruah, Sanjib. *India against Itself: Assam and the Politics of Nationality*. New Delhi: Oxford University Press, 1999.

Baruah, Sanjib. *Durable Disorder: Understanding the Politics of Northeast India*. New Delhi: Oxford University Press, 2005.

Baruah, Sanjib. *Beyond Counter-insurgency: Breaking the Impasse in Northeast India*. New Delhi: Oxford University Press, 2009.

Baruah, Sanjib. 'The Partition's Long Shadow: The Ambiguities of Citizenship in Assam, India'. *Citizenship Studies* 13, no. 6 (2011): 593–606.

Baruah, Sanjib. 'Stateless in Assam'. *The Indian Express* (19 January 2018). https://indianexpress.com/article/opinion/national-register-of-citizens-5030603/.

Baruah, Sanjib. 'The Missing 4,007,707'. *The Indian Express* (2 August 2018). https://indianexpress.com/article/opinion/columns/assam-nrc-draft-list-names-citizenship-5287213/.

Baruah, Sanjib. 'Defining Thousands as Non-citizens Will Create a New Form of Precarious Citizenship: People with Fewer Rights, Entitlements'. *The Indian Express* (31 August 2019). https://indianexpress.com/article/opinion/columns/a-more-precarious-citizenship-assam-nrc-list-jammu-kashmir-5949158/.

Basu, Deepankar, and Debarshi Das. 'Assam's Politics and the NRC'. *Economic & Political Weekly* 55, no. 5 (1 February 2020): 61–63. https://www.epw.in/system/files/pdf/2020_55/5/DI_LV_5_010220_Deepankar_Basu.pdf.

Basumatary, J. *Quest for Peace in Assam: A Study of the Bodoland Movement*. New Delhi: KW Publishers, 2014.

Bezbaruah, Ranju. *The Pursuit of Colonial Interests in India's North East*. Guwahati: EBH Publishers, 2010.

Bharatiya Janata Party, Assam. *Assam Vision Document 2016–16*. 2016. https://mmscmsguy.assam.gov.in/sites/default/files/swf_utility_folder/departments/mmscmsguy_webcomindia_org_oid_2/this_comm/vision-document.pdf.

Bhattacharjee, Chandana. *Ethnicity and Autonomy Movement. A Case of Bodo Kacharis of Assam*. New Delhi: Vikas Publishing House, 1996.

Bhattacharjee, Malini. 'Tracing the Emergence and Consolidation of Hindutva in Assam'. *Economic & Political Weekly* 51, no. 16 (16 April 2016): 80–87. https://www.epw.in/journal/2016/16/strategic-affairs/tracing-emergence-and-consolidation-hindutva-assam.html.

Bhattacharya, Rakhee. *Developmentalism as Strategy: Interrogating Post-Colonial Narratives on India's North East*. New Delhi: SAGE Publications, 2019.

Bhattacharyya, Rajeev. 'Is the Assam Govt. Shielding IPS Officers "Involved" in Rhino Killings, Chit Fund Scam?' The Wire, 26 September 2018. https://thewire.in/rights/assam-sarbananda-sonowal-rhino-killings-saradha-chit-scam-ips-officers.

Bhattacharyya, Rajeev. 'Saffron Wave in Assam: Ekal Vidyalayas Helped BJP, RSS Establish Strong Roots in Assam's Tribal Areas, Tea Estates'. Firstpost, 24 May 2019. https://www.firstpost.com/politics/saffron-wave-in-assam-ekal-vidyalayas-helped-bjp-rss-establish-strong-roots-in-assams-tribal-areas-tea-estates-6696851.html.

Bhattacharyya, Rituparna. 'Living with Armed Forces Special Powers Act (AFSPA) as Everyday Life'. *Geo Journal* 83, no. 1 (2018): 31–48. https://link.springer.com/article/10.1007/s10708-016-9752-9

Bhaumik, S. *Troubled Periphery: Crisis of India's North East*. New Delhi: SAGE Publications, 2009.

Bora, Sangita. 'Violence and Memory: The Communal Riots at Nagabandha during 1983'. Unpublished PhD thesis, 2017, Department of Political Science, Gauhati University.

Borah, Dhruba Jyoti. *Jatiya Prasna Aru Atmaniyantran* [The Nationality Question and Self-determination]. Guwahati: Radiant Impression, 1993.

Borbora, Arup. *All about PCG & Talks*. Guwahati: Aank-Baak, 2010.

Brass, P. *Language, Religion and Politics in North India*. London: Cambridge University Press, 1974.

Chakravartty, Anupam. 'Baghjan Blowout Verdict: NGT Flags Violations by OIL, Offers Respite to Affected'. *Down to Earth* (10 August 2020). https://www.downtoearth.org.in/news/environment/baghjan-blowout-verdict-ngt-flags-violations-by-oil-offers-respite-to-affected-72738.

Chandhoke, Neera. *Contested Secessions: Rights, Self-determination, Democracy, and Kashmir*. New Delhi: Oxford University Press, 2012.

Chandra, Kanchan. Why Ethnic Parties Succeed: Patronage and Ethnic Headcounts in India. New York, NY: Cambridge University Press, 2004.

Chaube, S. K. *Hill Politics in Northeast India*. Patna: Orient Longman, 1999.

Choudhury, A. C. *Koch-Rajbanshi Jaatir Itihaax Aaru Sanskriti* [History and Culture of the Konch-Rajbonshi Nationality] (Assamese). Bongaigaon: Unique Printers, 2011.

Choudhury, Angshuman, and Suraj Gogoi. 'A Narrow Nationalism Again'. *The Hindu* (12 September 2019). https://www.thehindu.com/opinion/op-ed/a-narrow-nationalism-again/article29394298.ece.

Choudhury, Angshuman, and Suraj Gogoi. 'Citizenship Amendment Act and NRC Are Two sides of Same Coin; Both Seek to Alienate India's Muslims'. Firstpost, 17 December 2019. https://www.firstpost.com/politics/

citizenship-amendment-act-and-nrc-are-two-sides-of-same-coin-both-seek-to-alienate-indias-muslims-7781461.html.

Choudhury, Angshuman, and Suraj Gogoi. 'Re-contextualising the NRC: A Response to Hiren Gohain'. Counter Currents.Org, 10 September 2019. https://counter-currents.org/2019/09/re-contextualising-the-nrc-a-response-to-hiren-gohain/

Choudhury, R. Dutta. 'Clause 6 Panel Recommends Land Rights to Indigenous'. *The Assam Tribune* (13 August 2020).

Choudhury, Ratnadeep. 'Nellie Massacre and "Citizenship": When 1,800 Muslims Were Killed in Assam in Just 6 hours'. *The Print* (18 February 2019). https://theprint.in/india/governance/nellie-massacre-and-citizenship-when-1800-muslims-were-killed-in-assam-in-just-6-hours/193694/.

Choudhury, Sujit. *The Bodos: Emergence and Assertion of an Ethnic Minority*. Shimla: Indian Institute of Advanced Studies, 2007.

Communist Party of India (Marxist). 'CPIM (M) Memorandum on Citizenship (Amendment) Bill, 2016'. 23 September 2016. Guwahati.

Countercurrents.org. 'The Final Draft of State Sponsored Statelessness: NRC and the 4 Million "Stateless People" of India'. 1 August 2018. https://countercur-rents.org/2018/08/the-final-draft-of-state-sponsored-statelessness-nrc-and-the-4-million-stateless-people-of-india/.

Das, Hemen. *Asamor Communist Andolanar Chamu Itihas* [A Short History of the Communist Movement of Assam]. Guwahati: Navayog Prakashan, 2014.

Das, Samir Kumar, ed. *Bristers on Their Feet: Tales of Internally Displaced Persons in India's North East*. New Delhi: SAGE Publications, 2008.

Deka, Basanta. *The Design, the Betrayal, the Assam Movement*. Guwahati: Orchid Publication, 2015.

Donthi, Praveen. 'How Assam's Supreme Court-mandated NRC Project Is Targeting and Detaining Bengali Muslims, Breaking Families. *Caravan* (2 July 2018). https://caravanmagazine.in/politics/assam-supreme-court-nrc-muslim-families-breaking-detention.

Dreze, Jean, and Amartya Sen. *An Uncertain Glory: India and Its Contradictions*. New Delhi: Penguin Books, 2013.

Dutta, Akhil Ranjan. 'BJP's Consolidation, AIUDF's Polarization and Congress' Defeat in Assam'. In *India's 2014 Elections: A Modi-led BJP Sweep*, edited by Paul Wallace, 381–403. New Delhi: SAGE Publications, 2015.

Dutta, Akhil Ranjan. 'The ULFA and the Indian State'. In *Unheeded Hinterland: Identity and Sovereignty in Northeast India*', edited by Dilip Gogoi, 186–208. New York, NY: Routledge, 2016.

Dutta, Akhil Ranjan. 'BJP's Electoral Victory in Assam, 2016: Co-opting the Khilonjiyas'. *Social Change* 47, no. 1 (2017): 108–124. https://journals.sage-pub.com/doi/abs/10.1177/0049085716683114?journalCode=scha.

Dutta, Akhil Ranjan. 'Political Destiny of Immigrants in Assam: National Register of Citizens'. *Economic & Political Weekly* 53, no. 8 (24 February 2018): 18–21. https://www.epw.in/journal/2018/8/commentary/political-destiny-immigrants-assam.html.

Dutta, Akhil Ranjan. 'Preventive Detention under Judicial Scrutiny: Akhil Gogoi v the State of Assam'. *Economic & Political Weekly* 53, no. 12 (24 March 2018): 20–23. https://www.epw.in/journal/2018/12/commentary/preventive-detention-under-judicial-scrutiny.html

Dutta, Akhil Ranjan. 'Conservation vs. Peoples' Entitlements: Contestations in Kaziranga National Park'. In *Developmentalism as Strategy: Interrogating Postcolonial Narratives on India's North East*, edited by Rakhee Bhattacharya, 280–303. Sage Studies on India's Northeast. New Delhi: SAGE Publications, 2019.

Dutta, Akhil Ranjan. 'Assam's 2019 Verdict and the Anti-CAB Mobilisations'. *Economic & Political Weekly* 54, no. 51 (28 December 2019): 27–32. https://www.epw.in/journal/2019/51/perspectives/assams-2019-verdict-and-anti-cab-mobilisations.html.

Dutta, Akhil Ranjan. 'Assam and the NRC: A Political Reading'. *Economic & Political Weekly* 55, no. 39 (26 September 2019): 55–58. https://www.epw.in/system/files/pdf/2020_55/39/DI_LV_39_260920_Akhil%20Ranjan%20Dutta.pdf.

Dutta, Nadana. *Questions of Identity in Assam: Location, Migration, Hybridity*. New Delhi: SAGE Publications, 2012.

Economic & Political Weekly. 'Quandary of National Register of Citizens'. Editorial, 54, no. 37 (14 September 2019). https://www.epw.in/journal/2019/37/editorials/quandary-national-register-citizens.html.

Eleventh Column. 'Crisis of Citizenship: A Critical Reading List on Assam's NRC and Beyond'. 1 March 2020. https://www.eleventhcolumn.com/2020/03/01/crisis-of-citizenship-a-critical-reading-list-on-assams-nrc-and-beyond/.

Fanari, Eleonora, and Pranab Doley. 'As Kaziranga Expands, the Fate of Grazing Communities Hangs in the Balance'. The Wire, 26 February 2018. https://thewire.in/environment/contested-boundaries-eviction-in-the-sixth-addition-of-kaziranga-national-park.

Fernandes, Walter, Gita Bharali, and Vemedo Kezo. *The UN Indigenous Decade in Northeast India*. Guwahati: NESRC, 2008.

Forum against Citizenship Act Amendment Bill. 'A Memorandum on Bill Moved in Parliament to Amend the Citizenship Act 1955 on July 15, 2016 to Hon'ble Joint Parliamentary Committee on Citizenship Amendment Bill, during a Public Hearing in Guwahati on May 7, 2018'. 7 May 2018. Guwahati.

Gogoi, Akhil. *Parivartanor Akhara* [Rehearsal for Change]. Guwahati: Akhara Prakash, 2014.

Gogoi, Akhil. *Asomiya Jatiyatabad: Swadhikar Pratisthar Sangram* [Assamese Nationality: The Struggle to achieve Self-right]. Guwahati: Banlata, 2018.

Gogoi, Dilip, ed. *Unheeded Hinterland: Identity and Sovereignty in Northeast India*. New York, NY: Routledge, 2016.

Gogoi, Mayuri. 'Kaziranga under Threat: Biodiversity Loss and Encroachment of Forest Land'. *Economic & Political Weekly* (11 July 2015). https://www.epw.in/journal/2015/28/reports-states-web-exclusives/kaziranga-under-threat.html.

Gogoi, Suraj, and Abhinav P. Borbora. 'Assam's NRC Consensus: Lack of Public Disorder after Draft List Didn't Mean Absence of Violence'. Scroll.in, 13

December 2019. https://scroll.in/article/944214/inside-the-nrc-consensus-the-lack-of-public-disorder-does-not-mean-the-absence-of-violence.

Gogoi, Suraj, and Parag Jyoti Saikia. 'NRC and Intellectual Racism'. Sabrang, 29 August 2018. https://sabrangindia.in/article/nrc-and-intellectual-racism.

Gohain, Hiren. 'Cudgel of Chauvinism'. *Economic & Political Weekly* 15, no. 18 (23 February 1980): 418–420. https://www.epw.in/journal/1980/8/our-correspondent-columns/assam-cudgel-chauvinism.html.

Gohain, Hiren. 'Fall-out of Underdevelopment'. *Economic & Political Weekly* 15, no. 22 (22 March 1980): 589–590. https://www.epw.in/system/files/pdf/1980_15/12/from_our_correspondents_assam_fall_out_of_underdevelopment.pdf.

Gohain, Hiren. 'Tangled Theories'. *Economic & Political Weekly* 15, no. 16 (19 April 1980): 733–735. https://www.jstor.org/stable/4368579.

Gohain, Hiren. 'Little Nationalism Turned Chauvinist: A Comment'. *Economic & Political Weekly* 16, no. 9 (28 February 1981): 339–340. https://www.epw.in/system/files/pdf/1981_16/9/special_articles_little_nationalism_turned_chauvinist.pdf.

Gohain, Hiren. *Assam: A Burning Question*. Guwahati: Spectrum, 1985.

Gohain, Hiren. 'Livelihood Losses and National Gains'. *Economic & Political Weekly* 45, no. 51 (18 December 2010): 79–80. https://www.epw.in/journal/2010/51/discussion/livelihood-losses-and-national-gains.html.

Gohain, Hiren. *Hiren Gohain Rachanawali*. Vol. 2. Guwahati: Katha Publications, 2014.

Gohain, Hiren. 'The Assamese People Do Not Really Know the Guests That They Have Welcomed with Open Arms'. The Wire, 20 May 2016. https://thewire.in/politics/the-assamese-do-not-really-know-the-guests-they-have-welcomed-with-open-arms.

Gohain, Hiren. 'The BJP's Plans for Assam: An RSS-run School in Every Panchayat'. The Wire, 15 June 2016. https://thewire.in/communalism/the-bjps-plans-for-assam-an-rss-run-school-in-every-panchayat.

Gohain, Hiren. 'Debate: The NRC Is What Will Allow Assam to Escape from the Cauldron of Hate'. The Wire, 13 August 2018. https://thewire.in/politics/debate-the-nrc-is-what-will-allow-assam-to-escape-from-the-cauldron-of-hate.

Gohain, Hiren. 'It's Important to Know the History of the NRC before Passing Judgment on It'. The Wire, 8 August 2018. https://thewire.in/rights/assam-nrc-history-immigration.

Gohain, Hiren. 'Debate: Colonial Policy Created the Northeast's Citizenship Problem'. The Wire, 8 February 2019. https://thewire.in/rights/debate-colonial-policy-created-the-northeasts-citizenship-problem.

Gohain, Hiren. 'It Is Important to Contextualise the NRC'. *The Hindu* (5 September 2019). https://www.thehindu.com/opinion/op-ed/it-is-important-to-contextualise-the-nrc/article29334764.ece.

Gohain, Hiren. *Struggle in a Time Warp: Essays and Observations on the Northeast's History and Politics with Particular Reference to Assam*. Guwahati: Bhabani Books, 2019.

Gohain, Hiren. 'Citizenship Amendment Bill Is A Vicious Ploy to Aggravate Communal Division'. *Outlook* (23 December 2019). https://www.outlookindia.com/magazine/story/india-news-opinion-citizenship-amendment-bill-is-a-vicious-ploy-to-aggravate-communal-division/302494.

Gohain, Hiren. 'Discussion: Linking Excesses in NRC Process to Assamese Xenophobia Is Unwarranted'. *Economic & Political Weekly* 55, no. 9 (29 February 2020). https://www.epw.in/engage/article/discussion-linking-excesses-nrc-process-assamese?0=ip_login_no_cache%3Dba2f84792dcce0e5abfc1f8be34927de.

Goswami, Sandhya. *Language Politics in Assam*. Delhi: Ajanta Publications, 1997.

Goswami, Sandhya. 'Assam: Mandate for Peace and Development'. *Economic & Political Weekly* 46, no. 23 (4 June 2011): 20–22.

Government of Assam. 'White Paper on Foreigners' Issue'. October 2012. https://cjp.org.in/wp-content/uploads/2018/10/White-Paper-On-Foreigners-Issue-20-10-2012.pdf.

Government of Assam. *Assam State Human Development Report* (Managing Diversities, Achieving Human Development). 2014. https://sita.assam.gov.in/portlets/assam-human-development-report-0.

Government of Assam. 'Budget Speech 2016–17'. 2016. https://finance.assam.gov.in/sites/default/files/porlets/Budget%20Speech%20%28English%29%202016%20-%202017.pdf.

Government of Assam. 'White Paper on Assam State Finances' (As on 24th May 2016). 2016. https://finance.assam.gov.in/sites/default/files/A%20White%20Paper%20On%20Assam%20State%20Finances%20%28English%29.pdf.

Government of Assam. 'Budget Speech 2017–18'. 2017. https://finance.assam.gov.in/portlets/assam-state-budget-2017-18.

Government of Assam. 'Budget Speech 2018–19'. 2018. https://finance.assam.gov.in/documents-detail/budget-speech-2018-19-english.

Government of Assam. 'Budget Speech 2019–20'. 2019. https://finance.assam.gov.in/portlets/assam-budget-2018-19.

Government of Assam. 'Budget Speech 2020–21'. 2020. https://finance.assam.gov.in/portlets/assam-budget-2020-21.

Government of Assam. *Report on Economy of Assam in the Backdrop of COVID-19 Pandemic*. Prepared by State Innovation and Transformation Aayog (SITA), Government of Assam, in collaboration with OKD Institute of Social Change and Development, Guwahati, 2020.

Government of Assam. *Economic Survey 2019–20*. Guwahati: Government of Assam, 2020.

Government of Assam. *Report of the Advisory Committee for Revitalisation of Economy of Assam in the Backdrop of Situation Arising Out of COVID-19 Pandemic & Consequent Lockdown*. Guwahati: Government of Assam, 29 May 2020.

Government of India. 'Immigrants (Expulsion from Assam) Act, 1950 (10 of 1950)'. 1950. www.assam.gov.in, Annexure 2.

Government of India. *The Constitution of India*. New Delhi: Universal Law Publishing, 2016.

Gudavarthy, Ajay. 'Neoliberalism Is Killing the Very Idea of citizenship in India'. Quartz India, 3 September 2019. https://qz.com/india/1700542/neoliberalism-is-killing-the-very-idea-of-citizenship-in-india/.

Guha, Amalendu. 'Little Nationalism Turned Chauvinist: Assam's Anti-foreigner Upsurge 1979–80'. *Economic & Political Weekly* (25 October 1980): 41–43 (Special number): 1699–1720. https://www.epw.in/system/files/pdf/1980_15/41-42-43/national_question_in_assam_little_nationalism_turned_chauvinist.pdf.

Guha, Amalendu. *Planter Raj to Swaraj: Freedom Struggle & Electoral Politics in Assam*. New Delhi: Tulika, 2014.

Gupta, Shekhar. 'Blood, Bodies and Scars: What I Saw after the 1983 Nellie Massacre in Assam'. *The Print* (18 February 2019). https://theprint.in/opinion/blood-bodies-and-scars-what-i-saw-after-the-1983-nellie-massacre-in-assam/194662/.

Harvey, David. *The New Imperialism*. New York, NY: Oxford University Press, 2003.

Harvey, David. *A Brief History of Neoliberalism*. New York, NY: Oxford University Press, 2005.

Hazarika, Sanjoy. *Strangers No More: New Narratives from India's Northeast*. New Delhi: Aleph Books, 2018.

Hobsbawm, Eric. *Age of Extremes: The Short Twentieth Century*. New Delhi: Penguin India, 2018.

Hussain, Monirul. *The Assam Movement: Class, Ideology and Identity*. New Delhi: Manak Publications, 1993.

Hussain, Monirul. 'Ethnicity, Communalism and State-Barpeta Massacre'. *Economic & Political Weekly* (20 May 1995). https://www.epw.in/journal/1995/20/commentary/ethnicity-communalism-and-state-barpeta-massacre.html.

Indigenous Forum, Assam. 'Memorandum to the Hon'ble Chairman, Joint Parliamentary Committee on the Citizenship (Amendment), Bill, 2016'. 7 May 2018. Guwahati.

Joshy, P. M., and K. M. Seethi. *State and Civil Society Under Siege: Hindutva, Security and Militarism in India*. New Delhi: SAGE Publications, 2015.

Kapur, Devesh, and Pratap Bhanu Mehta. *Public Institutions in India: Performance and Design*. New Delhi: Oxford University Press, (2005) 2014.

Kashyap, Samudra Gupta. 'Give Me Love in This Election, I Will Give You 5 Years of Development: PM Modi in Assam Election Rally'. *The Indian Express* (9 April 2016). http://indianexpress.com/article/elections-2016/india/india-news-india/pm-narendra-modi-assam-election-rally-country-suffered-due-to-remote-control-state-should-not/.

Kashyap, Samudra Gupta. 'The Politics of Cleaning Up Kaziranga'. *The Indian Express* (26 September 2016). https://indianexpress.com/article/india/india-news-india/kaziranga-eviction-drive-assam-elections-bjp-sonowal-government-politics-dead-3051774/.

Kothari, Rajni. *Politics and the People: In Search of a Humane India*. Vol. I. Delhi: Ajanta Publications, 1990.

Kothari, Rajni. *Rethinking Development: In Search of Humane Alternatives*. Delhi: Ajanta Publications, 1990.

Kothari, Rajni. *Transformation and Survival: In Search of Humane World Order*. Delhi: Ajanta Publications, 1990.

Kothari, Smitu, and Ramananda Wangkheirakpam. 'Dams in the North-east Will Also Ruin Livelihoods'. *Down to Earth* (7 June 2015). https://www.downtoearth.org.in/coverage/dams-in-the-northeast-will-also-ruin-livelihoods-13890.

Krishak Mukti Sangram Samiti, Assam. 'Memorandum to the Honourable Chairman, Joint Parliamentary Committee on the Citizenship (Amendment), Bill, 2016'. 7 May 2018. Guwahati.

Lok Sabha Secretariat. *Report of the Joint Committee on the Citizenship (Amendment) Bill, 2016*. 7 January 2019. https://www.prsindia.org/sites/default/files/bill_files/Joint%20committee%20report%20on%20citizenship%20%28A%29%20bill.pdf.

Mahanta, Nani Gopal. 'Assam: Politics of Peace-making'. *Economic & Political Weekly* 40, no. 1 (1 January 2005): 25–27. https://www.epw.in/journal/2005/01/commentary/assam-politics-peace-making.htm.

Mahanta, Nani Gopal. *Confronting the State: ULFA's Quest for Sovereignty*. New Delhi: SAGE Publications, 2013.

Mahanta, Nani Gopal. 'Politics of Space and Violence in Bodoland'. *Economic & Political Weekly* 48, no. 23 (8 June 2013): 49–58. https://www.epw.in/journal/2013/23/special-articles/politics-space-and-violence-bodoland.html.

Makenzie, Alexander. *The North-east Frontier of India*. New Delhi: Mittal Publications, 2010.

Mander, Harsh. 'The Forgotten Nellie Massacres'. *The Hindu* (14 December 2008). http://www.sacw.net/article423.html.

Mander, Harsh. 'Assam's Tragedy'. *The Hindu* (25 August 2012). https://www.thehindu.com/opinion/columns/Harsh_Mander/assams-tragedy/article3820732.ece.

Mander, Harsh. 'It's Time We Listened to the Plight of Assam's "Foreigners"'. *Al Jazeera* (4 August 2018). https://www.aljazeera.com/indepth/opinion/time-listened-plight-assam-foreigners-180803143309823.html.

Mander, Harsh. 'A Flawed Process That Pleased None'. *The Hindu* (2 September 2019). https://www.thehindu.com/opinion/op-ed/a-flawed-process-that-pleased-none/article29317452.ece.

Mehta, Pratap Bhanu. 'A BJP-dominant System'. *The Indian Express* (20 May 2016). https://indianexpress.com/article/opinion/columns/bjp-assam-elections-sarbananda-sonowal-tarun-gogoi-kerala-elections-2809631/.

Ministry of External Affairs, Government of India. 'Statement by MEA on National Register of Citizens in Assam'. 2 September 2019. https://www.mea.gov.in/Speeches-Statements.htm?dtl/31782/Statement+by+MEA+on+National+Register+of+Citizens+in+Assam.

Ministry of Home Affairs, Government of India. 'The Gazette of India— Extraordinary (2015) F. No. 25022/50/2015-F.I & [F. No. 25022/50/2015-F.l].' 2015. https://indianfrro.gov.in/frro/Notifications_dated_7.9.2015.pdf.

Ministry of Home Affairs. *Report of the Committee on Implementation of Clause 6 of the Assam Accord.* Guwahati: Government of Assam, 10 February 2020.

Misra, Udayon. 'Little Nationalism Turned Chauvinist: A Comment'. *Economic & Political Weekly* 16, no. 8 (21 February 1981): 290–292. https://www.epw.in/system/files/pdf/1981_16/8/special_articles_little_nationalism_turned_chauvinist.pdf.

Misra, Udayon. 'Army Killings in Assam'. *Economic & Political Weekly* 30, no. 15 (15 April 1995): 793. https://www.epw.in/system/files/pdf/1995_30/15/commentary_army_killings_in_assam.pdf.

Misra, Udayon. *The Periphery Strikes Back: Challenges to the Nation-State in Assam and Nagaland.* Shimla: Indian Institute of Advanced Studies, 2000.

Misra, Udayon. 'ULFA: Beginning of the End'. *Economic & Political Weekly* 44, no. 52 (26 December 2009): 13–16. https://www.epw.in/journal/2009/52/commentary/ulfa-beginning-end.html.

Misra, Udayon. 'A New Edge to People's Protests in Assam'. *Economic & Political Weekly* 46, no. 28 (9 July 2011): 16–18. https://www.epw.in/journal/2011/28/commentary/new-edge-peoples-protests-assam.html.

Misra, Udayon. 'Victory for Identity Politics, Not Hindutva in Assam'. *Economic & Political Weekly* 51, no. 22 (28 May 2016). https://www.epw.in/journal/2016/22/2016-state-assembly-elections/victory-identity-politics-not-hindutva-assam.html.

Misra, Udayon. 'National Register of Citizens: Beginnings and endings'. *The Indian Express* (7 August 2018). https://indianexpress.com/article/opinion/columns/nrc-assam-aasu-bangladesh-assamese-bengali-1971-national-register-of-citizens-beginnings-and-endings-5294784/.

Misra, Udayon. 'Why Many in Assam See the National Register of Citizens as a Lifeline'. The Wire, 24 August 2018. https://thewire.in/history/history-nrc-assam.

Misra, Udayon. *Burden of History: Assam and the Partition: Unresolved Issues.* New Delhi: Oxford University Press, 2018.

Misra, Udayon. 'Assam's Humanitarian Conundrum'. *The Hindu* (15 August 2019). https://www.thehindu.com/opinion/lead/assams-humanitarian-conundrum/article29095073.ece.

Mitra, Dola, Debarshi Dasgupta, and Uttam Sengupta. 'A Bridge Too Far'. *Outlook India* (13 August 2012). https://magazine.outlookindia.com/story/a-bridge-too-far/281840.

Murty, T. S. *Assam: The Difficult Years.* New Delhi: Himalayan Books, 1983.

Nag, Sajal. *Roots of Ethnic Conflict: Nationality Question in North-east India.* New Delhi: Manohar Publications, 1990.

Nag, Sajal. *Beleaguered Nation: The Making and Unmaking of the Assamese Nationality.* New Delhi: Manohar Publications, 2017.

Naqvi, Sadiq. 'Assam Pollution Control Board seeks Baghjan Shut Down, OIL Plans to Move Court'. *Down to Earth* (20 June 2020). https://www.downtoearth.org.in/news/pollution/assam-pollution-control-board-seeks-baghjan-shut-down-oil-plans-to-move-court-71880.

Palshikar, Suhas. *Indian Democracy* (Oxford India Short Introductions). New Delhi: Oxford University Press, 2017.

Parashar, Utpal. 'Terming It Anti-northeast, Assam Groups and Parties Up Ante against Draft EIA 2020'. *Hindustan Times* (18 July 2020). https://www.hindustantimes.com/india-news/terming-it-anti-northeast-assam-groups-and-parties-up-ante-against-draft-eia-2020/story-973anIqcppVby9lDtcN6WP.html.

Patnaik, Prabhat. *Whatever Happened to Imperialism and Other Essays*. New Delhi: Tulika, 1995.

Patnaik, Prabhat. 'Economics and the Two Concepts of Nationalism'. Peoples' Democracy, 18 June 2015. https://peoplesdemocracy.in/2015/0618_pd/economics-and-two-concepts-nationalism.

Phukan, Girin, ed. *Inter-ethnic Conflict in Northeast India*. New Delhi: South Asian Publishers, 2005.

Pisharoty, Sangeeta Barooah. 'Assam on the Boil Again, This Time over Hindu Migrants from Bangladesh'. The Wire, 13 September 2015. http://thewire.in/10622/assam-on-the-boil-again-this-time-over-hindu-migrants-from-angladesh/.

Pisharoty, Sangeeta Barooah. 'Oil and "Outsiders": Outrage in Assam over the BJP's Decision to Privatise Oil Fields'. The Wire, 10 July 2016. https://thewire.in/politics/bjp-assam-oil-privatisation.

Pisharoty, Sangeeta Barooah. 'Citizenship and Assam: An Explainer on the Legal Questions That Still Loom Large'. The Wire, 25 November 2019. https://thewire.in/rights/citizenship-and-assam-the-legal-questions-that-still-loom-large.

Pisharoty, Sangeeta Barooah. 'Why Is BJP Changing Tack on NRC in Assam?' The Wire, 30 August 2019. https://thewire.in/politics/bjp-change-tack-nrc-assam.

Pisharoty, Sangeeta Barooah. *Assam: Accord, The Discord*. Gurgaon: Penguin Random House, 2019.

Prabhakara, M. S. *Looking Back into the Future: Identity & Insurgency in Northeast India*. New Delhi: Routledge, 2012.

Rafibadi, H. N. *Assam: From Agitation to Accord*. New Delhi: Genuine Publications & Media, 1988.

Ramesh, Jairam. 'The Two Cultures Revisited: The Environment-Development Debate in India'. *Economic & Political Weekly* 45, no. 42 (16 October 2010): 13–16. https://www.epw.in/journal/2010/42/commentary/two-cultures-revisited-environment-development-debate-india.html.

Rowlatt, Justin. 'Kaziranga: The Park That Shoots People to Protect Rhinos'. BBC News India, 10 February 2017. https://www.bbc.com/news/world-south-asia-38909512.

Roy, Anupama. 'Ambivalence of Citizenship in Assam'. *Economic & Political Weekly* 51, nos 26–27 (25 June 2016): 45–51. https://www.epw.in/journal/2016/26-27/perspectives/ambivalence-citizenship-assam.html.

Roy, Anupama. 'Between Encompassment and Closure: The "Migrant" and the Citizen in India'. *Contributions to Indian Sociology* 42, no. 2 (2018): 219–248.

Roy, Anupama. 'The Citizenship (Amendment) Bill, 2016 and the Aporia of Citizenship'. *Economic & Political Weekly* 54, no. 49 (14 December 2020): 28–34. https://www.epw.in/system/files/pdf/2019_54/49/PE_LIV_49_141219_Anupama_Roy.pdf.

Saha, Abhishek. 'Explained: What Is the Assam Police SI Recruitment Examination Scam?' *The Indian Express* (22 October 2020). https://indianexpress.com/article/explained/assam-police-recruitment-exam-scam-6757704/.

Saikia, Arunabh. 'In Assam, a Massive Eviction Drive Throws New Light on Old Pressures on Land'. Scroll.in, 1 December 2017. https://scroll.in/article/859806/in-assam-a-massive-anti-encroachment-drive-throws-new-light-on-old-pressures-on-land.

Saikia, Arupjyoti. *A Century of Protests: Peasant Politics in Assam since 1900*. New Delhi: Routledge, 2014.

Saikia, Jaideep, ed. *Frontier in Flames: North East India in Turmoil*. New Delhi: Penguin Books, 2007.

Sarma, Himanta Biswa. *Bhinna Samay, Abhinna Mat* [Changing Times Consistent Views]. Guwahati: Saraswati Printers, 2019.

Sethi, Rajat and Shubhrastha. *The Last Battle of Saraighat: The Story of the BJP's Rise in the North-east*. New Delhi: Penguin, 2017.

Shah, Ghanshyam, ed. *Social Movements and the State*. New Delhi: SAGE Publications, 2002.

Shah, Ghanshyam. *Social Movements in India: A Review of Literature*. New Delhi: SAGE Publications, 2004.

Sharma, Ditilekha. 'Determination of Citizenship through Lineage in the Assam NRC Is Inherently Exclusionary'. *Economic & Political Weekly* 54, no. 14 (6 April 2019). https://www.epw.in/engage/article/determination-citizenship-through-lineage-assam-nrc-exclusionary.

Sharma, Jayeeta. *Empires Garden: Assam and the Making of India*. New Delhi: Permanent Black, 2012.

Simlai, Trishant, and Raza Kazmi. 'Grasslands of Grey: How the BBC's Flawed Kaziranga Muckraker Has Done Harm'. The Wire, 23 February 2017. https://thewire.in/culture/kaziranga-bbc-rhino-survival.

Simlai, Trishant, and Raza Kazmi. 'Grasslands of Grey: The Kaziranga Model Isn't Perfect—But Not in the Ways You Think'. The Wire, 24 February 2017. https://thewire.in/environment/kaziranga-bbc-shoot-poaching.

Singh, Satyajit. *Taming the Waters: The Political Economy of Large Dams in India*. New Delhi: Oxford University Press, 1997.

Singh, Ujjwal Kumar, and Anupama Roy. *Election Commission of India: Institutionalising Democratic Uncertainties*: New Delhi: Oxford University Press, 2019.

Stiglitz, Joseph. *The Price of Inequality*. New Delhi: Penguin Books, 2012.

Supreme Court of India. *Assam Sanmilita Mahasangha & Ors vs Union Of India & Ors* (WP ©No 562 0f 2012, WP © No 274 of 2009 & WP © 876 of 2014), 17 December 2014. https://indiankanoon.org/doc/50798357/.

Supreme Court of India. *Kamalakhya Dey Pukayastha and Others vs Union of India & Others*. (Writ Petition (Civil) No 1020/2017), 5 December 2017. https://indiankanoon.org/doc/132044439/.

Supreme Court of India. *Rupjan Begum vs Union of India & Others* (Special Leave Petition (Civil) No 16441/2017), 5 December 2017. https://indiankanoon.org/doc/7961750/.

Supreme Court of India. *Assam Public Works vs Union of India* (Writ Petition(s) (Civil) No(s) 274/2009), 13 August 2019. https://indiankanoon.org/doc/135202420/.

Talukdar, Sushanta. 'Dehing Patkai: Land Claimed by NBWL as "Unbroken" Has Already Been Mined or Cleared, Reveals RTI'. *The Wire*, 24 May 2020. https://science.thewire.in/environment/dehing-patkai-elephant-reserve-nbwl-mining/.

Teltumbde, Anand. 'Saffron Neo-liberalism'. *Economic & Political Weekly* 49, no. 31 (2 August 2014): 11. https://www.epw.in/journal/2014/31/margin-speak/saffron-neo-liberalism.html?0=ip_login_no_cache%3D5ea38a5c9b317e2310d941d9079bce20.

The Gauhati High Court. *Kaziranga National Park vs Union of India & Others*, PIL (suo moto) 66/2012, 67/2012; and WP(C) 648/2013 and 4860/2013, 9 October 2015. available at http://ghconline.gov.in/Judgment/PIL662012.pdf.

The Gauhati High Court. *Manowara Bewa vs The Union of India and Others* (WPC 2634/2016), 28 February 2015. https://indiankanoon.org/doc/105245883/.

The Gauhati High Court. *Akhil Gogoi (Petitioner) vs The State of Assam & 2 Ors* (W.P. (Crl) 14 of 2017), 21 December 2017. http://ghconline.gov.in/Judgment/WPCrl142017.pdf.

Wallace, Paul, ed. *India's 2014 Elections: A Modi-led BJP Sweep*. New Delhi: SAGE Publications, 2015.

Wallace, Paul, ed. *India's 2019 Elections: The Hindutva Wave and Indian Nationalism*. New Delhi: SAGE Publications, 2019.

ABOUT THE AUTHOR

Akhil Ranjan Dutta, Professor and presently Head in the Department of Political Science at Gauhati University, Assam, India, is one of those social scientists of India's north-east whose research has been motivated by political and cultural aspirations of people at the grassroots. A familiar face in Assam's intellectual circle, Professor Dutta is known for his endeavours to build an organic link between academia and the larger society—a passion born of his academic trajectory. His political, cultural and ideological orientations have been moulded by his early encounters with the common citizen's struggles in the rural setting of his childhood in a remote village of Assam's Lakhimpur district; his subsequent exposure to the diverse, secular and inclusive academic and cultural atmosphere of Cotton College, Guwahati; and the rich and progressive intellectual setting of the University of Delhi.

A bilingual author (in Assamese and English) and a political commentator, Professor Dutta is closely connected with the social and cultural movements in Northeast India and is a popular columnist in several leading Assamese dailies. He is a regular commentator and contributor on Assam's politics in leading national and international journals, including the *Economic & Political Weekly,* and serves as the Executive Editor of *Natun Padatik,* a sociocultural magazine published from Guwahati. A passionate advocate of interdisciplinary social science scholarship, Professor Dutta presently serves as the honorary Chairperson of Brahmaputra Institute of Research and Development (BIRD), Guwahati, and is the President of the Social Science Research Community (SSRC), India—Transcending Boundaries for Sustainable

Alternatives. In his two decades of teaching at Gauhati University, he has also served the Gauhati University Teachers' Association (GUTA) as its general secretary for three tenures, its vice-president for two tenures and its president in the year 2019–2020.

A Rotary World Peace Fellow (2009) at the Rotary International Center for Peace and Conflict Studies, Chulalongkorn University, Bangkok, Thailand, Professor Dutta led the Indian think tank delegation to China in June 2017 on the invitation of the Chinese Embassy in India and the Institute of Chinese Studies, New Delhi. He also received visiting fellowships at the Centre for Political Studies, Jawaharlal Nehru University, in March 2017 and in the Department of Political Science, University of Delhi, in March 2020. He is also the recipient of the Second Bhabananda Dutta Memorial Social Science Research Award 2020.

Apart from his research publications in reputed international journals like *Social Change*, *Studies in Indian Politics* and *Advances in Applied Sociology*, Professor Dutta has authored and edited several books in both Assamese and English. Some of his significant edited volumes include *Human Security in North-East India: Issues and Policies* (Ed., 2009); *Political Theory: Issues, Concepts and Debates* (Ed., 2011); *Culture, Ideology, Politics* (Ed., 2012); *Indian Politics: Issues, Institutions and Processes* (Ed., 2013); *The Conscientious Statesman: Gaurisankar Bhattacharyya in Assam Legislative Assembly* (Ed., 2015); and *Asomor Jatiya Jivanat Lakshminath Bezbaruah Aru Anyanya Prabandha* (Assamese, 2015).

INDEX